ILLINOIS CLASSICAL STUDIES, VOLUME III

ILLINOIS
CLASSICAL
STUDIES.

VOLUME III

1978

Miroslav Marcovich, *Editor*

UNIVERSITY OF ILLINOIS PRESS

Urbana Chicago London

© 1978 by the Board of Trustees of the University of Illinois
Manufactured in the United States of America
ISBN: 0-252-00654-2

9/13/79

MARK NAOUMIDES
(1931–1977)

Professor of Classics in the University of Illinois at Urbana (1962–1977)

IN MEMORIAM

Preface

In addition to regular contributions, Volume III (1978) of *Illinois Classical Studies* contains enlarged versions of papers presented at the First Illinois Classical Symposium, held at Urbana 29–30 April 1976 and dedicated to problems in Papyrology. Hence the predominant emphasis, in this volume, is on Greek topics rather than on Latin. I am indebted to the papyrologist Professor Gerald M. Browne, who served as assistant to the editor for the volume.

The publication of this volume was possible thanks to a substantial grant by an extremely generous private donor who prefers to remain anonymous. My gratitude to the donor is sincere and immense.

The volume is dedicated to the memory of Mark Naoumides (1931–1977), Professor of Classics in the University of Illinois at Urbana (1962–1977).

Opinions expressed by contributors are not necessarily shared by the editor.

Urbana, 4 July 1977   Miroslav Marcovich, *Editor*

Contents

1

Xenophanes on Drinking-Parties and Olympic Games[1]

MIROSLAV MARCOVICH

Unlike the early Presocratics (Thales, Anaximander, Anaximenes), the thinkers between 550 and 450 B.C. (Pythagoras, Xenophanes, Heraclitus, Parmenides, Empedocles) all had the ambition of being enlighteners. In their endeavors, some even invoked divine assistance and authority (Pythagoras, Parmenides, Empedocles).

The traveling sage Xenophanes of Colophon lived a long life of at least ninety-five years (ca. 570–475). He himself attests to his writing elegiac poetry at the age of ninety-two (B 8 Diels-Kranz). Of his rich harvest, however, only 120 lines survive. They fall into three categories. (1) A philosophical poem in hexameters, probably called Περὶ φύσιος ἁπάντων ("On the essence of all things"), dealing with God, with human knowledge, and with natural phenomena (only 28 lines are extant). (2) At least four or five books of Σίλλοι, short parodies in hexameters and iambics, ridiculing almost everybody: Homer and Hesiod, Epimenides (B 20), Pythagoras (B 7), Simonides (B 21), Lasos of Hermione (A 16), and others (only 24 lines survive). (3) The lion's share, however, belongs to Xenophanes' elegiac poetry (with 68 extant lines). This is a poetry of exhortation and good advice, and I think it is this παραινετικὸν γένος which enabled the wandering sage to keep soul and body together, while traveling from one Greek city to another and reciting his *practical philosophy in verse-form*, all the way from Colophon and Paros to Zancle, Catana, and the rich court of Hieron of Syracuse in Sicily. Thanks to Athenaeus two of his elegies survive complete (or almost complete). But for some reason

[1] This is an enlarged version of a lecture delivered at the Johns Hopkins University, at the Center for Hellenic Studies in Washington, and at the University of Illinois at Urbana. I am indebted to Professors Bernard M. W. Knox, Georg Luck, James H. Oliver, and James W. Poultney for kindly giving me the opportunity for delivering this lecture.

scholars have not hitherto attempted to assess their literary and philosophical impact.

I. Xenophanes on Drinking-Parties: b 1 dk (ap. Athen. 462 c)[2]

Νῦν γὰρ δὴ ζάπεδον καθαρὸν καὶ χεῖρες ἁπάντων
A

καὶ κύλικες· πλεκτοὺς δ᾽ ἀμφιτιθεῖ στεφάνους,   R
B

ἄλλος δ᾽ εὐῶδες μύρον ἐν φιάληι παρατείνει·
C

4   κρατὴρ δ᾽ ἕστηκεν μεστὸς εὐφροσύνης·
D   E

ἄλλος δ᾽ οἶνος ἑτοῖμος, ὃς οὔποτέ φησι προδώσειν,
D   D

μείλιχος ἐν κεράμοις, ἄνθεος ὀζόμενος·   R ?
B   C

ἐν δὲ μέσοις ἁγνὴν ὀδμὴν λιβανωτὸς ἵησιν,
F   C   F

8   ψυχρὸν δ᾽ ἐστὶν ὕδωρ καὶ γλυκὺ καὶ καθαρόν·
A

παρκέαται δ᾽ ἄρτοι ξανθοὶ γεραρή τε τράπεζα
F

τυροῦ καὶ μέλιτος πίονος ἀχθομένη·
D

---

2 ἀμφιτιθεῖ Dindorf: -τιθείς A   4 κρητήρ Hermann   5 ἄλλος δ᾽ οἰνός ἐστιν codd.:
ἄλλος δ᾽ οἶνος Eustathius, Musurus: {ἄλλος} οἶνος δ᾽ ἐστὶν Hermann, Ludwig   6 ὀζομένοις
ci. Ziegler   9 παρκέαται Wackernagel: πάρκεινται codd.: πάρκειται (schema Pindaricum)
ci. West

---

2 Here is a selective working literature on B 1 and/or B 2: K. Reinhardt, *Parmenides und die Geschichte der griechischen Philosophie* (Bonn, 1916; reprint 1959) 126–135. C. M. Bowra, "Xenophanes on songs at feasts," *Class. Philol.* 33 (1938) 353–367, and "Xenophanes and the Olympian Games," *Amer. Journ. of Philol.* 59 (1938) 257–279, = *Problems in Greek Poetry* (Oxford, 1953) 1–14 and 15–37. E. Diehl, *Anthologia Lyrica Graeca* (rev. R. Beutler, Leipzig, 1949). H. Diels–W. Kranz, *Die Fragmente der Vorsokratiker* (6th ed., Berlin, 1951), I, 113–139 plus *Nachträge* (16th reprint 1972). M. Untersteiner, *Senofane: Testimonianze e Frammenti* (Florence, 1956). H. Herter, "Das Symposion des Xenophanes," *Wiener Studien* 69 (1956) 33–48 (= *Festschrift Albin Lesky*). H. Fränkel, *Hermes* 60 (1925) 177–178, = *Wege und Formen frühgriechischen Denkens* (2nd ed., Munich, 1960) 335–337. J. Defradas, *Les Élégiaques Grecs* (Paris, Collection Érasme, 1962) 74–81. *Idem*, "Le banquet de Xénophane," *Revue des Études Grecques* 75 (1962) 344–365. H. Fränkel, *Dichtung und Philosophie des frühen Griechentums* (2nd ed., Munich, 1962) 372–376 = *Early Greek Poetry and Philosophy* (transl. by M. Hadas and J. Willis, New York, 1975) 326–330. K. Ziegler, "Xenophanes von Kolophon, ein Revolutionär des Geistes," *Gymnasium* 72 (1965) 289–302. D. A. Campbell, *Greek Lyric Poetry* (London, 1967) 74–76 and 331–339. D. E. Gerber, *Euterpe* (Amsterdam, 1970) 238–239 and 243–249. M. Eisenstadt, *The Philosophy of Xenophanes of Colophon* (Diss U. Texas at Austin, 1970) 37–78 and 186–195. M. L. West, *Iambi et Elegi Graeci*, II (Oxford, 1972) 163–165. *Idem, Studies in Greek Elegy and Iambus* (Berlin, 1974) 189.

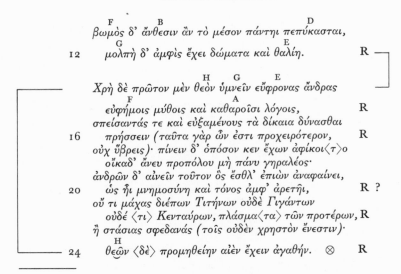

βωμὸς δ' ἄνθεσιν ἂν τὸ μέσον πάντηι πεπύκασται,

12   μολπὴ δ' ἀμφὶς ἔχει δώματα καὶ θαλίη.

Χρὴ δὲ πρῶτον μὲν θεὸν ὑμνεῖν εὔφρονας ἄνδρας

εὐφήμοις μύθοις καὶ καθαροῖσι λόγοις,

σπείσαντάς τε καὶ εὐξαμένους τὰ δίκαια δύνασθαι

16   πρήσσειν (ταῦτα γὰρ ὦν ἐστι προχειρότερον,

οὐχ ὕβρεις)· πίνειν δ' ὁπόσον κεν ἔχων ἀφίκοι⟨τ⟩ο

οἴκαδ' ἄνευ προπόλου μὴ πάνυ γηραλέος·

ἀνδρῶν δ' αἰνεῖν τοῦτον ὃς ἐσθλ' ἐπιὼν ἀναφαίνει,

20   ὡς ἧι μνημοσύνη καὶ τόνος ἀμφ' ἀρετῆι,

οὔ τι μάχας διέπων Τιτήνων οὐδὲ Γιγάντων

οὐδέ ⟨τι⟩ Κενταύρων, πλάσμα⟨τα⟩ τῶν προτέρων,

ἢ στάσιας σφεδανάς (τοῖς οὐδὲν χρηστὸν ἔνεστιν)·

24   θεῶν ⟨δὲ⟩ προμηθείην αἰὲν ἔχειν ἀγαθήν. ⊗

13 δὴ ci. Bergk, ft. recte ὑμνὲν A, ὕμνεν epitome, corr. C   17 ὕβρεις A (om. epitome), def. West: ὕβρις Musurus cett.   ἀφίκοιτο ci. West: ἀφίκοιο A: ἀφίκηαι Wilamowitz   19 ἐσθλ' ἐπιὼν Untersteiner (conl. Xenophan. B 7): ἐσθλὰ πιω A (πιὼν E): ἐσθλ' εἰπὼν H. Fraenkel   ἀναφαίνηι Hermann   20 ἧι Ahrens: η A (ἧ E): οἱ Koraes: ὥς οἱ μνημόσυν' ἧι Bergk   τόνος Koraes [cf. Pind. Pyth. 11.54 ἀμφ' ἀρεταῖς τέταμαι]: τὸν ὃς codd.: πόνος Schneidewin: νόος Hermann   ἀρετῆι Wilamowitz: ἀρετῆς codd.   21 οὔ τι codd.: οὐδὲ ci. West   διέπων Fraenkel: διεπειν A, διεπει E   22 τι add. Meineke   πλασμάτων codd., corr. Schweighaeuser   23 σφεδανὰς Osann: φενδόνας A   24 δὲ add. Casaubon   ἀγαθὸν Fr. Franke, Hermann

TRANSLATION

For now the floor is swept clean; clean are the hands of every man, clean are their cups. A servant sets fresh-woven garlands around everyone's head, another hands around sweet-scented unguent in a saucer. The mixing-bowl stands waiting, brimful of good cheer. And another wine is ready, which promises never to run out—a soft-tasting one, redolent of its flower-bouquet in the jars.

(7) In the middle of the room the frankincense sends forth its scent pure-and-holy, and there is water, cold and sweet and pure. Ready lie at hand the brown loaves and the respectful table with a load of cheese and thick honey. The altar in the center is covered all round with flowers; and singing and good cheer fill the hall.

(13) Now it is meet for men of good cheer first of all to sing a hymn to the god with reverent tales and pure words, after pouring libations and praying for strength [or, for faculty] to do the right (for this is indeed a

more obvious thing to pray for, not acts of violence). Then it is meet to drink as much as one can take and still reach his home without the help of a slave-boy, unless he be very old.

(19) It is also meet to praise that man among the guests who is able to engage in showing forth noble deeds, according as his memory serves him and his zeal [or, striving] for moral excellence enables him, while avoiding to deal with the fights of Titans or Giants or Centaurs—fictions of our forbearers—or with the violent civil strife, in which there is no wholesome use. Finally, it is meet always to keep a good regard for the gods.

Bowra seems to be right (against Bergk first, Snell last) in believing that one introductory couplet of the poem is missing. For no poem is likely to begin with a γάρ (*Iliad* 10.173 Νῦν γὰρ δὴ being no exception to this). On the contrary, Fränkel (*EGP* 328) seems to be wrong in assuming that the end of the poem is missing ("It is a pity that the fragment breaks off here: the positive recommendations which followed have not been preserved"). For, unless I am mistaken, θεῶν of line 24 deliberately resumes θεόν of line 13, within a rudimentary ring-composition (compare also the link between lines 12 and 13, and Xenophanes B 2, *infra*). One should start with god and end with god: σὲ δ' ἀοιδὸς . . . πρῶτόν τε καὶ ὕστατον αἰὲν ἀείδει (*Hymn to Apollo* [21] 3 f.; compare Hesiod *Theog.* 34; Theognis 1–4).

The extant twenty-four lines easily fall into two parts of six couplets each (lines 1–12 against lines 13–24). The first part of the poem describes the external, physical, preliminary conditions for an ideal symposium, and the second part sets forth ethical and religious precepts for the participants. The poet plays the role of a toast-master at the drinking-party (συμπο-σίαρχος, *arbiter bibendi*). As such, he already had given orders to the servants, before the poem started, about the proper mixture of water and wine (say, 3:1, or 2:1, or maybe even 3:2). For we find the mixing-bowl already brought in, brimful of cheerful wine (4, μεστὸς ἐυφροσύνης. Of course, the audience will easily recall οἶνον εὔφρονα from *Iliad* 3.246). Soon our ποταρχῶν will prescribe how much wine each of the company will be allowed to drink (say, nine rounds from small cups, followed by seven rounds from the bigger ones: Diogenes Laërtius 1.104). But being a sage, Xenophanes will tell this too in his own philosophical way (lines 17–18).

We enter the hall at the moment when everything is ready for the initial ceremony at a drinking-party (libations, prayer, paean). Namely, (1) The floor has been swept clean after the dinner, the guests have already washed their hands after the meal, and their cups too are cleaned from the dinner-libation. One slave is still busying himself with putting garlands around each guest's head, while another servant is passing around a saucer with perfumes. So much for the guests (lines 1–3). (2) We pass now to the wine (lines 4–6). A less expensive wine is already in the mixing-bowl; another, more expensive and sophisticated, soft-tasting and flower-scented, stands by in jars. And notice that there is plenty of this good wine too, if the phrase ὃς οὔποτέ φησι προδώσειν (5) means (as I think it does), "which promises never to betray the guests by running dry," (compare the Herodotean phrase (7.187), "the streams of some rivers betray us by running dry" [προδοῦναι τὰ ῥέεθρα τῶν ποταμῶν ἔστι ὧν]).[3] Less likely, the phrase may mean, "the wine promises to remain loyal to his friends by not intoxicating them." The water for this good wine is at hand, cool and sweet and pure (line 8). (3) Next, the snacks necessary for a long drinking-party lie ready on the table, and again in large quantities—crunchy loaves, cheese and rich thick honey (lines 9–10).

(4) A small altar stands in the center of the hall, banked all round with flowers, and there is a pot with frankincense, also in the center, most probably on the altar itself (lines 11 and 7). (5) Finally, the sound of a pious song (12, μολπή) spreads over the hall, probably coming from a hired musician, since the presence of a lyre-player and a flute-player is at any rate necessary for the forthcoming libation and paean.

To sum up, the atmosphere in Part I is drenched with cleanliness, purity, holiness, fragrance, flowers, abundance and, above all, good cheer and merriment. Each key-word is repeated three times. In the Greek text printed above, A stands for cleanliness and purity (lines 1, 8, 14); B, for flowers (2, 6, 11); C, for scent (3, 6, 7); D, for abundance and plenty (4, 5, 10, 11); E, for good cheer (4, 12, 13); F, for holiness and piety (7, 9, 11, 14); finally, G stands for singing (12 and 13). In addition, Wine is personified (he can speak, φησί, 5),[4] and the table has the epithet "reverend" (γεραρή, 9), probably because it holds bread—the holy γέρας of Demeter—not because it would hold the offerings to the gods, as would a τράπεζα ἱερά (against Defradas' translation, "une table d'offrandes" ("Banquet," pp. 348 and 355).

Before we pass to Part II (13–24), we should consider the links between both parts. There seem to be three of them. (1) *Purity* (καθαρός, 14): external cleanliness (καθαρός in lines 1 and 8) leads us to purity of heart,

[3] This interpretation goes back to J. N. Bach, *Jahrbücher für Philologie und Pädagogik* 9 (1829) 317: "Wein, der niemals ausgehen wird" (= *deficere*, not *deserere*), and was adopted by Simon Karsten, *Xenophanis Colophonii carminum reliquiae* (Amsterdam, 1830), fr. 21, p. 70 f.: "vinum copiosum, quod ipsum spondet se convivis non defecturum."

[4] Οἶνος appears as an old man (along with 'Οπώρα and 'Αγρός) on a third-century mosaic panel from Daphne (The Antioch Project, Art Gallery at Baltimore).

thought and speech, and is matched by another key-word, *holiness* or *godliness* (marked with F): εὔφημοι (14) corresponds to ἁγνή (7) and γεραρή (9), to βωμός (11) and λιβανωτός (7).

(2) The subject of all of Part II, εὔφρονες ἄνδρες (13), "men of good cheer and festive spirit," matches merriment (θαλίη) in the last line of Part I (in addition to the phrase μεστός εὐφροσύνης in line 4). The word εὔφρων need not mean here more than "man of good cheer," as befits participants in a symposium (so Eduard Fraenkel, *Agamemnon*, II, 366 f.). Compare Theognis 765–767:

> ὧδ' εἶναι καὶ ἄμεινον, εὔφρονα θυμὸν ἔχοντας
> νόσφι μεριμνάων εὐφροσύνως διάγειν
> τερπομένους.[5]

(3) Finally, ὑμνεῖν (13) resumes μολπή also from the end of Part I: apparently, an appropriate song sung by the lyre-player serves as a prelude leading to the singing of the ritual paean by the guests. In short, Part I shows a progressive linear movement leading to a climax: from the floor (line 1), via the altar (7 and 11), to the hall as a whole (δώματα, 12); from physical cleanliness (1) to singing and merriment (12). The same linear movement is present also in Part II.

If my text is acceptable, Part II of the poem consists of one single sentence, all four infinitives (ὑμνεῖν in 13, πίνειν in 17, αἰνεῖν in 19, and ἔχειν in 24) depending on the moral precept implied by χρὴ δὲ εὔφρονας ἄνδρας in 13: "For men of good cheer it is meet: (1) to sing a paean to the god; (2) to drink with moderation; (3) to provide an entertainment leading to the moral excellence; (4) finally, *always* to be mindful of gods." This one-sentence structure seems to enhance the unity of Xenophanes' moral message. But the unity of Part II is at any rate clear: first, thanks to the ring-composition (13 θεόν ∽ 24 θεῶν); second, by agglomeration of the pentameter-rhyme (marked with R in the right margin facing lines 14, 16, 20, 22, 24). And notice that this rhyme is almost entirely absent in Xenophanes' emotional and polemical B 2 (*infra*). It seems then quite likely that Xenophanes had put special emphasis on his moral message starting with χρή (13) and ending with ἀγαθήν (24). West, however, seems to take the infinitives in lines 17, 19, and 21 (reading διέπειν) as absolute: "as for the drinking, you (he) should take . . ."; "as for the guests, applaud him whose skolion is edifying . . ."; "your skolion should

---

[5] Against such translations as "man of sound mind, reasonable" (LSJ), "righteous men" (W. K. C. Guthrie, *A History of Greek Philosophy*, Cambridge, I, 1962, 360), "recht-gesonnene," "verständige," "wohlgesinnte Männer" (Reinhardt, Diels, Kranz).

not . . ." (*Studies* 189). Both interpretations are possible; but the difference is of no vital importance to my point.

Xenophanes' prescriptions deal with: (1) libations, prayer and the paean (13–17a); (2) drinking instruction (17b–18); (3) the right entertainment at a symposium (19–23); finally (4), propemptic good advice before adjourning (24). The topics follow Greek symposiac customs.

(1) *Libation.* At the end of the dinner and before the floor was cleaned, the guests had poured a libation of pure wine to Ἀγαθὸς Δαίμων (as Karl Kircher had shown).[6] Now, at the beginning of the drinking-party, the guests most probably will pour a triple libation of wine: to Zeus Ὀλύμπιος and the Olympians, to the heroes, and to Zeus Σωτήρ.[7] Evidently, Bowra (7) is wrong when writing: "Xenophanes seems to place the libation after the paean, and the Ionian practice may have differed in this respect from the Athenian." It did not; notice the difference in tense between σπείσαντάς τε καὶ εὐξαμένους (aorist) and ὑμνεῖν (present); this implies that the libation and prayer preceded the paean (compare Herter 35 n. 8).

(2) *Prayer.* "Pray for the strength or faculty to act justly, not for acts of violence." I think West is right in defending ὕβρεις (17) against ὕβρις (introduced by Marcus Musurus in the Aldine edition of Athenaeus, of 1514, and adopted by all scholars). For, as West (189) correctly pointed out, if Xenophanes really wanted to say, "It is no sin to drink as much as . . .," he could easily have said οὐδ᾽ ὕβρις avoiding such a violent postponement of δέ. What seems to be more important: it is questionable whether the phrase οὐχ ὕβρις can yield the required sense, "fas est bibere" (Karsten), "it is no sin to drink" (Guthrie), "it is no presumption to drink" (Fränkel), "dann soll's keine Sünde sein, zu trinken" (Reinhardt), "ist's kein Übermut so viel zu trinken" (Diels-Kranz), etc. On the contrary, the opposition of ὕβρεις ("acts of violence," predominantly on the battlefield) to τὰ δίκαια seems to be easy in early Greek. West refers to Hesiod, *Opera* 145 f., where the third generation of mortal men is said to have cared only for woeful works of Area and deeds of violence (οἷσιν Ἄρηος | ἔργ᾽ ἔμελε στονόεντα καὶ ὕβριες).

Bowra (2) wrote in support of ὕβρις: "Nor was it unusual to regard too much drinking as ὕβρις. For even Anacreon subscribes to this belief, when he regulates the amount of water to be mixed with wine that he may hold his revels ἀνυβρίστως (fr. 43.5 Diehl)." I do not think Anacreon's regulation is relevant here. If we read Anacreon *PMG* 356 so: ὡς ἀνυβρίστως

---

[6] *Die sakrale Bedeutung des Weines im Altertum* (RGVV IX, 2, Giessen, 1910) 13 ff.

[7] E. Buchholz, *Anthologie aus den Lyrikern der Griechen*, 4th ed. (Leipzig, 1886), I, 64. A. B. Cook, *Zeus*, II, Appendix (Cambridge, 1925) 1123 f. n. 7.

(Pauw: ἂν † ὑβριστιῶς † Athen.) | ἀνὰ δηῦτε βασσαρήσω, it may yield the sense, "to revel in a decorous way, so that I may keep drinking without engaging in disorderly acts." But Xenophanes' phrase is different. I think the only sense the phrase οὐχ ὕβρις (sc. ἐστὶ) πίνειν κτλ. could give is, "moderate drinking does not involve acts of violence" (which is out of place here), not "it is no sin or outrage to drink."[8] At least, it cannot be paralleled.

Next, the word προχειρότερον (16) is puzzling. Possibly, it implies, "it is an easier way for men to pray for strength to act justly than to pray for success in deeds of violence," this "easier way" implying "preferable." For, in the end Δίκη always defeats Ὕβρις, and a fool who does not know this will have to learn through suffering: παθὼν δέ τε νήπιος ἔγνω (Hesiod Opera 216–218).

The most original idea of the prayer, however, seems to reside in δύνασθαι (15), "strength or faculty to do what is just." Reitzenstein[9] had referred to Ion's prayer to Dionysus (fr. 1.15 f. West): "Give me long life, and to drink, and to play, and to be mindful of right things (καὶ τὰ δίκαια φρονεῖν)," which coincides with Hipparchus' inscription (apud Plato Hipparch. 229 a), στεῖχε δίκαια φρονῶν. But to think or purpose the right thing is not the same as to have the strength to accomplish it, as Reinhardt (128) had correctly pointed out; he refers to an anonymous poet in Plato's Meno (77 b 2), who defined the ἀρετή as χαίρειν τε καλοῖσι καὶ δύνασθαι, "to be fond of noble things and be able to provide or achieve them" (δυνατὸν εἶναι πορίζεσθαι, explains Plato).[10]

Here too Bowra (8) had underestimated Xenophanes: "His prayer is for strength to do the right things, and these are what almost any Greek aristocrat would regard as belonging to his code." For, πρήσσειν (16) most probably implies "to achieve, accomplish, bring about, fulfil," (as Reinhardt, Snell, and Fränkel had seen), and δύνασθαι (15) is best explained as hinting at a man's *intellectual capacity* to choose the right thing to do: "die innere Kraft zum sittlichen Handeln" (Ziegler 293). By stressing the need for divine assistance in a man's moral decision-making (possibly implying freedom from delusion-Ἄτη) Xenophanes radically differs from the authors of traditional prayers.

---

[8] Incidentally, Eduard Buchholz (n. 7, *supra*) already seemed to have sensed the violent postponement of δέ here; he prints: ταῦτα γὰρ ὧν ἐστι προχειρότερον, οὐχ ὕβρις. But his rendering is weak in sense, "denn diese ist die höchste Pflicht, nicht frevle Überhebung."

[9] R. Reitzenstein, *Epigramm und Skolion* (Giessen, 1913; reprint 1970) 50. Reinhardt 127 f.

[10] "Mit anderen Worten: wenn der Mensch auch noch so sehr das Gerechte denkt und will, es zu vollbringen ist doch nicht in seine Macht gegeben; er bedarf dazu der göttlichen Hilfe." The rest of Reinhardt's interpretation (128–131) is far from convincing.

(3) *Paean*. Most likely, it is sung either to Apollo or to Dionysus, and not "to the god to whom the altar in the middle of the hall is dedicated." For the probability is that this indoor-altar is dedicated to no god at all; it is simply a small portable *terracotta arula*, "too small to support a sacrificial fire, but rather intended to receive merely a few hot coals" for burning incense, as archaeological material from both Greece and Magna Graecia have shown.[11]

Probably μῦθος refers to the content of the paean, λόγος to the verbal expression. The chosen story or tale should be reverent, and it must be expressed in adequate hymnic diction, *contra* Bowra (5): "... he means that in hymns to the gods the tales told must be εὔφημοι and the subjects treated καθαροί." The epithet καθαρός (14) may have been deliberately chosen in order to resume καθαρός from lines 1 and 8. Language should match the occasion.

We now come to a problem. Starting from the fact that singing a song (μολπή, 12) before the performance of the paean (θεὸν ὑμνεῖν, 13) is not known from Greek symposiac literature, Professor Herter (in 1956) advanced the interpretation that μολπή *is* actually the paean sung by the guests. While the guests sing the paean (=μολπή, 12), Xenophanes takes the opportunity of telling us what the content of an ideal paean should be (χρὴ δέ). "Vor allem bedeutet das Wort [μολπή] ja gar nicht Musik, sondern Gesang und kann daher nur das normale Festlied meinen [with reference to *Iliad* 1.472–474]." "... es bleibt dabei, will man genau sein, dass die Ermahnung [i.e., lines 13–24] während des Gesanges gesprochen wird. Damit zeigt sich aber, wozu sie da ist: sie soll eine Vorstellung von dem Paian geben, der selber nicht reproduziert wird." (36). Herter then saw in Xenophanes' elegy the earliest example of the device called *Zeitraffung* ("Time snatching"), which became so dear to later Hellenistic and Roman poets: a selective discontinuity of the logical succession of events in time, a clear example being Tibullus' *Ambarvalia* poem (2.1).[12]

I am in strong disagreement with Herter's ingenious interpretation: μολπή is not ὕμνος. I prefer to think that Part I (1–12) describes *only the preparations* for the symposiac ritual (libation, prayer, paean). Notice the difference in tense between Part I and Part II (13–24). In Part I all the verbs are in the present (or in the perfect-present) tense. What they describe is what is actually happening. Starting with line 13, Xenophanes *qua* συμποσίαρχος takes the floor and gives his instructions for the *ensuing* ritual, drinking, and entertainment: χρή followed by infinitives. Accordingly, the paean is *never* sung in this poem: it *will* be sung after Xenophanes

---

11 C. G. Yavis, *Greek Altars* (St. Louis, 1949) §54 (p. 137 f.) and §65 (pp. 171–175).
12 Herter (n. 1, *supra*) 37 ff.

finishes his instructions. Then μολπή must refer to some prelude to the real paean, most probably sung by the hired lyre-player.

I have two main objections to Herter's interpretation. First: as is known, libation and prayer precede the paean. Now if the guests had already reached the stage of the paean in μολπή (12), the toast-master's belated instructions about libation and prayer in lines 15–17 become unmotivated, even pointless. What is the point in telling the guests how to pray if they had already prayed and are now singing the paean?

Second: Plutarch (*Quaest. conviv.* 7.8.4 p. 712 F) writes: "The *lyre* has been of old, both in Homer's times and today, an intimate member of the banquet. Now it is not fair to dissolve an intimate friendship of such a long standing: all we need do is request the singers to drop too many dirges and laments from their repertory and to sing cheerful songs appropriate to men of festive spirit (εὔφημα καὶ πρέποντα θαλιάζουσιν ἀνθρώποις ἄιδοντας). As for the *flute*, we could not drive it away from the table even if we wanted to: it is as essential to our libation as is the garland, and it helps impart a religious tone to the singing of the paean (αἱ γὰρ σπονδαὶ ποθοῦσιν αὐτὸν ἅμα τῶι στεφάνωι καὶ συνεπιφθέγγεται τῶι παιᾶνι τὸ θεῖον)." (Compare *Septem sap. conviv.* 150 D.) And in Plato Comicus (fr. 69 Kock, ap. Athen. 665 B–D) a flute-girl is urged to get ready her flute at once and start playing *a prelude* to the libation (τῆι παιδὶ τοὺς αὐλοὺς ἐχρῆν ἤδη πρὸ χειρὸς εἶναι | καὶ <u>προαναφυσᾶν</u>). My point is: if the presence of a lyre-player and a flute-player at the drinking-party was necessary for the coming ritual and entertainment, and if a flute-girl could produce a prelude (προαναφυσᾶν) to the libation, why could a waiting lyre-player not do the same while singing an appropriate prelude to the ensuing ritual? And this prelude is the μολπή of line 12.

(4) *Drinking instruction.* It is worthy of an Enlightener: "Be your own judge of how much wine to take without bringing shame upon yourself. For it is shameful for an *adult* man indeed to be led home drunk by an *unfledged* slave-boy (πρόπολος)." Xenophanes' spiritual son Heraclitus says much the same (B 117 DK = 69 Marcovich): "A *man* when he is drunk stumbles and is led home by a *beardless boy*, not knowing whither he goes; for his soul is wet." Compare also Plato *Symposium* 176 e 4, τοῦτο μὲν δέδοκται, πίνειν ὅσον ἂν ἕκαστος βούληται, ἐπάναγκες δὲ μηδὲν εἶναι.

(5) *The right entertainment* (19–23). It will be provided, not by hired artists but by the participants themselves, who will in turn recite either the traditional scolia or pieces of epic and elegiac poetry. In view of the fact that Memory (μνημοσύνη, 20), mother of the Muses and guardian-angel of epic poets, is invoked (compare *Hymn to Hermes* 429 f.; Hesiod *Theog.*

53 f.; Alcman 8.9 Page; Solon 13.1 f. West), one would think that the later Attic short scolia or glees are ruled out. Longer symposiac scolia (by Alcaeus, Anacreon and Pindar) are sometimes mentioned in the later literature,[13] and Philochorus (ap. Athen. 630 F) tells us that Tyrtaeus' elegies were recited at banquets in Sparta. Reinhardt (133) suggested that Xenophanes may have had in mind his own type of moralistic elegiac poetry (such as B 1 and B 2), and the force of such key-phrases as ἐσθλὰ ἀναφαίνειν (19) and τόνος ἀμφ' ἀρετῆι (20) may well hint at the genre of Solon's elegies (Xenophanes himself may have borrowed diction from Solon; compare B 2, infra, and n. 21.)

The point is that any Titanomachy, Gigantomachy, or Centauromachy must be banned from the program, along with, say, Alcaeus' στασιωτικά (Diels). For they all sing of deeds of violence (17, ὕβρεις; 21, μάχαι; 23, στάσιες), which have no place at such a holy celebration as a symposium. The traditional element in this kind of ban has been well pointed out by Reitzenstein (50), Reinhardt (133), Bowra (3), and others. And Karsten (in 1830) had already referred to Anacreon fr. 96 Diehl:

Οὐ φιλέω, ὃς κρητῆρι παρὰ πλέωι οἰνοποτάζων
νείκεα καὶ πόλεμον δακρυόεντα λέγει,
ἀλλ' ὅστις Μουσέων τε καὶ ἀγλαὰ δῶρ' Ἀφροδίτης
συμμίσγων ἐρατῆς μνήσκεται εὐφροσύνης.

Karl Bielohlawek[14] rightly remarked that Εὐφροσύνη (4) and Θαλίη (12) happen to be names of two Χάριτες, and χάρις is exactly what is required at an ideal drinking-party.

There may be more to that. Xenophanes' condemnation of stories about violent acts of gods and men may well have the objective of suppressing the natural tendencies of drunkenness toward violence: such stories homeopathically excite ὕβρις in the audience. (Remember the misbehavior of the drunken Centaurs at the wedding-party of Peirithous, Odyssey 21.295–304.) As Eisenstadt (57) has recently suggested: "The theory behind Xenophanes' censorship might well be called one of homeopathic sociology in the sense that he believed stories of violence elicit violent acts from an audience which is intoxicated and therefore more liable to such a tendency."

True as these reasons may be, they seem to be too narrow for an Enlightener. Xenophanes' standpoint is pragmatic and utilitarian: safety and prosperity of the whole πόλις is what comes first. The phrase at the

---

13 Reintzenstein (n. 9, supra) 43 f.
14 Wiener Studien 58 (1940) 22.

end of his instructions for a noble entertainment, τοῖς οὐδὲν χρηστὸν
ἔνεστιν (23), implies simply: "there is no wholesome use for the city in
them." The force of this χρηστόν was well pointed out by Bowra (10 f.):
"So when Xenophanes says that certain themes have nothing χρηστόν in
them, he means that they are not suited to the god citizen. . . . So Xenophanes' objection is based primarily on grounds of public good. He dislikes
themes of στάσις because they are politically unprofitable." The same is
true of the word πιαίνει in the closing line of his B 2, οὐ γὰρ πιαίνει ταῦτα
μυχοὺς πόλεως, i.e., "the victorious athlete is not what *fattens* the chambers
of the city." And the same political overtone can be detected in the word
ἀνωφελέας of his B 3 (ap. Athen. 526 A), where the Colophonians are said
to have behaved this way:

> ἁβροσύνας δὲ μαθόντες ἀνωφελέας παρὰ Λυδῶν,
>   ὄφρα τυραννίης ἦσα⟨ν ἄ⟩νευ στυγερῆς,
> ἤιεσαν εἰς ἀγορὴν παναλουργέα φάρε᾽ ἔχοντες,
> 4   οὐ μείους ὥσπερ χ⟨ε⟩ίλιοι ὡς ἐπίπαν,
>   αὐχαλέοι, χαίτ⟨η⟩ισιν ἀγαλλόμεν(οι) εὐπρεπέεσσιν,
>   ἀσκητοῖς ὀδμὴν χρίμασι δευόμενοι.

"While they were still free from the loathsome tyranny, after having
learned from the Lydians any kind of *useless refinement*, they used to come
to the place of assembly [*or*, to the agora] wearing garments made all of
purple, no fewer than one thousand of them, as a rule, with boastful mien,
delighting in their elaborate coiffure with locks, drenched with ointments
of refined fragrance." Lydian luxury is called "useless," for such a boastful
display of wealth and intemperance in public, by one thousand oligarchs
in Colophon, proved to be fatal to the city: either it led to an internal
upheaval of the poor with a subsequent tyranny, or it made the citizens
so enervated and defenseless that they became an easy prey for the Median
tyranny (after 546 B.C.). Compare Theopompus (115 F 117 Jacoby, ap.
Athen. 526 C), τοιγαροῦν διὰ τὴν τοιαύτην ἀγωγὴν ἐν τυραννίδι καὶ στάσεσι
γενόμενοι αὐτῆι πατρίδι διεφθάρησαν, and Theognis 1103–1104, ὕβρις καὶ
Μάγνητας ἀπώλεσε καὶ Κολοφῶνα | καὶ Σμύρνην· πάντως Κύρνε καὶ ὔμμ᾽
ἀπολεῖ.[15]

There seem to be two different reasons for Xenophanes to ban poetry
dealing with theomachy and civil strife, one political, or pragmatic; the
other theological, or theoretical. The political reason: in any theomachy
gods engage in fighting *against their own kith and kin*, thus encouraging the
citizens to imitate them by doing exactly the same (in στασιωτικά such an

---

[15] On B 3 see C. M. Bowra, *Class. Quarterly* 35 (1941) 119–126; Eisenstadt 32–36.

example is self-evident). And any civil strife endangers the very existence of the city. This point was well stressed by Herter (46 f.): "Jene Geschichten sind unwahr, weil sie der Würde der Götter widersprechen, und das tun sie, weil sie ihnen Kämpfe gegen ihresgleichen zumuten: nicht nur in der Titanomachie, sondern auch in der Gigantomachie standen die Olympier gegen Verwandte, und auch Herakles' Kampf gegen die Kentauren war zum mindesten durch die unheilbare Verwundung des gerechten Cheiron belastet. So betrachtet liegen diese Götterzwiste auf derselben Linie wie die ebenfalls verpönten στάσιες unter den Menschen."

The theological reason: such stories about the gods are sheer lies, fabrications of Homer, Hesiod, and the Epic Cycle (πλάσματα τῶν προτέρων), morally unworthy of a supreme being. For, contrary to what Homer and Hesiod teach us, gods do not steal, commit adultery or deceive each other. And they certainly do not engage in acts of violence against their own kin. Here Xenophanes the religious reformist is speaking. Compare his B 11, where the word ἀνέθηκαν ("Homer and Hesiod have *attributed* to the gods everything that is a shame and reproach among men: stealing and committing adultery and deceiving each other") clearly implies "falsehood, lie:"

> πάντα θεοῖς ἀνέθηκαν Ὅμηρός θ' Ἡσίοδός τε
> ὅσσα παρ' ἀνθρώποισιν ὀνείδεα καὶ ψόγος ἐστίν,
> κλέπτειν μοιχεύειν τε καὶ ἀλλήλους ἀπατεύειν.

Pindar (*Ol.* 9.40 f., μὴ νῦν λαλάγει τὰ τοιαῦτ'· ἔα πόλεμον μάχαν τε πᾶσαν | χωρὶς ἀθανάτων) may or may not be under the spell of Xenophanes' ban of theomachies, but Plato (*Republic* 2, 377 b–378 d; *Euthyphro* 6 bc) certainly is.[16] Both Xenophanes' reasons for the ban appear in Plato: (1) such stories about the gods are untrue, οὐδὲ γὰρ ἀληθῆ (378 c 1), μύθους τοῖς ἀνθρώποις ψευδεῖς συντιθέντες ἔλεγόν τε καὶ λέγουσι (377 d 5), μύθους πλασθέντας ἀκούειν τοὺς παῖδας (377 b 6, where πλασθέντας recalls Xenophanes' πλάσματα, as Eisenstadt 58 had suggested). (2) They are politically harmful while encouraging the youths to engage in civil strife, οὐδέ γε (sc. δοκεῖ ἐπιτήδεια εἶναι λέγειν νέωι ἀκούοντι) τὸ παράπαν ὡς θεοὶ θεοῖς πολεμοῦσί τε καὶ ἐπιβουλεύουσι καὶ μάχονται ... εἴ γε δεῖ ἡμῖν τοὺς μέλλοντας τὴν πόλιν φυλάξειν αἴσχιστον νομίζειν τὸ ῥαιδίως ἀλλήλοις ἀπεχθάνεσθαι—πολλοῦ δεῖ γιγαντομαχίας τε μυθολογητέον αὐτοῖς καὶ ποικιλτέον, καὶ ἄλλας ἔχθρας πολλὰς καὶ παντοδαπὰς θεῶν τε καὶ ἡρώων πρὸς συγγενεῖς τε καὶ οἰκείους αὐτῶν.

16 As H. Diels, *Poetarum philosophorum fragmenta* (Berlin, 1901) 35, J. Adam, *The Republic of Plato* (Cambridge, 1902; 2nd ed. 1963), I, 114, and recently Eisenstadt 58, and especially in *Hermes* 102 (1974) 145 f., have pointed out.

(6) *Lines 19 and 20.* If this interpretation of lines 21–23 holds good we may be able to understand better why Xenophanes expects the singers "to strive for moral excellence." Because such a zeal fits a singer's knowledge about the *true* nature of the gods (being exactly the opposite of the "fabricated stories," πλάσματα, of Homer and Hesiod) and about the *real* value (χρηστόν) for the city.

The success of a guest's performance, then, seems to depend on two things: on his memory (μνημοσύνη) and on his moral endeavor (τόνος ἀμφ᾽ ἀρετῆι). The former quality is part of his technical poetic skill, the latter is much more than that. (Therefore Reinhardt's interpretation of ἀρετή as "der musikalische Teil des Vortrages" [p. 133] cannot be correct.)

The text of line 20 no longer seems to present difficulty. I prefer Ahrens' ἧι to Koraes' οἱ for the simple reason that an omitted dative can be more easily understood than an omitted verb, and a parallel case is at hand: Xenophanes B 2.8, where σῖτ᾽ εἴη stands for σῖτ᾽ οἱ εἴη. Koraes' emendation τόνος seems to be well established since J. Sitzler (*Berl. philol. Woch.* 1921, 1053) referred to Pindar *Pyth.*11.54 ξυναῖσι δ᾽ ἀμφ᾽ ἀρεταῖς τέταμαι, against the defense of the transmitted τὸν ὅς by Wilamowitz (*Hermes* 71 [1926] 278 f.), by T. W. Allen (*Revue de philologie* 8 [1934] 239 n. 11), by Bowra (8), and by Untersteiner (104 f.). For, if we adopt Wilamowitz's "two-singers theory" while translating, "Above all men praise this man who after drinking tells noble thoughts as his memory serves, and that man who tells about excellence" (Bowra, reading καὶ τὸν ὅς ἀμφ᾽ ἀρετῆς), we will find ourselves in the awkward position of distinguishing between "noble deeds" (ἐσθλά) and "moral excellence" (ἀρετή).

West (189) advanced a different interpretation of lines 19 f.: "As for the guests, applaud him whose skolion is edifying, so that the company's reflection on things past, and their effort in the future, may be concentrated on goodness" (ὡς ἧι μνημοσύνη καὶ τόνος ἀμφ᾽ ἀρετῆι). I am at a loss to see the point in the request that a man's reflection on things past be concentrated on goodness. In addition, the change of subject from "the singer" (in 19) to "the company as a whole" (in 20) seems to destroy the deliberate opposition between ἐσθλὰ ἀναφαίνειν (19) and μάχας διέπειν (21). Consequently, I prefer to understand the line as translated above (compare, e.g., Campbell 336, "as his memory and his enthusiasm for the virtue enable him").

More difficult is the text of line 19. My reason for banning πιών is not so much the breach of Hermann's bridge (Xenophanes violates it at B 1.17; at B 15.2 ἔργα τελεῖν ἄπερ ἄνδρες, and at B 34.2 ἄσσα λέγω περὶ πάντων), nor the strange position of πιών (as pointed out by Fränkel,

EGP 327 n. 3), but the very association of πιών with ἐσθλὰ ἀναφαίνει. Scholars adopting πιών explain it as standing in opposition to ἀναφαίνει: "who although he has drunk reveals noble thoughts" (Gerber 246); "his performance is good, although he has been drinking" (Campbell 336); "si la place des mots est inhabituelle, c'est que le poète met en valeur le participe concessif πιών" (Defradas, "Banquet" 348 n. 2). But I think such an opposition is trivial and unworthy of the rest of Xenophanes' message. As I have just stated, the excellence of a singer's performance will depend on two things only: on his memory, and on his drive for moral excellence. It does *not* depend on how strong his body is in resisting intoxication. Theognis' instruction (491 f.), ἀνίκητος δέ τοι οὗτος, ὃς πολλὰς πίνων μή τι μάταιον ἐρεῖ, is a platitude: it speaks of a common drinker (cf. 481 μυθεῖται δ' ἀπάλαμνα, τὰ νήφοσι γίνεται αἰσχρά), not of a noble singer of tales.

For a close parallel to the corruption of ἔσθλ' ἐπιὼν into ἐσθλὰ πιὼν compare Parmenides B 8.4: ἠδὲ τελεστόν (A. Covotti) for the transmitted ἠδ' ἀτέλεστον (an error possibly caused by ἀγένητον in the preceding line).

(7) *Line* 24. Finally, Xenophanes provides good advice for tomorrow (notice αἰέν): "It is meet always to keep a good regard for the gods." Herter, however, after referring to the Pythagorean injunction, "Be well disposed toward the divine race" (Iambl. *VP* 100, ἔτι πρὸς τούτοις περί τε τοῦ θείου καὶ περὶ τοῦ δαιμονίου καὶ περὶ τοῦ ἡρωικοῦ γένους εὔφημόν τε ⟨εἶναι ex Porph. add. C. Rittershausen⟩ καὶ ἀγαθὴν ἔχειν διάνοιαν = Porphyr. *VP* 38),[17] suggested that Xenophanes' drinking-party may well be a spiritual conventicle of the Eleatics: "Ist es zu kühn, den letzten Vers der Elegie des Xenophanes—es war sicher der letzte—als Reflex eines ähnlichen Schlusswortes aufzufassen?" (37). "Will man dies annehmen, so müsste man vielleicht an ein Konventikel geistiger Menschen denken, und was läge dann näher als die Philosophengemeinschaft, die sich in Elea bildete?" (48).

Six years later, Defradas gave a new twist to Herter's interpretation. Xenophanes not only "évoque sans doute la réunion d'un thiase philosophique éléate." He even criticizes and corrects Pythagoras' excessive asceticism. Pythagoras had commanded, μήτε οἶνον ὅλως πίνειν: Xenophanes corrects him, οὐχ ὕβρις πίνειν . . . ("Banquet" 363–365). Defradas' gratuitous enlargement of Herter's interpretation may well be left alone.

My objections to Herter's own interpretation (though scholars usually

---

[17] Compare Iambl. *VP* 149 ἐχρῆτο δὲ καὶ εὐφημίαι πρὸς τοὺς κρείττονας καὶ ἐν παντὶ καιρῶι μνήμην ἐποιεῖτο καὶ τιμὴν τῶν θεῶν; Diog. Laërt. 8.24.

refer to D⸃fradas, not to Herter: Campbell 334; Gerber 243) is as follows. First, the tenet, "Always be mindful of god" expresses common Greek sentiment, and need not go back to Pythagoras. Doubtless such common Greek names as Μνησίθεος or Θεόμνηστος ("Mindful of God") are not Pythagorean creations. And second, there is no historical evidence for a link between Xenophanes and the city of Elea. The text of Diogenes Laërtius (9.18) which Diels printed in his *FV*, Οὗτος [Xenophanes] ἐκπεσὼν τῆς πατρίδος ἐν Ζάγκληι τῆς Σικελίας ⟨διέτριβε καὶ τῆς εἰς Ἐλέαν ἀποικίας κοινωνήσας ἐδίδασκεν ἐκεῖ suppl. Diels⟩, διέτριβε δὲ καὶ ἐν Κατάνηι, is his own creation and should read, Οὗτος ἐκπεσὼν τῆς πατρίδος ἐν Ζάγκληι τῆς Σικελίας διέτριβε {δὲ om. P²F} καὶ ἐν Κατάνηι. Another testimony of Diog. Laërt. about Xenophanes and Elea (9.20), ἐποίησε δὲ ... καὶ τὸν εἰς Ἐλέαν τῆς Ἰταλίας ἀποικισμὸν ἔπη δισχίλια, is no more than a "Spielerei" by Lobon of Argos.[18]

Finally, the infinitive ἔχειν depends on the general injunction implied in χρή (13), as do the infinitives ὑμνεῖν (13), πίνειν (17), and αἰνεῖν (19); its subject is εὔφρονες ἄνδρες (13). Fränkel (*EGP* 327 n. 3) and Eisenstadt (38; 188), however, were not happy with the meaning of προμηθείη ("consideration, regard, respect"), and suggested the change of θεῶν δὲ to χρεὼν δὲ (Fränkel), or to τῶνδε (Eisenstadt, referring to the stories about violence mentioned in lines 21–23: "Of such things always have a virtuous providence"). Neither change is justified. Fränkel wrote: "θεῶν προμηθείην ἔχειν could only mean 'have consideration for the well-being of the gods' . . . and this is nonsense. I propose: χρεὼν δὲ προμηθείην αἰὲν ἔχειν ἀγαθήν . . . = 'one should always have a good purpose before one's eyes' (poetry should not only *delectare*, but also *prodesse*)." But Karsten (75) had already referred to Herodotus 1.88 (Κῦρος δὲ αὐτὸν [sc. Κροῖσον] . . . κάρτα ἐν πολλῆι προμηθίηι εἶχε), where προμηθίη clearly means "consideration, regard," "*observantia, reverentia*." The verb προμηθεῖσθαι has the same sense of "showing consideration or regard for" in Herodotus 2.172; 9.108.

II. XENOPHANES ON OLYMPIC GAMES: B 2 DK (ap. Athen. 413 F)

⊗ Ἀλλ' εἰ μὲν ταχυτῆτι ποδῶν νίκην τις ἄροιτο (1)
    ἢ πενταθλεύων, ἔνθα Διὸς τέμενος (2)

---

[18] As Wilamowitz (*Hermes* 61 [1926] 281), Jacoby, and especially M. Gigante (*Parola del Passato* 25 [1970] 236–240) have seen. Compare Untersteiner CCL–CCLIV; P. Steinmetz, "Xenophanesstudien," *Rhein. Mus.* 109 (1966) 28 n. 47. In the same vein, Bias is credited with a poem of two-thousand hexameters Περὶ Ἰωνίας (Diog. Laërt. 1.85) on the ground of a story in Herodotus (1.170).

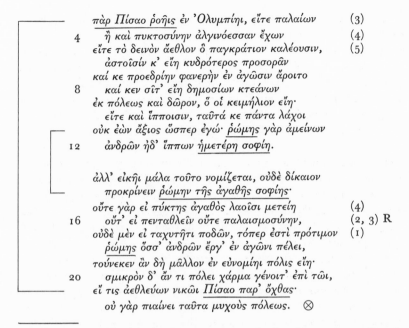

πὰρ Πίσαο ῥοῇις ἐν ᾿Ολυμπίηι, εἴτε παλαίων (3)

4 ἠ καὶ πυκτοσύνην ἀλγινόεσσαν ἔχων (4)

εἴτε τὸ δεινὸν ἄεθλον ὃ παγκράτιον καλέουσιν, (5)
ἀστοῖσίν κ᾿ εἴη κυδρότερος προσορᾶν
καί κε προεδρίην φανερὴν ἐν ἀγῶσιν ἄροιτο

8 καί κεν σῖτ᾿ εἴη δημοσίων κτεάνων
ἐκ πόλεως καὶ δῶρον, ὅ οἱ κειμήλιον εἴη·
εἴτε καὶ ἵπποισιν, ταῦτά κε πάντα λάχοι
οὐκ ἐὼν ἄξιος ὥσπερ ἐγώ· ῥώμης γὰρ ἀμείνων

12 ἀνδρῶν ἠδ᾿ ἵππων ἡμετέρη σοφίη.

ἀλλ᾿ εἰκῆι μάλα τοῦτο νομίζεται, οὐδὲ δίκαιον
προκρίνειν ῥώμην τῆς ἀγαθῆς σοφίης·
οὔτε γὰρ εἰ πύκτης ἀγαθὸς λαοῖσι μετείη (4)

16 οὔτ᾿ εἰ πενταθλεῖν οὔτε παλαισμοσύνην, (2, 3) R
οὐδὲ μὲν εἰ ταχυτῆτι ποδῶν, τόπερ ἐστὶ πρότιμον (1)
ῥώμης ὅσσ᾿ ἀνδρῶν ἔργ᾿ ἐν ἀγῶνι πέλει,
τούνεκεν ἂν δὴ μᾶλλον ἐν εὐνομίηι πόλις εἴη·

20 σμικρὸν δ᾿ ἄν τι πόλει χάρμα γένοιτ᾿ ἐπὶ τῶι,
εἴ τις ἀεθλεύων νικῶι Πίσαο παρ᾿ ὄχθας·
οὐ γὰρ πιαίνει ταῦτα μυχοὺς πόλεως. ⊗

---

5 εἴτε τό Wakefield: εἴτέτι A 6 προσεραν A, corr. Jacobs 8 σιτειη A, corr. Turnebus: σίτησιν Kaibel 9 et 22 πόλιος Schneidewin 10 κ᾿ εἰπάντα A, corr. Schweighaeuser 15 λαοῖσιν ἔτ᾿ εἴη A, corr. Stephanus

---

TRANSLATION

Nay, should a man win victory by the swiftness of his feet, or in the five-contest (*pentathlon*), there where the precinct of Zeus stands, by the streams of the river of Pisa [i.e., Alpheus] in Olympia; or else in wrestling, or by possessing skill in the painful boxing, or again in that dreadful contest which they call *pankration*: he would be more glorious [sc. than others] to look upon, in the eyes of his fellow-citizens; and he would win the privilege of a conspicuous first-seat at the contests; he also would have bread from the public stores, granted to him by the city; and even a present to serve him as his heirloom. Even if he won with his horses, he would obtain all these though he is not worthy of such rewards as much as I am.[19] For our art [*or* wisdom] is better than the strength of men and horses.

[19] Line 10 f.: εἴτε καὶ ἵπποισιν (sc. νίκην τις ἄροιτο from line 1), ταῦτά κε πάντα λάχοι: so W. E. Weber and J. N. Bach (*Jahrbücher für Philologie und Pädagogik* 9 [1829] 315). The sense seems to be, "And even if his victory was due only to the strength of his horses, not his own, he would still obtain all these rewards though not being worthy of them as much

(13) Nay, this is an utterly gratuitous custom, and it is not right to prefer strength to the useful art [*or* wisdom]. For suppose there is a man among the people good at boxing, or at wrestling, or at the five-contest, or even in swiftness of his feet (which is most honored of all men's deeds of strength in the contest): not for that reason would the city enjoy a better government. Shortlived, indeed, is the source of joy for a city coming from a victorious athlete in the contest at the banks of the river of Pisa: for this is not what fattens the chambers of the city.

Xenophanes' rebellious attack on the traditionally highly esteemed Ὀλυμπιονῖκαι seems to be a complete poem, easily falling into two parts: lines 1–12 against lines 13–22. For a poem beginning with ἀλλά, compare Tyrtaeus 11 West; Timocreon 727 *PMG*; Theognis 97, 341, 583, 843, 889, 1055 (and Campbell 140 f.). The unity of the poem is enhanced by the ring-composition. At the end (line 21), Πίσαο παρ' ὄχθας (a Homeric phrase, *Iliad* 12.313) resumes πὰρ Πίσαο ῥοῆις in line 3. Doubtless the poet is trying to tell the audience: "My targets are the very Olympic victors." In the middle of the poem, the preference given to ἡμετέρη σοφίη over ῥώμη in lines 11–12 leads to the preference given to ἡ ἀγαθὴ σοφίη over ῥώμη in line 14, clearly implying that "*our* art (*or* wisdom)" is an "effective (*or* wholesome) art (*or* wisdom)." Moreover, there are no less than *nine* negative particles or expressions in the last six couplets (lines 11, 13, 15, 16, 17, 22, plus 13: εἰκῆι, and 20: σμικρόν = "hardly any"); these negatives indicate that this is a strongly polemic poem indeed.

---

as I am." This interpretation derives support from the fact that chariot-racing is mentioned separately from "the deeds of strength of men," in lines 1–5, clearly implying that the strength of horses is even less worthy of reward than that of athletes.

Consequently, Fränkel's interpretation (advanced in 1925, and adopted by Jaeger, Untersteiner, and Gerber), "Oder wenn es auch nur seine Rosse waren die den Sieg gewannen, so erhält er alle diese Ehren" (*Wege* 69 and 334 f.), should be given preference to that of Diels ("ja mag er selbst einen Wagensieg erringen, so würde er trotz aller dieser gewonnenen Preise ihrer doch nicht so würdig sein wie ich") and of W. J. Verdenius, "even if his victory will be with horses [which won a man the highest fame among the Greeks], he will not deserve to receive all these honours, whereas I do deserve to receive them" ("Emphatic use of the participle," *Mnemosyne* ser. 4, 9 [1956] 234).

For, the fact that victory in chariot-racing enjoyed the highest rank among the Greeks is of no interest to Xenophanes. Building upon the opposition between "physical strength" (ῥώμη) and "wholesome wisdom" (σοφίη), Xenophanes takes into consideration primarily "strength and endurance" of both men and horses (ῥώμη in lines 11, 14, 18), not the athletes' skill as well. He himself states that foot-racing ranks the highest (τόπερ ἐστὶ πρότιμον, 17) among men's deeds of strength in competitions. And from the word-order in line 12 (ἀνδρῶν ἠδ' ἵππων) it becomes clear that strength of horses is of less value than that of men.

What is emphatically rejected is "physical strength," ῥώμη (three times: 11, 14, 18). What is very much on the poet's mind is πόλις (four times: 9, 19, 20, 22). A clear voice for *reappraisal* of traditional values in the city is raised, a firm request for reform is unmistakable. The well-established custom (νομίζεται, 13) of highest rewards for victorious athletes is both utterly arbitrary (εἰκῆι μάλα) and unjust (οὐδὲ δίκαιαν, 13). Euripides (fr. 282 Nauck², from *Autolycus*, ap. Athen. 413 C) had correctly understood Xenophanes' message (as Athenaeus had already seen):

(1)   Κακῶν γὰρ ὄντων μυρίων καθ' Ἑλλάδα
      οὐδὲν κάκιόν ἐστιν ἀθλητῶν γένους.
(13) ἐμεμψάμην δὲ καὶ τὸν Ἑλλήνων νόμον,
      οἳ τῶνδ' ἕκατι σύλλογον ποιούμενοι
      τιμῶσ' ἀχρείους {ἡδονὰς} δαιτὸς ⟨ἐπιδόντες⟩ χάριν.[20]

And why is the established custom of high rewards for Olympic winners wrong and unjust? Because it reverses the scale of values in the city by placing "physical strength" (ῥώμη) above "wholesome wisdom" (ἡ ἀγαθὴ σοφίη, 14). For there can be no *prosperity* for a city (εὐδαιμονίη, implied by the plain utilitarian phrase, "this is not what *fattens* the chambers of the city," 22) without a *good government* (εὐνομίη, 19). And no athlete can provide such a government (no matter how strong and successful at the contests he may be): it can come only from citizens *instructed* by such enlightening bard-sages as Xenophanes himself (ἡμετέρη σοφίη, 12) or, say, as Solon.[21] In short, the message of the whole poem boils down to this: "Only a useful wisdom (such a one as my own) can bring about good government (on which the well-being of the city depends): no athlete's strength can."

Both the Platonic Socrates and Euripides shared Xenophanes' view. Socrates (Plato *Apology* 36 d 5, referred to by Buchholz, I, 66), claimed that an *educator* of the citizens deserves to be awarded the public σίτησις much more than do Olympic winners; for he makes the citizens happy in

20 "The Greeks call an assembly for the athletes' sake and pay the honor to these useless men after granting them the favor of free feast [i.e., ἐν πρυτανείωι σιτεῖσθαι]." The text as transmitted does not seem to make sense. C. B. Gulick (*Athenaeus*, Loeb, IV, p. 373) translates: "and pay them the honour of useless pleasures to grace a feast." The word ἡδονὰς seems to be out of place here—probably a makeshift introduced after ἐπιδόντες had been mistakenly dropped. Another makeshift is to be found in line 23 (*infra*): {στὰς} for the lost ⟨ἀλλ'⟩ ἄνδρας (Nauck).

21 εὐνομίη (19) may or may not be reminiscent of Solon 4.32 West Εὐνομίη, but δημοσίων κτεάνων (8) does seem to recall κτεάνων... δημοσίων of Solon 4.12, as E. Diehl and more recently A. Lumpe (*Rhein. Mus.* 98 [1955] 378) have pointed out. And Xenophanes may have known of Solon's reform imposing limits on the rewards for victorious athletes (see *infra*).

full truth, while the athletes do so only in seeming: οὐκ ἔσθ' ὅτι μᾶλλον . . .
πρέπει οὕτως ὡς τὸν τοιοῦτον ἄνδρα [scil. as Socrates the educator is, 36 c 5
ἐπιχειρῶν ἕκαστον ὑμῶν πείθειν κτλ.] ἐν πρυτανείωι σιτεῖσθαι, πολύ γε μᾶλλον
ἢ εἴ τις ὑμῶν ἵππωι ἢ συνωρίδι ἢ ζεύγει νενίκηκεν Ὀλυμπίασιν· ὁ μὲν γὰρ ὑμᾶς
ποιεῖ εὐδαίμονας δοκεῖν εἶναι, ἐγὼ δὲ εἶναι.[22] Euripides (fr. 282.23–28),
expanded Xenophanes' thought:

　　　⟨ἀλλ'⟩ ἄνδρας – x χρὴ σοφούς τε κἀγαθοὺς
　　　φύλλοις στέφεσθαι χὥστις ἡγεῖται πόλει
　(25)　κάλλιστα σώφρων καὶ δίκαιος ὢν ἀνήρ,
　　　ὅστις τε μύθοις ἔργ' ἀπαλλάσσει κακὰ
　　　μάχας τ' ἀφαιρῶν καὶ στάσεις. τοιαῦτα γὰρ
　　　πόλει τε πάσηι πᾶσί θ' Ἕλλησιν καλά.[23]

In addition, Isocrates (*Paneg.* 4.1–2, referred to by Karsten, 64) and
Diodorus of Sicily (9.2.5) seem to echo the sentiment of Socrates and
Euripides. Isocrates does so by proclaiming, τῶν μὲν γὰρ ἀθλητῶν δὶς
τοσαύτην ῥώμην λαβόντων οὐδὲν ἂν πλέον γένοιτο τοῖς ἄλλοις, ἑνὸς δὲ ἀνδρὸς εὖ
φρονήσαντος ἅπαντες ἂν ἀπολαύσειαν οἱ βουλόμενοι κοινωνεῖν τῆς ἐκείνου διανοίας,
while Diodorus states, ὅτι ὁ Σόλων ἡγεῖτο τοὺς μὲν πύκτας καὶ σταδιεῖς καὶ
τοὺς ἄλλους ἀθλητὰς μηδὲν ἀξιόλογον συμβάλλεσθαι ταῖς πόλεσι πρὸς σωτηρίαν,
τοὺς δὲ φρονήσει καὶ ἀρετῆι διαφέροντας μόνους δύνασθαι τὰς πατρίδας ἐν τοῖς
κινδύνοις διαφυλάττειν.

Now, the fact that the well-being of a city depends on its good government was common knowledge in Xenophanes' time:

　　　αὐτοὶ δ' εὐνομίηισι πόλιν κάτα καλλιγύναικα
　　　κοιρανέουσ', ὄλβος δὲ πολὺς καὶ πλοῦτος ὀπηδεῖ.
　　　　　　　　　　(*Homeric Hymn* 30.11 f.)

But the idea that good government depends on wholesome instruction by
an enlightener, not on glory of reigning Olympic victors, seems to be
Xenophanes' original contribution.

At this point we should dismiss an exaggerated notion, introduced by
Bowra (28 f.), shared by H. Bengtson,[24] and expanded by Eisenstadt
(68 f.)—that unjustified rewards for the athletes will encourage ὕβρις on
the part of dissatisfied citizens. Bowra wrote, "In general δίκαιος means
that which belongs to the established order of things and is for that reason

---

[22] Compare, e.g., Aeschylus *Septem* 592, οὐ γὰρ δοκεῖν ἄριστος, ἀλλ' εἶναι θέλει (Plato,
Republic 2, 361 b 7).

[23] Eisenstadt 71 f. seems to go too far in making Euripides depend on Xenophanes
B 1.21–23.

[24] *Die olympischen Spiele in der Antike* (Zurich, 1971) 68.

to be approved. Its opposite, ἄδικος, is applied to whatever breaks this order and is associated with κόρος and ὕβρις." "For him [i.e., Solon] Εὐνομίη is practically a state of mind, or at least a political condition produced by a state of mind. And it is something like this to which Xenophanes refers when he says that athletic success does not put a city μᾶλλον ἐν εὐνομίηι. He means that so far from creating that modest frame of mind which is the essence of social stability, the honours paid to athletes will encourage ὕβρις."

But this is not what we have in Xenophanes' text. I have in mind especially lines 15 and 19:

> οὔτε γὰρ εἰ πύκτης ἀγαθὸς λαοῖσι μετείη,
> τούνεκεν ἂν δὴ μᾶλλον ἐν εὐνομίηι πόλις εἴη.

As I have already said, Xenophanes' position is that of a *pragmatic utilitarian*. No παιδοτρίβης or γυμνασίαρχος can teach an athlete the art/wisdom (σοφίη) of how to govern well a city. All he can impart to him is "physical strength and fitness" (ῥώμη), which is simply not good enough. As a consequence, the presence of a victorious athlete in the city-government (even though he be famous Milon of Croton, athletically active ca. 540–512 B.C.) will produce neither εὐνομίη nor the ensuing εὐδαιμονίη. Only the presence in the government of citizens instructed by such a σοφός as Xenophanes can assure this result. That is why an "effective sage" (ἀγαθὸς σοφός) should be valued by the city more highly than an "effective boxer" (πύκτης ἀγαθός), contrary to the established practice (εἰκῆι μάλα τοῦτο νομίζεται, 13). The current reversal of values proved to be counter-productive in practice. That is why it is unjust (οὐδὲ δίκαιαν, 13).

Eisenstadt gave a new twist to Bowra's ὕβρις-interpretation of the poem: "The violence of athletic strength, exemplified in the person of the *Olympionikês*, is not a fit object of public honor because of its disturbing effect on the passions of the audience. At the very least, the sight of the athlete is not the best paradigm of emotional tranquillity and hence the city is not 'more in good order.'" Against such a narrow interpretation of the poem it suffices to say that it leaves unexplained the presence of such a key-phrase as πιαίνειν μυχοὺς πόλεως (22), and that the presence in the city of an excellent foot-racer (notice the preference given to "swiftness of foot," lines 1 and 17–18) does not suggest any "disturbing effect on the passions of the audience."

Σοφίη (12 and 14). Ever since Karsten's remark of 1830, "σοφίη dicitur poëtarum ars et sapientia, qua olim omnis tam privatarum quam publicarum rerum disciplina continebatur" (*Xenophanis reliquiae* 63), scholars have been divided in trying to decide which sense prevails here—"poetic skill and art" or its content, "a practical wisdom." (Untersteiner's rendering, "capacità di conoscere," "abilità conoscitiva," 113–115, may well be left alone.) J. Burnet, O. Gigon ("Dichterkunst"), G. S. Kirk, D. A. Campbell and many others have preferred the former, and W. K. C. Guthrie writes, ". . . claiming that their [the athletes'] physical feats are of far less worth than 'my art.' . . . This claim is characteristic of a poet of the time, and would have been made equally by Solon or Theognis."[25] On the other hand, Diels ("Wissen"), Reinhardt ("Weisheit"), J. Defradas ("science") and others have preferred the latter meaning.

Having in mind this very genre of paraenetic elegies (such as B 1 and B 2), Fränkel and Bowra happily combined both senses. The former rendered σοφίη with "Weisheitskunst" ("skill or wisdom");[26] the latter wrote (18): "Since he was writing a special kind of poetry, it must be to his excellence in this that he refers, and we are wrong to assume that he meant either poetry as such or knowledge as such. He meant the philosophical and critical poetry which he himself wrote and which he believed to be worthy of better rewards than it got."

I prefer, however, to believe that "wisdom" prevails here over "poetic skill," if ἀγαθός in line 14 (ἡ ἀγαθὴ σοφίη) means much the same as in line 15 (πύκτης ἀγαθός)—"effective, capable," thus reflecting Xenophanes' utilitarian pragmatism. It is the content of his poetry which promises to enlighten the citizens, teaching them how to govern their city so that prosperity may follow. In short, Xenophanes' ἀγαθὴ σοφίη says much the same as "his traveling thought," βληστρίζοντες ἐμὴν φροντίδ᾽ ἀν᾽ Ἑλλάδα γῆν (B 8.2).[27] The practical wisdom of a sage may be meant.[28]

Xenophanes is evidently at pains to give a fairly complete list of Olympic events. He does so by listing them in chronological order, not in the sequence of contests at Olympic Games (where the chariot-race was the opening, not the last event).[29] The only exception is the chariot-race, the

[25] A History of Greek Philosophy, I (Cambridge, 1962) 364.

[26] Dichtung und Philosophie 375 f. and 607 (English translation, 330 and 528, but "wisdom" on p. 329).

[27] M. Marcovich, Antiquité Vivante 1 (1951) 117–120, against "care, anxiety" (LSJ); "meine Sorge" (Diels-Kranz); "my cares" (Guthrie, HGP I, 363); "mein sorgenschweres Herz," "Sorge und Not" (Ziegler, n. 1, supra, 289 n. 1 and 290).

[28] The sentiment that "wisdom" here prevails over "poetic skill" is shared by Boris Gladigow, Sophia und Kosmos (Diss. Tübingen, 1962), Hildesheim, 1965 (Spoudasmata, 1) 35, and by Friedrich Maier, Der Σοφός-Begriff etc. (Diss. Munich, 1970) 40–43.

[29] Fränkel (Wege 336) is half wrong, half correct when writing: "Es ist die Reihenfolge in der sich die Kämpfe abspielten, und zugleich die historische Reihenfolge der Einsetzung."

mention of which is postponed probably because it involves the ῥώμη of horses, not of men. Incidentally, Xenophanes refers only to the four-horsed chariot-race (unlike the distinction made by Socrates in Plato *Apology* 36 d 5), for the two-horsed one was introduced to the Olympic Games long after Xenophanes' death (in 408 B.C.). Most probably, the "fleetness of foot" comprises all running events (after all, Xenophanes is writing poetry, not an Olympic program). Therefore, Bowra's dating of the poem before 520 B.C., the year in which the race in armor—absent in Xeno-phanes—was introduced to the Olympic Games (*Problems* 16), need not be accepted: this running event too may be implied by "swiftness of foot."[30] The chronological order of events (1, 2, 3, 4, 5) in lines 1–5 is inverted to some extent in lines 15–17 (with the omission of the *umbilicus*—pankration—possibly because it consists of wrestling plus boxing, which have already been mentioned), forming a chiastic scheme (4, 2, 3, 1), as Fränkel had pointed out.[31] Here is a table of Olympic events.[32]

Olympiad	Year B.C.	Athletic event first introduced	Xenophanes B 2
1	776	One-stade foot-race	1
14	724	Two-stade foot-race (*Diaulos*)	1
15	720	Long-distance race (*Dolichos*)	1
18	708	*Pentathlon.* Wrestling	2 and 3
23	688	Boxing	4
25	680	The four-horsed chariot-race	6
33	648	*Pankration.* Horse-race	5 and 0
37	632	Foot-race and Wrestling of youths	0
41	616	Boxing of youths	0
65	520	Race in armor	1 or 0
93	408	The two-horsed chariot-race	0

"*Educator is above Athlete*" (Xenophanes B 2) against "*Soldier is above Athlete*" (Tyrtaeus 12 West). One final problem remains. High rewards for the 'Ολυμπιονῖκαι reflected genuine and common sentiment through-out the Hellenic world. How original and realistic then is the voice of protest coming from our maverick sage? There are two known attempts before Xenophanes to curb the traditional glory of the Olympic winners, one by Tyrtaeus (12), the other by Solon (Diog. Laërt. 1.55; Plutarch *Solon* 23.3). Both of them gave preference to *good soldier* over *good athlete*. Not long after 650 B.C. the Greeks must have realized the striking

[30] So Fränkel 337 (as an alternative), Defradas (n. 1, *supra*, 79), Gerber 248, Bengtson (n. 24, *supra*, 68).

[31] *Wege* 69 f. and 336 n. 3. This is an old device. Compare *Odyssey* 11.170 ff.: Odysseus asks Anticleia about his mother, father, son, and wife. She answers in the reversed order: wife, son, father, mother.

[32] Bengtson 35. Bowra's chronology (16 n. 1) is wrong.

difference between athletic skill and military fitness. In spite of such common disciplines as javelin-throwing, horse-racing, and race-in-armor, athletic training failed to provide skilled, brave and enduring soldiers, able to stand the hardships of war. As Plutarch (*Philopoemen* 3.2–4) summed it up, ἀθλητικὸν στρατιωτικοῦ σῶμα καὶ βίον διαφέρειν τοῖς πᾶσι, μάλιστα δὲ δίαιταν ἑτέραν καὶ ἄσκησιν εἶναι. It would be no surprise if this difference was first discovered at Sparta. Now Tyrtaeus wrote:

> (1)   Οὔτ' ἂν μνησαίμην οὔτ' ἐν λόγωι ἄνδρα τιθείην
>   οὔτε ποδῶν ἀρετῆς οὔτε παλαιμοσύνης,
>   οὐδ' εἰ Κυκλώπων μὲν ἔχοι μέγεθός τε βίην τε,
>   νικώιη δὲ θέων Θρηίκιον Βορέην . . .
> (9)   οὐδ' εἰ πᾶσαν ἔχοι δόξαν πλὴν θούριδος ἀλκῆς·
> (15)   ξυνὸν δ' ἐσθλὸν τοῦτο πόληί τε παντί τε δήμωι,
>   ὅστις ἀνὴρ διαβὰς ἐν προμάχοισι μένηι
>   νωλεμέως . . .

Jaeger argued that Xenophanes B 2 was "obviously inspired" by Tyrtaeus 12 ("offenbar von ihm inspiriert").[33] He adduced two reasons for this assumption: (1) The first lines of Xenophanes' elegy show a striking similarity with the elegy of Tyrtaeus ("Der Eingang . . . ist von schlagender Aehnlichkeit mit der Elegie des Tyrtaios"). And (2), what is decisive is that both of them use the same reason for the preference given to the true ἀρετή: the welfare of the polis, "Was aber für den Einfluss des Tyrtaios auf Xenophanes entscheidend ist, das ist die Begründung des Vorrangs der σοφίη vor den agonalen ἀρεταί [Xenophanes B 2.15–22]. Auch hier ist das Wohl der Polis zum Massstab des Werts der ἀρετή gemacht."

Neither reason is decisive. The similarity between the beginning lines of both elegies is not striking, and the criterion of "what is profitable to the common welfare of the polis" ("der Nutzen für das gemeine Wohl der Polis") is not sufficiently emphasized in Tyrtaeus. For, line 15 (built upon Homeric formulas, ξυνὸν δὲ κακὸν πολέεσσι plus πατρί τε σῶι μέγα πῆμα πόληί τε παντί τε δήμωι, *Iliad* 16.262 and 3.50, as E. Diehl had pointed out) does not bear the same force in Tyrtaeus' poem as does the final line of Xenophanes' message, οὐ γὰρ πιαίνει ταῦτα μυχοὺς πόλεως.[34]

But even if Xenophanes knew of Tyrtaeus' poem, there are significant

---

[33] W. Jaeger, "Tyrtaios über die wahre ἀρετή," *SB Berlin*, 1932, 23, 537–568, esp. 556 ff. = *Scripta Minora* (Rome, 1960), II, 100 ff. = *Five Essays* (Montreal, 1966) 128 ff.

[34] Compare also Campbell 178, "Jaeger's view that for Tyrtaeus 'there is only one standard of true areté—the state' is also misleading . . .," and C. M. Bowra, *Early Greek Elegists* (Harvard U.P., 1938) 66, "In Hector, Homer certainly created a man like Tyrtaeus' ideal. . . ."

differences between them. First, Tyrtaeus gives preference to "fierce courage on battlefield" (9, θοῦρις ἀλκή) over athletic skill, while Xenophanes replaces "warlike prowess" by "wholesome wisdom": there is none of the martial ethics of Tyrtaeus and Heraclitus in Xenophanes (compare B 1).[35] And second, Xenophanes proves to be much more *realistic* than Tyrtaeus (for who in Greece would think of abolishing all awards for the Olympic winners?). Tyrtaeus' first line is radical, "No public memory in poetry, and certainly no esteem whatsoever for the best athlete unless he is a good warrior too." Xenophanes is pragmatic and moderate instead: the words οὐκ ἐὼν ἄξιος ὥσπερ ἐγώ and ἡμετέρη σοφίη ἀμείνων (B 2.11–12) do not imply "no rewards for the Olympic winners whatsoever," but only "they deserve lower rewards than those to be given to a good educator." All Xenophanes wants is a *reappraisal* of the values traditionally (but wrongly and unjustly) established in the polis.

Xenophanes shared this social need for *moderate* reform with Solon, who is reported to have introduced a measure curtailing excessive rewards for victorious athletes by fixing the allowance at 500 drachmai for an Olympic winner, 100 for an Isthmian one, and so on; and Diogenes Laërtius continues (l. 55), "For it is in bad taste to increase the rewards for these victors, but rather only those for the fallen in battle, whose sons, in addition, should be maintained and educated at the state's expense" (ἀπειρόκαλον γὰρ τὸ ἐξαίρειν τὰς τούτων τιμάς, ἀλλὰ μόνων ἐκείνων τῶν ἐν πολέμοις τελευτησάντων, ὧν καὶ τοὺς υἱοὺς δημοσίαι τρέφεσθαι καὶ παιδεύεσθαι).

While Plato, in *Apology* 36 d 5 and *Republic* 2, 377 b–378 d, was doubtless under the spell of Xenophanes' elegies (B 2 and B 1), no such influence is visible in *Republic* 3 and in *Laws* 7 and 8, where Plato deals with the physical education of the future soldiers only to dismiss athletic training as inappropriate. It is now Tyrtaeus who inspires him with his *virtus bellica*. Plato calls him Τύρταιον τὸν φύσει μὲν Ἀθηναῖον and twice quotes from his elegy 12 (*Laws* 1, 629 ab; 2, 660 e–661 a). Here is the way Plato feels about the athletic training: περὶ ἁπάντων τῶν ἀγώνων τῶν γυμνικῶν, ὡς ὅσα μὲν αὐτῶν πρὸς πόλεμόν ἐστιν ἀγωνίσματα ἐπιτηδευτέον καὶ θετέον ἆθλα νικητήρια, ὅσα δὲ μή, χαίρειν ἐατέον (*Laws* 8, 832 e 1). Καὶ δὴ τά γε κατὰ πάλην ἃ μὲν Ἀνταῖος ἢ Κερκύων ἐν τέχναις ἑαυτῶν συνεστήσαντο φιλονικίας ἀχρήστου χάριν, ἢ πυγμῆς Ἐπειὸς ἢ Ἄμυκος, οὐδὲν χρήσιμα ἐπὶ πολέμου κοινωνίαν ὄντα, οὐκ ἄξια λόγωι κοσμεῖν (*Laws* 7, 795 e 7). Ἦ οὐχ ὁρᾶις ὅτι καθεύδουσί τε τὸν βίον (sc. οἱ ἀθληταί) καί, ἐὰν σμικρὰ ἐκβῶσιν τῆς τεταγμένης

[35] Compare Fränkel (*Early Greek Poetry and Philosophy* 338), "The elegist, like Xenophanes, vigorously controverts the devotion to athletics, but he follows a very different line. He has no notion of claiming a leading role for the intellect, and he cares little for skill in words: *aretê* for him is most fully realized in courage shown in battle."

διαίτης, μεγάλα καὶ σφόδρα νοσοῦσιν οὗτοι οἱ ἀσκηταί· Ὁρῶ. Κομψοτέρας δή τινος, ἦν δ' ἐγώ, ἀσκήσεως δεῖ τοῖς πολεμικοῖς ἀθληταῖς ... (Republic 3, 404 a 5). Αὐτά γε μὴν τὰ γυμνάσια καὶ τοὺς πόνους πρὸς τὸ θυμοειδὲς τῆς φύσεως βλέπων κἀκεῖνο ἐγείρων πονήσει μᾶλλον ἢ πρὸς ἰσχύν, οὐχ ὥσπερ οἱ ἄλλοι ἀθληταὶ ῥώμης ἕνεκα σιτία καὶ πόνους μεταχειριεῖται (410 b 5).

Of course, these passages also reflect the reaction of fifth-century medical literature to the shortcomings of athletic training, with its over-specialization and exaggerations in dietetics; this reaction is best summarized by Hippocrates De alimento 34, διάθεσις ἀθλητικὴ οὐ φύσει· ἕξις ὑγιεινὴ κρέσσων ἐν πᾶσι ("The physical condition of the athletes is not natural: a healthy state of body is superior in every respect," appropriately quoted by Galen, Protrept. 10 and 11), and by Socrates ap. Xenophon, Symp. 2.17, ἀλλὰ παντὶ διαπονῶν τῶι σώματι πᾶν ἰσόρροπον ποιεῖν.[36]

But long before Plato connected Xenophanes' "wisdom of an educator of citizens" with Tyrtaeus' virtus bellica and contrasted them with athletic training and skill, Euripides had done the same in his Autolycus, where he combines lines echoing Xenophanes' B 2 (fr. 282.13–15 and 23–25, quoted above) with verses of Tyrtaean sentiment:

(16) Τίς γὰρ παλαίσας εὖ, τίς ὠκύπους ἀνὴρ
ἢ δίσκον ἄρας ἢ γνάθον παίσας καλῶς
πόλει πατρώιαι στέφανον ἤρκεσεν λαβών;
πότερα μαχοῦνται πολεμίοισιν ἐν χεροῖν

(20) δίσκους ἔχοντες ἢ δι⟨χ'⟩ ἀσπίδων χερὶ
θείνοντες ἐκβαλοῦσι πολεμίους πάτρας;
οὐδεὶς σιδήρου ταῦτα μωραίνει πέλας. {στάς}[37]

University of Illinois at Urbana

[36] Compare H. Kanter, "Platos Anschauungen über Gymnastik," Progr. Gymn. Graudenz (Leipzig, 1886) 3–22. J. Jüthner, Philostratos über Gymnastik (Leipzig, 1909; reprint 1969) 30–43 and 51–59.

[37] For sure, the Euripidean eclectic cento also reflects Hippocratic attacks on over-eating as part of athletic training and diet (well summed up by Galen, Proptrepticus 11), in the same way in which Plato, Republic 3, 404 a 5 (quoted above), ridicules the required over-sleeping of the athletes: πῶς γὰρ ὅστις ἔστ' ἀνὴρ | γνάθου τε δοῦλος νηδύος θ' ἡσσημένος | κτήσαιτ' ἂν ὄλβον εἰς ὑπερβολὴν πατρός;

2

Philoctetes and Modern Criticism

P. E. EASTERLING

Philoctetes has attracted more critical attention in the ʹlast fifteen years than any other play of Sophocles, more perhaps than any other Greek tragedy. This may be partly because its themes—alienation and communication, ends and means—are familiar and important to modern readers, partly because it is a play of remarkable complexity which presents a special challenge to the interpreter. What follows is a brief attempt to take stock, to see how far there are areas of common agreement and where the important problems now seem to lie.

I begin with dramatic technique, on which much of the best recent work has been concentrated,[1] leading us to a deeper understanding of the play's extremely refined and subtle design. We can now make a number of fairly confident assumptions without having to argue from scratch about the nature of Sophocles' methods:

1. Here as in the other extant plays Sophocles releases the crucial information on which the action turns in a piecemeal and ambiguous way. If pressed too literally, as if it were historical evidence, it turns out to be inconsistent; but this is how he gives himself scope for effects of suspense and surprise and progressive revelation. The prophecy of Helenus is expounded in a way which leaves its detail uncertain until late in the play, and (as Robinson has pointed out)[2] Sophocles makes his characters respond to it as people would in real life, interpreting the cryptic revelation of the future according to their sense of what is actually feasible in the circumstances.

Thus in the Prologue Odysseus argues, from his knowledge that Philoctetes is a man with both a bitter grievance against the Greeks and

---

[1] Following the trail blazed by Tycho von Wilamowitz in 1917 (*Die dramatische Technik des Sophokles*).

[2] D. B. Robinson, "Topics in Sophocles' *Philoctetes*," *C.Q.* 19 (1969) p. 47.

an unfailing bow, that neither persuasion nor force will have any effect
(103). To him at this juncture there is only one conceivable approach to
Philoctetes, stealth. This attitude is echoed in the False Merchant's story
(whether true or false is not important) that when Helenus said that
Philoctetes must be persuaded to go to Troy Odysseus volunteered to
fetch him: most likely he would do it by persuasion, he said, but if
persuasion failed, by force (617 f.). Odysseus is approaching the prophecy
in the pragmatic spirit that you do the best you can towards fulfilling what
is foretold, crossing your fingers that whatever is beyond your control will
somehow fall into place. This is what the Chorus are doing at 833 ff.,
when they urge Neoptolemus to make off with the bow while Philoctetes
sleeps. When he refuses, saying that the god demanded Philoctetes as well
as his bow, their answer is "The god will see to that: you get the bow while
you can." This flexibility of response is not only convincing; it is also a
great source of dramatic interest, which would simply be precluded if the
dramatist and his characters treated the future deterministically.

2. It used often to be argued (and here Bowra's[3] interpretation was
especially influential) that the point of the varying responses to the
prophecy was moral and religious, that the real focus of the action was the
impious neglect by Odysseus of the god's command. But detailed analysis
has shown the weaknesses in this approach; and in any case modern
criticism of the other plays of Sophocles has made us more and more aware
that a simple moralistic formula is unlikely to work. The impiety of
Odysseus as the "real subject" of *Philoctetes* is as inadequate as the *hubris*
of Ajax as the key to that play.

3. Analogous with Sophocles' ambiguous treatment of the prophecy is
the ambiguity in his treatment of the characters' motivation. What, for
example, does Odysseus really want, and what has he in mind at successive
points in the play? Is he bluffing or not when he says that with the bow
safely in Neoptolemus' possession Philoctetes can be left behind on
Lemnos (1054 ff.)? How much truth is told by the False Merchant? Most
important of all, how far is Neoptolemus carrying out his plan to deceive,
and how far is he moved by pity and shame, *before* the moment at which
he breaks? Recent criticism collectively demonstrates how little the
audience actually knows—either about the prophecy or about the motivation of everyone but Philoctetes—until late in the play.

In the case of Neoptolemus, Steidle[4] in particular has drawn attention
to a great many places where his words or his silence may hint that he is

---

[3] C. M. Bowra, *Sophoclean tragedy* (1944) pp. 261 ff.
[4] W. Steidle, *Studien zum antiken Drama* (1968) pp. 169 ff.

unhappy with the role he is playing; we must also remember that the suffering figure of Philoctetes makes a very powerful impact on our emotions, and therefore, we may suppose, on the emotions of Neoptolemus. But the important point is that almost every detail in Neoptolemus' behaviour can be variously interpreted. For example, at 461 ff., when he says he had better be going: is this simply a device for furthering the deceit, precipitating a plea for rescue on Philoctetes' part by pretending that the interview is over, just like the other interviews with casual callers in the past, or is Steidle right to see in it a hint of Neoptolemus' passivity and reluctance to take more positive action?[5] The answer is that we have no means of knowing for certain, though each critic or producer or actor will have a strong individual response and feel sure of the tone of voice in which it should be played.

4. Finally, there is the visible stage action. Recent work has taught us to recognise more readily that what we see on the stage is crucially important for the interpretation of the play. Taplin,[6] for example, has shown how the action of Neoptolemus in physically supporting Philoctetes links two highly significant scenes: 877 ff., where Philoctetes leans on Neoptolemus as he makes ready to leave Lemnos, and 1402 ff., where the same sequence follows Neoptolemus' final agreement that he will take him home. In both cases the action brings the essential situation—Philoctetes trusting Neoptolemus—as directly as possible before our eyes, and the parallelism between the two scenes deepens the meaning of 1402 ff.: *this* time Philoctetes' trust is not misplaced. Seale's[7] work on the repeated pattern of departures that turn out not to be departures points in the same direction: the play exhibits symmetries of design that ought to make us wary of the once popular view that it is all stops and starts ("Sophocles Improvises" is the title Waldock chose for his chapter on *Philoctetes*).[8]

There is another consideration which in my view needs to be recognised as fundamental, one so obvious that it is easily overlooked. This is that the technique of "deceiving" the audience, or of withholding information in order to build up suspense or create surprise effects, must be sharply distinguished from anything that could be described as confusion. The most striking feature of *Philoctetes* as (I would argue) of all Sophocles' plays is, paradoxically enough, its lucidity. The audience are never allowed to be perplexed by the way the action is presented, though the issues may be

[5] *Op. cit.*, p. 178.

[6] O. Taplin, "Significant actions in Sophocles' *Philoctetes*," *G.R.B.S.* 12 (1971) pp. 27 ff.

[7] D. Seale, "The element of surprise in Sophocles' *Philoctetes*," *B.I.C.S.* 19 (1972) pp. 94 ff.

[8] A. J. A. Waldock, *Sophocles the dramatist* (1951) Ch. X.

left extraordinarily imprecise. In the Prologue, for example, the notorious ambiguity created by Sophocles as to the object of the mission—is it the bow alone, or the bow and Philoctetes?—is not perplexing because it is not even noticeable as the scene is played. Its function is to give Sophocles room for manoeuvre later, certainly not to present the audience with a puzzle to be worried over at this stage. At each point in the action the engagement of the audience's emotions is such that they have little attention to spare for questions of conflicting evidence. But audiences *can* be distracted by obscurity or implausibility and will refuse to suspend disbelief if they are; so that this impression of clarity where the situation is in fact shifting and complex depends on very considerable sleight of hand by the dramatist.

There is a good example in the scene with the False Merchant. The detail about the crucial importance of persuasion is made prominent by being set in a context where the means of winning Philoctetes are discussed at some length (610–619), and later in the play it is reaffirmed as an essential requirement by Neoptolemus (1329 ff.), but at this stage, since it is set in a speech which we know to be partly a lie, and spoken by a bogus character, we cannot be sure how valid a point it is. Thus, as Gellie[9] rightly says, "we know, and we do not know, that Philoctetes must go willingly to Troy." The gloss I wish to add is that we are not therefore perplexed or confused. This speech certainly confirms our feeling of distrust for Odysseus' methods, which took its cue from Neoptolemus' reactions in the Prologue, but what most occupies our thoughts here is the ordeal of Neoptolemus: is he, or is he not, going to be able to carry through the deception? His progressive insight will be a guide to our own.

It is worth considering how Sophocles creates this impression of lucidity. One important factor is his psychological sureness of touch. There is nothing an audience finds more baffling than motiveless behaviour, but if what the characters do is susceptible of explanation, even of multiple explanation, then we accept it because this is what we are used to in real life. Take the scene where Odysseus goes off saying "We don't need you: we have the bow, and there are good archers like Teucer and myself who know how to use it" (1054 ff.). The situation is so recognisable that we do not need to look for an answer to the question whether Odysseus convinces himself as well as Philoctetes that he really is leaving Lemnos. Different actors will give different nuances to the scene—more or less calculation, more or less frustration and anger on the part of Odysseus— but the real dramatic point is of course the effect of his behaviour on

9 G. H. Gellie, *Sophocles: a reading* (1972) p. 144.

Philoctetes. For the audience this must be something absolutely serious, even if at the back of their minds they feel that the play cannot end here, like this.

Another factor which is inseparable from the lucid impact of the play is its structure. Garvie[10] has convincingly shown that there is an essential three-part structure: the parts all overlap, but are still clearly to be seen as three distinct phases in the dramatic movement. First, deceit, which fails because the agent, Neoptolemus, cannot bring himself to carry it through; second, violence, which fails because the person who tries to use it, Odysseus, never succeeds in getting the bow; third, persuasion, which fails when it encounters the full force of Philoctetes' will. Garvie treats the epiphany of Heracles as extraneous to this pattern, but I prefer to see the moment when Philoctetes listens to Heracles' words as the ultimate and paradoxical success of persuasion. Even if we leave aside for the moment the question of the end of the play, it seems clear that at least up to 1407 there is what Garvie calls a "totality of dramatic design,"[11] not a mere episodic sequence of stops and starts: the Prologue states the three options (101–103) and the play enacts the trial of each in turn.

This apprehension of the play's plan very much sharpens, or so I have found, the questions of meaning to which we must now turn. If we consider what is the function of the tripartite structure certain obvious answers suggest themselves. For example, that it gives shape to the central sequence of events, the developing relationship between Neoptolemus and Philoctetes, with the result that we are made to think very hard about communication between human beings and about ends and means, facing the question *What really matters?* This is pretty clear and uncontroversial, but there is a harder question which demands an answer: if the structure also has the function of relating the human interaction of Neoptolemus and Philoctetes and Odysseus to a broader scheme of things, as it does, through the prophecy and Heracles, what weight does Sophocles give to this broader scheme, or suprahuman level? Is the prophecy a purely formal device, or does it mean something; and if so, what?

Sophocles was not after all obliged to use the prophecy. Admittedly it was there in the myth, the datum that Philoctetes and his bow were essential for the capture of Troy, and he had to find some way of motivating the expedition to fetch Philoctetes. But it would have been possible to

---

[10] A. F. Garvie, "Deceit, violence, and persuasion in the *Philoctetes*," *Studi Classici in Onore di Quintino Cataudella* vol. I (1972) pp. 213 ff. J.-U. Schmidt, *Sophokles Philoktet, eine Strukturanalyse* (1973) pp. 249 ff. also analyses the play into three phases although his interpretation differs in detail.

[11] *Art. cit.*, p. 214.

manage without Helenus and his prediction. For example, Odysseus and Neoptolemus can have come at the instance of the Greek generals, who have decided that they must secure the aid of Philoctetes because he is the most effective archer they know, by virtue of being armed with the bow of Heracles which took Troy once before. Odysseus opts for trickery as the only possible method; when that fails because of the inability of Neoptolemus to carry it through he would like to use force, but Neoptolemus refuses to co-operate; at last Neoptolemus tries the method most congenial to him, persuasion, and offers Philoctetes the promise of glory at Troy. Even without the prophecy this could be made very convincing ("come to Troy and we will find you the best doctors, give you the greatest honours . . ."). Only in the Exodos would Sophocles really have needed a revelation of the future, when Heracles makes his dispositions. The crucial interaction of Neoptolemus and Philoctetes, the real focus of our interest and sympathy, would hardly be affected by the suppression of the prophecy.

The dramatist, however, thought the prophecy worth the price of fairly major inconsistencies. Why?

The reason can hardly be that this was his only means of conveying the sense of compelling necessity which must be part of the dilemma of Neoptolemus. The struggle within the young man's conscience would be just as real—if anything more immediately recognisable by a modern audience, at least—if that sense of necessity were equated with patriotic duty. If it was loyalty to the state that demanded the ruthless exploitation of Philoctetes then there would still be a fine moral dilemma for Neoptolemus. And clearly (following the lead of Euripides) Sophocles could have made a much more political play out of this story. As it is, he treats the theme of duty with some reserve: Schmidt[12] has pointed out, for example, that in the crucial exchange at 1222 ff. Odysseus has no moral arguments, only threats, in answer to Neoptolemus' claim that it is δίκαιον to hand back the bow.

Nor does it seem that Sophocles is using the prophecy in the same way as he treats oracles in *Trachiniae* and *OT*, to make an overt contrast between divine and human knowledge which ironically illustrates the frailty and vulnerability of man. But irony is certainly there, and this perhaps is the direction in which we ought to be looking for a clue to Sophocles' interest in the prophecy.

It has, I think, to be accepted that the final exposition of the future by Heracles is authoritative, and that this validates retrospectively the

[12] Schmidt, *op. cit.* (n. 10 above), pp. 221 ff.

account given by Neoptolemus at 1326 ff. The message is that Troy *will* fall, by the joint endeavour and freely willed co-operation of Philoctetes and Neoptolemus, and that Philoctetes will be cured. (The audience know that these things did happen.) All through the play we witness human attempts to achieve these ends, attempts which are based on reasonable, though humanly limited, assessments of the situation, such as Odysseus' claim in the Prologue that nothing but trickery will work. But these attempts successively frustrate themselves. Neoptolemus speaks more truly than he knows at 431 f.: ἀλλὰ χαὶ σοφαὶ | γνῶμαι, Φιλοκτῆτ', ἐμποδίζονται θαμά. His own impassioned attempt to persuade is "tripped up" by the trickery he has earlier employed. There is deep irony in the exchange at 1362 ff. when Philoctetes expresses surprise that he should want to go to Troy and help the Atridae who are his enemies, and Neoptolemus can only say, lamely, λέγεις μὲν εἰκότα (1373) without daring to reveal the whole truth.[13]

There is another sort of irony in the false departures that we witness on stage, particularly in the latter part of the play: Odysseus and Neoptolemus with the bow apparently abandoning Philoctetes (1068 ff.); Philoctetes and Neoptolemus leaving for Malis (1402 ff.). These departures contradict what the audience, reminded by the prophecy, must know actually happened. So in each case we feel that this cannot be the real ending and that something more ought to happen, but it is hard to see what it can be. This is particularly true of the great moment when Neoptolemus sacrifices his own interests to those of Philoctetes, which is enormously deepened by the sense that Neoptolemus is abandoning his destiny. We have to believe in his serious rejection of his future even though we remember that Troy fell. It is an insoluble contradiction, until Heracles comes and solves it.

This final stage in the action seems to me unintelligible if it is not genuinely organic, if it is only Sophocles making a gesture towards the received tradition. The logic of the play's structure and the ironical use of the prophecy surely point to the view that Philoctetes' assent to Heracles in fact fulfils the requirements of Helenus' prediction, though of course in a quite unexpected way. (Unexpected, but not unprepared; many critics have noted the trouble Sophocles has taken to make the visible presence of Heracles the culmination of a major theme.) But is Philoctetes "persuaded" by Heracles, or is he not? This can easily turn into a rather pointless debate if we allow ourselves to be mesmerised by English terminology and make a rigid distinction between obedience to a command

[13] Cf. Schmidt, pp. 234 ff.

and compliance in response to argument: the Greeks after all used πείθομαι for both ideas. When Philoctetes says to Heracles οὐκ ἀπιθήσω τοῖς σοῖς μύθοις (1447) and later speaks of the γνώμη ... φίλων (1467) that is one of the causes of his going to Troy, we should surely see the fulfilment of Helenus' words: Philoctetes is going willingly—and his whole tone in the closing anapaests is one of positive, even joyful, acceptance. It is a quibble to insist that he is not persuaded; but there is a larger and more difficult question to be answered: What is the meaning of that culminating persuasion?

If we accept the structural pattern suggested by Garvie, and further, the ultimate effectiveness of persuasion, then there is more sense in the stress that Sophocles seems to lay on Neoptolemus' growing understanding of the prophet's words. As Zwierlein[14] has pointed out, we must not treat the question of what Neoptolemus knows as an historical problem. If we press it logically we are forced to the unwelcome conclusion that despite his apparently ignorant questions in the Prologue Neoptolemus knew the details of the prophecy already. Certainly at the end of the play he can give Philoctetes a most circumstantial account of what Helenus has foretold, but the contrast between his knowledge then and his ignorance earlier emphasises not the factual inconsistency but Neoptolemus' acquisition of insight. He becomes more aware, through his contact with Philoctetes, of the meaning of the prophecy, making sense of what he had already heard but did not understand. Particularly at 839 ff., the famous "oracular" pronouncement in hexameters, Neoptolemus seems to be expressing his "seeing" something that he has not properly seen before: ἐγὼ δ' ὁρῶ . . . . This experience is a familiar part of the process of growing up, and it has often been noticed that in Sophocles' Neoptolemus we have a study of a young man coming to maturity through experience. But it is not enough to stop there and adopt a comfortable view of *Philoctetes* as a "character play": Neoptolemus' deepening insight must be seen as part of the play's dramatic movement and must bear on the larger question to which we are seeking an answer. Can his insight be a guide to our own? Does the prophecy have any truth to tell?

The prophecy *could* be offering some sort of illumination of the gods' purposes or some meditation on the relation between man and god, but I should be surprised if it were. The divine activity as such is far less significant in this play than in *OT* with its Apollo or *Trachiniae* with its Zeus; the lack of imaginative detail is striking by contrast. This is why I find it hard to see the real emphasis of *Philoctetes* as *either* on the ultimate

---

[14] O. Zwierlein, review of Steidle, in *G.G.A.* 222 (1970) pp. 208 ff.

rightness of the gods' purpose *or* on their cruelty in condemning Philoctetes to ten years' agony on Lemnos. Much more telling, it seems to me, is the stress given to the power of persuasion: Neoptolemus' response to Philoctetes, his willingness to be persuaded to sacrifice everything because he respects and pities Philoctetes, is matched by Philoctetes' culminating response to Heracles. And in each case it is the power of φιλία—the φιλία of χρηστοί, who know how to behave—that makes one man bend his will to another's. It is worth adding that Heracles seems to be more important as the φίλος and heroic mentor of Philoctetes than as representative of the gods.[15]

Steidle[16] perceptively notes the force of Heracles' words describing Neoptolemus and Philoctetes as a pair of lions each protecting the other (ἀλλ' ὡς λέοντε συννόμω φυλάσσετον | οὗτος σὲ καὶ σὺ τόνδ' 1436 f.): this is one sense in which the prophecy tells the truth, emphasising the importance of the relationship between Neoptolemus and Philoctetes; and their interdependence is visually demonstrated by Neoptolemus supporting Philoctetes as they go. This reading of the play, in which the words of Heracles are seen as the true climax of the dramatic movement, makes Sophocles affirm the values of φιλία—of pity and respect and human interdependence—in answer to his implied question What really matters?; but there is a final related problem which needs to be discussed, the meaning of Philoctetes' going to Troy. This after all is an important part of Heracles' revelation, and we must be able to make sense of it if we are to understand the play's morality.

Modern criticism is sharply divided: I quote a few representative views. Robinson[17] argues that the decision of Neoptolemus to take Philoctetes home is the first and "true" conclusion; the second is lighter and slighter, avoiding historical or theological issues, but explaining how Sophocles' version can be fitted into the myth while not essentially detracting from the serious meaning of the first conclusion. Jan Kott[18] goes much further and sees the end as the ultimate absurdity. Just as in *Ajax* there is no meaning in the making of a hero out of Ajax, so in this play Philoctetes' going to Troy is the final horror: "healing is always payment for submission." This attitude is shared by Poe,[19] for whom "Philoctetes' failure becomes a paradigm of the frustration and futility of mankind."

---

15 Cf. Taplin, *art. cit.* (n. 6 above), p. 39.

16 *Op. cit.* (n. 4 above), p. 187; cf. Schmidt, *op. cit.* (n. 10 above), p. 247.

17 *Art. cit.* (n. 2 above), p. 55.

18 J. Kott, *The eating of the gods* (1974) pp. 162 ff. The quotation is from p. 169.

19 J. P. Poe, *Heroism and divine justice in Sophocles' Philoctetes* (1974) = *Mnemosyne* Suppl. 34. The quotation is from p. 51.

At the other end of the spectrum there are the old-fashioned pietists, and more recently and interestingly Vidal-Naquet,[20] who sees Philoctetes' going to Troy as the re-integration of the wild man into the city, or Clare Campbell,[21] who brings out the importance of the themes of disease and cure: "When Heracles now says both men should go to Troy, not home, Philoctetes freely agrees—he has been healed in his social nature, so he can accept physical healing, and it is in the logic of his plight that it will happen at Troy, when he rejoins the Greek body politic which had cut him off just as in despair he used to want to cut off his own foot. . . ."

Since this is a drama we need to use the design of the action and its effect on the spectator's emotions as the basis of any interpretation. Sophocles was at liberty to make the Greeks at Troy stand for whatever he chose: they have no absolute significance independent of the dramatic context. Equally there is no need to suppose that he was concerned to assert the rightness of history because it happened. The important question is What do the audience want for each of the characters as they watch the play?

Philoctetes himself is the focus of nearly all the imagery: the desert island, the wound, the bow, the dead man, are all used as means of exploring his situation and of arousing our emotional response to him. This is overwhelmingly a reaction of pity: for his brute physical suffering, lavishly described and enacted on stage, and for his mental anguish in his isolation. His suffering is the main, almost the only, theme of the lyrics, and the sense of his pitiableness is reinforced by important moments in the action, as at 248 ff., when Neoptolemus pretends never to have heard of him, and Philoctetes is desolated by the thought that even his name has vanished from the memory of the Greeks. We also admire him for his dignity and strength, his generous warmth towards Neoptolemus, his concern at the fate of the other Greek heroes, his delight at the sound of Greek being spoken, his ingenuity in managing for himself on Lemnos, most of all perhaps for his refusal to kowtow.

We badly want him to be cured and to be rescued from isolation. At the same time we understand his hostility towards the Greeks, and we do not want him to sacrifice his self-respect as the price of being healed. His wound is *both* his bitterness and wildness *and* his dignity, just as the desert island symbolises not only his alienation, loneliness and animal-like life but also his purity. Thus our feelings are mixed: we want Philoctetes to be made whole and to be honoured by society, but we do not want him to

---

[20] P. Vidal-Naquet, "Le Philoctète de Sophocle" in J.-P. Vernant and P. Vidal-Naquet, *Mythe et tragédie en Grèce ancienne* (1973) pp. 161 ff.

[21] C. Campbell, "A theophany," *Theoria to theory* 6 (1972) pp. 82 f.

compromise with men whose methods the play makes us despise. To introduce the Christian notion of forgiveness and loving one's enemy would be to make Sophocles write a quite different play.

Or Sophocles might have written a different play again, in which going to Troy was a compelling patriotic duty: then Philoctetes' refusal would plainly be a matter of selfish pride; but he has not arranged things like this. The world of the Greeks at Troy is the ordinary world of unheroic politics, whose methods are illustrated by the behaviour of Odysseus and sharply contrasted with the noble standards of Philoctetes and Neoptolemus and the great dead: Achilles, Ajax, Nestor. . . .[22] When Philoctetes wants nothing to do with this world we cannot blame him.

But it is also true that when Neoptolemus appeals to Philoctetes *as a friend* to go to Troy we begin to fear that he is in danger of becoming inaccessible, permanently alienated, if he will not listen; and although we endorse Neoptolemus' willingness to renounce Troy altogether for his sake we surely must feel that going to Malis is a second best,[23] not because we much care about the fall of Troy, but because it is at Troy that the cure is to be found, and it is very important to us that Philoctetes be cured, both to assuage our pity and to convince us that he is reintegrated into society. For the healing must be a healing of mind as well as body: the language that associates the wound with death,[24] with the desert island,[25] with Philoctetes' hatred of his enemies,[26] requires us to see the cure as relating to his entire being. Being cured will mean coming back from the dead,[27] ceasing to be the solitary wild thing who is at the same time predator and prey of the island's beasts and becoming instead one of a "pair of lions, each guarding the other's life" (1436 f.).

As Schmidt has argued,[28] Neoptolemus' action in standing by his commitment to Philoctetes has given Philoctetes a new heroic community to which to belong: it is no longer true that all the "real" heroes are dead. So Troy can be used as a symbol *both* of the corrupt unheroic world of politics, which we applaud Philoctetes for rejecting, *and* of society, into which we want him to be reintegrated. This double significance is achieved in ways which illustrate the delicacy of Sophocles' technique. For example,

---

[22] Schmidt, *op. cit.* (n. 10 above), p. 94, brings out the importance of 410–452 for making these standards clear; Philoctetes' hostility is confined to the κακοί of the Greek army.

[23] Cf. B. M. W. Knox, *The heroic temper* (1964) p. 139.

[24] 796 f.; 861; 945 ff. (cf. 1018; 1030).

[25] 182 ff.; 265 ff.; 279 ff.; 311 ff.; 691 ff.

[26] 631 f.; 791 ff.; 1043 f.; 1113 ff.

[27] Cf. 624 f., 1198 f. and the passages cited in n. 24 above. Knox, *op. cit.* (n. 23 above), p. 141.

[28] *Op. cit.* (n. 10 above), p. 246.

he is careful not to raise the question of just how Philoctetes and say, Agamemnon, will greet each other at Troy. This absence of naturalism is essential to the success of the final scene, and the use of anapaests must help to create a distancing that makes credible the apparition of Heracles and the response of Philoctetes.

The double significance of Troy makes equally good sense in Sophocles' treatment of Neoptolemus. What the audience want for him is that he should be willing to be true at last to his real φύσις and sacrifice everything to his sense of what he owes to Philoctetes (καλῶς | δρῶν ἐξαμαρτεῖν μᾶλλον ἢ νικᾶν κακῶς 94 f.); but also that the two of them should do great deeds together. Neoptolemus, we feel, will not be truly fulfilled any more than Philoctetes will if he has no opportunity for the exercise of his ἀρετή in action. Sophocles is not inviting us to reject the whole idea of action in society as inevitably evil or futile, as a modern writer might. So our feelings are mixed for Neoptolemus, too: we want him to put Philoctetes first (and this is another reason why Sophocles makes comparatively little of the patriotic motive), but we also want him to be part of his society. Thus the prophecy can be seen to have more truth to tell than the value of φιλία: it also asserts the possibility of right action.

If this approach to the meaning of Troy is correct it throws some light on Sophocles' treatment of Odysseus. This ambiguous figure represents on stage the ambiguity of the world of the Greek army: he is by no means the simple embodiment of evil that he seems to Philoctetes. His goal, after all, is the restoration of Philoctetes in order that Troy shall be taken; this is the goal to which the prophecy points and which is ultimately achieved through the intervention of Heracles. But the meaning of this goal has been completely redefined by the action of the play, and at the end we are given no sense that Odysseus, to use Gellie's phrase, "has won, yet again;"[29] the inadequacy of Odysseus' arguments at 1222 ff. and his decisive defeat at 1293 ff. make it clear that Philoctetes at Troy will be doing neither his bidding nor that of the Atridae.[30]

The language of Philoctetes himself at the end of the play is not at all the abject language of the broken man who licks the boots of his exploiters: there is joy in his response to Heracles (ὦ φθέγμα ποθεινὸν . . . 1445) and Vidal-Naquet[31] suggests that in his address to Lemnos and its nymphs we see the wild island given a new significance: the scene is transformed and made almost pastoral, representing the re-entry of Philoctetes into the

[29] Op. cit. (n. 9 above), p. 157.
[30] Cf. Taplin, art. cit. (n. 6 above), p. 37; Schmidt, op. cit. (n. 10 above), pp. 231; 246.
[31] Art. cit. (n. 20 above), p. 179.

civilised world. Of course there *could* be a sinister irony in the joy of Philoctetes—the audience might be meant to think "poor fool" as the big battalions take over—but in that case it would be hard to explain the feelings that Sophocles has generated about Philoctetes' wound and the need for cure.

The only disturbing irony at the end of the play, it seems to me, is of a kind that Sophocles uses elsewhere: the hint at 1440 ff. of the subsequent history of Neoptolemus. "Only be careful," says Heracles, "to show reverence to the gods. . . ." It was Neoptolemus who killed Priam at the altar when Troy was taken, but we have not been reminded of this part of his story until this glancing hint very late in the play, and Kott is surely unjustified in treating him as a war criminal all along. Sophocles likes making these ironical references to other stories at the very end of his dramas; one might compare the end of *O.C.*, where Antigone asks to be allowed to go to Thebes in order to settle her brothers' quarrel (1769 ff.), or the reference at the end of the *Electra* to "the present and *future* ills of the Pelopidae" (1498).

Almost all critics, I suspect, would agree that the profoundest moment in the play is Neoptolemus' decision to take Philoctetes home, which as it is enacted on stage, with Neoptolemus supporting Philoctetes, is made more significant through its recall of the earlier scene of his breakdown. At once Neoptolemus' act of listening to a friend's persuasion is echoed by Philoctetes listening to Heracles, and Clare Campbell[32] is right, I think, to suggest linking these events very closely in the stage action, so that the one shall seem to precipitate the other. Certainly they are linked in meaning: they give the answer to the question What really matters? This answer takes us away from the familiar and perhaps too schematic image of the proudly lonely Sophoclean hero to something more complex, which is echoed in the themes of φίλος and ξένος in the *Coloneus*.[33]

Newnham College, Cambridge

[32] *Art. cit.* (n. 21 above), pp. 81 ff.

[33] An earlier version of this paper was delivered at the triennial conference of the Greek and Roman Societies on 31 July 1975. I am grateful for the criticisms and suggestions which were put forward in the discussion following the paper.

3

The *Bacchae* as Satyr-Play?

DAVID SANSONE

One of the most influential books on Euripides in perhaps the last thirty years has been A. P. Burnett's *Catastrophe Survived*.[1] One of the most interesting features of Burnett's treatment is the demonstration of the presence of satyr-play "motifs" or "elements" in certain of Euripides' tragedies, most notably the *IT*, *Helen*, *Ion* and *Alcestis*. This treatment conforms to a recent tendency among students of Euripides to regard these plays as strongly "satyric" in character.[2] What seems to have been overlooked is that these elements appear also in another of Euripides' tragedies, the *Bacchae*. In fact, when one considers only those elements which Burnett mentions in the course of her book, one finds that the *Bacchae* turns out to be the most "satyric" of all Euripides' surviving plays, *Cyclops* not excluded. Of twenty-eight satyr-play elements referred to by Burnett, the *Bacchae* can be seen to exhibit no fewer than twenty-three.[3]

[1] Oxford, 1971.

[2] For satyric elements in the *Ion* see already K. Horna, "Metrische Bemerkungen zur Prolog des *Ion*" *WS* 50 (1932) 175–179. Also P. Guggisberg, *Das Satyrspiel* (Zürich, 1947) 129, 44–48. Recent work which stresses the satyric affinities of various Euripidean tragedies includes (in addition to Burnett's work) J. Ferguson, "Tetralogies, Divine Paternity, and the Plays of 414" *TAPA* 100 (1969) 109–117, B. Knox, "Euripidean Comedy" in *The Rarer Action. Essays in Honor of Francis Fergusson* edited by A. Cheuse and R. Koffler (New Brunswick, N.J., 1970) and a number of papers by D. F. Sutton: "The Relation Between Tragedies and Fourth Place Plays in Three Instances" *Arethusa* 4 (1971) 55–72, "Satyric Qualities in Euripides' *Iphigeneia at Tauris* and *Helen*" *RSC* 20 (1972) 321–330 and "Satyric Elements in the *Alcestis*" *RSC* 21 (1973) 384–391 (note also W. M. Calder III, "A Pro-Satyric *Helen*? *Addendum*" *RSC* 21 [1973] 412).

[3] A note as to method: I consider only those features which are noted in Burnett's Index as "satyr-play elements" or "satyr-play motifs." It should be noted that there is some overlap of these two categories, nor can I discern the distinction Mrs. Burnett intends between "elements" and "motifs." My own powers of discrimination are not, however,

It is readily acknowledged that the *Alcestis* contains several features in common with satyr-play. "The disguise, the trick, the girl won at the games as a prize, the imputations of lustfulness to Admetus all come from satyr-play" (Burnett, p. 45). Apart from the girl,[4] these motifs are found also in the *Bacchae*. In fact, we find not one but two disguises in the *Bacchae*. Dionysus is himself disguised when he enters the stage; in line 4 he tells us that he has arrived in Thebes "having exchanged my divine form for that of a human." Later in the play Pentheus disguises himself as a woman to spy on the bacchae. Trickery and deception[5] also are to be found in the *Bacchae*. Pentheus is tricked into thinking he has imprisoned Dionysus (616) and deceived with the impression that his palace is aflame (624, note the δοκῶν which ends both lines). Pentheus also smites the air with his sword, thinking he is striking Dionysus (631), is tricked into donning women's clothing and, finally, is tricked into using a tree as vantage point for watching the maenads. And it is Pentheus who constantly imputes lustfulness to the bacchae and to Dionysus himself (225, 236–238, 686–688).

Other satyr-play elements which Burnett finds in the *Alcestis* are a preoccupation with food and wine,[6] the motif of hospitality[7] and the appearance on stage of the "monster" of the piece.[8] A preoccupation with food and drink is certainly to be found in the *Bacchae*: Dionysus is of course himself the god of wine and he is conspicuously paired (274–277) with Demeter, who is the patron of the dry aspect of nutrition. Near the end

---

yet at issue. Our only concern is that these are the features which Mrs. Burnett points to as giving evidence of the "satyric" nature of certain tragedies. In what follows I shall occasionally cite, in addition to the relevant references in *Catastrophe Survived*, the works mentioned in note 2 above, to indicate that, in some cases, Mrs. Burnett is not alone in regarding certain features as "satyric." I concern myself primarily with Burnett, however, simply because hers is the longest list of "satyric elements" in Euripides' tragedies.

[4] A feature to be found referred to occasionally in plays dealing with members of the house of Pelops, e.g., *Helen* 386 f. and *IT* 1 f. See also Burnett, p. 32 n. 9.

[5] For these as features of satyr-play see also Sutton, *RSC* 20 (1972) 326 and 21 (1973) 388–389.

[6] Wine: Burnett 31–32, 72 n. 23. (Drunkenness: Sutton *RSC* 21 [1973] 390.) Banqueting: Burnett 45. Food and drink: Knox "Euripidean Comedy" 72–74. (It should be noted that Knox makes no distinction between "satyric" and "comic.")

[7] Burnett 31, Sutton *RSC* 21 (1973) 387–388.

[8] Burnett 31. Another motif in the *Alcestis* is the appearance on stage of Heracles (see Burnett 38 and 232, Guggisberg 45, Sutton *RSC* 21 [1973] 389–390). This is not a feature of the *Bacchae*, but neither is it a feature of the *Cyclops*. It is, of course, a prominent feature of Sophocles' *Trachiniae* and of Euripides' *HF*, from which play, according to Burnett (180–181, 232), satyr-play elements are missing.

of the play Agave invites the Chorus (1184) to partake of a glorious banquet in celebration of the successful hunt.[9] Hospitality too is a motif of the *Bacchae*. Indeed the action of the plot is given its impetus by the fact of Dionysus' inhospitable reception in the very city of his birth and by his own relatives. Finally Pentheus, like Thanatos in the *Alcestis*, certainly appears on stage. But in what respect is Pentheus portrayed as a "monster"? To quote E. R. Dodds (on lines 537–541): "References to P.'s curious ancestry are strikingly frequent in the play (cf. 265, 507, 995 f., 1025 f., 1155, 1274 ff.). . . . The Chorus . . . draw here and at 995 the . . . conclusion that like the earthborn giants who fought against the gods he comes of a monstrous, inhuman stock and is therefore the natural enemy of what is divine." Indeed, considering his rôle and his ancestry, Pentheus' nearest literary kin is the δράκων, or διάβολος, of Revelation 12.

Mrs. Burnett mentions (31–33) two more features which the *Alcestis* shares with satyr-play: an "overt physical conflict" (comparing Phrynichus' *Alcestis*, which is not, to my knowledge, a satyr-play) with the result that "the monster is not killed but maimed" (comparing the *Cyclops*). The *Bacchae* certainly contains an overt physical conflict, somewhat frustrated by the divinity and mutability of the protagonist, as reported in Dionysus' trochaic speech 616–637. But this is surely as much a characteristic of tragedy (or comedy) as it is of satyr-play. As to the next feature, I am sure Mrs. Burnett does not mean that it is necessarily a feature of satyr-play that the monster is not killed (but only maimed). It happens, as Mrs. Burnett points out, that the monsters in the *Cyclops* and in the *Alcestis* are not killed. In the former Euripides was constrained to follow his Homeric model, in the latter the death of the monster would provoke in the audience the utmost incredulity. We must, then, for once modify Mrs. Burnett's formulation. For convenience we may adopt Sutton's more comprehensive phrase, "the discomfiture and defeat of an ogre, monster or villain."[10] Pentheus is first maimed, then killed. The villain in the *Alcestis* is neither maimed nor killed.

According to Burnett, the *Iphigenia in Tauris* also can be regarded as in some sense a satyr-play. Elements in that play which provoke such an identification include: reference to the infancy of a god or hero, mention of the gifts and inventions of a god, the release of the entire Chorus from servitude, the pastoral setting of the messenger speech and the indecisive-

---

[9] For the themes of wine and food in the *Bacchae* see R. P. Winnington-Ingram, *Euripides and Dionysus* (Cambridge, 1948) 48–50 and 25–27.

[10] *RSC* 20 (1972) 323. Sutton's references show that the killing of the monster is a frequent feature of satyr-play. In addition, some of the villains whom Sutton cites are, like Pentheus, *contemptores divum*: Salmoneus, Erysichthon.

ness of the cowherds as reported in that messenger speech.[11] The infancy of Dionysus is prominently mentioned, in the *Bacchae*, in the Chorus' parodos (the "second birth" of Dionysus: 88–98; see also 288–297) as is the infancy of Zeus (in the cave of the Curetes: 120–134). The benefactions of Dionysus are even more prominently referred to: Teiresias informs Pentheus that Dionysus discovered wine (279) and that he also, like Apollo in the *IT*, is one who grants prophecy to mortals (298–301). In the course of the play the Chorus of bacchants are miraculously released from the prison in which Pentheus attempted to keep them (443–448). One of the glorious features of the poetry of the *Bacchae* is the pastoral setting of not one but two brilliant messenger speeches.[12] And in the first messenger speech there is an incident exactly analogous to that in the *IT*: the herdsmen are at first indecisive, but finally one man persuades them (compare *Ba.* 721 εὖ δ' ἡμῖν λέγειν | ἔδοξε with *IT* 279 ἔδοξε δ' ἡμῶν εὖ λέγειν τοῖς πλείοσι) to capture the bacchants (compare *Ba.* 719 θηρασώμεθα with *IT* 280 θηρᾶν) and bring them to the king. Apparently also satyric, according to Burnett (citing *Dictyulci*), is the call for help which the herdsmen set up in the *IT*. In the *Bacchae* it is not the herdsmen but Agave who calls out for help (731). The final satyric characteristic of the *IT*, the deception of the monster (Burnett 72 n. 23, comparing *Cyclops*), has been dealt with above and shown to be characteristic of the *Bacchae* as well. If the *Iphigenia in Tauris* is satyric, the *Bacchae* most certainly is.

The *Helen*, according to Burnett, exhibits the following satyric characteristics: representation of cowardice, inappropriate dress, "consciousness of genre," a gatekeeper scene and an adventurer-hero. In addition, the salvation of Helen and Menelaus, "like that of a satyr-play, has been granted to creatures at once excessively flawed and excessively fortunate, to mortals who are plainly the darlings of the gods."[13] As in the *Helen*, we

[11] Burnett 71–72 with notes 21 and 22. For gifts and inventions see also Guggisberg 74. For release from bondage see also Burnett 31 (*Cyclops*), Guggisberg 60–63 and Sutton *RSC* 20 (1972) 324–326 and *RSC* 21 (1973) 386–387 (*Eurystheus, Omphale, Inachus* and others). In this connection Burnett does, in fact, refer to *Bacchae* and *Philoctetes*.

[12] See especially 677–686 and 1051–1057. It is interesting to note the similarity between line 1051 and a line from an unknown *satyr*-play quoted in the scholia to Hephaestion (p. 183 Gaisford). Indeed Porson thought the anonymous line to be a variant of *Ba.* 1051.

No cave is mentioned in these messenger speeches. If a cave is the satyric element Mrs. Burnett thinks it is (it is a feature of the *Cyclops*) we will have to make do with the aforementioned cave of the Curetes. A cave features also in the *Ion* and the *Philoctetes*.

[13] Cowardice: Burnett 81–82 (Menelaus in *Helen*, Phrygian in *Orestes*), 72 n. 22 (cowherds in *IT*), 142 and 232 (Menelaus in *Andromache*), 222 (Orestes in *Orestes*). Dress: Burnett 82 ("If the champion won't dress the part, the poet seems to say, anything can happen."). Knox also ("Euripidean Comedy" 71–74) remarks on the preoccupation with

find cowardice exhibited in the *Bacchae* by men in the face of women. The herdsmen are put to flight by mere women (734, 763 ἀπενώτιζον φυγῇ | γυναῖκες ἄνδρας) and Pentheus relents from his blustering intention of a frontal attack (781–786), recognizes the prudence of Dionysus' suggestion of infiltration (838) and finally decides, king though he is, to slink unseen through the streets of Thebes in fear of being seen and ridiculed (840–843). And the ridicule Pentheus fears is on account of his proposed dress which is, on any account, inappropriate. Surely men dressing in women's clothing is an element of comedy (e.g., *Thesmophoriazusae*) and satyr-play[14] rather than of tragedy. As to Mrs. Burnett's "consciousness of genre," I do not think the *Bacchae* shares this feature, unless the subject of the play itself be regarded as a retort to the proverbial οὐδὲν πρὸς τὸν Διόνυσον.[15] We may not, however, be constrained to regard this feature as a *characteristic* of satyr-play merely on the basis of Mrs. Burnett's reference to the *Cyclops*. A gatekeeper-scene also is not found in the *Bacchae*, although the entrance of Cadmus is prepared by a brief speech (170–177) in which Teiresias calls to the servants inside and asks them to inform Cadmus of his presence. In fact, this should qualify, as it is the same kind of scene as A. *Choe.* 652–667, which Mrs. Burnett *does* cite, the only difference being the presence in the latter of a reference to knocking—apparently a comic element.[16] Dionysus is, to a certain extent, an "adventurer-hero," although perhaps more so in Nonnus than in Euripides. At any rate, he has come, like the Odysseus of *Cyclops*, to whom Burnett compares Menelaus, from afar in search of hospitality. Indeed the arrival of Dionysus corresponds to the "action of return" which Mrs. Burnett sees as the "praxis" of the *Ion*, and for which she compares, among others, the satyr-play *Sphinx* (102 n. 2). Finally, we see in the *Bacchae* that salvation of flawed and fortunate darlings of the gods which Mrs. Burnett regards as a satyric element in the *Helen* and *Orestes*. At the

---

clothing in the *Electra* as being a satyric characteristic. "Consciousness of genre": Burnett 92 n. 10 (comparing *Cyclops*). Gatekeeper scene and adventurer-hero: Burnett 81. Salvation of "darlings of the gods": Burnett 99 (*Helen*) and 222 (*Orestes*).

14 Perhaps the Omphale-plays of Achaeus and Ion? See Guggisberg 134–136. It is not recorded that the *Scyrioi* of either Sophocles or Euripides is a satyr-play, nor is it certain what the subject-matter of either was. For a transvestite satyr see Fig. 69 in F. Brommer, *Satyrspiele*[2] (Berlin, 1959). I owe this last reference to Dana Sutton.

15 For which, see the *Suda s.v.* οὐδέν.

16 See G. W. Bond (ed.), *Euripides' Hypsipyle* (Oxford, 1963) 59: "The details of door-knocking occur frequently in comedy. They are mostly passed over in tragedy, doubtless as οἰκεῖα πράγματα more suited to comic scenes. . . . W. W. Mooney, *The House-Door on the Ancient Stage*, pp. 19 f. quotes only two instances from tragedy, A. *Cho.* 653 . . . and *IT* 1304. . . . Even *Hel.* 435 ff., a comic scene, has none."

end of the play Dionysus predicts that Cadmus (his own grandfather) and Harmonia (daughter of Ares) will be translated, after some difficulties, to the "land of the blessed" (1338–1339). Cadmus is nothing if not flawed, and his lasting fate is perhaps better than the character who spoke lines 333–336 deserves:

> κεἰ μὴ γὰρ ἔστιν ὁ θεὸς οὗτος, ὡς σὺ φῄς,
> παρὰ σοὶ λεγέσθω· καὶ καταψεύδου καλῶς
> ὡς ἔστι Σεμέλης, ἵνα δοκῇ θεὸν τεκεῖν,   335
> ἡμῖν τε τιμὴ παντὶ τῷ γένει προσῇ.

Four final satyr-play elements or motifs (according to Burnett) remain: the marriage-motif, the Chorus "carried off to Dionysus," dancing and an apotheosis.[17] I can find no hint of the "marriage-motif" in the *Bacchae*, but at the end of the play the Chorus, whether represented as the collective spouse of Dionysus or not, surely go off with their patron deity. The Chorus are Asiatic women who have come out of Lydia with Dionysus (55–57) and Thebes is the first Greek city they have visited (23). Therefore, although they are nearly silent in the final scene and although Dionysus does not mention their fate (perhaps some reference was made in the long lacuna after 1329), we can only assume that they continue their journey in company with Dionysus. Dancing is naturally mentioned frequently in the *Bacchae*. We even see the beginnings of the pas-de-deux (184–185, 195: Cadmus and Teiresias) which Burnett finds in the *Orestes*. The final element, an apotheosis, I include not because it is necessarily a satyr-play motif but, for completeness, because of a comment of Mrs. Burnett's. She correctly points out that satyr-play elements are absent from Euripides' very serious and very tragic *Heracles* and she characterizes that play as "a tetralogy that has lost its satyr play" (180). At the end, however, with the expected apotheosis of the hero, "the heavenly satyr play begins at last, though only on the inner stage of [the spectator's] imagination" (182). Dionysus does, in the *Bacchae*, undergo an apotheosis of sorts. He arrives on stage at the start of the play in human form (4) and expresses his intention that he will be recognized as a god: θεὸς γεγὼς ἐνδείξομαι 47. This purpose is fulfilled in the final scene when, for the first time in the play,[18] Dionysus appears on the roof of the scene-building.

---

[17] Marriage: Burnett 31, 45, 232 (*Cyclops, Alcestis*). Chorus carried off to D.: Burnett 31 (*Cyclops*). Dancing: Burnett 222 (*Orestes*). Apotheosis: Burnett 182 (*HF*).

[18] The prologue is spoken from the stage; see N. C. Hourmouziades, *Production and Imagination in Euripides* (Athens, 1965) 163. The lines of Dionysus in the "earthquake scene" (576–595) were spoken by the protagonist off stage (so Dodds, p. 147). For a different view see J. Roux, *REG* 74 (1961) 41 and also her edition of the *Bacchae* (Paris, 1970) I, 97.

In closing, then, this contrast between the *Bacchae* and the *HF* is especially instructive. In these two dramas we have two works which have never been suspected of being "satyric," and yet the one contains (perhaps) the fewest "satyric elements" and the other surely the largest number. Either, therefore, the *Bacchae*, this most tragic of plays, has been consistently and grossly misunderstood, or the practice of discovering satyr-play elements in the "non-tragic" tragedies of Euripides should be replaced with a more fruitful one.

University of Illinois at Urbana

4

Apollonius Rhodius and the Papyri*

MICHAEL W. HASLAM

"Papyri of Apollonius Rhodius have been remarkably productive of valuable readings." So Grenfell and Hunt in 1908.[1] Since then the material has multiplied many times over, and the statement is as true as ever. What is a valuable reading? Of most obvious value is a reading which is both new—that is to say, unattested in any other manuscript—and true. Such a reading directly and immediately ameliorates the text—unless it stands already in the text by conjecture, in which case there may be value in having ancient testimony for it. Hermann Fränkel, in his brilliant and monumental OCT of 1961, admitted a good number of conjectures that had not found a place in the texts of his predecessors, and some of them, including one or two of his own, have since been confirmed by papyri. This is a most encouraging vindication of Fränkel's approach to the text,[2] and very striking to anyone familiar with the much more meagre returns yielded by, say, the Euripides papyri. There is always the epistemological problem, of course, the problem of knowing truth, and in particular there is the danger, especially acute in an author as linguistically self-conscious as Apollonius, of what Paul Maas calls deceptive confirmation:[3] an ancient reading is not automatically rendered true by virtue of its having been proposed by a modern scholar. But for the moment, let me merely say that I see no need to refuse ever to talk of a papyrus confirming a conjecture. Far more harm is done, to my mind, by the opposite and more prevalent fallacy, that if a papyrus agrees with the medieval

* This paper was written before I learned of Hermann Fränkel's death. Now it can only be offered to his memory.

[1] *P.Oxy.* VI 874, intro., speaking of Oxyrhynchus papyri. Cf. Grenfell in *JHS* 39 (1919) 23. *Contra* A. Lesky, *A History of Greek Literature* (English translation, London, 1966) 737: "The papyri yield little."

[2] See the preface to his OCT, and his *Einleitung zur kritischen Ausgabe der Argonautica des Apollonios* (Göttingen, 1964), hereafter referred to as *Einleitung*. "permulta novavi, temere quod sciam nihil" (OCT praef. xx) looks provocatively back at Wellauer's "contra librorum consensum nihil novare ausus sum."

[3] *Textkritik* §37.

manuscripts at a place where a conjecture has been put forward, the text of the manuscripts is thereby proved sound.

As well as the direct application, simple inferences can be made. If the medieval tradition should be shown to be more corrupt than had been thought in every place where it can be tested, it would be reasonable to suppose that it is in a similar state elsewhere. By exposing unsuspected defects in the medieval tradition, the papyri put us in a position to reassess its condition. In this way they serve as a complement to the extraordinarily rich indirect tradition, represented mainly by quotations in the lexicographers. In his OCT praefatio (vii, cf. *Einleitung* 18), Fränkel calculated that the papyri bettered the text on average about once in every ten verses, allowing a generous margin of error either side of that figure. That represents of course a *minimum* proportion of corruption in the medieval manuscripts, for it leaves common errors out of account. Over the last fifteen years the amount of *Argonautica* extant on papyrus has increased severalfold, and Fränkel's assessment has held up. H. Erbse, however, who reviewed the OCT for *Gnomon*, had more faith in the medieval tradition. He did not question Fränkel's judgment that the papyri bettered the text as often as Fränkel thought. But he nonetheless said (I translate): "Presumably the text transmitted by the manuscripts [he means the medieval manuscripts, of course, not the ancient manuscripts] is nothing like as bad as the . . . editor thinks."[4] It is one thing to emphasize that the evidence may be unreliable and should not be pressed too hard: it is altogether another to throw the evidence overboard and resort instead to presumption. The value of the papyri is precisely that they allow such presumptions to be tested. They are by way of being a control—however deficient a control —on the authority, the Glaubwürdigkeit, of the medieval tradition.

(It is a good general rule, even apart from the papyri, that our modern texts are in a worse condition than they appear to be. How could it be otherwise than that there are some corruptions which give no sign of being such? A practical rule among editors and critics is that the reading of the manuscripts should not be abandoned unless it has to be. But as E. J. Kenney has remarked, "There is an important difference between using the *status quo* as a methodological convenience and regarding it as true."[5] The papyri are a constant reminder that even an apparently sound text is not necessarily sound, that a conjecture does not have to be necessary in order to be true—though admittedly it has to be necessary in order to be *known* to be true.)

---

[4] *Gnomon* 35 (1963) 18: "Vermutlich ist der handschriftlich überlieferte Wortlaut der *Argonautica* bei weitem nicht so entstellt, wie der gelehrte und konjekturenfreudige Herausgeber annimmt."

[5] *The Classical Text* (Berkeley–Los Angeles–London, 1974) 25.

The establishment of the fact and minimum amount of corruption in the medieval tradition: that is a valuable if discomforting contribution of the papyri stated in static, synchronic terms. But we are bound to introduce the historical dimension—I mean, to ask How come? The corruptions revealed by the papyri might show something of the sorts of way in which the text was peculiarly *liable* to corruption, and that in turn might facilitate the uncovering of the still hidden corruptions and guide the critic's feet when he takes what Fränkel graphically terms the "step into the void," "der Schritt ins Leere," i.e., resorts to conjectural emendation; unless, of course, it merely imposes a recognition that detection and healing are beyond us, and that we shall have to be content after all with simple and unsatisfying diagnostic statements such as that the text has suffered from Homeric normalization. The question "How come?" can also be formulated in more expressly transmissional terms: how did the medieval tradition come to *be* the medieval tradition?

Perhaps it will be as well to get a handle on some of these abstractions by taking a summary look at an actual papyrus text. Below is printed fr. 2 of *P.Oxy.* XXXIV 2700, attributed to the third century. The papyrus is no. 1, as coming nearest the beginning of the Argonautica, in the list of papyri conveniently published by F. Vian in his new and admirable Budé text; it is also described by its editor, P. Kingston, as offering "the text most difficult to evaluate" of all the twelve Argonautica papyri in that volume. It could not be said to be untypical of the Argonautica papyri, except perhaps insofar as it is a plain text, without alternative readings or marginalia of any kind.

To the left of the transcription, reproduced as in the ed. pr., I detail any and all divergencies from the united medieval mss. To the right I list the cases where the medieval tradition is split and the papyrus agrees with one or another part of it; these will be taken up later.

For ease of reference I reproduce on the opposite page the text and apparatus as offered in Fränkel's OCT (compiled before the papyrus was known), with the differences between that text and the text of the papyrus alongside. (There will almost certainly have been more such differences, for the survival of the papyrus for this passage is only partial.)

Sigla as follows: m = LA, w = SG, k = EJP.[6] We are at the end of the catalogue of Argonauts, as they go down to the beach to the ship.

---

[6] L, the first representative of m, is the famous cod. Laur. gr. 32.9, nowadays dated ca. 960–980 (Irigoin, *REG* 74 [1961] 514). The w family is associated with Maximus Planudes. Much progress has been made with k, the "Cretan recension," since the OCT: see Vian, *Rev. Hist. Textes* 2 (1972) 171–195. It is basically a sub-family of m; Vian has found P to be a descriptus of J, which is in turn a descriptus of E.

	......]α.[		
	......]επικλη[		
	......]εηππό[		
	.....]ηντοη[	205	
	.....]ϱℓ..]τη[		
207 Φ[ω]κεί[ων: Φωκήων codd.	......]φ[·]κει[		
	......]ουεκ[		
	...]εβη·π.[.]ωδ[		
	.....]λιησ·τοθιγ[	210	
	....]αυκαλαῖσ[		
	......]ερεχθη.[		
	......]ηθρηκ[...]υ[·]χ.[.].ερ.[		
	θρηκιοσβορεησανερεψατοκε[		ἀνερέψατο w (-θρεψ- G):
215 Εἰλεισοῦ:'Ιλισσοῦ codd.	ειλεισοῦπρ[.]παροιθεχορωενιδι[	215	ἀνερείψ- m k test
(Εἰλισσοῦ J)	καιμιν[.]γωνεκαθενσαρπηδ[.]ηἱ[		
	κλειουσ[..]ποταμιοιοπαρα[...].[		
218 Λυγκαιος: λυγαίοις codd.	λυγκαιοσ[..].μασσεπερινεφ.ε[..]ι.[		
(Λυγκαίοις coni. Livrea)			
219 ἐ[πὶ κρ]οτάφοισι: ἐπ'	τὼμενε̱[....]οταφοι[.]ιποδων⟨θ'⟩εκα[		
ἀκροτάτοισι codd. Σ (ἐπ'			
ἀστραγάλοισι coni.			
Fränkel conl. Σ ⟨θ'⟩			
Kingston			
220 ἀειρ[ο]μένας (sic): -μενω codd.	σειοναει[..]μεναιπτερύ[...]μεγ[	220	
πτερύ[γας (hoc accentu):	χρυσειαισφολιδεσσιδια[		
πτέρ- codd.	κραατοσε[		
223 om.			
	ουδεμενουδα[		
	ἴφθιμ[..]πελι.[................].εοιο	225	ἑοῖο w: ἑῆος m k
	μιμμ[..].ινα[.............]ερ.[...]θηνη[		
	αλλαρ[....]τὼμ[......]νικρ[......]ιομ[		
228 τ[ό]σσαι: τόσσοι codd.	τ[.]σσαιαραισον[..]ησυνυμησ[		
συνμησ[(i.e., σὺν μῆσ-?):	τουσμε[..]ρισ[...]σμινύασπ[		
συμμήστορες codd. Σ	κικλησκ[.]νμαλαπαντα̱[	230	
	οιπ.[.]ιστο.καιαριστοιασφα[		
	εμμ[....].[....]αιαυτον[		
	.]λκι[.........]ησμιννη[		
	...........]εσσινεπαρτέα.[		
235 ἐπήρεες: ἐπαρτέα k, -τέες m w	...........]ονταιεπηρεεσ[	235	
	...........]ανδρασ[.]πειρ'αλαν[		
	...............]αστεοσενθ.[		
	...............]νήτιδεσ·αμ[		
239 ? σπερχομένου]σ: ἐπερχο-	...........]σαμυδισθεεν·οι[		θέεν m w: θέον k
μένων codd., σπερχ-	...............]μετεπρ[.]πον ωδ[	240	
Meineke	...............]χεσιγαι[		
242 τοῖ[ο]ν (sic): τόσσον codd.	..................]σσονομ[		
	..................]κτ[		

Ἐκ δ' ἄρα Φωκήων κίεν Ἴφιτος, Ὀρνυτίδαο   φ[ω]κει[ων
Ναυβόλου ἐκγεγαώς· ξεῖνος δέ οἱ ἔσκε πάροιθεν,
ἦμος ἔβη Πυθώδε θεοπροπίας ἐρεείνων
ναυτιλίης, τόθι γάρ μιν ἑοῖς ὑπέδεκτο δόμοισι.   210
Ζήτης αὖ Κάλαΐς τε Βορήιοι υἷες ἱκέσθην,
οὕς ποτ' Ἐρεχθηὶς Βορέη τέκεν Ὠρείθυια
ἐσχατιῇ Θρήκης δυσχειμέρου· ἔνθ' ἄρα τήνγε
Θρήικιος Βορέης ἀνερείψατο Κεκροπίηθεν,   ἀνερεψατο
Ἰλισσοῦ προπάροιθε χορῷ ἔνι δινεύουσαν,   215   ειλεισοῦ
καί μιν ἄγων ἔκαθεν, Σαρπηδονίην ὅθι πέτρην
κλείουσιν ποταμοῖο παρὰ ῥόον Ἐργίνοιο,
λυγαίοις ἐδάμασσε περὶ νεφέεσσι καλύψας.   λυγκαιος
τὼ μὲν ἐπ' ἀστραγάλοισι ποδῶν ἑκάτερθεν ἐρεμνάς   ε[πικρ]οταφοισι
σεῖον ἀειρομένω πτέρυγας, μέγα θάμβος ἰδέσθαι,   220   -μενας
χρυσείαις φολίδεσσι διαυγέας· ἀμφὶ δὲ νώτοις
κράατος ἐξ ὑπάτοιο καὶ αὐχένος ἔνθα καὶ ἔνθα
κυάνεαι δονέοντο μετὰ πνοιῇσιν ἔθειραι.   v.om.
Οὐδὲ μὲν οὐδ' αὐτοῖο πάις μενέαινεν Ἄκαστος
ἰφθίμου Πελίαο δόμοις ἔνι πατρὸς ἑῆος   225   εοιο
μιμνάζειν, Ἄργος τε θεᾶς ὑποεργὸς Ἀθήνης,
ἀλλ' ἄρα καὶ τὼ μέλλον ἐνικρινθῆναι ὁμίλῳ.
Τόσσοι ἄρ' Αἰσονίδῃ συμμήστορες ἠγερέθοντο.   -αι   συν
τοὺς μὲν ἀριστῆας Μινύας περιναιετάοντες
κίκλησκον μάλα πάντας, ἐπεὶ Μινύαο θυγατρῶν   230
οἱ πλεῖστοι καὶ ἄριστοι ἀφ' αἵματος εὐχετόωντο
ἔμμεναι, ὣς δὲ καὶ αὐτὸν Ἰήσονα γείνατο μήτηρ
Ἀλκιμέδη Κλυμένης Μινυηίδος ἐκγεγαυῖα.
Αὐτὰρ ἐπεὶ δμώεσσιν ἐπαρτέα πάντ' ἐτέτυκτο
ὅσσα περ ἐντύνονται †ἐπαρτέα ἔνδοθι νῆες,   235   επηρεες
εὖτ' ἂν ἄγῃ χρέος ἄνδρας ὑπεὶρ ἅλα ναυτίλλεσθαι,
δὴ τότ' ἴσαν μετὰ νῆα δι' ἄστεος, ἔνθα περ ἀκταί
κλείονται Παγασαὶ Μαγνήτιδες· ἀμφὶ δὲ λαῶν
πληθὺς σπερχομένων ἄμυδις θέον, οἱ δὲ φαεινοί   -μενου]σ   θεεν
ἀστέρες ὣς νεφέεσσι μετέπρεπον. ὧδε δ' ἕκαστος   240
ἔννεπεν εἰσορόων σὺν τεύχεσιν ἀίσσοντας·
"Ζεῦ ἄνα, τίς Πελίαο νόος; πόθι τόσσον ὅμιλον   τοι[ο]ν
ἡρώων γαίης Παναχαιίδος ἔκτοθι βάλλει;

213 neque ἔνθα neque ἄρα satis aptum   214 ἀνερείψατο LAPE: -ερέψ- (-εθρέψ- G) SG;
cf. ii.503, ubi ἀνερειψάμενος omnes, contra iv. 918 ἀνερέψατο L²ASG: -ρύσα- PE (ex 861?);
Ap. vel altera vel altera vel utraque forma usus esse potest (v. Platt 33. 30)   215 marg. ἄλλο
κιφισοῦ γράφουσι PE (cf. schc, lin. 16), male   217 παρὰ(ρ) LSGPE: παραὶ p. corr. V, A
219 ἀστραγάλοισι Fr: ἀκρατάοισι libri (ex 183): gl. ἐπ' ἀκρ. π.· τοῖς σφυροῖς ἢ τοῖς
ἀστραγάλοις sch^LP   ἐρεμνὰς APE sch: ἐρυμνὰς SG: utrumque (ε supra υ scr.) L   220 θάμβος
LASG: θαῦμα PE: cf. 1307   225 ἑῆος LAPE: ἑοῖο SG (cf. 667, ii. 656, al.)   235 ἐπαρτέα
PE: -τέες LASG; ex 234   239 σπερχομένων Meineke (ad Theocr. 21. 49): ἐπερχ- libri
θέον PE: θέεν LASG: v. ad iv. 689

Ignoring orthographica (which are interesting but of minor importance),[7] in two cases the papyrus brings indubitable truth where the text
had been suspected but not put right:

(i) In 219 we find ἐ[πὶ κρ]οτάφοισι for ἐπ' ἀκροτάτοισι. The Boreads
had two pairs of wings, one at their feet and the other at their
temples; this is known not only from Hyginus and Statius and
visual representations but actually from the so-called Orphic
Argonautica, which is closely derived from Apollonius and ought
really to have given the clue. As for ἐπ' ἀκροτάτοισι, it seems
incredible—in hindsight—that it should have been printed with
scarcely a hint of suspicion right up until Fränkel. Fränkel
thought that he had in fact recovered the correct reading from
the scholium here: ἐπ' ἀστραγάλοισι, at their ankles. One suspects
that if he had not had the dubious benefit of the scholium, he
would have reached the true solution. (The papyrus shows the
corruption part-way there: note the omission of θ, probably by
haplography.)

(ii) In 235, ἐπαρτέα had been defended by more than one editor.
With scepticism now shown to be well justified, Fränkel daggered.
ἐπήρεες is clearly right.[8]

So much for indubitable truth. Let us go to the other end of the scale,
to indubitable error, and then move into the more slippery middle ground.

(iii) The omission of v. 223 is self-evidently due to homoearchon
(KPA: KYA).

(iv) τ[ό]σσαι in 228, of the catalogue of Argonauts, is a quirky little
blunder. Perhaps induced by Αἰσονίδη following, by a simple
kind of phonetic attraction?

(v) In 220, the editor read αει[..]μεναι, which would be completely
unintelligible. But on the plate (Pl. V) what I see is αειρ[ο]μενας.
Due, I suppose, to straightforward attraction to ἐρεμνάς . . .
πτέρυγας. (But I dare say if ἀειρομένας alone had been transmitted, it would have found its defenders.)

(vi) In 218, λυγαίοις and Λυγκαιος make an intriguing pair of
alternatives. The editor strongly championed the papyrus'

---

[7] (i) In 215 Εἰλισσοῦ is the right reading: εἰλισσ - δινεύουσαν (see Campbell, CQ
21 [1971] 404 f.). (ii) Φωκείων (207) is a v. l. for Φωκήων at Il. 2.517, and may have been
Aristarchus' reading (cf. schol. ad loc.). (iii) πτερύγας (220) is the accentuation prescribed
by Herodian.

[8] Cf. Fränkel, OCT praef. vii, Einleitung 39, R. Renehan, Greek Textual Criticism, 19.

Λυγκαιος, but otherwise there seems to be general agreement, which I share, that λυγαίοις should be allowed to stand[9]. I will not repeat the reasons, merely observe that Λυγκαιος, which on the face of it is a very difficult reading to account for *unless* it is genuine, might be the scribe's inadvertent portmanteau of Λυγκεύς and 'Αγκαῖος: Lynceus was mentioned just above at 151 and 153, and Ancaeus twice since; add that at 125 Λυρκήιον "Αργος appears as Λυγκήιον "Αργος in all the mss.[10]

(vii) συνμηστορες at 228 might simply be dissimilation. If it is not, but represents συν prepositional with Aἰσονίδη, I think it is wrong; but I shall not spend time arguing about it.[11]

(viii) In 239, there is only a single letter left of the supposed σπερχο-μένου]ς, but what else could it have been? σπερχομένους should definitely be preferred to σπερχομένω, which is quite redundant with θέον.[12] The corruption to the genitive is perfectly natural after λαῶν πληθύς. (The corruption at the beginning of the word in the mss., the unmetrical ἐπ- for σπ-, will be a separate, unconnected error. The papyrus may have had it or not.)

(ix) Finally, τοῖ[ο]ν in 242: the reading was reported in an addendum, and seems to have escaped notice. It is surely better than τόσσον.[13] At 228 above, τόσσοι and only τόσσοι is appropriate, in the summing-up line for the catalogue, but here in 242 what impresses the natives is not the quantity of the heroes—there are not so very many of them, after all—but their quality, as just described in 239–241. There is hardly need to ask for a specific cause of the corruption of τοιον to τοσσον, but it would be ungracious to refuse the one that is offered us: ἀίσσοντας immediately above (cf. ἐπαρτέα in 235).

To sum up: in this short passage the papyrus corrects four errors common to the medieval mss.;[14] two of them in previously suspected but

[9] Vian, *Rev. Et. Gr.* 82 (1969) 232 and Budé text; Del Corno, *Gnomon* 45 (1973) 545; Campbell, *CQ* 21 (1971) 405.

[10] The scholium *ad loc.* attests to both readings. Λυγκήιον was defended by Brunck and anew by D. N. Levin (*GRBS* 4 [1963] 9–17).

[11] The fact that the compound is unhomeric is hardly an argument against its being Apollonian. Cf. e.g., ὑφήτορες 1.22 (I do not know whether it has been noted that this is modelled on ἀφήτορος, of controversial interpretation at *Il.* 9.404).

[12] So Vian in a *note complémentaire* to his Budé text, p. 250.

[13] Mr. A. H. Griffiths, to whom I am very grateful for discussion, disagrees. He would defend τόσσον by reference to πουλὺν ὅμιλον at *Il.* 10.517.

[14] Vian would agree with this assessment, except insofar as he missed τοῖον; I would hope that Fränkel would too.

unmended places. It also has some errors peculiar to itself; but these do not matter so much, nor would any number of them vitiate the true readings. Scribal blunders are often invoked in order to discredit good readings, as if the presence of a blunder in one place were somehow incompatible with the preservation of truth in another. Some papyri are better than others, of course; a schoolboy's text will probably be less reliable than a scholar's. But however bad a text may be, however stupidly copied and uncontrolled, it is still liable to carry truth that was later to be lost. And we are not setting up a contest between the ancient ms. and the medieval ones, but trying to form some idea of the absolute state of the paradosis.

Nearly all the errors noted above, both those of the medieval tradition and those of the papyrus, are of the simple transcriptional kind that any of us might commit in copying out the text. (Though what is easily committed may not be so easily detected.) They are produced by factors of palaeography and sense combined, and that is all. Things are not always so simple.

Grenfell and Hunt pointed the way, Fränkel followed it. Prejudice against new papyrus readings (together with its counterpart, undue and unfounded faith in the transmitted text) has impeded restoration of Apollonius' text of the Argonautica less than is the case with some other authors. Individual papyrus readings have on the whole been well evaluated. There are perhaps one or two instances where a reading has not quite been given its due. Here is one which bears on the rationale of corruption.

4.445 f.   (In this and all subsequent quotes, I quote from Fränkel's text.)

> Σχέτλι' "Ερως, μέγα πῆμα, μέγα στύγος ἀνθρώποισιν,
> ἐκ σέθεν οὐλόμεναί τ' ἔριδες στοναχαί τε γόοι τε
> τ' non habet P.Oxy. XXXIV 2694 (II)[15]   πόνοι pap.

In 446 the papyrus is without the elided τε presented by the medieval mss. Fränkel suggests that an inadvertent omission is likelier than an inadvertent addition (*Einleitung* 15), and subsequent editors have followed him in his retention of the particle. But who said the corruption was inadvertent? τ' was surely put in to avert the hiatus, as frequently in Apollonius and elsewhere. There is no objection to the hiatus, of course: cf.

> 4.1011   κούρη δ' οὐλομένῳ ὑπὸ δείματι κτλ.
> *Il.* 20.253   αἴτε χολωσάμεναι ἔριδος πέρι θυμοβόροιο
> *Od.* 11.410   ἔκτα σὺν οὐλομένῃ ἀλόχῳ κτλ.

[15] II = 2nd cent. of our era; similarly below.

(πόνοι for γόοι would take more time to discuss, and is less to my purpose. I will just say that I am less sure than Fränkel that it is wrong, and the *utrum in alterum* principle is in favour of it.)[16]

Certainly, a lot of the corruption in the Argonautica is due to scribal inadvertence, and not always of the every-day kind committed or exposed by *P.Oxy.* 2700. Homer was always more popular than Apollonius, and a scribe set to copy out the Argonautica might well write down the Homeric phrase out of his head instead of what stood before him in his exemplar. Confronted with δέπας ἀμφοτέρῃσιν, "(he took) the cup in both hands," the scribe of *P.Oxy.* XXXIV 2695 (or a predecessor) wrote δέπας ἀμφικύπελλον: the collocation δέπας ἀμφ- triggered the familiar continuation. At 1.781 most modern readers were perfectly happy with Jason going "in front of the city along the path," πρὸ πόληος ἀνὰ στίβον, as the medieval mss. have him do, until a papyrus turned up with προπόλοιο κατὰ στίβον, "in the footsteps of the handmaid."[17] The unhomeric προπόλοιο had given place to the Homeric πρὸ πόληος.

Invasion from Homer is a well-known phenomenon in the Argonautica, and it is not always the straightforward substitution of the ordinary Homeric phrase for the Apollonian variation of it. The insidious pressures exerted by the more readable and memorable epics are perhaps to be seen at work in the following two cases.

3.1299 ff.   ὡς δ᾽ ὅτ᾽ ἐνὶ τρητοῖσιν εὔρρινοι χοάνοισιν
φῦσαι χαλκήων ὀτὲ μέν τ᾽ <u>ἀναμαρμαίρουσιν</u>
πῦρ ὀλοὸν πιμπρᾶσαι, ὅτ᾽ αὖ λήγουσιν ἀυτμῆς,
δεινὸς δ᾽ ἐξ αὐτῶν πέλεται βρόμος, ὁππότ᾽ ἀίξῃ
νειόθεν—ὡς ἄρα, κτλ.

αν]αμωρμυρουσιν P. Mil. Vogl. III 121 (IV), *voluit sane* αναμορ-, *q. coniecerat Ruhnken*

This is one of the few places where Fränkel had retained a ms. reading in the face of a true conjecture.[18] We are in an elaborate simile comparing the fire-breathing bulls to the bellows of a furnace. ἀναμορμύρω occurs once and once only in Homer: it is what Charybdis did. *Od.* 12.237 ff.:

ἦ τοι ὅτ᾽ ἐξεμέσειε, λέβης ὡς ἐν πυρὶ πολλῷ
πᾶσ᾽ ἀναμορμύρεσκε κυκωμένη· ὑψόσε δ᾽ ἄχνη
ἄκροισι σκοπέλοισιν ἐπ᾽ ἀμφοτέροισιν ἔπιπτεν.
ἀλλ᾽ ὅτ᾽ ἀναβρόξειε θαλάσσης ἁλμυρὸν ὕδωρ, κτλ.

[16] Cf. Vian, *Rev. Et. Gr.* 82 (1969) 232 (and ap. Livrea's ed. of bk. 4 *ad loc.*). Cod. C, one of Demetrius Moschus' mss., has πόλεμοί τε μάχαι τε (*GRBS* 15 [1974] 120), no doubt a wilful alteration.

[17] Grenfell, *JHS* 39 (1919) 23, Wilamowitz, *Hermes* 58 (1923) 73, Fränkel, *AJP* 71 (1950) 113–114 n. 1 (and connoisseurs of the horrific should see Dain, *Rev. Phil.* 17 [1943] 56–61).

[18] As he would himself now agree (see *P. Mil. Vogl. III*, p. 18).

In the Odyssey passage there is an alternation between the belching out and the sucking in, as here between the bellows blowing and—ceasing to blow (ὅτέ . . . ὅτέ).[19] ἀναμαρμαίρουσιν, the reading of the medieval tradition, is quite inappropriate: there is no justification for the preverb, and bellows do not gleam. (I am aware that this is a rather summary dismissal, but I think it is fair.) It is wrong: but how did it originate? The verb is not attested anywhere else. I should guess that χαλκήων . . . ἀναμορμύρουσιν, by foggy phonetic association, stirred up such Homeric phrases as χάλκεα μαρμαίροντα, and thus the copyist unwittingly wrote μαρμαιρουσιν instead of μορμυρουσιν. (Cf. ἐπικροταφοισι → ἐπακροτατοισι at 1.219, p. 52 above: perhaps that would not have happened but for Homer's ἐπ᾽ ἀκροτάτῳ, ἐπ᾽ ἀκροτάτῃ, etc.)

1.1201 ff.   ὡς δ᾽ ὅταν ἀπροφάτως ἱστὸν νεός, εὖτε μάλιστα
χειμερίη ὀλοοῖο δύσις πέλει Ὠρίωνος,
ὑψόθεν ἐμπλήξασα θοὴ ἀνέμοιο κατάιξ
αὐτοῖσι σφήνεσσιν ὑπὲκ προτόνων ἐρύσηται, κτλ.
]οασα PSI X 1172 (I) (ἐμπλήσασα G)

ἐμπλήξασα is guaranteed, as Fränkel points out, by Aratus 422–424, εἰ δέ κε νηί/ ὑψόθεν ἐμπλήξῃ δεινὴ ἀνέμοιο θύελλα/ αὔτως ἀπρόφατος, κτλ. Fränkel suggests that the papyrus reading was ἐμπρήσασα.[20] With ἱστόν up above awaiting a verb, and θοὴ ἀνέμοιο κατάιξ following, it is then difficult to resist the thought that there has been some contamination from epic phrases like the following:

Il. 1.481   ἐν δ᾽ ἄνεμος πρῆσεν μέσον ἱστίον . . .
Od. 2.427   ἔπρησεν δ᾽ ἄνεμος μέσον ἱστίον . . .
H. Bac. 33   ἔμπνευσεν δ᾽ ἄνεμος μέσον ἱστίον . . . (ἔμπρησεν temptaverim[21])

But it is perhaps more likely that the papyrus read ἐμπλήσασα, as G, in which case Homer is nihil ad rem.

Then there are a number of variants whose origin I would be tempted to find less in the Homeric permeation of scribes than in the Homeric erudition of scholars.

1.374 f.   αἰεὶ δὲ προτέρω χθαμαλώτερον ἐξελάχαινον
στείρης· ἐν δ᾽ ὁλκῷ ξεστὰς στορέσαντο φάλαγγας.
ἐξ- codd. et PSI XV 1478 (I/I): ἀμφ- P.Berol. 11690 (III)

---

[19] Both passages involve a simile, too: Charybdis ἀναμορμύρεσκε like a cauldron on the boil.

[20] Einleitung 20.

[21] ἔπρησεν Gemoll. One or the other must surely be read: ἐμπνέω is never used thus. (LSJ's entry for ἐμπνέω II.1 should be deleted.)

The Argonauts are digging a trench in the beach for the launching of the Argo. The word Apollonius uses is ἐξελάχαινον, an apparent coinage evidently derived from the one and only occurrence of a (-)λαχαίνω verb in Homer, namely *Od.* 24.242, where Laertes is busying himself in his garden "digging around a plant:" ἦ τοι ὁ μὲν κατέχων κεφαλὴν φυτὸν ἀμφελάχαινεν. A third-century Berlin papyrus proffers ἀμφελάχαινον in the Apollonius passage.[22] Now there can be no doubt that ἐξελάχαινον is right; that is made quite clear by the use of the word and the simplex by Apollonius and by other Hellenistic poets.[23] The ἀμφι compound is a *hapax*, and it seems extremely unlikely that the displacement of ἐξ- by ἀμφ- in the papyrus should be due to the copyist's unconscious substitution of a *hapax*, however thoroughly steeped in Homer he may have been. Is not its origin more likely to be a commentary or marginal scholium noting what any self-respecting modern commentary would, namely the dependence of Apollonius' ἐξελάχαινον on Homer's ἀμφελάχαινεν?[24]

> 3.1225 καὶ τότ' ἄρ' Αἰήτης περὶ μὲν στήθεσσιν <u>ἕεστο</u>
> θώρηκα στάδιον
> ἕε]σσεν P.Berol. 17020 (VII–VIII)

Aeetes put on his breastplate. ἕεστο, with two epsilons, is attested only once in Homer: *Il.* 12.464, λάμπε δὲ χαλκῷ/ σμερδαλέῳ, τὸν ἕεστο περὶ χροΐ κτλ. A papyrus codex dated to the seventh or eighth century (this is very interesting, as showing that there were mss. around in this late period with significant readings not found in the medieval tradition) has ἕεσσεν. (The beginning of the word is lost, but it is hardly open to doubt.) This form, if the apparatuses are to be trusted, is not attested in Homer at all[25]—but the single-epsilon form ἕσσεν is, and always in circumstances where the substitution of ἕεσσεν would be metrically possible.[26] ἕεσσεν is just as respectable a form as the middle ἕεστο. Presumably the middle is

[22] *P.Berol.* 11690; *Forsch. und Berichte Staatl. Museum von Berlin, Arch. Beitr.* 10 (1968) 123 f.

[23] Ap. Rh. 4.1532 αἶψα δὲ χαλκείῃσι βαθὺν τάφον ἐξελάχαινον. For the simplex see Pfeiffer at Callim. fr. 701. Zenodotus read ἐλάχεια for λάχεια (etymologized as παρὰ τὸ λαχαίνεσθαι) in Homer (*Od.* 9.116, 10.509), but we do not know whether anyone ever made out that the verb was ἐλαχαίνω. (Ch. de Lamberterie, *Rev. Phil.* 49 [1975] 236 f. discusses the etymology.)

[24] The scholia are constantly comparing the linguistic usages of the Argonautica with those of Homer. They adduce Homeric models, they illustrate Homer's use where it differs from Apollonius', and so on. (Deviation from Homeric usage is castigated: hence textual normalization.)

[25] Bekker introduced it, however.

[26] ἕεσσεν (or rather ἕεσσεν, or rather again ἕϝεσσεν) will be the older form. Cf. the parallel middle parts ἑέσσατο/ἕσσατο as mutual vv. ll. at *Il.* 10.23.

right, since Aeetes is putting the breastplate not on someone else but on himself. How then did it get replaced by ἔεσσεν? Substitution of active endings for passive is common enough, but not when it results in a *vox nihili*. Some little disquisition on the past forms of ἔννυμι in Homer could be responsible.

(Something similar seems to have happened at 3.454, the well-known αὐτός θ᾽ οἷος ἔην οἵοισί τε φάρεσιν εἶτο (*k*: ἧστο *mw*: ἔστο *d*). Fränkel compares *Od.* 11.191, where the mss. offer variously (χροὶ εἵματα) εἶται, εἷσται, ἧται and ἧσται (so Zenodotus, test. schol.: ἧστο Aristarchus). There seems little chance of establishing what Apollonius wrote.)

An alleged occurrence of one such form elsewhere in this book prompts me to make an elementary methodological point. At 3.263, Chalciope is pathetically greeting her sons:

δειλὴ ἐγώ, οἷον πόθον Ἑλλάδος ἔκποθεν ἄτης
λευγαλέης Φρίξοιο ἐφημοσύνῃσιν ἔνεσθε
πατρός.

-σι]ϝεϝεϛ[θε (*ut leg. Zuntz*) *vel* -σι]ϝϙλεϛ[θε (*ut leg. Grenfell–Hunt*; -σιν ἔλεσθε *coniecerat Brunck*) *P.Oxy. VI 874* (II/III): -σι νέεσθαι (*mk*) *vel* -θε (*w*) *codd.*[27]

The question at issue is the verb. "Ah me, what a desire for Greece you ___ at the behest of your father."[28] Brunck had conjectured ἔλεσθε for the nonsense of the mss., and *P.Oxy.* 874 has either that or, as Professor Zuntz would prefer to read, ἔνεσθε.[29] A pamphlet has recently been published in which the reading offered by cod. G is taken to be ἔεσθε, which is then defended: "you put on desire."[30] ἔεστο at 3.1225 is adduced to support the tense (pluperfect), and φρεσὶν εἱμένος ἀλκήν at *Il.* 20.381 is adduced to support the sense, the extended meaning. Such far-flung analogical procedures seem to me a sure way of perpetuating any grotesquerie that the mss. might happen to hand down. No mention is made of the dative that regularly attends the verb: Apollonius does not mean to say, "you put desire on the behests of Phrixus." And with νέεσθαι as verse-ending I do not know how many times in Homer and in the Argonautica, the *ratio corruptelae* stares one in the face.[31]— And what is said of the papyrus? Nothing at all, it is simply ignored. It might as well not have been found. In the same pamphlet are defended other readings of the medieval mss. where a conjecture has been proposed which is now known to be an ancient reading. Now it could be that they are all instances

[27] In cod. G (which with cod. S effectively constitutes *w*) ἔεσθαι is written in an erasure after ν (i.e., the *w* reading was altered to the *mk* reading).

[28] Read λευγαλέης? [Mr. A. H. Griffiths now tells me this was proposed by Platt.]

[29] I have seen a photograph, on which λ looks better than ϙ; but I have not seen the original. Not θ (ἔθεσθε coni. Fränkel, *Noten* 341).

[30] G. Giangrande, *Zu Sprachgebrauch Technik und Text des Apollonios Rhodios, Classical and Byzantine Monographs* 1 (Amsterdam, 1973) 21 f.

[31] It is the commonness of γαῖαν ἱκέσθαι as verse-ending that lends plausibility to Fränkel's bold suggestion at 3.775.

of "deceptive confirmation."[32] But a papyrus reading is at least *evidence*, and should enter the discussion. A procedure which cuts out half the evidence—and that the only half known to be ancient—is not best calculated to lead to the truth.

T. S. Kuhn, investigating the resistance which new scientific truths invariably encounter, observes that "normal" science (as he terms it) "often suppresses fundamental novelties because they are subversive of its basic commitments."[33]

1.798 εὖτε Θόας ἀστοῖσι πατὴρ ἐμὸς ἐμβασίλευε
? ἶφι] ἄνασσε *P.Oxy. XXXIV 2698* (II)

The medieval mss. have ἐμβασίλευε, the papyrus ..ασσε, which the editor suggested was ἄνασσε; and what can this be in fact but ἶφι ἄνασσε? Neither can be a gloss upon the other. I suppose ἐμβασίλευε is right. Homer never uses ἶφι ἀνάσσω (as opposed to simple ἀνάσσω) with dat. pers. ἐμβασιλεύω occurs twice in the Iliad, once in the Odyssey—there preceded by πατὴρ ἐμός: τῇσιν δ' ἀμφοτέρῃσι πατὴρ ἐμὸς ἐμβασίλευε (*Od*. 15.413).

A still more striking case of such equivalents or quasi-equivalents is at the mourning of Cyzicus:

1.1057 ἤματα δὲ τρία πάντα γόων τίλλοντό τε χαίτας
κείρον[το *P.Oxy. XXXIV 2696* (II)

τίλλοντο vs. κείροντο. Each of these words, in this form, is *hapax legomenon* in Homer, in each case preceding τε χαίτας. (*Od*. 10.567 ἑζόμενοι δὲ κατ' αὖθι γόων τίλλοντό τε χαίτας; *Od*. 24.46 δάκρυα θερμὰ χέον Δαναοὶ κείροντό τε χαίτας.) Whichever is right (and this time I think it is probably the papyrus version),[34] I should imagine the other to be due ultimately to the deliberate adduction of the Homeric doublet.

2.135 f. ὡς οἵγ' οὐκέτι δὴν μένον ἔμπεδον ἀλλὰ κέδασθεν
εἴσω Βεβρυκίης, Ἀμύκου μόρον ἀγγελέοντες
αγγελλ[ον]τε[ς *P.Oxy. XXXIV 2697* (III)

The Bebrycians are spreading the news of their king Amycus' death at the hands of the Argonauts. The issue is between the future participle and the present. There is room for argument as to which is the more appropriate

[32] I should be surprised if anyone but Giangrande is prepared to retain αἶψα μέλαν τεταγὼν πέλεκυν μέγαν ἠδὲ κελαινόν at 2.119, however. [Cf. now E. Livrea, *Gnomon* 47 (1975) 354 f.] ἀντεταγών might have been "eine aus der Luft gegriffene Form" (Giangrande *op. cit.* 49, n. 3) when Sanctamandus proposed it, but it is now in *P.Oxy. XXXIV* 2697 *ad loc.* (αντεταγ(ων) in marg.).
[33] *The Structure of Scientific Revolutions* (Chicago, 1970), 151.
[34] Discussed by Vian, *Rev. Et. Gr.* 82 (1969) 231; Del Corno, *Gnomon* 45 (1973) 544; Vian, Budé ed. p. 100. At *Od*. 24.46 κείροντο is v. l for κείραντο.

to the situation.[35] Despite first appearances, it is unlikely that ἀγγέλλοντες is a simple corruption from ἀγγελέοντες. The feminine fut. part. ἀγγελέουσα is very common in Homer, and so far as I know that never gets corrupted to the present; any corruption tends to go the other way (under metrical influence?). The only masculine participle of ἀγγέλλω in an oblique case in Homer is at *Il.* 17.701, at verse-end as here, of Antilochus bearing the news of Patroclus' death to Achilles. (Do we again have a deliberate contextual affinity?) And there too there are variant readings: the medieval manuscripts have ἀγγελέοντα, a third-century papyrus ἀγγέλλοντα.[36] In Apollonius at least I think we should print the *spondeiazon*. Whether the alternative owes its existence more to scholarship or to accident I should not like to say, but scholarship (if that is not too grand a word for concern to impose Homeric norms) should not be ruled out.

A more intriguing choice is posed by an Amherst papyrus at 1. 777, as Jason makes his radiant way to the city of Lemnos.

1.774 ff.　Βῆ δ' ἴμεναι προτὶ ἄστυ, φαεινῷ ἀστέρι ἶσος,
　　　　　　ὅν ῥά τε νηγατέῃσιν ἐεργόμεναι καλύβῃσιν
　　　　　　νύμφαι θηήσαντο δόμων ὕπερ ἀντέλλοντα,
　　　　　　καί σφισι κυανέοιο δι' αἰθέρος ὄμματα θέλγει
　　　　　　καλὸν ἐρευθόμενος, κτλ.
　　　　αιθερος P.Amh. II 16 (II/III): ἠέρος codd. (ηρερος L)

The papyrus' δι' αἰθέρος is actually printed by Fränkel, though I cannot imagine anyone else printing it, and I suspect the main reason Fränkel did was to encourage radical thinking. Apollonius is fond of δι' ἠέρος (see Ardizzoni *ad loc.*), and often makes a point of using it in contexts where Homer would say δι' αἰθέρος.[37] But it would be strange if a scribe were so steeped in Homer as to substitute subconsciously αἰθέρος and yet not steeped enough to have been deterred by κυανέοιο: what could be less Homeric than dark aether? (I will not complicate the discussion still further by introducing the scholium, which glosses κυανέοιο with νῦν

35 Cf. Fränkel, *Noten* 164 n. 28, Vian *Rev. Et. Gr.* 82 (1969) 231.

36 It is interesting to find Homeric vv. ll. recurring as vv. ll. in the text of the Argo-nautica. So with ἑοῖο/ἑῆος at 1.225 (p. 50 above), ἐσσεύαντο/-οντο at 2.121 and *Il.* 11.549, and cf. the vv. ll. at 3.454 (p. 58 above). So too e.g., ἔπλετ' ἀϋτή (Et. Gen.) vs. ἔπλετο φωνή (codd.) at 1.1249, in parallel with ἵκετ' ἀϋτή (Aristarchus) vs. ἵκετο φωνή (codd.) at *Il.* 11.466; cf. 2.124 (πολιοί/πελιοί), 1.275 (ὀρεχθεῖ/ἐρεχθεῖ). Homeric hypomnemata influenced not only the original formation of the text of the Argonautica (Erbse, *Hermes* 81 [1953] 163–196) but also its subsequent transformations.

37 Similarly Callimachus locates stars in the ἀήρ, fr. 110.7, hy. 4.176. On ἀήρ and αἰθήρ in Apollonius, see H. Faerber, *Zur dicht. Kunst in Ap. Rh. Argonautica* 77. Cf. M. L. West at Hesiod *Theog.* 697 and N. J. Richardson, *The Homeric Hymn to Demeter*, 52.

λαμπροῦ, "here 'bright'"!) It would be folly to insist on absolute con-
sistency for Apollonius, and I can see a nice case being made for a nonce
Apollonian *reversal* of the one time that Homer does in fact say δι' ἠέρος
and not δι' αἰθέρος. But whichever is opted for, the other could well owe
its presence to a comparison with Homeric usage.[38]

It should not be thought that the above corruptions are representative.
What we saw when comparing *P.Oxy.* 2700 with the medieval mss. were
more run-of-the-mill affairs, such as might befall the text of any author.
But over and above these there are the sorts of corruption to which the
Argonautica was peculiarly liable by its very nature, and it is the pathology
of some of this more particular class that I have tried to illustrate above.
There are many other interesting doublets that I have not touched on,
such as ἄντρῳ ἐνὶ ζαθέῳ (*P.Oxy.* XXXIV 2691) and ἄντρῳ ἐν ἠγαθέῳ
(codd.) at 4.1131, or θυμὸν ἀποπνείων (*P.Oxy.* XXXIV 2694) and θυμὸν
ἀναπνείων (codd.) at 4.472; πλατὺ νῶτον (*PSI* X 1172) for πλατὺν ὦμον
(codd.) at 1.1198 is an aberration paralleled at Theoc. 24.125. Perhaps
I have seen significance where none exists; but in a text like the Argonautica, it is probably better to see too much significance than too little.

All this reminds us, if we have forgotten it, that for a proper appreciation
of Apollonius it is necessary to know Homer off by heart, inside out and
back to front. (I do not lay claim to a proper appreciation of Apollonius.)
We can be unhappily sure that there is much in our text that does not
proceed from Apollonius, and that much of that is perfectly undetectable;
we shall have to live with the knowledge of a certain irreducible minimum
of corruption that may be greater than in most of our authors. But en-
lightened despair need not be absolute. Emendation is not yet played out,
and thanks to the papyri we are somewhat better placed both for identifying corruption and even for removing it.

There is a potential complication. I have talked so far as if, given
alternative readings, one at least of them must be wrong. This is to reckon
without the possibility of *author's variants*. The notion of author-variants
in general is to my mind somewhat overplayed, but if it is respectable
anywhere, it is respectable in Apollonius. It is possible no longer to put off
the question of the *proecdosis*. For six passages of bk. 1, varying in extent
from one to eight lines, the scholia quote a different version from what is

---

[38] This assumes that no weight is to be attached to L's ηρεπος. If that is significant,
however, then the truth is αἰθέρος (ΑΙΘΕΡΟΣ → ΗΡΕΡΟΣ → ἠέρος is a one-way
progression). The reading is discussed by Pfeiffer, *Kallimachosstudien*, 12–13 n. 2, and
W. Ludwig, *Gnomon* 41 (1969) 256.

called the πρόεκδοσις, the "prior edition."[39] In three of the six passages the proecdosis version has a different number of lines. So we shall be particularly interested to see if the papyri have anything to offer by way of substantive discrepancies as compared with the medievally transmitted text. By substantive discrepancies I mean simply differences of an order comparable with what the scholia report from the proecdosis; these can be divided into two categories: disparity in the number of lines, and the radical reworking of an entire verse or group of verses.

The first result is simple enough. There are two cases where papyri overlap with a passage for which the scholia cite a different version from the proecdosis, and in neither place does the papyrus have the proecdosis version.

> 1.788 f. is partially extant in *P.Amh.* II 16 (2nd–3rd cent.).[40] 1.801 ff. is partially extant in *P.Oxy.* XXXIV 2698 (2nd cent.), a ms. which shows signs of collation and is therefore witness to the text of at least one ms. other than its own exemplar.

This is not too surprising, perhaps, but it is a datum worth having. There is in fact no evidence from the papyri that the proecdosis extended its peculiarities to the texts in ordinary circulation.

Indeed, there is little to encourage a belief that there were substantially different versions of the text current in antiquity. The papyri certainly do not. There are two cases in which papyri seem to present a different number of lines from the transmitted text,[41] but they are both pretty dubious.

[39] Ad 1.285, 515, 543, 725, 788, 801. The fourth of these is very fishy. According to the scholium, the proecdosis was without vv. 726 f.: ἐν τῇ προεκδόσει τῷ "τῆς μὲν ῥηῖτερόν κεν" (725 *init.*) ἑξῆς ἐστιν "ἄκρα δὲ πορφυρέη" (728 *init.*). This results in a nonsensical sequence. I suspect that 726 f. had been accidentally omitted in the copy available to the collator, perhaps through homoeomeson: 12 *litt.* + *ONKENE* 725, 11 *litt.* + *CHMENE* 727. (The traditional view, still subscribed to by Erbse, *Gnomon* 88 [1966] 160, is that the latter half of 725 was different in the proecdosis, but it is hard to believe that the collator would not have noted it if so, quite apart from the difficulty of devising a half-line that will give a satisfactory sequence. I find it equally hard to believe, *pace* Fränkel, *Einleitung* 8, that the omission is original or that it proves anything about the publication of the proecdosis.)

[40] There is a non-significant divergence between the paradosis and the papyrus. The medieval mss. have δι' ἀναστάδος (def. A. G. Tsopanakis, *Hellenika* 15 [1957] 112–121), but the true reading διὰ παστάδος, presented by the papyrus, had already been restored from the Et. Mag.

[41] I do not count obviously accidental omissions, such as that of 1.223 in *P.Oxy.* 2700 (p. 50 above). Homoearchon is evidently responsible for the omission of 1.1220 in *PSI* X 1172 (1220 αλλα, 1221 αυψα), near homoeoteleuton for the omission of 1.376 in *P.Berol.* 11690 (375 φαλαγγας, 376 φαλαγξιν). On 3.739 (om. *P.Oxy.* IV 690 et codd.) see below p. 66 f.

The first is in *P.Oxy.* XXXIV 2694 (2nd cent.). Between v. 944 and v. 946 of bk. 2 the papyrus is reported as having not v. 945 (Αἰγιαλὸν πρόπαν ἦμαρ ὁμῶς καὶ ἐπ' ἤματι νύκτα) but two verses and some interlineation, as follows:

$$\ldots\,]ψαντεσ[\qquad 944$$
$$ερτ$$
$$]ρο\iota\ldots\,[\,.\,]\,.\,[$$
$$]\,.\,η\,.\,\iota\lambda\iota\,.\,η\ldots\,[$$
$$\ldots\ldots\,]\underset{\cdot}{δ}α\underset{\cdot}{σ}συρ\iota\eta\sigma[\qquad 946$$

The second is *P. Mil. Vogl.* III 121 (4th cent.). After v. 1302 of bk. 3 the papyrus apparently has remains of three unknown verses, before it breaks off:

$$]ππoτ'α'[\iota]ξη\qquad 1302$$
$$]\underset{\cdot}{\iota}σασ[—\,—\,—]\qquad 1302a$$
$$]ησ\qquad 1302b$$
$$][—]\qquad 1302c$$

If these are in fact new verses, there is no way of knowing whether they are additional (i.e., 1302a–c (*et seqq.?*) were followed by 1303) or substitutional (i.e., stood instead of 1303 (ff.)).

In neither of these cases does the state of preservation inspire confidence. I cannot help suspecting myself that if the papyri were less mutilated, the apparent anomaly would somehow disappear, or at least be rendered insignificant.[42] Certainly it would be wrong simply to ignore these cases, but it would be equally wrong to put reliance on them. The justification that Fränkel finds here for his belief in the lacunose condition of the medieval mss. (*Noten* 444, on the Milan papyrus) is rather precarious.

It is true that the medieval mss. themselves provide evidence of a certain amount of instability in the tradition. There is a verse in bk. 2 (1116[A]) and another in bk. 4 (539[A]) which are at once incompatible with their surroundings and unevenly attested among the mss. themselves. These must be invaders from elsewhere, from other texts which had different versions of the passages concerned. But these are both special cases: they are evidently fillers designed to fill a gap consequent upon an inadvertent omission.

(i) 2.1115   αὐτίκα δ' ἐρράγη ὄμβρος ἀθέστατος, ὗε δὲ πόντον
    1116   καὶ νῆσον καὶ πᾶσαν ὅσην κατεναντία νήσου
    1116[A]   [νῆσον ἤπειρόν τε περαίης ἀγχόθι νήσου]
    1117   χώρην Μοσσύνοικοι ὑπέρβιοι ἀμφενέμοντο
        1116[A] *adest in* w L², *deest in* L¹A k

It is recognized that 1116[A] is a doublet of 1116 f. (predictably enough, it has been assigned to the proecdosis); what seems not to have been recognized is

42 Similarly F. Piñero, *Stud. Pap.* 14 (1975) 112–114, though his solutions are dubious.

that 1116 f. must have dropped out by homoeoteleuton (*ΕΠΟΝΤΟ̄, EMONTO*).[43]

(ii) 4.539   ὁ γὰρ οἰκία Ναυσιθόοιο
539[A]   [τυτθὸς ἐών ποτ᾽ ἔναιεν· ἀτὰρ λίπε νῆσον ἔπειτα] ...
547   ... ὑπ᾽ ὀφρύσι Ναυσιθόοιο
539[A] adest in m w (L1 inter 540 et 541, praefixis a L2 numeris ad vv. 540 539[A] 541), deest in k ignotusque Σ

Confected when 540–547 fell out, again by homoeoteleuton: see Fränkel, *Einleitung* 37, and Livrea ad v. 547.

Note the various stages, the same in either case: (1) in some ms. or other, some verses accidentally get left out; (2) a verse is confected to make good the omission; (3) the ms. with this defective text (α) is *collated* against a ms. with the non-defective version (β) and the α-verse is entered in the margin of β; (4) the supernumerary verse penetrates the text (though does not, in these two cases, permeate the tradition). We end up with a text fuller than the original: textual traditions tend to be acquisitive.

So much for the *numerus versuum*. What about other possible discrepancies? Papyri do once or twice offer divergencies which although of a fairly minor order do extend beyond a single word.

At 1.347 *PSI* XV 1478 (1st cent. B.C. or A.D.) gives ?ἔοι τοῦδ᾽ ἀρχ]ὸς ὁμίλου, where the medieval mss. have καὶ ἀρχεύοι ὁμάδοιο (see Fränkel, *Noten* 69). And at 3.269 a variant version of the line was quoted in the margin of *P.Oxy.* VI 874 (3rd cent.), introduced by ἐν τ(ισὶν) οὕ(τως) φέρετ[αι: the papyrus is damaged, so that all we know for certain is that the verse-ending κίεν Αἰήταο was common to both versions.

The indirect tradition should have led us to expect occasional divergencies such as these.

At 1.94, for instance, the mss. give Πηλεὺς δὲ Φθίῃ ἔνι δώματα ναῖε λιασθείς, while a Pindaric scholium gives Πηλεὺς δ᾽ ἐν Φθίῃ ἐριβώλακι ναῖε λιασθείς. This presents a difficult choice; as Fränkel observes (*Einleitung* 45 f.), it can be argued either way. Assuming ἐριβώλακι to be the true reading: δώματα was written in unwitting error under the influence of the Homeric δώματα ναῖε (οἰκία ναῖε is more frequent, but -βώλακι could have triggered δώματα), with δὲ ... ἔνι as a subsequent *sensus causa* alteration. But it is more likely, I think, that δώματα is the truth.[44] ἐριβώλακι could then have got in by unconscious reminiscence of Homer, inflected forms of ἐριβῶλαξ being fairly common in Homer, and always in this *sedes*; but then we have a rather odd coincidence: Φθίῃ occurs in the dative only once in Homer (*Il.* 1.155), and

---

[43] This cuts the ground from under the feet of an argument that readings of the proecdosis leaked out and contaminated the vulgate (cf. esp. Fränkel, OCT *app. crit. ad loc.*, and *Einleitung* 9).

[44] At Ap. Rh. fr. 12 (*Λέσβου κτίσις*) 16 we have Φθίῃ δ᾽ ἐν⟨ὶ⟩ δώματα ναίοι, but this would perhaps be a two-edged argument.

is on that one occasion followed by ἐριβώλακι. I suspect that the Homeric phrase may have been noted in the margin of a ms. of the Apollonian text, for purposes of comparative exegesis, and then displaced the original lexis just as an ordinary gloss might.[45] At all events, and whichever is right, enough has been said to show that there is no need to invoke the proecdosis. That is a cheap way of cutting the knot.

This, along with the single-word variants, is the extent of instability among the ancient mss. and between them and the medieval. How much of this variation should be assigned to the proecdosis? There is no knowing for certain, but I should say very little *if any*. We can draw a clear distinction between the constant small-scale fluctuation to which what we may fairly call the standard or vulgate text was liable, and the relatively radical divergencies of the proecdosis. There is certainly no justification for an old habit which is coming back into vogue, that of projecting even single-word alternatives back on to Apollonius himself. We have no reason for thinking that Apollonius made such small-scale changes; and such variants as we encounter in the vulgate are all explicable as having arisen in the course of post-Apollonian transmission. If they are particularly numerous, that is a reflexion of the particular kind of text that the Argonautica is: *habent sua fata*. We might not always be able to decide between them ourselves, but we are not entitled to use the proecdosis as a blanket to cover the deficiencies of our critical discrimination.

Interpolations can be as contentious as lacunae and transpositions. But few would doubt that after 4.348 a verse is interpolated from bk. 2.

εἴτε μιν εἰς πατρὸς χρειὼ δόμον αὖτις ἱκάνειν
[εἴτε μετ᾽ ἀφνειοῖο (-οῦ k) θείου (-ην fort. S) πόλιν Ὀρχομένοιο]
εἴτε (καί τε k) μεθ᾽ Ἑλλάδα γαῖαν ἀριστήεσσιν ἕπεσθαι.

348[A] = 2.1186 (*nisi quod hoc loco* μετὰ Φθ(ε)ίην *pro* μετ᾽ ἀφνειήν *codd.*)

Fränkel is at a loss to account for the flight of the verse over two books (*Einleitung* 36, cf. Livrea *ad loc.*), but its presence here is surely due to the ancient equivalent of a commentator's "cf. 2.1186." (Fränkel's "durch den Dichter, oder durch Schreiberversehn?" is a rather unreal choice; it cuts out the middle-man, the scholar.) Other repeated verses are to be similarly accounted for.

The first line of fr. 1 of *P.Oxy.* XXXIV 2691 (1st cent. B.C.) was read as:

..]τεμι̣[

---

[45] The author of the Orphic Argonautica appears to have read ἐριβώλακι (131 ἐνὶ Φθίῃ ἐριβώλῳ), but he could have had a corrupt text. Quintus Smyrnaeus read the corrupt ἀκηδέα at 1.556 (cf. Campbell, *CQ* 21 [1971] 407).

It is followed by vv. 349–356. It has since been stated as a matter of fact that the papyrus is without the interpolated verse. I am not so sure. The editor made no comment at all, and if he was collating against Fränkel's text he might not have realized what was at stake over the reading of the single dotted letter. I should rather expect the papyrus to share the interpolation that is common to the medieval mss., but it need not have done so.[46]

Now an interpolation is in an entirely different class of error from a lacuna. Interpolations are liable to propagate themselves: they will creep from margin into text, and from one text into another. Once in, they are not likely to be rooted out, and they may infiltrate the whole tradition. Their powers of dissemination are second to none. Lacunae are quite different creatures. They are not likely either to spread or to be long-lived. If a lacuna is not put right immediately, from the exemplar, it will be put right the moment the text is collated with another manuscript. The presence of lacunae, therefore, is highly significant; they will either be of recent origin, or be indicative of vertical descent in a closed tradition.

Having said that, I will now contradict it. For there is in all the medieval mss. a lacuna of a single verse at 3.739, and it is a lacuna that is shared by P.Oxy. IV 690, a manuscript of the third century. The verse is supplied from the scholia, and for all the powers of attraction for interpolation that are exercised by the ends of speeches, there can be no doubt that it is genuine.

3.737 ff. (End of speech of Medea)

$$\mathring{\eta}\rho\iota \ \delta\grave{\epsilon} \ \nu\eta\grave{o}\nu$$
$$\epsilon\emph{\i}\sigma o\mu\alpha\iota \ \epsilon\emph{\i}s \ \Hekáτ\eta s, \ \theta\epsilon\lambda\kappa\tau\acute{\eta}\rho\iota\alpha \ \phi\acute{\alpha}\rho\mu\alpha\kappa\alpha \ \tau\alpha\acute{\upsilon}\rho\omega\nu$$
$$oi\sigma o\mu\acute{\epsilon}\nu\eta \ \xi\epsilon\acute{\iota}\nu\wp \ \upsilon\pi\grave{\epsilon}\rho \ o\hat{\upsilon} \ \tau\acute{o}\delta\epsilon \ \nu\epsilon\hat{\iota}\kappa os \ \Hoρ\omega\rho\epsilon\nu.$$

738 εἴσομαι L²ᵛᵖ et Eᵖ·ᶜ·: οἴσομαι codd.
739 v. om. codd. et P.Oxy. IV 690 (III). Ita Σ: ἐν τισι φέρεται μετὰ τὸν "οἴσομαι εἰς Ἑκάτης θελκτήρια φάρμακα ταύρων" καὶ ἕτερος στίχος–"οἰσομένη ξείνῳ, οὕπερ τόδε νεῖκος ὄρωρε." ἐν τισι δὲ οὐ φέρεται, ὡς καὶ ἐνταῦθα.

But the omission is obviously due to homoearchon; and the text makes perfect sense without the verse. More than that: the text makes perfect sense *only* without the verse, for εἴσομαι was corrupted to οἴσομαι (even before the omission, if the scholium is to be trusted), so that then the

---

[46]Postscript: Dr. R. A. Coles has been kind enough to examine the papyrus for me, and reports that the letter in question "can easily be ε." The different corruptions in the verse at either place suggest that its presence in bk. 4 is of long standing. It would be interesting to know when the last verse of bk. 2 got put at the end of bk. 1 (cf. Fränkel's *app. crit.* ad 1.1363).

addition of 739 would have made nonsense, and there was a real disincentive to its reintroduction.

There are several passages now extant on papyrus which cover a place where Fränkel suspects a lacuna or transposition.[47] In every case the papyrus in question has the same succession of verses as the medieval mss. (As do the scholia.) The derangement cannot therefore be attributed to a defective archetype. Fränkel's hypothesis of numerous accidental lacunae and transpositions has become historically implausible, for one has to date their origin early, and it is difficult to imagine how a demonstrably defective text could have been so influential as to effect the removal of groups of verses from all other texts. Fränkel argued on internal grounds, of course, and he has been opposed by other scholars, notably Erbse, also arguing on internal grounds.[48] The external evidence of the papyri, viewed in the context of the transmissional process, supports the opposition.

The average reader of the Argonautica concerned himself with textual matters more than the average reader of the Iliad. A good proportion of the papyri bear signs not only of correction but also of collation: texts were compared with one another, and alternative readings, true and false alike, were entered and spread. Contamination is so ubiquitous as to become practically a meaningless term. It would be good to know if there were any fixed points in the tradition at all. There is of course that proecdosis. But that seems to have been isolated from the main stream; it was recognized as distinct, and must somehow have been safeguarded from vulgate intrusion, presumably kept esoterically under wraps at Alexandria. It is true that it was at some stage collated, for we have those scholia comparing it with the vulgate, but there is no evidence of textual penetration in either direction.[49] I see the proecdosis as existing in fossilized isolation, and not impinging in the slightest on the vicissitudes of the vulgate. Of formative editions we know nothing. The marginal notes attesting other readings never have a name attached to them (though one or two in the scholia do). An edition is conventionally credited to Lucillus of Tarrha, on the basis of a lexicographical reference to him ἐν τοῖς Ἀργοναυτικοῖς; but I doubt whether this means anything other than his commentary. What scholars published, I take it, was not texts but hypomnemata: their preferred readings will have been made known by way of the lemma.

---

[47] 1.332–333 *PSI* XV 1478 (I/I); 2.102–103 *P.Oxy.* IX 1179 (III); 3.739–740 *P.Oxy.* IV 690 (III); 3.1054–1055 *P.Oxy.* X 1243 (II); 3.1265 ff. *P. Mil. Vogl.* III 121 (IV); and I may have missed some.

[48] Erbse also makes the point that the ancient commentaries would have served to protect the sequence of verses (*Rh. Mus.* 106 [1963] 229 f.).

[49] *Pace* Fränkel and others. Cf. n. 43 above.

What we have in antiquity, then, is a dynamic, volatile tradition, steadily degenerating as false readings succeeded in ousting true; prone to superficial fluctuation, but reasonably stable in its main outlines, the number and the succession of the verses.

This leads us to the relation of the medieval mss. to the ancient. The passage of a text from antiquity to the middle ages is in most authors characterized by some sort of bottle-neck in the transmission, and Apollonius is no exception. The number of manuscripts of the ancient authors, which had been diminishing for some time, was drastically cut down in the course of the seventh and eighth centuries. The Argonautica came through. But many mss. of it were lost, and along with them were lost many readings, not all of which will have been false. There was in fact an enormous number of readings that did not reach our manuscripts. Some indication of their quantity—and quality—is provided by the indirect tradition, which abounds in otherwise unknown good readings, and also, of course, by the remnants of ancient mss. themselves, on papyrus and parchment. Many of these readings will still have been in circulation in late antiquity. A small scrap of an uncial parchment codex at Strassburg (unfortunately of unknown provenance) which is assigned to the eighth or ninth century has an extremely interesting reading at 3.158 of which there is no trace in our minuscule mss.[50] One wonders how much more was still extant at that date which failed to reach the haven of the Second Hellenism.

That is the first thing, then: a drastic diminution of the range of readings, entailing an overall textual pejoration. The second thing to note is the enormous number of readings that by good fortune did succeed in surviving, to stand side by side in the direct tradition. Details of their distribution are complex, but its most marked feature is the split between the two families known as m and w. The earliest member of m is the famous Laurentianus gr. 32.9, now assigned a date ca. 960–980, whereas w makes its first appearance in Laur. gr. 32.16 (called by Fränkel the Soloranus, S), commissioned by Maximus Planudes and dated 1280. The two families are often at variance with one another, and in many if not most cases the reading on either side almost certainly goes back to antiquity.

How to account for the multiplicity of transmitted variants? One way would be to suppose that two or more ancient mss. survived the dark ages to be transliterated in the ninth century or later. This would have the

---

[50] βῆ δὲ διὲκ μεγάροιο Διὸς πάγκαρπον ἀλωήν codd.: διος (εκ sscr.) μεγαλοιο θ[P. Argentorat. 173. I would read διὲκ μεγάλοιο θεοῦ (with D. N. Levin, Class. Phil. 58 [1963] 107–109).

advantage of explaining the division between *m* and *w*. Another way would be to suppose the survival of a single ms. liberally equipped with vv. ll. This is the hypothesis of an ancient archetype. A third way would be to effect a compromise between these two positions by supposing that two or more ancient mss. were somehow combined, say in the ninth century, to form a medieval archetype. None of these is quite right, I think.

Fränkel was the first to thread his way through the complexities of the multitudinous medieval mss. and elucidate their interrelationships.[51] In his stemma, which may be found on p. ix of his OCT, he incorporates a succinct and characteristically rational justification for postulating an archetype (of whatever date): he instances two significant and undoubted errors common to the whole of the medieval tradition—"significant" meaning of such a kind as would not be committed by two scribes independently and of such a kind as would not be deliberately substituted for the truth (this latter provision is to safeguard against the possibility of horizontal transmission). One is a sparkling case of a conjecture subsequently confirmed by a papyrus (πείρομεν οἶδμα κατὰ for the mss'. verbless τειρόμενοι ἄμ᾽ ἐπὶ at 2.1127),[52] the other a metrically ruinous omission of a word convincingly supplied by conjecture.

Absence of such errors would make the hypothesis of an archetype utterly implausible. Presence of them, though admitted as conclusively probative by even the most determined opponents of archetypes,[53] is perhaps not quite so unequivocal. The idea of an archetype for the Argonautica arouses misgivings. For one thing, the sheer number of variants makes for some uneasiness. The archetype will have to have had more variants besides those handed down by its various descendants, for not all of them will have been caught.[54] And as well as the quantity of them, there is the matter of their distribution. If *m* and *w* both derive from the same archetype-with-variants, why should there have been such a difference in their choice? Then there are the transmissional problems associated with other parts of the tradition, the so-called Cretan recension (*k*) and to a lesser extent Demetrius Moschus' little cluster of mss. (*d*). Though the basic affinity is with L, Fränkel postulated access to some lost

---

[51] *Nachr. Gött. Ges. d. Wiss.* 1929, 163–194.

[52] If it were not for the papyrus, no doubt there would still be scholars today ready to elucidate the mss. reading by invoking either (*a*) "participle for finite verb" (cf. G. Giangrande, *Zu Sprachgebrauch Technik und Text des Ap. Rh.*, 30 f.) or (*b*) the proecdosis.

[53] Cf. e.g., the opening of the chapter "Ci fu sempre un archetipo?" in Pasquali's *Storia della Tradizione e Critica del Testo* (p. 15); R. Dawe, *Collation and Investigation of Manuscripts of Aeschylus*, 160.

[54] Cf. W. S. Barrett, *Euripides Hippolytos*, p. 58, and more generally, pp. 53–61. I am much indebted to Barrett's account.

source as well, and subsequent investigators have endorsed as well as refined this opinion.[55] It is noticeable that Fränkel confines his stemma to *m* and *w*, even though by rights *k* and *d* belong in there too by virtue of their sharing the common errors.

The hypothesis of an archetype, then, puts a certain strain on credulity, and we shall be glad to abandon it if a more credible alternative is forthcoming. What we are after is the most plausible account of the medieval tradition, the account which seems best in accordance at once with the textual evidence of the extant manuscripts and with the history of books and scholarship. Its outlines might be somewhat as follows. More than one ancient manuscript—probably parchment codices written in uncial—survived the iconoclasm to surface in the ninth century or later. One of them (maybe more, but only one has left direct descendants) was copied into minuscule, the other (or one or more of the others) was collated. We could call the one that was transcribed a *manuscrit de base*, a base manuscript. It is a watered-down archetype: not all the readings of the medieval tradition will derive from it, for some, both true and false, will have come in from the collated ms(s). The collation(s) will not of course have been perfect: there will have been errors present in the base manuscript and/or its apograph which were not present in the ms(s). used for collation and yet which were left uncorrected.

This is a model of some considerable flexibility. Various collations may have been made at various stages, and in various parts of the tradition. If all collation with ancient mss. were complete before any copy was made of the first minuscule apograph, then we could still speak of a medieval archetype. But there is no anterior reason for imagining that this is what would have happened, and the evidence is against it. It is possible, indeed, that the tradition was unitary, dependent upon a single ancient ms., until the latter half of the thirteenth century, and that the *w* tradition is the product of Maximus Planudes' collation of an ancient codex against a text of the *m* tradition (the variants in L itself, if not entered subsequently, will in that case have been present in the base manuscript).[56] Quite a number of refinements suggest themselves, but I am not concerned here to elaborate the basic reconstruction, or to bring it more explicitly into relation with contemporary philological activity, but simply to propose a transmissional model which may be worthy of consideration as an alternative to the conventional postulate of an archetype.

---

[55] *k*: F. Vian, *Rev. Hist. Textes* 2 (1972) 171–195, and Budé ed., lxiii–lxv. *d* (no extra-stemmatic source?): G. Speake, *Proc. Camb. Phil. Soc.* 195 (1969) 90–93, Vian, Budé ed., lxv, Vian and Speake, *GRBS* 14 (1973) 301–318.

[56] Cf. R. Browning, *Bull. Inst. Class. Stud.* 7 (1960) 16 f.

Bound up with the history of the text, at least to a degree, is the history of the scholia. The transmitted scholia, as the subscription in L attests, are an amalgam from three sources: παράκειται τὰ σχόλια ἐκ τῶν Λουκίλλου Ταρραίου καὶ Σοφοκλείου καὶ Θέωνος. Now there is a chunk of text for which the scholia are missing: 80 verses of bk. 1 (321–400) are without scholia. Clearly the ms. containing the scholia lost the page or pages concerned. This led Carl Wendel, the excellent editor of the scholia, to assert that they must have had an independent existence in their conglomerate form, must have been transmitted on their own, without accompanying text, prior to their incorporation in the archetype; and he has been followed by subsequent scholars. But this cannot be so. An anonymous self-acknowledged conglomeration such as this can never have been autonomous. There was never a separate book of these multi-source cullings. They were collected, directly from the three discrete hypomnemata, in the margins of a text. For confirmation we have the wording of the subscriptio itself: παράκειται cannot refer to an independently existing hypomnema, it must refer to marginal annotation. The scholia in their transmitted conglomerate form, then, accompanied a text from the start; and if a portion of *them* was lost, the corresponding portion of text was lost along with it. But that portion of text is there, in all the mss., without a hint of there being anything amiss. Therefore there were at least two mss., one accompanied by scholia, damaged, and another with the text intact.

It is most probable that these two mss. were ancient uncial codices which survived into the middle ages. We can save the hypothesis of an archetype by putting them either earlier or later, but only at some cost to historical probability. (1) We could shift back into antiquity the copying out of amalgamated scholia from the margins of one text into the margins of another. But this is an activity that will be much more happily assigned to the age of Photius or Arethas. (2) We could move the whole process of compilation forward into the middle ages, by postulating the survival of the three commentaries themselves.[57] This would seem a rather self-defeating means of upholding the survival of a single ms. of the Argonautica. (3) Both mss. could be derived from the hypothetical medieval archetype, which suffered physical damage before the scholia were copied from it. But this postulated damage will have to have been inflicted on a precious minuscule codex in the philologically regenerated century or so before the copying of L: how much more vulnerable was a sixth-century ms. (say) in its precarious passage through the next three centuries.

A new account of the history of the text is offered by Vian in the introduction to his 1974 Budé text. Vian has laboured long and hard in the mss. tradition, and has done much to elucidate the parts of it left unclarified by Fränkel, shedding light in particular on the immediate

---

[57] Zuntz comes closest to this (*An Inquiry into the Transmission of the Plays of Euripides*, 272 n. 2), but understandably balks at it: he asserts that Sophocleius' commentary "embodied the comments of the other two," a view which is hard to reconcile with the wording of the subscriptio.

ancestry and the progeny of the Protocretensis. I sincerely hope it will not be thought churlish of me if I ignore these refinements at the lower end of the stemma and turn instead to the upper end.

Vian's stemma is more comprehensive than Fränkel's; nothing is left out. It is to be found on p. lxxxv of his edition.

Vian demands even more of his archetype than does Fränkel. It already staggers under the weight of the variants of the direct tradition, and now Vian, far from being concerned to relieve it of some of this load, burdens it still further by piling on to it all the readings of the indirect tradition as well. This, to be frank, is an absurdity. The indirect tradition is as rich as the papyri in readings unknown to the direct tradition, and is clearly a reflexion of the same state of affairs as is evidenced by the papyri. The lexicographers, at first or second or third hand, utilized the ancient commentaries. There is no reason on earth to imagine that their readings are derived from a single source, let alone that that source was the same ms. from which (allegedly) derive all the extant medieval manuscripts of the text.

X never existed; nor did Ψ; and it is far from sure that Ω did either. The upper reaches of Vian's stemma imply altogether too rigid a view of the early history of the text, one which takes no account of the fluidity of the transmissional process. The text was in a constant state of flux, and to apply stemmatics to the premedieval tradition is a waste of time.

To end where we began, with *P.Oxy.* 2700. In three instances the medieval mss. are split and the papyrus agrees with one of the transmitted readings. The editor noted that in two of the three cases, ἀνερέψατο 214 and ἑοῖο 225, the papyrus agrees with the same branch of the tradition, and he suggested that we are perhaps to see a "slight leaning" towards this branch in the papyrus. Now I am not sure what this means. If the two readings in question were false, as Fränkel believed when he compiled his OCT, this partial concord could conceivably be taken as evidence, however fragile, that the w tradition had some sort of distinct existence in antiquity (which would be interesting indeed). But the papyrus editor believes that they are true readings; and the day has yet to dawn when agreement in truth establishes affiliation between one ms. and another. Even in a closed tradition it would be virtually meaningless just to catalogue agreements between papyrus and medieval mss., but it is done by even the best editors. The most extreme application of the approach is to be found in a recent article which reaches the conclusion that the m and w hyparchetypes each antedates the third century[58]—a conclusion that might

[58] F. Piñero, *Studia Papyrologica* 14 (1975) 109–118.

have led the author to take a more critical look at the way it was arrived at. All that indiscriminate lists of agreement prove is that the readings in question are ancient, which is valuable if they were thought not to be,[59] but not otherwise. Since true readings are by definition ancient, this does not get us much further forward. But even if we confine ourselves to agreement in error, I cannot see that it is very likely to help us in a textual tradition as manifestly jumbled as that of the Argonautica in antiquity. There are errors in the medieval mss., either in all or in some of them, that occur too in ancient mss. (i.e., papyri);[60] but their distribution is not systematic, but more or less random, as indeed we would expect it to be, given the situation we see exemplified in the ancient mss. With the inter-action between one ms. and another that is directly attested by the presence of alternative readings in a single ms., false readings are not going to be magically protected from diffusion. Any attempt to trace lines of transmission, Ueberlieferungslinien, is practically doomed to failure, because stemmatic relationships are disrupted the moment one text is collated with another. It will never be possible to unravel different strands of tradition, for the simple reason that there are no such strands to unravel.

University of California, Los Angeles

[59] When literary papyri first came on the scene, their scattered agreement was perti-nently adduced to justify editorial eclecticism against undue reliance on a single ms. (cf. e.g., Grenfell, *JHS* 39 [1919] 35 f.).

[60] Throughout this paper I have used "manuscript" to mean "manuscript." This, as I am belatedly reminded, is an unorthodox usage, but it is one which is commended by more than mere pedantry, if it serves to temper reverence for "the manuscripts."

5

The Third-Century B.C. Land-Leases
from Tholthis*

JEAN BINGEN

The recent publication by Wolfgang Mueller of *BGU* X[1] drew my attention
to a set of Ptolemaic documents in the general framework of my preliminary studies on the social components of population in Hellenistic Egypt.
In the present paper I wish to deal with a small group of texts limited in
time, restricted to one village and confined to one juridical matter, the
leasing and subletting of klerouchic holdings.

In fact, the nucleus of the texts we will be considering today consists of a
series of land-leases and receipts of rents drawn up at Tholthis during the
7th, 8th, 9th and 10th years of Ptolemy Philopator. These documents come
from mummy cartonnages the yield of which is scattered in several
collections, especially in Berlin, Hamburg and Frankfurt.[2]

From the methodological point of view, it is both interesting and
dangerous to centre our attention on such a small and uniform group of
texts. It is interesting to study it separately mainly because I feel that as
far as the third century B.C. is concerned, we tend to consider the documentation for that period as a whole, whereas in fact it covers a century of
deep change in the way Greeks behaved in the Nile Valley, from the first
military occupation to the progressive development of a Greek urban
bourgeoisie. But it is not without danger to consider a small sample as a
valid model only because it is homogeneous, even if we restrict its appli-

---

* This paper was delivered as a lecture at the Papyrological Symposium (University of
Illinois at Urbana, 30 April 1976).

[1] *Papyrusurkunden aus ptolemäischer Zeit* (Berlin, 1970).

[2] *BGU* VI 1262–1265, 1268–1269, 1277–1278; *BGU* X 1943–1950, 1958–1962, 1965,
1969–1970; *P.Frankf.* 1, 2 (= *BGU* 1264), 4; *P.Hamb.* I 26 = II 189; *SB* 6302–6303;
P.Hamb. II 188 + *P.Iena* inv. 905 (Fr. Uebel, *Archiv für Papyrusf.* 22–23 [1974] 111–114);
P.Hib. I 90, II 263. There are many other documents of this period from Tholthis or in
general from the Oxyrhynchite nome.

cation to a limited period and area. Let Tholthis be taken as an example. All our documentation on third-century Tholthis comes from klerouchic circles. Does that imply for instance that there were large numbers of klerouchs at Tholthis, or that the land there consisted exclusively of klerouchic holdings? Furthermore do our land leases represent the normal way klerouchs were handling their holdings? We can agree, however, that Tholthis provides us with the possibility of studying the socio-economic conditions underlying cultivation of a certain number of klerouchic holdings.

With that restriction we may establish that our land-leases from Tholthis point to one type of cultivation of the κλῆροι: the surrender of the holding to third parties with part of the yield of the land coming back to the holder as rent in kind.

A first significant feature of this group of contracts covering years 7 to 10 of Philopator is the fact that the lessor of contracts is always a klerouch, with one half-noteworthy exception. This exception is a woman, but she is the mother of a klerouch, who is her kyrios in this affair.[3] These klerouchs, including the latter, are all either privates of one military unit, ἰδιῶται τῶν Φίλωνος, or else klerouchs οὔπω ὑφ' ἡγεμόνα. The lessees, on the contrary, are always individuals designated as τῆς ἐπιγονῆς, sometimes in partnership with one or two Egyptians or, in one case, with a klerouchos οὔπω ὑφ' ἡγεμόνα. Can this opposition, klerouch as lessor versus τῆς ἐπιγονῆς as lessee, be interpreted according to the classical social model whereby on the one hand, from the economic point of view, the holder of the land, here the klerouch, would be the strong party, while the lessee, here a τῆς ἐπιγονῆς, would be the weak party condemned to short-term contracts and to producing at least in part for a third person, the lessee? That would be an erroneous interpretation.

Let us briefly consider the status of the different parties at issue here. First of all, there are the holders of the land, the klerouchs who are part of the military or who are waiting for a military involvement; there are the τῆς ἐπιγονῆς (and on this point I agree with most of Oates' conclusions),[4] who are non-Egyptian civilians claiming a non-Egyptian origo, through a real or fake foreign origo—unlike the newcomers from Greece or elsewhere whose status was acquired by virtue of their birth abroad.

An analysis of the contracts indicates that the strong party, economically speaking, lies among the τῆς ἐπιγονῆς.

This appears quite clearly, for almost half of the contracts involve either

[3] BGU X 1944.
[4] John F. Oates, "The Status Designation: Πέρσης, τῆς ἐπιγονῆς," Yale Classical Studies 18 (1963) 1–129. See especially 60–61.

advance payment of rent or a loan to be repaid or subtracted from the rent. This brings us back to something familiar to the papyrologist: the various sorts of contracts which cover financial transactions warranted by the right of use, whether a house, fields or the work of human beings. The activity of the τῆς ἐπιγονῆς Aristolochos, son of Stratios, is indicative. Sometimes he acts alone,[5] sometimes with partners, among them a klerouch οὔπω ὑφ’ ἡγεμόνα,[6] but, and this is important, a klerouch who is going to give up his military title in order, in turn, to become τῆς ἐπιγονῆς in a later transaction.[7]

At the end of the 7th year, during the month of Peritios,[8] Aristolochos and Straton rent Zopyrion's kleros, according to a lease not in our possession. Zopyrion is a private τῶν Φίλωνος. At the same time, Aristolochos agrees with Zopyrion to an advance payment of rent. Repayment of the loan is entered into the rent accounts not only for the 8th year but also for the 9th. Several months later,[9] in Hyperberetaios in year 8, Aristolochos acts alone. He now supplies another klerouch (Μακεδὼν τῶν οὔπω ὑφ’ ἡγεμόνα) with wheat, and this as an advance to cover future rents. At the same time, he signs a lease for the kleros of this klerouch. An additional element comes into play here: the contract is concluded several months before the traditional time for doing so. It is clear that at this very moment the holding was leased to someone else; the loan therefore includes a long-term option on the kleros. In this document of year 8, the ἐκφόρια, or rent in wheat, are to be taken for and from the crop of year 10, and the balance eventually is to be carried over to year 11. This contract is important since it helps dispel our original uncertainty as to the meaning of the first part of the document. One might have interpreted the advance payment of the rent for the coming year as an additional requirement set by the lessor. But in the second case the advance payment is to be recovered over a long term, and this indicates that the traditional lessor/lessee relationship does not exist between the two parties. Instead their relationship is that of a creditor (the lessee) to a debtor (the lessor), or rather the relationship of the one who has economic means to produce (the lessee) to the one who has not. In addition, shortly afterwards, at the beginning of year 9, Aristolochos and Straton carry out a similar operation for the kleros of a different klerouch, a Πέρσης τῶν Φίλωνος ἰδιώτης.[10]

5 *BGU* X 1959, *P.Hamb.* II 188 + *P.Iena* inv. 905.

6 *P.Hamb.* I 26 = II 189, *BGU* X 1958, *BGU* VI 1265.

7 *BGU* X 1944.

8 *P.Hamb.* I 26 = II 189, *BGU* X 1958.

9 *BGU* X 1959.

10 *BGU* VI 1265.

They advance him 100 artabs of wheat as rent not for year 9 but for year 11. Furthermore we have two leases concerning other transactions of Aristolochos.

The first, *P.Hamb.* 188 + *P.Iena* inv. 905, is an ordinary one-year lease for the kleros of a triakontarouros. In the second document,[11] Aristolochos signs with Straton. But in the meantime, as I already pointed out, Straton has become a τῆς ἐπιγονῆς, and there is a third partner who is also a civilian. All three together lease, for one year, the land I mentioned earlier, the kleros belonging to a woman whose kyrios is her son, a klerouch τῶν Φίλωνος.

The group contains other documents accompanying such loans guaranteed by the right of cultivation of the plot and by the rents. They show two other variants at Tholthis. *SB* 6303 is a cession with loan of a piece of land by a private τῶν Φίλωνος to two τῆς ἐπιγονῆς. This lease exceptionally covers a period of two years. On the contrary, in two other cases, lease and loan are combined in one document. This time it is a question of a πρόδομα in silver. In one case, *P.Frankf.* 1, a τῆς ἐπιγονῆς lends 60 silver drachmas to a klerouch τῶν οὔπω ὑφ' ἡγεμόνα and leases the latter's entire kleros according to the usual terms: no loan of seeds, duration one year, harvest in year 10, and payment of the ἐκφόρια in Dystros of year 11. The loan in silver has to be repaid by the lessee before the rent is paid to him in wheat; otherwise the sum will be subtracted from the rent at the price of wheat on the threshing-floor. *BGU* VI 1262 is a similar document, very probably from Tholthis. Each of these contracts confirms our picture of the socio-economic relationship between the klerouch (weak party) and the τῆς ἐπιγονῆς (strong party), at least in our group of documents.

Is the τῆς ἐπιγονῆς to be considered the actual cultivator of the holding he leases, whether alone or in partnership? Does he use his economically stronger position to secure more land to be directly cultivated by himself? This would be strange, and nothing in the Tholthis contracts leads to the idea that this so-called lessee intended to work on the fields he leases.

In the Tholthis documents it seems that a situation I have noted elsewhere for the Fayum at Tebtynis can be found here as well. The τῆς ἐπιγονῆς of the contracts, at any rate, often seems to be a middleman who puts the land in the hands of Egyptian peasants. I should first like to examine the problem in the light of a contract from a neighboring village, Takona, found in the same cartonnages made from documents of klerouchs τῶν Φίλωνος. *BGU* VI 1266, dated in year 203, presents us with the case of a τῆς ἐπιγονῆς who has leased a kleros that is found under the name of

[11] *BGU* X 1944.

an orphan. He shares his rights to cultivate the kleros with three partners. There are several important factors in the provisions of the contract. First of all, we know one of the partners as a lender of money and wheat. Secondly, the profits and costs are divided among the four partners as follows: 1/5, 1/5, 1/5 and 2/5; this indicates that the share of profit obtained is not a function of direct common cultivation of the fields, but of differentiated investment in it. The third factor, which elucidates the second, is that the contribution which each partner is required to make concerns the supply of seed and operating expenses. We are dealing with a small-scale capitalist group intervening between the klerouch, or holder of the land, who either does not want to cultivate it or is unable to do so, and the peasant who has no means of production of his own, and who will till the land with heavier rent requirements than those provided in the lease between the kleros–holder and the middleman τῆς ἐπιγονῆς.

In an article published four years ago in the *Problèmes de la terre en Grèce ancienne* edited by Moses Finley,[12] I tried to discern, mainly through Tebtynis papyri, the general phenomenon of the absence from the land of an important part of the Greeks who are involved in administration and cultivation of land, and, *a contrario*, the effective role of Egyptian peasants on klerouchic land and on royal land leased by Greek middlemen. This phenomenon does not appear as clearly in the Tholthis contracts, but that is mainly due to the nature of documents resulting from transactions between Greek klerouchs and Greek middlemen τῆς ἐπιγονῆς. Even so, on that level, Egyptians are not absent from the Tholthis documents. In some of the contracts we find an Egyptian directly associated with a Greek as a lessee,[13] the latter being always a τῆς ἐπιγονῆς except in one case where the associate lessee is a klerouch. But are the two associates, the Greek and the Egyptian, on the same level? One might theorize that the Egyptian associate also belongs to the category of the middleman with a certain capital, and we cannot exclude this possibility. But, from what we know about the role of Egyptians in agriculture, it is far more probable that in many cases the Egyptian is associated with a Greek middleman not because he contributes his own capital, but because he brings to the partnership his own labour or that of a team of Egyptian peasants.

Furthermore, some of the texts advance our understanding of the role

---

[12] "Présence grecque et milieu rural ptolémaïque," in M. Finley, *Problèmes de la terre en Grèce ancienne* (1973) 215–222. Cf. my "Le milieu urbain dans la chôra égyptienne à l'époque ptolémaïque," *Proceedings of the XIV International Congress of Papyrologists* (1975) 367–373.

[13] *BGU* X 1943, 1946, 1947; *P.Frankf.* 2 (cf. *BGU* VI 1263 and 1264); *P.Frankf.* 4. Cf. *P.Hib.* II 263.

of Egyptians in the agricultural structure of the chora. *BGU* VI 1269, for instance, probably from Tholthis, shows how a τῆς ἐπιγονῆς Greek sublets to an Egyptian part of a kleros he leased from a klerouch.

In short, in the Tholthis land-leases a socio-economic system appears in clearer light than was the case in my recent study of the Tebtynis situation. There, in fact, I focused my attention on Greek/Egyptian relations, taking into account the frequent absence of the Greek from the soil and the physical presence of the Egyptian in the fields, with all consequences this situation could have, even if most of the Egyptians were exploited by the absent Greek. The Tholthis file makes it possible to be more precise in this description. The klerouch has the privilege of holding part of the available good soil. A class of Greek civilians, settled in the chora, has at its disposal some economic means with a certain flexibility in using these resources. The Greeks may grant loans in money or in wheat, but they can also use their capital to involve themselves in the cultivation of the soil, whether klerouchic land, as in the Tholthis documents, or royal land. This involvement is accepted, and even sought, by klerouchs. For various reasons, one of which is their military engagement, klerouchs may not be able themselves to cultivate the fields they received or to exercise direct control on the cultivation of this land by Egyptian peasants. Perhaps a certain degree of indebtedness of the klerouchs may have hastened the development of this situation. This is nothing new, and we could extend the dichotomy between klerouch and free Greek, free Greek originating from Greece or Asia Minor or free Greek τῆς ἐπιγονῆς, to other periods of the third and second century. And we are immediately reminded of the versatile activity of Zenon after the end of the Apollonios tenure in Philadelphia. But this generalization is not our purpose today.

In conclusion, I would simply like to emphasize that the social dichotomy I have demonstrated between klerouchs and, we may suppose, civil officials, on the one hand, and Greeks not in the service of the army or administration on the other hand, is a tendency, but is not a rule. For instance, *BGU* X 1943 reveals more complex structures. Hermias, a klerouch τῶν οὔπω ὑφ᾽ ἡγεμόνα has a kleros of 30 arouras. This kleros is leased to another klerouch, Πύρρος, also τῶν οὔπω ὑφ᾽ ἡγεμόνα, who in turn leases the kleros to a τῆς ἐπιγονῆς associated with an Egyptian shepherd, ᾽Οξυρυγχίτης ποιμήν, accompanying the lease with a loan of seeds. In this case, a τῶν οὔπω ὑφ᾽ ἡγεμόνα, in fact a klerouch with loose ties with the army, acts as a middleman between the landholder and the Egyptian and his Greek associate, who has at his disposal movables to invest in production. Here too we could easily find parallels in the third-century documents of other provenance. The case of Πύρρος would be an exception only if we were to take as a rule the relationship we found in Tholthis between a certain number of klerouchs and a certain number of τῆς ἐπιγονῆς. I was not searching for a rule, but I merely tried to put in the foreground a double facet of the social structure of Egypt at the end of the third century.

It would be a broader topic to insert this relationship in the interaction of two socio-economic elements: (a) on the one hand the inability of the klerouchs fully to assume the rôle of a production factor in the cultivation of the soil they had at their disposal; (b) on the other hand, the existence of a Greek (including Macedonian and Thracian) population with means to take economic initiative and to intervene in cultivation although they had no access to land holding. Taken even on a broader scale, this could be the beginning of a new approach to the study of the various levels of Greek population in Egypt in the third century. Two factors have conditioned papyrologists in this matter: first, the omnipresence in our documents of the king's administration and the king's holding of the land; second, the myth we have created of a Ptolemaic state economy. Analysis of groups of texts, such as the land-leases drawn up in Tholthis, will make increasingly evident the number of Greeks who were neither officials nor klerouchs, and will indicate that they were an important element in the development of the Greek community settled in the chora into the society of Greek notables of the Roman metropoleis.[14]

University of Brussels

[14] Cf. Cl. Préaux, *Les Grecs en Égypte d'après les archives de Zénon* (Brussels, 1947), where private types of economy developed by some Greeks are alluded to rather than specifically studied and described. See also a not quite satisfactory approach to the problem in M. Rostovtzeff, *The Social and Economic History of the Hellenistic World* I (1943) 328–332, on "tax-farmers," "Greek bourgeoisie" and "Foreigners of lower standing," with such statements as the following: "In any case a Greek bourgeoisie was in course of formation in Egypt. The Ptolemies were aware of the fact and opened the doors of their new economic system to this new class." Was the door ever closed? And is the class really new?

6

More of Nemesion's Notes: P. Corn. inv. 18*

JOHN F. OATES

Philadelphia   56 cm. × 23.5 cm.   ca. 55–60

This text belongs with the group whose provenience is the tax office of Philadelphia in the Fayum during the early years of Nero's reign. In itself the text does not provide important new information but it adds to our knowledge of Nemesion the πράκτωρ λαογραφίας in Philadelphia during this period. The most recently published of these papers are *P.Mich.* XII 638–642[1] and *P.Mich.*inv. 879,[2] and to be published shortly, *P.Corn.*inv. 10v.[3] The hand is that of *P.Corn.*inv. 10v, *P.Princ.* I, 14, *P.Corn.* 24 (inv. 10r), *P.Ryl.* iv, 595 recto, *P.Mich.*inv. 880v (ined.), *P.Mich.* xii, 638, 639, 642, and parts of 640 and 641. The writing is extremely fast and full of abbreviations, a veritable scribble; clearly the notes were intended solely for the use of the scribe himself in compiling other material. See my description in the edition of *P.Corn.* 10v in the *Festschrift Youtie* and that of Browne in his introduction to *P.Mich.* xii, 638–642.

This papyrus contains on the recto at the left one half column of names and one full column. The writing is much abraded and very illegible, but

---

* An earlier version of this paper was read at the International Papyrology Symposium hosted by the University of Illinois, 29 and 30 April 1976, at Urbana. I must express my thanks to Professors Miroslav Marcovich and G. M. Browne for the invitation and for their generous hospitality. The papyri purchased by Cornell University in 1921 and 1922 are now housed at the University of Michigan Library at Ann Arbor. I wish to thank Professor and Mrs. Youtie for all their help, particularly when I was in Ann Arbor in November of 1973. Most of the work on this text was done while I was holding a fellowship from the American Council of Learned Societies.

[1] Ed. G. M. Browne. *P.Mich.* xii = *Am. Stud. Pap.* xiv, 1975.

[2] Anne E. Hanson, "Lists of Taxpayers from Philadelphia (*P.Mich.* inv 879 and *P.Princ.* i,14.)," *ZPE* 15 (1975) 229–248.

[3] J. F. Oates, in *Collectanea papyrologica: Texts Published in Honor of H. C. Youtie*, edited by A. E. Hanson, I (Bonn, 1976), 189–196.

these columns are clearly the end of a tax list of the kind familiar from Philadelphia during this period and which occur in the Michigan and Princeton collections as well as the Cornell and Rylands collections. They were all purchased for these collections acting as a consortium by Sir Harold Bell in 1921 and 1922. I have not attempted a transcription of these lines. To the right of these lines there is a blank space of 19 cm. followed by a half column of writing, the recto text here transcribed. The final 15 cm. are left blank. The three columns of writing on the verso occupy the last 17.5 cm. of the papyrus. Clearly this piece of papyrus was torn from the end of a tax roll which was no longer current and used for note paper.

The text on the recto mentions a fourth year and a sixth year, that on the verso has to do with the dike tax of the fourth year. These are undoubtedly years of Nero, that is 57/58 and 59/60. The text on the recto contains a variety of entries; lines 1–3 concern a sum of 2,590 drachmas, 8 for Bacchias and 2,582 for the village, i.e., Philadelphia. Lines 4–10 concern payments or receipt of 232 drachmas for Philadelphia and five other villages in the Fayum; lines 11–15 concern payments of the pig tax for Philadelphia and three other villages totalling 21 drachmas in all. All of these numbers concern the sixth year, apparently; the last line mentions a sum of 340 drachmas for the dike tax in the fourth year.

The text on the verso concerns solely the dike tax from Choiach 1 in the fourth year and then for each month for the rest of the year, that from 27 November 57 to 23 August 58, for Philadelphia and a number of other villages in the Fayum. Presumably the figures represent receipts of tax payments which were then credited to the accounts of Philadelphia or other villages. Braunert has shown the great amount of mobility in this period among Fayum villages[4] and *P.Mich.* xii, 642 concerns some kind of payments in Philadelphia by residents of other villages. Line 1 of the verso gives a comprehensive figure of 1,853 drachmas, but this number bears no relation to the list itself. Lines 2 to 58 enter monthly from Choiach to Kaisareion payments, all of which are multiples of 6 dr. 4 obols as are the monthly totals in each case, the sum we know as the required dike tax payment. Line 59 is difficult to read and I have been unable to decipher it. Lines 60 to 64 concern three late payments of the dike tax. The total payments given in the month by month tabulation and the late payments add up to 1,066 dr. 4 ob., which represents 160 payments of the tax. This of course does not correspond with the figure in line 1 which does not represent a multiple of 6 dr. 4 ob. Furthermore, 1,066 dr. 4 ob. does not

4 H. Braunert, *Die Binnenwanderung*, Bonn, 1964.

relate in any way to the figures given in the last three lines of the verso. Neither 1,330 dr. 4 ob. nor 530 dr. 4 ob. are evenly divisible by 6 dr. 4 ob. The 700 dr. of the last line, however, represent 105 payments of the dike tax. The monthly accounts credit Philadelphia with 102 payments totalling 680 drachmas. If the three late payments are credited all to Philadelphia—two are certain and the third is likely—payments will total 700 drachmas.

These are what appear to be superficial relationships with some of the figures given in *P.Ryl.* iv, 595 also for the fourth year of Nero. That text lists 105 men as owing the dike tax for the fourth year. It has also a figure of 1,100 dr. owed for dike tax, although it lists just the 105 men. The 1,100 dr. is close to the figure of 1,066 dr. 4 ob. which is the sum of the payments listed in the month by month section of the verso. Nonetheless the Rylands text is an account of arrears and such a nature is inconceivable for our text; one does not list arrears in a running monthly account.

The following is a tabular account of the payments and topographical information about the sites mentioned. *P.Mich.* xii, 642 also concerns payments made in Philadelphia for men whose *idia* was elsewhere and I have noted below whether or not each site is also included there. Unless otherwise indicated column and line numbers refer to the verso.

Ἀλεξάνδρου Νῆσος   i.18 Mecheir   33 dr. 2 ob. 5 men
Not in *P.Mich.* xii, 642.
Near Theadelphia in the northwest corner of the Themistes meris.
See Calderini, *Dizionario dei nomi geografici*, i, 211–212 and *P.Mich.* 620.

Ἀφροδίτης Πόλις   ii.28 Phamenoth   13 dr. 2 ob. 2 men
                         ii.49 Pauni   6 dr. 4 ob. 1 man
Not in *P.Mich.* xii, 642.
There is more than one village of this name in the Fayum. There is one in the Polemon meris and one in Herakleides.

Ἀρσινόη   i.12 Mecheir   13 dr. 2 ob. 2 men
                         recto lines 5 and 12
In *P.Mich.* xii, 642.27, 7 men pay 20 dr. each.
Village in Herakleides meris.

Βακχιάς   ii.36 Pharmouthi   6 dr. 4 ob. 1 man
                         revised account
                         recto line 2
P.Mich. xii, 642.13 where it is joined with Hephestias which does not appear in *P.Corn.* inv. 18. 2 men pay 20 dr. each.
North of Philadelphia in the Herakleides meris.

Βούβαστος   i.21 Mecheir   20 dr. 3 men
                         iii.54 Epeiph   6 dr. 4 ob. 1 man
                         recto lines 8 and 14
P.Mich. xii, 642.94 5 men pay 20 dr. each.
Near Philadelphia in the Herakleides meris.

Εὐημέρεια   ii.39 Pharmouthi   213 dr. 2 ob. 32 men
                                                                      entry is erased
    Not in *P.Mich.* xii, 642.
    In the Themistes meris; excavated in 1898 by Grenfell and Hunt.
῞Ηρων   recto line 7
    P.Mich. xii, 642 ἐποίκιον ῞Ηρωνος 4 men pay 20 dr. each.
    Known only from these two references.

Ἱερὰ Νῆσος   i.13 Mecheir   13 dr. 2 ob. 2 men
                                   ii.26 Phamenoth   6 dr. 4 ob. 1 man
                                   ii.38 Pharmouthi   13 dr. 2 ob. 2 men
                                   revised account
                                   recto lines 6 and 13
    Not in *P.Mich.* xii, 642.
    In Herakleides meris; see *P.Petaus* 40 and 41.

Καρανίς   ii.30 Phamenoth   6 dr. 4 ob. 1 man
                                   ii.42 Pharmouthi   6 dr. 4 ob. 1 man
                                   revised account
                                   recto line 9
    P.Mich. xii, 642.61 4 men, 2 of whom pay 45 dr. 2 ob. What the others pay is uncertain.

Κερκεσοῦκα   i.7 Tybi   13 dr. 2 ob. 2 men
                                   i.11 Mecheir   46 dr. 4 ob. 7 men
                                   ii.35 Pharmouthi   66 dr. 4 ob. 10 men
                                                                      entry erased
    P.Mich. xii, 642.48 10 men pay 20 dr. each.
    The village near Karanis which never has a *Beiname* as other villages of the same name do.
    See *P.Petaus*, introduction pp. 25–27.

Κοιταί   ii.29 Phamenoth   6 dr. 4 ob. 1 man
    Not in *P.Mich.* xii, 642.
    In the Herakleides meris.

Παπίων   ii.40 Pharmouthi   6 dr. 4 ob. 1 man
                                   revised account
    Not in *P.Mich.* xii, 642.
    Not otherwise attested as a place name. It is a man's name and the designation might be
    Παπίωνος ἐποίκιον.

Πτολεμαὶς Νέα   i.6 Tybi   33 dr. 2 ob. 5 men
                                   i.16 Mecheir   20 dr. 3 men
                                   iii.53 Epeiph   13 dr. 2 ob. 2 men
    Not in *P.Mich.* xii, 642.
    In the Herakleides meris near Karanis.

Σεβέννυτος   i.5 Tybi   6 dr. 4 ob. 1 man
                                   i.17 Mecheir   6 dr. 4 ob. 1 man
                                   ii.46 Pachon   6 dr. 4 ob. 1 man
    P.Mich. xii, 642.88 3 men pay 20 dr. each, a fourth pays 29 dr. 2 ob.
    In the Herakleides meris; see *P.Petaus*, page 33, note 36.

Τάνις   i.14 Mecheir   26 dr. 4 ob. 4 men
                                   ii.45 Pachon   6 dr. 4 ob. 1 man
    Not in *P.Mich.* xii, 642.
    In the Herakleides meris; see *P.Petaus* 40 and 41.

Φαρβαῖθα   i.8 Tybi   20 dr. 3 men
                 i.15 Mecheir   6 dr. 4 ob. 1 man
                 ii.27 Phamenoth   6 dr. 4 ob. 1 man
Not in *P.Mich.* xii, 642.
In the Herakleides meris; see *P.Petaus*, introduction, pp. 32–33.

Ψενῦρις   ii.37 Pharmouthi   6 dr. 4 ob. 1 man
                                     entry erased
Not in *P.Mich.* xii, 642.
In the Herakleides meris; see *P.Petaus* 40 and 41.

Ψύα   i.22 Mecheir   6 dr. 4 ob. 1 man
P.Mich. 642.154 4 men pay 20 dr. each.
In the Herakleides meris.

Recto
ϛ (ἔτους) κώμ(ης) (δραχμαὶ) Βϕπβ
Βακ(χιάδος) (δρ.) η
     (γίνονται) (δρ.) Βϕϟ
τρ(απέζης) Φαῶϕι κώμη(ς) (δρ.) σλς
5   Ἀρσινόη(ς) (δρ.) ξ
    Ἱερᾶς Νήσου (δρ.) ιβ
    Ἥρωνος (δρ.) λς
    Βουβάστο(υ) (δρ.) μδ
    Καρανίδο(ς) (δρ.) μδ
10   (γίνονται) (δρ.) υλβ
    υἱκ(ῆς) κώμη(ς) ιζ (τριώβολον)
    Ἀρσινόη(ς) (δρ.) α (ὀβολός)
    Ἱερᾶ(ς) α (ὀβολός)
    Βουβά(στου) α (ὀβολός)
15   (γίνονται) (δρ.) κα
    δ (ἔτους) χωμα(τικοῦ) (δρ.) τμ

Verso, column i
ὑπὲρ χωματικ(οῦ) δ (ἔτους) Ἀωνγ
Χοίαχ κώμη(ς) κς (τετρώβολον)
    (γίνονται) (δρ.) κς (τετρώβολ.)
Τῦβι
5   Σ[εβ]εννύτο(υ) (δρ.) ϛ (τετρώβολ.)
    Πτολ(εμαίδος) Νέα(ς) (δρ.) λγ (διώβολον)
    Κερκε⟨σο⟩υχ(ων) (δρ.) ιγ (διώβολ.)
    Φαρβαίθω(ν) (δρ.) κ
    (γίνονται) (δρ.) ογ (διώβολ.)
10   Μεχείρ κώμη(ς) (δρ.) σξ
    Κερκε⟨σο⟩υχ(ων) (δρ.) μς (τετρώβαλ.)
    Ἀρσινόη(ς) (δρ.) ιγ (διώβολ.)
    Ἱερᾶς (δρ.) ιγ (διώβολ.)
    Τάνεως (δρ.) κς (τετρώβολ.)
15   Φαρβαίθ(ων) (δρ.) ϛ (τετρώβολ.)
    Πτολεμα(ίδος) Νέα(ς) (δρ.) κ
    Σεβε(ννύτου) (δρ.) ϛ (τετρώβολ.)

'Αλεξάνδρ(ου) Νή(σου) (δρ.) λγ (διώβολ.)
Πολέμω(νος) μερίδ(ος) διὰ
20 'Ηρακλή(ου) το(ῦ) Θέω(νος) (δρ.) ϛ (τετρώβολ.)
Βουβάστο(υ) (δρ.) κ
Ψύων (δρ.) ϛ (τετρώβολ.)
    (γίνονται) (δρ.) υξ

Verso, column ii
Φαμενώ(θ)
25 κώμη(ς) (δρ.) ρμϛ (τετρώβολ.)
    'Ιερᾶ(ς) Νήσο(υ) (δρ.) ϛ (τετρώβολ.)
    Φαρβαίθ(ων) (δρ.) ϛ (τετρώβολ.)
    'Αφροδ(ίτης) Πόλ(εως) (δρ.) [ι]γ (διώβολ.)
    Κοιτῶ(ν) (δρ.) ϛ (τετρώβολ.)
30 Καρανίδ(ος) (δρ.) ϛ (τετρώβολ.)
    (γίνονται) (δρ.) ρπϛ (τετρώβολ.)
    Φαρ[μ]οῦ(θι)
    κώμη(ς) [[(δρ.) λγ (διώβολ.)]]
    (δρ.) μϛ (τετρώβολ.)
35 Κερκε⟨σο⟩υχ(ων) [[(δρ.) ξϛ (τετρώβολ.)]]
    Βακχ(ιάδος) (δρ.) ϛ (τετρώβολ.)
    [[Ψενύρεω(ς) (δρ.) ϛ (τετρώβολ.)]]
    'Ιερᾶς Νήσο(υ) (δρ.) ιγ (διώβολ.)
    [[Εὐημερεί(ας) (δρ.) σιγ (διώβολ.)]]
40 Παπίωνο(ς) (δρ.) ϛ (τετρώβολ.)
    [[(γίνονται) τκ]]
    Καρανίδο(ς) (δρ.) ϛ (τετρώβολ.)
    (γίνονται) (δρ.) π
    Παχ(ών) κώμη(ς) (δρ.) μϛ (τετρώβολ.)
45 Τάνεο(ς) (δρ.) ϛ (τετρώβολ.)
    Σεβενύτου (δρ.) ϛ (τετρώβολ.)
    (γίνονται) ξ
    Παῦνει
    'Αφροδ(ίτης) Πόλ(εως) (δρ.) ϛ (τετρώβολ.)
50 (γίνονται) (δρ.) ϛ (τετρώβολ.)

Verso, column iii
['Επείφ]
κώμης (δρ.) ρκ
Πτολεμαίδος Νέα(ς) (δρ.) ιγ (διώβολ.)
Βουβάστο(υ) (δρ.) ϛ (τετρώβολ.)
55 (γίνονται) (δρ.) ρμ
[Κα]ισαρείου
κώμη(ς) (δρ.) ιγ (διώβολ.)
    (γίνονται) (δρ.) ιγ (διώβολ.)
    . . . . ϛ (ἔτους)
60 ὑπὲρ δ (ἔτους)
κώμη(ς) (δρ.) ιγ (διώβολ.)
ἄλ(λου) (δρ.) ϛ (τετρώβολ.)

$(\gamma \acute{\iota} \nu o \nu \tau \alpha \iota)\ (\delta \rho.)\ \kappa$
$\lambda \alpha o \gamma \rho \alpha (\varphi \acute{\iota} \alpha s)\ \mu \delta$ . .
65　　$(\gamma \acute{\iota} \nu o \nu \tau \alpha \iota)\ (\delta \rho.)\ \xi \gamma\ (\delta \iota \acute{\omega} \beta o \lambda.)$
　　　$(\gamma \acute{\iota} \nu o \nu \tau \alpha \iota)\ (\delta \rho.)\ {}'A \tau \lambda\ (\tau \epsilon \tau \rho \acute{\omega} \beta o \lambda.)$
$[[\lambda o(\iota \pi \alpha \grave{\iota})\ (\delta \rho.)\ \varphi \lambda\ (\tau \epsilon \tau \rho \acute{\omega} \beta o \lambda.)]]$
　　　$(\gamma \acute{\iota} \nu o \nu \tau \alpha \iota)\ (\delta \rho.)\ \psi$

NOTES

Recto 7　Apparently the scribe wrote $\lambda \epsilon$ and then changed it to λs which is necessary for correct arithmetic.

Verso i.7　This scribe frequently omits the syllables $-\sigma o-$ and $-\sigma \iota-$. Whether this is the result of fast writing or something in his hearing or speech is unclear. See the comments of G. M. Browne, *P.Mich.* xii, pages 44–45.

ii.29–30　The numerals are very dim but must be as read for the arithmetic to be correct.

ii.33–43　One set of entries was written then struck through with lines cancelling them; then a new set was added in the spaces between the cancelled ones. There is a sharp difference between the two sets.

iii.51　No trace of Epeiph is left.

iii.53　Only $N \acute{\epsilon} \alpha (s)$ is readable in the name of the village but the traces before it are compatible with $\Pi \tau o \lambda \epsilon \mu \alpha \acute{\iota} \delta o s$.

iii.59　It is not clear to me what this line should have contained. At the very end one would read $\iota s\ (\acute{\epsilon} \tau o u s)$ but that makes no sense in context.

iii.64　There is further ink after the δ which appears to be part of two letters or numbers. Following the trace a strip 2 to 3 mm. wide is missing.

Duke University

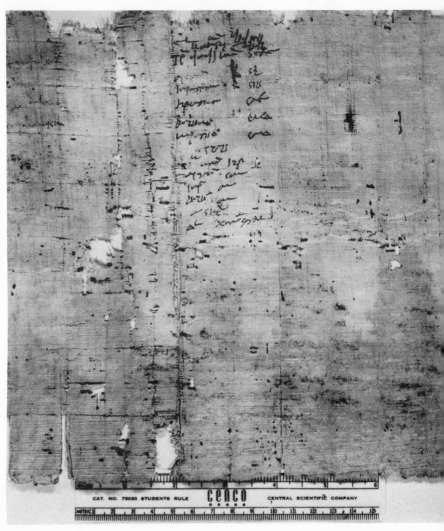

*P.Corn.*inv. 18, Recto.

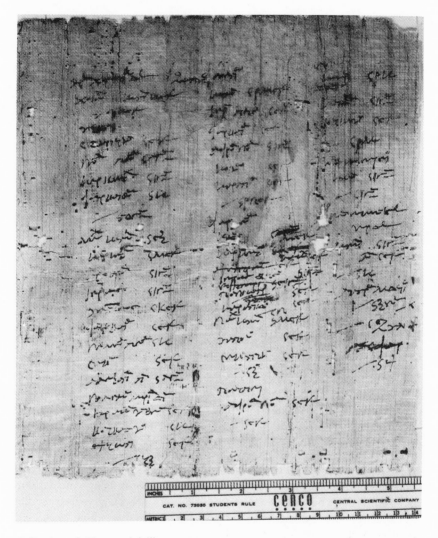

*P.Corn.*inv. 18, Verso, col. i–iii.

7

Grenfell's Gift to Lumbroso

HERBERT C. YOUTIE

In the year 1896 Bernard Grenfell presented to his friend Giacomo Lumbroso three small papyri, together with a sheet on which he had written out his own transcription of the texts. These were published from Grenfell's transcription in the following year by Lumbroso as an appendix to a review article of *P.Grenf.* II.[1] They were reprinted some two decades later by Preisigke in *Sammelbuch* I 5746–5748. In the years that followed, the three papyri disappeared from view, and they were only recently found again among papers given by Lumbroso to the Biblioteca della Società Economica di Chiavari. These texts have now been published a third time, again from Grenfell's transcription, but with consultation of the originals, by Amelotti and Migliardi, who have included them as Nos. 48–50 in their edition of papyri in the collection of the University of Genoa.[2] They have also rendered the great service of providing photographs of the papyri as well as a reproduction of Grenfell's autograph transcription.[3]

Of the three texts only No. 49 will retain our attention here.[4] This papyrus preserves the first nine lines of a letter from a certain Diogenes to his father Stratippus. The new editors have improved Grenfell's transcription at a number of points, but in either version the text presents nothing of importance. The editors, perhaps for this very reason, have devoted the introduction to a statement of their position on a matter which has teased the minds of scholars for over sixty years.

Lines 4–6 of the letter have an example of the *proskynema* formula directed to Sarapis:

τὸ προσκύνημά σου ποιῶ παρὰ τῷ κυρίῳ Σαράπιδι κατ᾽ ἑκάστην ἡμέραν.[5]

---

[1] *Rendiconti Accad. Lincei* 6, 1897, 77 f.

[2] For a brief but sensitive and moving account of the recent history of these papyri, see *PUG*, pp. 103 f. (cf. p. vi).

[3] Plates 28–31.

[4] My comment on No. 50 has appeared in *ZPE* 23, 1976, 109 ff.

[5] Read καθ᾽ ἑκάστην ἡμέραν.

It is this clause which has induced the editors to provide a very brief but perspicuous summary of opinion on the point at issue, i.e., the localization of the *proskynema*. I repeat their comment: "Interessante, anche se trova riscontro in altri testi epistolari, è la menzione del *proskynema* a Sarapis e questo elemento potrebbe far pensare ad Alessandria quale luogo di provenienza della lettera: ma la tesi—formulata dal Wilcken ed anche accettata dallo Schubart—secondo la quale i papiri, ove si legge τὸ προσκύνημα τῷ Σαράπιδι proverrebbero necessariamente da Alessandria è oggi riveduta dalla critica più recente. Gli studiosi moderni—Koskenniemi, Zaki Aly, Geraci, ecc.—sostengono infatti che le lettere contenenti tale formula possono ben provenire da altre località dell' Egitto, in cui furono fondati dei Serapei, divenuti altrettanti famosi come quello alessandrino. E questo può essere il caso del papiro qui esaminato, in cui mancano elementi più precisi per l'identificazione del luogo di provenienza."

The final words of this summary—"mancano elementi più precisi per l'identificazione del luogo di provenienza"—are, as I shall show later, symptomatic of a basic weakness in the new theory regarding the diverse localities to which the epistolary *proskynema* to Sarapis may be assigned. For the moment, however, it seems desirable to review the history of scholarship on this question. As long ago as 1912 Wilcken posited a direct link between the epistolary *proskynema* to Sarapis and the city of Alexandria. He held that letters sent from Alexandria were for the most part identifiable because the writers employed the *proskynema* formula applied to Sarapis.[6] In support of his contention he submitted a few examples for which he considered an Alexandrian origin to be explicitly attested, and a few for which he thought it probable.[7] His view found favor with Schubart, who reported it approvingly in 1918, when he published his introduction to papyrology.[8] Almost ten years later, however, he reprinted, with a short commentary,[9] a letter originally published by Bell in 1919,[10] and his interpretation of that text now induced him to restrict the application of Wilcken's doctrine. Admitting that the *proskynema* to Sarapis was especially fitting in Alexandria, where the god had his most famous temple and his most sacred image, he restates Wilcken's view that letters which contain the *proskynema* to Sarapis were written in Alexandria, and he grants that this principle of localization would apply for the most part, but he finds that it does not suit the letter with which he is immediately concerned.

---

[6] Wilcken, *Grundzüge* 122 f.

[7] *Op. cit.* 123, n. 1.

[8] Schubart, *Einführung* 368.

[9] *Idem, Griech. Pap.: Text*, No. 44, *Kommentar*, p. 54.

[10] Bell, *Rev. Égypt* 1, 1919, 203–206; reprinted *Sammelbuch* III 6263.

This letter was written by Sempronius to his mother Saturnila. Lines 4–6 have the *proskynema* formula:

$$ἄμα δὲ τὸ προσκύ-$$
5 νημα ὑμῶν ποιοῦμε[11] ἡμερησίως παρὰ τῷ κυρί-
ῳ Σεράπιδι.

After the usual complaint about his mother's failure to write (6–11) and a list of salutations (11–12) ending καὶ ʿΕλένην καὶ τοὺς αὐτῆς, he writes the following sentence in lines 12–14:

12   μετάδος
αὐτῇ ὅτι ἐκομεισάμην Σεμπρωνίου ἐπειστολὴν[12]
ἀπὸ Καππαδοκίας,

literally, "tell her that I received a letter of Sempronius from Cappadocia." He then resumes the salutations and shortly concludes his letter.

The writer thus interrupted the series of salutations to introduce an instruction to his mother which is in effect a parenthesis. She is to convey to Helen a piece of information, which he must have supposed would be welcome news. Bell had understood this sentence in what might be thought to be the obvious way: "Tell her that I have had a letter from Sempronius from Cappadocia," i.e., "Tell her that I (the Sempronius who am writing this letter) have had a letter from the (other) Sempronius (writing) from Cappadocia." In another sentence the writer complains that he had written to his mother a number of times without receiving a single letter in reply, even though many travellers had come down the river: τοσούτων κατα-πλευσάντων. This Greek phrase elicited from Bell the following comment: "It appears from line 8 (καταπλευσάντων) that the writer was living lower down the river than his correspondents; and his mention of the arrival of a letter from Cappadocia makes it not improbable that he was at Alexandria."

Schubart was not satisfied with Bell's interpretation of the Greek, and he states categorically that the reference to "a letter from Sempronius from Cappadocia" makes sense only if it refers to this very letter from Sempronius to his mother Saturnila.[13] In effect, then, Schubart sees the words "I have had a letter from Sempronius from Cappadocia" as a sentence to be spoken by Saturnila to Helen. What Schubart overlooked

[11] Read ποιοῦμαι.

[12] Read ἐκομισάμην, ἐπιστολήν.

[13] Schubart takes ὅτι as recitative and encloses the following clause in quotation marks, thus fixing it as direct discourse. The same interpretation underlies his remark made several years earlier (1923) in *Ein Jahrtausend am Nil*, p. 104: "Sempronius schreibt aus Kleinasien . . ."

in saying this, was the very great importance of epistolary salutations in the emotional life of ancient families.[14] Since the letter holds a salutation for Helen, this would necessarily have been conveyed to her by Saturnila, and with it of course the news that Sempronius had written a letter including the salutation. The insertion of a special admonition that this news should be given to Helen, is indeed pointless.

At any rate, Schubart's revision of Bell's interpretation remained without consequence. Hunt and Edgar, who included this letter in the first volume of their *Select Papyri* in 1932, followed Bell, not Schubart,[15] and Wilcken, writing in 1937, showed no awareness of Schubart's desire to modify his thesis regarding the *proskynema* to Sarapis. In a review devoted to a group of four letters in the collection of Columbia University published by C. W. Keyes,[16] Wilcken declares with total confidence: "Von dem dritten Brief (Columb. Inv. Nr. 321) nehme ich wegen des προσκύνημα παρὰ τῷ κυρίῳ Σαράπιδι an, dass er in Alexandrien geschrieben ist. Mir ist nicht bekannt, dass diese Schlussfolgerung, auf die ich in meinen Grundzügen S. 122 f. hinwies, widerlegt oder auch nur bestritten wäre. Mir ist sie inzwischen an der Hand neuer Beispiele immer sicherer geworden."[17] Both Bell and Wilcken proceeded as if they had never seen Schubart's admittedly too brief exposition of another approach to the problem. The limit of irony, even though totally without conscious intention, is reached in Bell's contribution to a volume in honor of Schubart, published in 1950.[18] Bell here republishes, as part of a family archive, the letter of Sempronius to his mother Saturnila. He gives not the least hint that he ever saw the pages on which Schubart assigned this letter to Cappadocia, and he repeats substantially the view that he had expressed in 1919: "Sempronius was evidently at Alexandria; this may be inferred both from his invocation of Serapis and from the fact that he mentions a letter he has had from a certain Sempronius in Cappadocia."

On this last point he is certainly right. As I have shown above, the Sempronius who wrote a letter to his mother, and the Sempronius who wrote from Cappadocia, are different persons. Bell may also be right when he suggests that the latter is the husband of Helen, now a long way from home and communicating with his family through his brother-in-law

[14] Cf. the sentiment expressed in *P.Giss.* 78, 7 f.; *P.Grenf.* I 53 = Wilcken, *Chrest.* 131, 9–12.

[15] Cf. *P.Mich.* VIII 476, 4–5 note.

[16] *Class. Phil.* 30, 1935, 141 ff.; reprinted in *Sammelbuch* V 7659–7662.

[17] *Archiv f. Papyrusforschung* 12, 1937, 83.

[18] *Aus Antike u. Orient*, ed. S. Morenz, pp. 38–47. Cf. Bell, *Cults and Creeds* (Liverpool, 1953), pp. 20 f.

Sempronius, who happens to be at Alexandria.[19] Whatever the personal relationship may be, it is at least clear that this letter was not written from Cappadocia, and even though it provides no sure ground for placing the writer at Alexandria, it also gives no help for placing him elsewhere. And Schubart went astray in attempting to use it as a means of restricting the application of Wilcken's thesis on the relation of Alexandria to the *proskynema* formula.

As it happens, Wilcken himself was, on one occasion at least, unmindful of his own theory. In his introduction to the Bremen papyri, published in 1936, he notes that several of the texts, among them No. 49, although found together with the archive of the strategos Apollonius at Hermopolis, were not written there. They were written elsewhere and sent to Hermopolis.[20] But in his discussion of No. 49, he makes a quite different approach. The text is a letter from a young man named Hermaeus to the gymnasiarch Aelius Apollonius. In lines 13–16 he writes a mysterious piece of Greek: τῶι θεῶι με ἐχαρίσω, παρ' ὧι τὸ προσκύνημά σου ποιῶ μετὰ τῶν σῶν πάντων, "you made a gift of me to the god, before whom I make obeisance for you and all your people." In an attempt to explain what is meant here by making "a gift of me to the god," Wilcken has elaborated a complex background, in which "the god" becomes the great god Sarapis, who had a temple in the gymnasium of Hermopolis.[21] In these conditions, the *proskynema* would be directed to Sarapis of Hermopolis, not to Sarapis of Alexandria. And if Wilcken were demonstrably right about this letter, we would be spared the need of further discussion, since he would have proved himself wrong about the exclusively Alexandrian connections of the *proskynema* to Sarapis. There is, however, no indication in the letter that it was written at Hermopolis, or that "the god" is Sarapis.[22]

Of greater potential consequence for Wilcken's theory are *P.Sarapion* 89c and 90. The first of these is a letter sent by Heliodorus, one of the sons of Sarapion, to his mother Selene on May 2, presumably in A.D. 108.[23] In lines 3–5 Heliodorus gives a unique twist to the *proskynema* formula: τοῖς καλοῖς Σαραπείοις τὸ προσκύνημά σου καὶ τῶν τέκνων ποιήσαντες,

---

[19] So also A. Deissmann, *Licht vom Osten* (1923), p. 160, n. 13.

[20] *P.Bremen*, pp. 9 f.: "Sind doch auch manche der Briefe, die nicht an Apollonios gerichtet sind, nach Hermopolis hin geschrieben (vgl. Nr. 48–53)."

[21] *P.Bremen*, p. 117: "Wenn der Brief, wie mir aus allgemeinen Gründen wahrscheinlich ist, aus Hermopolis stammt, so war dieser Gott nach meinen obigen Ausführungen zu Nr. 46 (S. 110) 'der grosse Sarapis,' der ein Heiligtum im Gymnasium dieser Stadt hatte."

[22] Geraci, *Aegyptus* 51, 1971, 196, wisely disregards Wilcken's discussion. His own statement is non-committal: the letter "dimostra inoppugnabilmente che con ὁ θεός si può intendere menzionare il dio del luogo."

[23] Cf. *P.Sarapion*, p. 243.

"having made obeisance for you and your children at the splendid festival of Sarapis." It is not said specifically that the *proskynema* was directed to Sarapis, but that is an entirely reasonable, even necessary inference. Nor are we told where the letter was written. But its date, as well as the information provided in lines 7–8, where Heliodorus refers to the falling market value of gold,[24] link it to No. 90, a letter written by the same Heliodorus to his brother Eutychides two days later, on 4 May. Here there is lengthier and more explicit talk about gold prices and the intervention of the prefect.

Of considerable importance for our theme are the words that Heliodorus uses in No. 90 about the Prefect's arrival on 20 April: Σέρουιον Σουλπί-κιον Σίμιλιν τὸν ἀγαθώτατον ἡγεμόνα ἐπι[δ]ε͟δη[μ]ηκέναι τῆι κ̅ε̅ τοῦ Φαρμοῦθι, "Servius Sulpicius Similis, the excellent Prefect, stopped here on the 25th of Pharmouthi." Heliodorus is known to have resided for a long time in Memphis,[25] and if the reading of the verb were secure, we might very well share the editor's conviction that the Prefect came to Memphis late in April,[26] very much later in fact than his normal annual schedule would suggest. The terms ἐπιδημέω and ἐπιδημία are regularly used of officials on tour and refer to the breaks in the journey on the way out or on the way back.[27] These words are not used to mark a prefect's return to Alexandria. But the reading is something less than secure. Instructive is Bilabel's comment in a note to the editio princeps: "'Ἐπι[δ]ε͟δ͟η͟μ͟ηκέναι scheint zu den dürftigen Spuren—es sind solche von den Spitzen der Buchstaben erhalten—am besten zu passen, ohne dass absolute Sicherheit zu erreichen ist."[28] It is in consequence decidedly unsafe to use this reading of *P.Sarapion* 90 in order to place Heliodorus at Memphis when he wrote the letter to his mother from the same place. The latter would then be the only epistolary attestation of a *proskynema* to Sarapis at Memphis. We must go slowly here because other scholars have attributed *P.Sarapion* 90 to Alexandria,[29] or if not to Alexandria, in any case not to Memphis.[30] It is wise for the time being to suspend judgment about both letters and to hold that their place of origin is uncertain.

---

24 Cf. *P.Sarapion*, p. 242.

25 J. Schwartz, *Bull. Fac. Lettres Strasb.* 28, 1949–1950, 154; *Chr. d'Ég.* 68, 1959, 355.

26 In spite of his note to *P.Sarapion* 90, 5: "La venue d'un préfet fin avril à Memphis a quelque chose d'anormal . . ."

27 Cf. Wilcken, *Grundzüge* 33.

28 *P.Baden* II 37, 5 note.

29 A. C. Johnson, *Egypt and the Roman Empire* (Ann Arbor, 1951), 20 f.

30 G. F. Talamanca, Ricerche sul processo nell' Egitto greco-romano (Milan, 1974), 112 f.

Nevertheless, even if the doubtful reading in *P.Sarapion* 90 were taken to be correct and the papyrus assigned to Memphis, the unusual turn given to the *proskynema* formula may well have significance of its own. It departs radically from the customarily simple statement used elsewhere. The obeisance is said to have been performed at the time of the Sarapis festival. Since the occasion was exceptional, it may be precisely this which was thought to lend the *proskynema* a degree of persuasive power otherwise reserved for this act only when it took place in the Serapeum at Alexandria, the chief seat of Sarapis in this world. Comparable to the situation depicted in *P.Sarapion* 90 are the circumstances described in *P.Bremen* 15 as background for a *proskynema* directed to Isis. This letter was written in the Hermopolite nome, where the patron deity was Hermes, who is in fact mentioned in the *proskynemata* of four other letters on papyrus from the same nome.[31] The writer states in lines 31–34 that he performed the obeisance πρὸς ταῖς θυσίαις τῆς Ἴσιδος τῆι νυκτὶ γενεσί[οι]ς αὐτῆς, "at the sacrifices made to Isis at night on her birthday."[32]

One other text deserves a moment's attention. It is a letter dated to the third century. In lines 3–4 it has the familiar formula: τὸ προσκύνημα ὑμῶν ποιῶ παρὰ τῷ μεγάλῳ Σαράπιδι. And in lines 5–6 the writer communicates information which appears to have a certain importance for him: ἡ μήτηρ μου οὐχ ἥκι[33] ε[ἰς Σ]εναώ οὐδ' ἐλεύσεται, "my mother has not come to Senao, nor will she come." Senao is a village in the Oxyrhynchite nome, and if the text is correctly restored, the writer is living in Senao and has made the *proskynema* to Sarapis at an otherwise unknown temple in that village. But ε[ἰς Σ]εναώ is not obligatory, and ἐ[κ Σ]εναώ is at least equally possible. The writer would then be saying: "my mother has not come from Senao, nor will she come." And he would then not be writing from Senao, but from elsewhere, possibly even from Alexandria. This letter also we must put among those whose place of origin is unknown.

Although Schubart went wrong in trying to assign to Cappadocia the letter that Sempronius wrote to his mother Saturnila, he laid out a pattern of thought for letters containing the *proskynema* to Sarapis that recent writers on this subject have exploited much more fully. Outstanding among them are Koskenniemi, Zaki Aly, and Geraci.[34] Koskenniemi is

---

[31] Geraci, *op. cit.* 188 f.

[32] Geraci, *op. cit.* 183. The only other epistolary *proskynema* involving Isis associates her with Apollo (= Horus) and the σύνναοι θεοί (*P. Ross. Georg.* III 4, 3–5). This letter was sent to Alexandria, but its place of origin is not disclosed.

[33] Read ἥκει.

[34] H. Koskenniemi, *Studien zur Idee u. Phraseologie des griech. Briefes* (Helsinki, 1956), 139–145; Zaki Aly, *Ét. de Pap.* 9, 1971, 173 f., 215 f.; G. Geraci, *Aegyptus* 51, 1971, 172–180, 203 f.

cited with approval by Geraci, who finds that a number of letters which certainly came from Alexandria mention a *proskynema* to Sarapis,[35] but he sees in this no proof that all the others in which the place of origin is not indicated, whether directly or indirectly, must also have been written in Alexandria. Some of them may come from other localities in Egypt where temples of Sarapis are known to have existed and prospered.[36]

In putting the matter in this way, the newer scholars make substantially the same claim that motivated Schubart's remarks. They say in effect that Wilcken exceeded the possibilities of the evidence. Nevertheless, Wilcken has received strong support in our day from a notable historian. It has been demonstrated by Braunert that Alexandria for a variety of reasons—commercial, judicial, and religious, was the most frequent goal of travelers in Egypt, and nothing was more natural for such persons than to visit the great Serapeum, both to see the sights and to invoke the favor of Sarapis. In the course of his discussion Braunert has made a telling use of the private letters and their *proskynemata*.[37]

And so it will do no harm to point up the fact that Schubart and his successors have also pushed their conclusion beyond the potentialities of the evidence. Starting with Geraci's useful list of *proskynemata* mentioned in papyri,[38] and adding a few more from recent publications, we obtain a total of 155 letters which have the *proskynema* formula. Of these 72 mention Sarapis,[39] and of this number 22, or almost one-third, either tell us directly that they were written at Alexandria or are so intimately connected with other letters known to have come from Alexandria, that an Alexandrian origin is in the highest degree probable. Of the other 50, not one reveals either directly or indirectly its place of origin. A similar result is obtained for *proskynemata* involving Apis, the bull god of Memphis, even though only two occurrences are known. For one of these we are told in the letter itself

[35] Geraci, *op. cit.* 12–26, argues strongly that προσκύνημα, a word restricted to Egyptian Greek, is not simply an equivalent of προσκύνησις, "obeisance," but designates the graffiti inscribed on the walls and the stelae set up in the precincts of a temple to give permanence to the obeisance. With this thesis it becomes necessary, in view of the various wording of the epistolary formula, to distinguish between *proskynemata* actually embodied in inscriptions and others inserted into private communications on papyrus as formal although valued compliments. This is too complex a subject for brief discussion, and I hope to return to it on another occasion.

[36] Geraci, *op. cit.* 173.

[37] H. Braunert, *Binnenwanderung* (Bonn, 1964), 146 f. Cf. *P.Tebt.* II 416 = Wilcken, *Chrest.* 98, 3–8; *P.Oxy.* VII 1070, 2–8; *P.Brem.* 48, 29–31.

[38] Geraci, *op. cit.* 203–208.

[39] To Geraci, *op. cit.* 203 f., add *P.Oxy.* XLIII 3094; *P. Soc. Ég. Pap.* Inv. 253 and 254 (*Ét. de Pap.* 9, 1971, 172 f., 166).

that the writer is at Memphis. For the other no such information is provided, and here again Geraci is tempted to extend the topographical scope of the text: "La lettera è stata redatta in un luogo in cui si trovava un sacello di Apis, forse a Memphis, come la precedente, forse in un' altra città, sede di un tempietto locale del dio . . ."[40]

It is significant that when we know where letters were written, the places indicated are such as might have been predicted for the deities who are mentioned. We have already seen that this is true for Sarapis and Apis. It is true also for Hermes. Four letters have the *proskynema* formula with Hermes as its object. These have come down to us as parts of the archive of the strategos Apollonius, and they were all written at Hermopolis.[41] One letter with a *proskynema* to Zeus Kasios was written at Pelusium, whose patron deity he was.[42] In another, which leaves no doubt that it comes from Coptus, the writer performs the *proskynema* παρὰ τοῖς τριχώμασι ἐν Κοπτῷ. The hair was the hair of Isis, which she had cut off in mourning when she heard at Coptus of the death of Osiris. It was exhibited there as a sacred relic of the great goddess, and it was the object of a cult.[43]

The evidence is accordingly of such a nature that it constrains us to caution in estimating the validity of the rival contentions regarding the epistolary *proskynema* to Sarapis. Wilcken may have overstepped the mark in extending the Alexandrian origin attested for approximately one-third of the letters which have the *proskynema* to Sarapis, also to others which yield no topographical clues.[44] But it is at least equally excessive to broaden the possibilities the moment a text with no information on this topic is being considered. It will be time enough for that when at least one letter appears which on internal evidence can be assigned definitely to a place other than Alexandria. So far this has not happened.[45] Until it does happen, we must grant that Wilcken's seemingly daring hypothesis has still a good chance of proving to be true, and Braunert's explanation of the

[40] Geraci, *op. cit.* 185 f.

[41] Cf. Geraci, *op. cit.* 188 f. A group of inscriptions from Pselkis also have the *proskynema* to Hermes (*Sammelbuch* V 7911, 7921, 7926, 7932, 7934, 7942, 7944), and we must reckon with the possibility of different conventions governing epigraphic and epistolary *proskynemata*. This aspect of the problem needs further investigation.

[42] Cf. Geraci, *op. cit.* 181 f.

[43] Cf. Geraci, *op. cit.* 182 f. See *P.Mich.* VIII 502, 5 note.

[44] A few of them refer to travel up and down the river in a manner suitable for someone writing at Alexandria, but this is not sufficient to prove an Alexandrian origin. See *Sammelbuch* III 6263, 7 f.; *P.Merton* I 22, 10 ff.; *P.Princeton* II 70, 5, 9, 11; *PSI* XIII 1331, 17 f., 21 f.; *BGU* I 333 = Wilcken, *Chrest.* 489, 3–5; *BGU* II 601, 16 f.

[45] Cf. E. G. Turner, *Rech. de Pap.* 2, 1962, 119, n. 2.

frequency of the formula may then be seen to be true also.[46] We must keep in mind that sixty-four years have passed since Wilcken first enunciated his doctrine, and although much new evidence has made its appearance over this span of more than half a century, not one piece of it has yet brought the proof that Schubart needed in 1927 to support his own contrary doctrine and his successors now need with equal urgency.

Ann Arbor

[46] See footnote 37. It is notable that Sarapis is rarely mentioned in epigraphic *proskynemata*. He is almost but not quite absent from the numerous pages (35–162) devoted to them by Geraci, *op. cit.* Cf. E. Bernand, *Inscr. gr. Philae* II, p. 109: "La mention de Sarapis à côté d'Isis est une rareté dans les inscriptions de Philae." See footnote 41.

8

Two Greek Documents from Provincia Arabia

NAPHTALI LEWIS

One of the most productive archaeological sites of the Judean desert was the northern cliff of Naḥal Ḥever. Cave 5/6 (so designated for its two entrances) was first explored in 1953. During the 1960 campaign there was found in it a bundle of fifteen letters—14 in Hebrew and Aramaic, 1 in Greek—relating to the famous Bar Kochba[1] revolt of A.D. 134. The following year "the Cave of the Letters," as it was now dubbed, yielded thirty-five more documents—6 Nabatean, 3 Aramaic, 17 Greek and 9 Greek with Aramaic or Nabatean signatures. These range in date from A.D. 93 to 132, i.e., the last dozen years of the Nabatean monarchy under King Rabel II and the first quarter century during which the area formed part of the new Roman province of Arabia.

Brief summaries of some of the documents were given in the reports of the finds.[2] Three of the Greek texts have since been published in toto, with translation and commentary in modern Hebrew.[3] No. 1, dated in A.D. 125, is a double document drawn up before witnesses; in it a mother proposes to the guardians of her orphan son an arrangement which would result in tripling the amount of money spent on his maintenance. No. 2, dated seven years later, is a receipt issued by the same mother to one of the guardians for three months' maintenance money. No. 3 is a Greek

---

[1] These letters use his real patronymic, Bar Kos(e)ba. A simple velarization of the sibilant produced the more familiar Bar Kochba, "son of a star," his messianic sobriquet as leader of the revolt.

[2] *Israel Exploration Journal* 11 (1961) 36–52, 12 (1962) 227–262; *Jaarbericht Ex Oriente Lux* 17 (1963) 227–241. See also E. Koffmahn, *Die Doppelurkunden aus der Wüste Juda* (*Studies on the Texts of the Desert of Judah* 5, 1968).

[3] H. J. Polotsky, *Eretz Israel* 8 (1967) 46–51. A privately produced English translation of some of Polotsky's notes was made available to me through the kind offices of Professor Gerald M. Browne. *SB* X 10288 reprints the Greek texts together with English translations (by Y. Yadin) of the Aramaic and Nabatean signatures.

rendering—in duplicate—of the Latin formula of an *actio tutelae*, parallel-ing the examples recorded in Gaius 4.40–51.

The many-faceted interest and importance of the three documents were promptly signalized in a review (the only one to date, as far as I know) by E. Seidl,[4] who concluded his brief account by calling on paleographers, philologists and historians to join in the study of these unique texts. But until now only jurists have responded to his appeal, and their principal concern, understandably, has been with No. 3.[5] The present article considers No. 3 only incidentally and concentrates on Nos. 1 and 2.

I. *The Hands.* The hands of the three documents show no essential differ-ences from those of contemporary documents written in Egypt. This observation comes as no surprise, but adds new confirmation to what had become apparent early in the history of papyrology: as Schubart put it fifty years ago, the Avroman parchments and a Berlin papyrus (*BGU* III 913) from Myra in Asia Minor had revealed "dass die Schrift überall in der griechischen Welt sich annähernd gleich weiter gebildet hat."[6] This is not to deny, as Schubart immediately added, the evidence of local or individual characteristics.

Each of the three documents under discussion is clearly the work of a skilled writer of Greek. Nos. 1 and 2, though not by the same hand, are both upright scripts making limited use of ligature, not unlike *P.Gr.Berol.* 22a in general appearance but less elegant or regular. No. 3 is a more rapid and slanting cursive.

II. *The People.* The men and women who appear in these documents are not Roman citizens but provincials, *peregrini*. With the possible exception of the writer of No. 2, they all bear Semitic names. The one exception may be more apparent than real: since his father's name was Judas it is more than likely that Germanos, as he signs himself, was but a Helleniza-tion of a Semitic given name.

Some of the names are simply transliterated into Greek, e.g., Βαβαθᾶ, Βαβελί. Others, like Μαναῆμος and Ἐλεάζαρος, are familiar Biblical

---

[4] *SDHI* 33 (1967) 550–552. A concise and penetrating appraisal is the one-paragraph bibliographical notice by J. Modrzejewski, *RHD* 46 (1968) 159 (quoted in part below, note 10).

[5] E. Seidl, *Studi in onore di G. Grosso* II (Turin, 1968) 345–361; M. Lemosse, *The Irish Jurist* 3 (1968) 363–376 and *RHD* 47 (1969) 291–293; A. Biscardi, *Studi in onore di G. Scherillo* I (Milan, 1972) 111–152 and *Atti del seminario romanistico internazionale* (Perugia, 1972) 45–61; H. J. Wolff, *Aufstieg und Niedergang der römischen Welt* II (forthcoming: cf. *Sav. Zeitschr.* 91 [1974] 409 n. 11 and 412 n. 24). [See Postscript.]

[6] W. Schubart, *Griechische Paläographie (Handbuch der Altertumswissenschaft* I.4, 1925), p. 72.

names which, while indeclinable in the LXX and in the NT when referring to OT figures, appear here with Greek declensional endings, in keeping with normal contemporary practice.[7] The names Ἰούδας, Ἰωάνης, Ἰωσῆπος and Σίμων appear in their familiar declensional forms, but Ἰησοῦς, which in the NT has the genitive Ἰησοῦ, appears here in two other declensions, Ἰησοῦτος and Ἰησούου.[8] Interesting also is the form Χαθουσίων, which renders Ktushion (as it appears in an Aramaic signature) by a metathesis of aspirates.[9]

III. *The Language.* However its presence among these papers is interpreted, No. 3 constitutes startling evidence of Roman law being invoked or applied in a remote Semitic milieu of Rome's remotest eastern province. Other elements in these proceedings, as the legal commentators have emphasized, do not conform to Roman procedure and are presumably governed by or attributable to Greek or local practice.[10]

The Greek idiom of these documents displays a similar mixture, containing some demonstrable Semitisms and some turns of phrase that look strikingly like translations of Latin.

A. Semitisms. The most obvious Semitism occurs in No. 1.3–5 and 17–20, ἐμαρτυροποιήσατο Βαβαθᾶ . . . λέγουσα. The addition of the participle is one of the most familiar Hebraisms of the LXX and NT.[11] Equally striking is the repeated omission of the definite article in places where normal Greek usage requires it, e.g., ὑπὸ βουλῆς in Nos. 1.5 and 19 and 2.7. Again, in lines 6 and 21 of No. 1 we read τροφῖα πρὸς τὴν δύναμιν τόκου ἀργυρίου αὐτοῦ, "maintenance in proportion to the amount of interest on his money." The omission of the article with nouns governing a genitive is a Semitism found in the LXX and NT,[12] and the quoted phrase—the more striking as the text continues in normal Greek

---

[7] So already in Josephus and the NT: cf. e.g., R. W. Funk, *A Greek Grammar of the New Testament* §§53, 55; A. Debrunner, *Geschichte der griechischen Sprache* II, 2d ed. by A. Scherer (Sammlung Göschen 114/114a), p. 90.

[8] According to Y. Yadin, *Jaarbericht Ex Oriente Lux* 17 (1963) 235, one of the unpublished documents has the variant Ἰασσούου.

[9] Normally, of course, the Greek simply drops the Semitic aspirations, for which it has no counterpart: thus Yeshua Ἰησοῦς, Yoḥana Ἰωάνης, etc.

[10] Cf. E. Seidl, *loc. cit.* (note 5) 356; M. Lemosse, *The Irish Jurist* 3 (1968) 367 and *RHD* 47 (1969) 291. In the words of J. Modrzejewski, *RHD* 46 (1968) 159, "Ces textes grecs . . . témoignent, par leur langue, d'une forte hellénisation et, quant au fond, d'une pénétration très poussée du droit romain dans les milieux juifs de Palestine à la veille de la révolte de Bar Kochba."

[11] See e.g., R. W. Funk, *op. cit.* §§397(3) and 420 (cf. esp. John 1:32, ἐμαρτύρησεν λέγων).

[12] *Ibid.* §259.

with the article (καὶ τῶν λοιπῶν ὑπαρχόντων αὐτοῦ)—is perhaps an instance of that usage. Both in literature (e.g., Polybius 3.14.10) and in the *koine* of the papyri from Egypt, corresponding expressions generally omit the article before δύναμις or its equivalent but include it before the following nouns. This is not, however, an absolute rule: in *P.Lond.* 1164k.10 (A.D. 212), for example, a debt is described as κεφαλαίου δραχμῶν δισχειλίων καὶ τόκων [α]ὐτῶν.[13] Later in No. 1 (lines 7, 9, 22–23 and 26) we find τόκον τοῦ ἀργυρίου, where the first noun remains without the article but the second has it in the normal Greek style. Again, lines 12 and 30 have εἰς δικαίωμα κέρδους ἀργυρίου, with no articles. The expression μακαριωτάτοις καιροῖς omits the article in line 10 but has τοῖς in line 27.

Another kind of Semitism found in the NT is the omission of the article with an abstract noun.[14] This usage may explain the following locutions in No. 1 where the want of the article is felt: πρὸς ὁμειλίαν (6 and 22), καιροῖς ἡγεμωνείας (10 and 27), περὶ τῆς ἀπειθαρχείας ἀποδόσεως (11 and 28). Also suggestive of non-Greek influence is the grammatical construction of the body (lines 5–13 = 20–31) of No. 1, a series of clauses loosely strung together, seemingly into a single clumsy sentence. See further below, 8 = 24–25 n.

B. Possible Latinisms. In attempting to discern the reason or reasons for such frequent omission of the Greek article, consideration should also be given to the possibility that some of the relevant expressions were translated from, or influenced by, Latin originals, where there would of course be no articles. However unexpected or startling the information may be, No. 3 leaves no room to doubt the presence of legal Latin in the area; to which we can add, of course, the Latin of the governor's office and of his army of occupation.

In addition to the omission of the definite article, other elements in documents Nos. 1 and 2 that may reflect Latin influence are the following:[15]

a) 1.1 and 14–15, 2.1. Dating by the Roman consuls and calendar was uncommon in the Greek East prior to the middle of the third century. In the papyri from Egypt there are more than two dozen consular dates from 43 B.C. to the death of Hadrian, and all but three are in Latin documents (mostly relating to military affairs). Of the three Greek documents, two (*BGU* IV 1074, *P.Oxy.* XXVII 2476), though they refer to the consuls of A.D. 43, were actually written in the middle of the third century; and the

[13] The article is also omitted when the rate of interest is specified: τόκων δραχμιαίων, τόκου τριωβολείου, etc.

[14] Funk, *op. cit.* §258.

[15] I must leave to the competence of others to say whether any of these can be traced to local language or custom.

third (*BGU* I 140 = *Chrest.Mitt.* 373 = *FIRA* I 78; A.D. 119), Hadrian's letter to the prefect Rammius Martialis regarding inheritance rights of the children of soldiers who die intestate, identifies itself at the outset as ἀν[τί]γρα(φον) ἐπιστ[ολ(ῆς) τοῦ κυρίου με]θηρμ[ην]ευμένης [ἐκ τῶν ʿΡω-μαικ]ῶ[ν.

Thus, the dating by the Roman consuls in these transactions among non-Romans may reflect a wider and earlier use of Latin formula, perhaps under the impact of a military occupation (see also *e*, below), than papyri and inscriptions from other parts of the Roman East would lead us to expect. Two Greek documents from the Murabb'at caves, drawn up in the neighboring province of Judaea some 150 kms. from the Ma(h)oza of Nos. 1 and 2, also have consular dates. *P.Jud.Des.* 114 (A.D. 171?), a loan between parties at least one of whom is a soldier λεγεῶνος δ[εκάτης (and hence also a Roman citizen), has only the consular dating; *P.Jud.Des.* 115 (A.D. 124), a marriage contract between Jews, has the regnal year of Hadrian (in the same titulature as 1.1 and 14, cf. note *ad loc.*) followed by the consular dating.[16]

b) 1.6 and 21. In the papyri from Egypt (which regularly have the idiomatic κατὰ δύναμιν) the expression πρὸς δύναμιν does not occur before the fifth century, by which time the Greek *koine* shows many Latin intrusions. Does πρὸς τὴν δύναμιν in 1.6 and 21 render the Latin *ad valorem*? In *Corp.Gloss.Lat.* κατὰ δύναμιν is equated with *pro viribus*. While the expression δύναμις χρημάτων is not unknown in Greek,[17] our text may be rendering *vis argenti*, a Latin expression that occurs, for example, in Cicero.[18]

c) 1.7 and 23. To express a rate such as "one half-denarius (τροπαικόν) per hundred denarii" the *koine* uses ἀνά, ἐκ and ὡς (as in lines 9 and 26), never εἰς.[19] Nor can our text be explained in terms of classical Greek usage, where εἰς preceding a numeral expresses an upper limit or approximation.[20] Is εἰς here perhaps a translation of Latin *ad*?[21]

d) In the documents from Roman Egypt the legal guardian of a child is called ἐπίτροπος (= *tutor*), but a (non-Roman) woman transacts

---

[16] The texts are reprinted in E. Koffmann, *op. cit.* (note 2), pp. 90 and 126. Comparable evidence from Dura-Europos is later in date, the excavation having yielded no Greek documents from the first Roman occupation of A.D. 115–117. The earliest relevant document is *P.Dura* 25, of A.D. 180, which is dated by the consuls, the emperor's regnal year and the local (Seleucid) era.

[17] It occurs, for example, in Herodotus 7.9, and is restored in *Chrest.Mitt.* 284.

[18] *De prov. cons.* 2.4 and *Tusc. disp.* 5.32.91.

[19] Cf. E. Mayser, *Grammatik* II.2, 44 and index s.vv.

[20] Cf. *LSJ* s.v. III.2.

[21] Cf. εἰς ἔτος = *ad annum*, *Corp. Gloss. Lat.* s.v.

business μετὰ κυρίου τοῦ δεῖνα. This κύριος is normally her husband if she has one and he is on the scene, but we find the role filled by all manner of men, including even sons who are minors. In the Babatha archive only her husband is styled κύριος,[22] apparently a literal use of the term, since he alone is her "lord." In Nos. 1 and 2, where she is a widow, her transactional guardian is styled ἐπίτροπος, the same term that is used for the guardians of her young orphan son. This identity of terminology corresponds to Roman usage, where the same word, *tutor*, serves in both kinds of guardianship, *tutor impuberis* and *tutor mulieris*.

e) 1.38. *Librarius* is not only a Latin word, but its only previous occurrences in papyri earlier than the fourth century have been as military secretaries.[23] It is thus at least possible, and perhaps likely, that there was a military detachment in the immediate area and No. 1 was drawn up for the illiterate parties by the secretary of the detachment adding to his income by a bit of "moonlighting."[24]

IV. *The Provincial Administration.* Arabia, annexed to the empire in A.D. 106 after being seized by a Roman army under A. Cornelius Palma, is the Roman province about which our information is scantiest. The new information contained in the documents from "the Cave of the Letters," as outlined in the preliminary reports, includes distinct evidence of administrative changes introduced when the area passed from Nabatean to Roman rule.[25]

If—and it is still a very big if—the language of these documents does turn out to reflect Latin influences, the establishment of such a fact, coupled with the undoubted element of Roman law recorded in No. 3, would amount to a quantum leap in our knowledge of the provincial administration, suggesting a significant parallelism between Arabia and the other new province that Trajan organized at almost the same time,

[22] Cf. Y. Yadin, *loc. cit.* (note 8) 239.

[23] *BGU* 423 = *Chrest.Wilck.* 480.29; *P.Mich.* VIII 466.27 and 29; *SB* X 10530.11–12.

[24] The legionary headquarters were at Bostra, but detachments were garrisoned at other strategic points in the province: cf. *R-E* 12, col. 1511, *P.Mich.* VIII 466, and for the same practice in Roman Egypt see now R. S. Bagnall, *BASP* 12 (1975) 135–144, esp. 138, and *O. Florida* (*GRBS Monograph* 7, 1976), pp. 23–29. On the identity of the legion in Arabia at this time (previously thought to be the III Cyrenaica [*R-E* 12, col. 1510, *P.Mich.* VIII 466.29 note]), see now below, note 25.

[25] Cf. above, note 2, and esp. Y. Yadin, *loc. cit.* (note 8) 231. The evidence on the annexation date and the identity of the initial garrison of the new province was recently reviewed by G. W. Bowersock, *ZPE* 5 (1970) 37–47. He concludes that the date was in fact A.D. 106, and that Legio III Cyrenaica, still attested in Egypt in A.D. 127, was transferred to Arabia a few years later, "in connection with the revolt of Bar Kochba" (p. 43).

Dacia. Although Dacia lay east of the Adriatic, adjacent to that half of the Roman empire which remained Greek in language and institutions, its peoples had been but lightly touched by Hellenic influences; it was, accordingly, organized like the Latin-speaking western instead of the Greek-speaking eastern provinces. For Arabia the first published documents from "the Cave of the Letters" offer a suggestion of a similar, though not identical, pattern of organization: the *lingua franca* of the area was of course and remained Greek, but Roman legal institutions—expressed in Greek and adapted to local custom, to be sure—were spread into this hitherto sparsely populated region along with the new Roman military presence.[26]

Texts[27]

N.B. Interchange of ει and ι, frequent in both documents, is not separately noted in the apparatus.

No. 1

Ca. 33 × 30 cm.   October 11 or 12, A.D. 125

[῎Ετους ἐν]άτου Αὐτοκράτορο[ς] Τραιανοῦ Ἀδριανοῦ Καίσαρος Σεβαστοῦ
ἐπὶ ὑπάτων Μάρκου Οὐαλερίου Ἀσιατικοῦ τὸ β̄ καὶ Τιτίου Ἀκυλείνου πρὸ
τεσσ[ά-]
2 [ρων εἰ]δῶν Ὀκτωβρίων, κατὰ δὲ τὸν ἀριθμὸν τῆς ἐπαρχείας Ἀραβίας
ἔτους εἰκοστοῦ μηνὸς Ὑπερβερεταίου λεγομένου Θεσρεὶ τετάρτῃ καὶ εἰκά-
[δι, ἐν Μα]ωζα περὶ Ζοαραν ἐπὶ τῶν ἐπιβεβλημένων μαρτύρων ἐμαρτυροποιήσατο Βαβαθᾶ Σίμωνος τοῦ Μαναήμου κατὰ Ἰωάνου Ἰω-
4 [σήπου το]ῦ̣ ⟨καὶ⟩ Ἐγλᾷ [κ]αὶ Ἀβδοοβδα Ἑλλουθα ἐπιτρόπων Ἰησοῦ
Ἰησοῦτος υἱοῦ αὐτῆς ὀρφανοῦ κατασταθέντων τῷ αὐτῷ ὀρφανῷ ὑ[πὸ]
[βο]υλ[ῆ]ς̣ {β[ου]λῆς} τῶν Πετραίων, π[α]ρόντων τῶν αὐτῶν ἐπιτρόπων,
λέγουσα· διὰ τὸ ὑμᾶς μὴ δεδωκέναι τῷ υἱῷ μ[ου ± 6]
6 [± 8] τροφῖα πρὸς τὴν δ[ύ]ναμιν ʼτ[όκ]ουʼ ἀργ[υ]ρίου αὐτοῦ καὶ τῶν
λοιπῶν ὑπαρχόντων αὐτοῦ καὶ μάλιστα πρὸς ὁμειλίαν ἣν .ικο. [2–3]
[± 8]ου [κ]αὶ μὴ χ[ορ]η[γ]εῖν αὐτῷ τόκον τοῦ ἀργυρίου εἰ μὴ τροπαι-
εικὸν ἕνα εἰς ἑκατὸν δηνάρια, ἔχουσα ὑπάρχοντα ἀξιό-
8 [χρεα τούτ]ου τοῦ ἀρ[γυρίο]υ οὗ ἔχετε τοῦ ὀρφανοῦ, διὸ προεμαρτυροποίησα
ἵνα εἰ δοκεῖ ὑμεῖν δοῦναί μοι τὸ ἀργύριον

---

[26] Such an organizational concept would explain at least some of the apparent legal anomalies of the documents, e.g., "la condition des parties, qui ne sont pas citoyens romains et qui s'adressent à la juridiction du légat d'Arabie, la procédure utilisée . . . qui, à Rome, est en droit classique du ressort de la procédure *extra ordinem* et non de *l'actio tutelae*" (M. Lemosse, *RHD* 47 [1969] 291).

[27] In addition to the plates of the *ed. pr.* (above note 3), I was able to use a pair of excellent photographs very kindly lent me by Professor H. J. Polotsky. My text does not seriously differ from that of the *ed. pr.* in No. 2; the differences in No. 1 are noted in the appropriate places.

[δι' ἀσφαλείας περὶ ὑποθήκης τῶ]ν ὑπαρχόντων μου χορηγοῦσα τόκον τοῦ
ἀργυρίου ὡς ἑκατὸν δην[α]ρίω[ν δηνάριν ἓν]

10 [ἥμισυ, ὅθεν λαμπρῶς διασω]θῇ μου ὁ υἱὸς εὐχ[αρι]στοῦντα μακαριωτάτοις
καιροῖς ἡγ[ε]μων[εί]ας Ἰ[ουλίο]ν ['Ιουλιανοῦ ἡγε-]
[μώνος ἐπὶ οὗ περὶ τῆς ἀπειθαρ]χε[ί]ας ἀποδόσεως τῶν τροφίων παρ-
ην[γ]ειλ. τε ἡ Βαβαθᾶ Ἰωάνῃ [τ]ῷ προγ[εγ]ρ[αμμένῳ]

12 [ἑνεὶ τῶν ἐπιτρόπων τοῦ ὀρφαν]οῦ. [[καὶ]] ʽε̣ὶ δὲ μή, ἔσται' τοῦτο τὸ
μαρτυροποίημα [[ἐγένετο]] εἰς δικαίωμα κέρδους ἀργυρίου τοῦ ὀρφα-
[νοῦ   ] vacat

14 ["Ετους ἐνάτου Αὐτοκράτορος] Τραιανοῦ Ἁδριανοῦ Καίσαρος Σεβαστοῦ
ἐπὶ ὑπάτ[ω]ν [Μάρκου Οὐαλερίου]
[Ἀσιατικοῦ τὸ β̅ καὶ Τιτίου Ἀκυλεί]νου πρὸ τ[εσσάρων] εἰδῶν ['Οκ]τ[ω-
βρίων, κατὰ δὲ τὸν ἀριθμὸν τῆς ἐπαρχείας]

16 [Ἀραβίας ἔτους εἰκοστοῦ μηνὸς Ὑ]περ[βε]ρ[εταίου λεγομένου Θεσρε]ὶ̣
[τ]ε̣[τά]ρ̣[τῃ καὶ εἰκάδι ἐν Μαωζα περὶ
[Ζοαραν ἐπὶ τῶν ἐπιβεβλη]μένων μαρτύρων ἐμαρτυροποιήσατο Βαβαθᾶ
Σίμωνος τοῦ Μανα-

18 [ἤμου κατὰ Ἰωάνου Ἰωσή]που τοῦ ⟨καὶ⟩ Ἐγλᾶ καὶ Ἀβδοοβδα 'Ελλουθα
ἐπιτρόπων 'Ιησοῦ 'Ιησοῦτος
[υἱοῦ αὐτῆς ὀρφανοῦ κατασ]ταθέντων τῷ αὐτῷ ὀρφανῷ ὑπὸ βουλῆς τῶν
Πετραίων, παρόντω[ν]

20 [τῶν αὐτῶν ἐπιτρόπων,] λέγουσα· διὰ τὸ ὑμᾶς μὴ δεδωκέναι τῷ υἱῷ [μου]
....δ. [1–2].[vacat?
[τροφῖα πρὸς τὴν δύν]αμιν τόκου [ἀ]ργυρίου [αὐ]τοῦ [κ]α̣ὶ [τῶν] λοιπῶ[ν]
ὑ[παρχόντων αὐτοῦ]

22 [κ]α̣[ὶ μ]ά̣λ[ιστα πρὸς ὁμειλία]ν ἦν [± 10]ο̣υ[± 6 καὶ μὴ χορηγεῖν
αὐτῷ τόκον]
το[ῦ] ἀρ[γυρ]ίου ε[ἰ μὴ τροπαι]εικὸν ἕνα εἰς ἑκατὸν δηνάρια, ἔ[χουσ]α
ὑπάρχο[ντα] ἀξι[όχρεα]

24 το[ύτ]ου [τοῦ ἀργυρίου] οὗ ἔχετε τοῦ ὀρφανοῦ, διὸ προεμαρτυροποίησα ἵνα
εἰ δοκεῖ
ὑμεῖν δοῦναί μ[οι τὸ] ἀργύριον δι' ἀσφαλίας ʽ.....' περὶ ὑποθήκης τῶν
ὑπαρχόντων μου χορη-

26 [γ]οῦσα τόκον τοῦ [ἀργυρίο]ν ὡς ἑκατὸν δηναρίων δηνάριν ἓν ἥμισυ, ὅθεν
λαμπρῶς διασω-
θ[ῇ μου] ὁ υἱὸς εὐχαριστῶν τοῖς μακαριωτάτοις καιροῖς ἡγεμωνε[ίας]
'Ιουλ[ί]ου 'Ιουλιανοῦ

28 ἡγεμώνος ἐπὶ οὗ περὶ τῆς ἀπειθαρχείας ἀποδόσεως τῶν τροφίων παρήνγειλα ἐγὼ Βα-
βαθᾶ 'Ιωάνῃ τῷ προγεγραμμένῳ ἑνεὶ τῶν ἐπιτρόπων τοῦ ὀρφανοῦ. εἰ δὲ
μή, ἔσται

30 τοῦτο [τὸ μαρτυρο]ποίημα εἰς δικαίωμα κέρδους ἀργυρίου τοῦ ὀρφανοῦ
εἰ διδόντες
η..εμα[± 4 ἐμαρ]τυροποιήσατο ἡ Βαβαθᾶ ὡς προγέγραπται διὰ
ἐπιτρόπου αὐτῆς τοῦδε

10 l. εὐχαριστῶν (cf. line 27).   10, 11, 27, 28 l. ἡγεμον-.   24 ἵνα Pap.   27 ιουλιου
Pap.

32　τοῦ πράγματο[ς Ἰούδου Χα]θουσίωνος ὃς παρὼν ὑπέγραψεν. (2nd hd.)
　　Βαβαθᾶς Σίμωνος ἐμαρτυροποιησάμη⟨ν⟩
　　κατὰ Ἰωάνου Ἐγλᾶ καὶ Ἀ⟨βδ⟩αοβδα Ἑλλουθα ἐπιτρώπων Ἡσοῦς
　　υ⟨ἱ⟩ο⟨ῦ⟩ μου ὀρφανοῦ δι' ἐπιτρόπου μου Ἰούδα
34　Χαθουσίωνος ἀκολ[ο]ύθως τα⟨ὶ⟩ς προγρεγραμμένα⟨ι⟩ς ἐρέσασιν. Ἐλεάζ-
　　αρος Ἐλεαζάρου ἔγραψα ὑπὲρ αὐτῆς
　　ἐρωτηθεὶς διὰ τὸ αὐτῆς μὴ ε⟨ἰ⟩δένα⟨ι⟩ γράμματα. vacat
36　(1st hd.) καὶ ἐπεβάλοντο μάρτυρες ἑπτά.　　　　Aramaic signature
　　　　　　　　　　　　　　　　　　　　　　　　　　　Nabataean signature
38　　　ὁ δὲ γράψας τοῦτο Θεενᾶς Σίμωνος λιβλάριος.　Aramaic signature

32 ὑπέγραψεν: ψ corrected.　　33 l. ἐπιτρόπων, Ἰησοῦ.　　34 l. αἱρέσασιν.　　35 l. αὐτήν.

TRANSLATION

In the ninth year of Imperator Traianus Hadrianus Caesar Augustus, in the consulship of M. Valerius Asiaticus for the second time and Titius Aquilinus four days before the Ides of October, and according to the reckoning of the province Arabia in the twentieth year the twenty-fourth of the month Hyperberetaios (locally) called Thisri, in Maḥoza-by-Zoara, before the attesting witnesses,

Babatha daughter of Simon son of Menaḥem testified against John son of Joseph *alias* Egla(s?) and Abdobdat son of Illuta, guardians of her orphan son Jesus son of Jesus appointed for the said orphan by the town-council of Petra, in the presence of the said guardians, declaring:

In view of the fact that you have not provided my orphan(?) son with suitable(?) maintenance money in proportion to the quantity of interest on his money and the rest of his property—and especially in relation to . . .— and that you allocate to him no interest on the money except one half-denarius per hundred denarii—

Now, I have property equivalent in value to this money of the orphan that you hold (in trust), wherefore I previously testified to the effect that, if you agree to give me the money on security of a mortgage of my property, I will furnish interest on the money at one and a half denarii per hundred denarii, whence my son can be maintained splendidly, rendering thanks to the(se) most blessed times of the governorship of the governor Iulius Iulianus, before whom I, Babatha, sought a summons against the afore-mentioned John, one of the guardians of the orphan, for his refusal to pay out the (appropriate) maintenance money. Otherwise, this attestation will serve as legal evidence of profit from the money of the orphan if they give . . .

Babatha has testified as aforestated through her guardian for this matter, Judas son of Ktushion, who was present and subscribed. (2d hand)

I, Babatha daughter of Simon, have testified through my guardian Judas son of Ktushion against John son of Egla(s?) and Abdobdat son of Illuta, guardians of my orphan son Jesus, according to the aforestated conditions. I, Eleazar son of Eleazar, have written for her at her request, in view of the fact that she is illiterate. (1st hand) And there were applied (the signatures of) seven witnesses.

(Aramaic) Yehudah son of Ktushion "lord of Babatha" in his presence testified Babatha according to the written above. Yehudah has written this.

(Nabatean) Abdobdat son of Illuta, in my presence and in the presence of my colleague Yohana the son of Egla, we wrote this testimony according to the above written. Abdobdat has written this.

(Aramaic) Yehohanan the son of Alex in the hand of Yehoseph his son. He who wrote this is Theēnas son of Simon, *librarius*.

NOTES

1 (and 14)   This version of Hadrian's nomenclature is found only here and in *P.Jud.Des.* 115, the closest parallels elsewhere being ὁ κύριος Τραιανὸς Ἀδριανὸς Καῖσαρ and Imp. Traianus Hadrianus: cf. P. Bureth, *Les titulatures impériales.*

On the consular dating see above, §IIIB.

1–2   There is a discrepancy of one day in the date. In the calendar of Rome "four days before the Ides" designates October 12th; in that of the province of Arabia, Hyperberetaios 24th corresponds to October 11th (cf. *R-E* 10, col. 1595; A. E. Samuel, *Greek and Roman Chronology* [*Handb.d.Altertumswiss.* I.7] 177). A note in the *ed. pr.* suggests that the discrepancy may be due to the fact that A.D. 124 was a leap year. It is hardly likely, however, that the intercalary day would still affect the calendar ten months after the end of the leap year.

2   εἰκά[ς *ed. pr.*, noting the occurrence of the nominative in another (unpublished) document written on the same day.

3 (and 16)   The village name Ma(ḥ)oza is new. Zoara, here a first-declension feminine, appears in No. 2 as Zoora, apparently neuter plural. According to Ptolemy's map, it lay southeast of and not far from Petra. Details (including a different localization by some modern scholars) are summarized by M. Lemosse, *The Irish Jurist* 3 (1968) 366 n. 3.

3 (and 17)   ἐπιβάλλω does not occur in this context in the papyri from Roman Egypt (where we find e.g., διὰ τῶν ὑπογεγραμμένων μαρτύρων, *P.Oxy.* 2131. 3), but *P.Dura* 26.5 has ἐπὶ τῶν ἐπιβεβλημένων καὶ ἐσφραγεισμένων ἀνδρῶν, and in *P.Dura* 18.34 there is among the witnesses' signatures the notation ἐπεβαλόμην: see further the Dura editor's comments pp. 103, 140.

3–4 (and 18)   Ἔγλᾶ: a new name, with nominative presumably in -ας (but the Nabatean signature in line 38 has Egla).

The filiation stated here is John son of Joseph son of Eglas. Everywhere else, both in Greek and in Aramaic (1.33 and 38, 2.6 and 11–12), he is styled John son of Eglas *or* John son of Joseph. This suggests that Joseph and Eglas are alternative names, and that we should accordingly read Ἰωσήπου τοῦ ⟨καὶ⟩ Ἔγλᾶ in 1.3–4 and 18.

4 (also 12, 18–19, 29, 33)   ἐπιτρόπων . . . ὀρφανοῦ: There is no indication of how old

the boy was at this time, but he was still under guardianship seven years later, when No. 2 was written.

4–5 (and 19–20)   In Roman Egypt guardians were appointed by the grammateus (metro)poleos, the strategos, or the exegetes (usually acting for a higher official): see most recently *BASP* 7 (1970) 116–118. At Rome and elsewhere appointment was normally by municipal magistrates, but possible involvement of the municipal council is suggested by a quotation from Ulpian in *Digest* 27.8.1. pr., *si a magistratibus municipalibus tutor datus sit, non videtur per ordinem electus*. Thus, while the present instance of appointment by the boule of Petra is unprecedented in extant documents, it may not be "une règle tout-à-fait particulière" (M. Lemosse, *loc. cit.* 368; similarly "jamais d'un conseil," 369). Cf. E. Sachers' monograph-length article "Tutela" in *R-E* 7A, esp. col. 1514.

5 (and 20)   M. Lemosse's suggestion (*loc. cit.* 366 n. 4), however qualified, that the words λέγουσα διὰ may indicate a sworn declaration seems far-fetched. On λέγουσα see above, §IIIA.

5   At the end supply perhaps ὀρφανοῦ, paralleling the expression in lines 4 and 33. See further below, 20 n.

5–6 (and 20–22)   The obligation that Babatha here charges the guardians with violating is succinctly expressed in one of the *Adriani sententiae* (Ἁδριανοῦ ἀποφάσεις): *Adrianus dixit curatori: "propter hoc ergo datus es, ut fame neces pupillum? pro modo ergo facultatis alimenta ei praesta."* (Ἁδριανὸς εἶπεν τῷ φροντιστῇ· διὰ τοῦτο οὖν ἐδόθ⟨η⟩ς, ἵνα λιμῷ πν⟨ί⟩ξῃς τὸν ὀρφανόν; κατὰ δύναμιν οὖν τῆς ὑποστάσεως τροφῖα αὐτῷ πάρεχε.) *Corp. Gloss. Lat.* III, 36, 5–14.

6   The restoration ἐπιτήδεια] is suggested by the sense and perhaps by the remnants at the corresponding point in line 20.

6 (and 22)   After ὁμειλίαν in line 6 eta is clear. The following letter, according to the indications of line 22, ought to be nu; if so it is a curiously distorted nu, the only such example of a letter that is formed quite regularly throughout. In what follows the letters ικο stand out clearly, preceded by a letter, clear but with its top gone, which may be gamma or sigma or tau, and followed by the bottom tip of a letter that may be iota, sigma, tau, upsilon (most likely) or even chi. The attempt to read the beginning as ει (yielding e.g., ϵἰκότ[ως) finds its obstacle in the fact that the presumed iota does not descend below the line, which it does everywhere else in the ει combination. [See Postscript.]

The loss of what follows leaves unclear whether ὁμιλία refers here to general local practice or more specifically to this wealthy family's social standing (compare ὑπόστασις in the *Adriani sententia* above).

7 (and 23)   The word for one-half denarius, here masculine, has previously occurred as a neuter.

Assuming that the interest is here stated *per mensem* (the standard Greek and Roman practice),[28] Babatha's complaint is that the guardians, who are presumably receiving interest at least at the standard rate of one per cent per month, are spending only half of that on her son's maintenance. See further below, 12 n.

8 (and 24–25)   As Polotsky points out in a footnote of the *ed. pr.*, the ἵνα clause is a hybrid conflate of two constructions, (1) εἰ δοκεῖ ὑμῖν δοῦναι and (2) ἵνα, εἰ δοκεῖ ὑμῖν, δῶτε.

9 (and 26)   On the Greek ending -ιν for -ιον, in evidence from at least the third century B.C., see E. Mayser, *Grammatik* I.2, pp. 15–16.

---

[28] Cf. e.g., *WB* s.v. τόκος, *CIL* III p. 930 no. 3 = *FIRA* III 123.

9–10 (and 26)   In contrast to the guardians, whom she accuses of spending far less than the interest actually received on the invested funds (cf. above, 7 n.), Babatha here offers to pay out three times as much if the administration of the funds is turned over to her. It may be that this higher-than-normal rate is evidence of frontier conditions, with investment capital scarce and at a premium. See further below, 12 n.

10 (and 27)   Although Iulius Iulianus "cannot be identified with certainty with any of the known bearers of that name,"[29] it is at least worth noting that he may have been a son or grandson (*R-E* 10 col. 158, no. 61) of Ti. Iulius Alexander. Favoring such an identification are the longstanding business interests of the family in the Red Sea region,[30] and evidence of prominent governmental careers exercised wholly or nearly so in the Egypt–Judea–Arabia geographical triangle: We have long known, for example, that Ti. Iulius Alexander was first epistrategos of the Thebaid and then procurator in Judea before becoming prefect of Egypt; and now we find in one of the unpublished documents from "The Cave of the Letters" that the governor of Arabia in A.D. 130 was named Haterius Nepos,[31] no doubt the son of the prefect of Egypt of A.D. 120–124. Such a regional policy in governance may well have been the concomitant or counterpart of Hadrian's well-known regionalization of Rome's far-flung military units. Such a policy may also be reflected in the shuffle of legions that took place between ca. A.D. 120 and 140, when the III Cyrenaica, which had been stationed in Egypt from Augustus to Hadrian, was moved to Arabia, to be replaced in Egypt by the II Traiana, which had probably been stationed in Syria under Trajan and Hadrian.

11 (and 28)   παραγγέλλω normally expresses the action of the presiding judge in issuing a summons: cf. *WB* s.v. Here, with Babatha (the complainant) as its subject, the verb presumably conveys that the summons was issued at her request.

11–12 (and 28–30)   παρήνγειλα ἐγώ ed. pr. This reading is clear in line 28, but line 11 had something different, related to the crossed-out words of line 12. Of the seven letters before Βαβαθᾶ in line 11 the middles are lost in a break caused by a horizontal fold of the papyrus. The very bottoms of the letters are preserved, together with dots of ink from the tops of four of the letters. The three letters before Βαβαθᾶ cannot be εγω but look most like the remnants of τεη. The letter before those three ought—as in line 28, and because the statement has since line 5 = 20 been in the first person—to be alpha, i.e., the ending of παρήνγειλα, but if so it is an alpha smaller than normal for this hand; epsilon would fit the space and remaining trace of ink much more comfortably.

In sum, it appears that the scribe first wrote παρήγγειλέ τε ἡ Βαβαθᾶ 'Ιωάνῃ . . . καὶ τοῦτο τὸ μαρτυροποίημα ἐγένετο εἰς δικαίωμα. He then drew a horizontal line through καί and ἐγένετο, canceling those words (whether he also canceled anything before Βαβαθᾶ cannot be determined because of the horizontal break in the papyrus), and inserted εἰ δὲ μή, ἔσται interlinearly. In lines 28–30 he wrote only the corrected text.

According to a note in the ed. pr., the παραγγελία, written on the same day, is extant among the as yet unpublished documents: cf. above, 2 n.

12 (and 30)   εἰς . . . ὀρφανοῦ: The meaning is far from clear. I suspect that Babatha, after chiding against the guardians for spending on her son's maintenance only a fraction of the interest yielded by his money (cf. above, 7 n., 10 n.), is here accusing the guardians of profiting from their trust by pocketing the rest of the interest themselves. Some such

---

[29] H. J. Polotsky, *Israel Exploration Journal* 12 (1962) 259.

[30] Cf. A. Fuks, *JJP* 5 (1951) 214–216, or the brief summary by E. G. Turner, *JRS* 44 (1954) 59.

[31] Cf. H. J. Polotsky, *loc. cit.*

malversation was presumably the basis of the *actio tutelae* envisaged in document No. 3. But the matter was presumably settled out of court, since No. 2 shows the guardians paying for the boy's maintenance seven years later.

20 *ad fin.* β ... δω[.. s ed. pr.* Of the first letter only the top loop or hook is left. The *ductus* of the ink stroke seems to me to give φ as another possible reading: ὀρ]φạṇọῦ? [See Postscript.]

25   The interlinear insert is blurred. The second letter may be lambda, less likely delta.

31   η at the beginning of the line may be π.

32   According to a note of the *ed. pr.*, after πράγματος some of the documents of the Babatha archive have and others omit χάριν (for which the lacuna here has no room).

33   *Ησουουο, ed. pr.*

36   The statement calls for seven witnesses, but the signatures that follow name at most five men.

No. 2

Ca. 13 × 19 cm.   August 19, A.D. 132

ἐπὶ ὑπάτων Γαίου Σερρίου Αὐγορείṇου καὶ Πουπλίου Τρεβίο[υ Σεργ]ị[ανο]ῦ
[π]ρọ̀
δεκατεσσάρων καλανδῶν Σεπτεμ[β]ρίων κατὰ τὸν τῆς νέας ἐ[πα]ρχίας
Ἀραβί-
ας ἀριθμὸν ἔτους ἑβδόμου εἰκοστο[ῦ] μηνὸς Γορπιαίου πρώτ[ῃ ἐ]ν Μạωζα
περιμέτρῳ Ζοορων. Βαβαθα{s} Σίμω[ν]ος, συμπαρόντος αὐτῇ [ἐπιτρόπου]
κ[α]ị̀
5   ὑπὲρ αὐτῆς ὑπογράφοντος Βαβελị[s] Μαναήμου, ἀμφότε[ροι τ]ῆ[s] ạὐτῆς
Μạω-
ζας, Σίμωνι κυρτῷ Ἰωάνου Ἐγλᾷ [τῆ]ṣ αὐτ[ῆ]ṣ Μαωζας χαίρị[ν.] σọῦ
δευτέρου ἐπι-
τρόπου κατασταθέντọς [± 16] ὑπ[ὸ βουλῆς Πετρ]αίων Ἰησọ[ύ-]
ου Ἰησούου ὀρφανοῦ υ[ἱοῦ] μọυ, ἀπ[έσχ]ọν π[αρ]ὰ σ[ο]ῦ ἰς λόγọ[ν τρ]οφίων
καὶ ἀμφị-
αζμοῦ τοῦ αὐτοῦ Ἰησọύọυ υ[ἱοῦ] μ[ου] ἀργυρίου δηναρίων [ἐξ] ạ[π]ọ̀ μηνὸς
10   Πανήμου πρώτη⟨s⟩ τοῦ αὐτοῦ ἔτου⟨s⟩ ἑβδόμου εἰκοστοῦ μέχρι Γορπι-
[αίο]υ τριακά-
δι, μηνῶν τελίων τρὶς. ←————————— Aramaic signature ←————
←————————————————————— Aramaic signature ←————
←————————————————————— Aramaic signature ←————
                                    Aramaic signature ←————
15   ἑρμηνία{s} Βαβαθᾶς Σίμωνος· ἀπέσχον παρὰ Σίμωνι κυρτῷ Ἰωάου
ἐπίτροπος Ἰησούου υἱῷ μου ἰς λό[γ]ọν τ[ρο]φίων κạὶ ἀμφιαζμοῦ αὐτοῦ
ἀργυρίου δηναρίων ἑξ ἀπὸ μηνὸς Πανήμου πρώτης μέχρι Γορπιαίου
τριακάδι ἔτους
ἑβδόμου εἰκοστοῦ, αἵ εἰσιν μῆνες [τέλιοι τρ]ị̂ṣ. [διὰ ἐπιτ]ρọ́ṗου αὐτῆς
Βαβελις Μαναήμου.
Γ̣ερμαṇ[ὸ]ṣ Ἰούδ[ο]υ ἔγραψα.

1 Αὐγουρίνου.   4 περιμέτρου.   8-9 ἀμφιασμοῦ.   9 δηνάρια.   10-11 τριακάδος.
11 τριῶν.   15 Σίμωνος κυρτοῦ.   16 ἐπιτρόπου, υἱοῦ, ἀμφιασμοῦ.   17 δηνάρια, τριακάδος.

TRANSLATION

In the consulship of C. Serrius Augurinus and P. Trebius Sergianus fourteen days before the Kalends of September, according to the reckoning of the new province Arabia in the twenty-seventh year the first of the month Gorpiaios, in Maḥoza-by-Zoora. Babatha daughter of Simon, with her guardian present and subscribing for her, both of the said Maḥoza, to the hunchback Simon son of John son of Eglas, greeting. You having been appointed by the town council of Petra to be [in place of your father?] the second guardian of my orphan son Jesus son of Jesus, I have received from you, toward the account of maintenance and clothing of the said Jesus my son, six denarii of silver (for the period) from the first of the month Panemos of the said twenty-seventh year up to the thirtieth of Gorpiaios, three complete months.

(Aramaic) Babatha the daughter of Simeon has received from Simeon the son of Yohana the son of Yehoseph the epitropos of my son Yeshua for clothing and food of my son Yeshua, six silver dinars, from the first of Tamuz until the thirtieth of Elul year twenty-seven, which are three full months. Babeli the son of Menahem has written this.

Translation of (the statement of) Babatha daughter of Simon: I have received from Simon the hunchback son of John, guardian of my son Jesus, toward the account of his maintenance and clothing, six denarii of silver (for the period) from the first of month Panemos up to the thirtieth of Gorpiaios of the twenty-seventh year, which are three complete months. By her guardian Babeli son of Menahem.

I, Germanos son of Judas, have written (this).

NOTES

4   Ζοορων: presumably the genitive of a neuter plural form (cf. above, 1.3 n.).

6–7   On the duration of the boy's guardianship see above, 1.4 n.

5 (and 18)   Βαβελις: As the Aramaic (line 14) gives the nominative of Babatha's guardian's name as Babeli, the ending in -ις is apparently intended as a genitive (presumably following the homophonous -η, -ης declension).

7   Perhaps the lacuna had something like ἀντὶ τοῦ πατρός σου. The substitution of the son raises interesting questions. (1) Had the father died, or simply asked the boule to appoint his son in his stead? We have no way of knowing, but a priori the former seems likelier. (2) Greek and Roman practice was normally content with a single guardian, but the orphan Jesus appears to have been under the constant tutelage of two (so too in *P.Cattaoui* verso = *Chrest.Mitt.* 88 I.26–28, II.13–15). Was this required by local custom (each to serve as a check on the other?), or merely an ad hoc arrangement here, perhaps at the insistence of one of the parties? Again we have no way of knowing, but a priori the former again seems likelier.

8–19 and 16   ἀμφιαζμοῦ: on zeta for sigma see E. Mayser, *op. cit.* I, p. 204.

10 πρώτῃ: In contrast to the general tendency in postclassical Greek for datives to be replaced by genitives (cf. e.g., A. Debrunner, *op. cit.*, pp. 110–113), here and later (10–11 and 17 τριακάδι, 15 Σίμωνι κυρτῷ) the writer of No. 2 uses a dative where a genitive is required. In the numerals πρώτῃ and τριακάδι the error is readily understandable, since days of the month on which documents are drawn up are expressed in the dative.

15 ἑρμηνία defines what follows as a Greek translation of the acknowledgment of receipt that Babatha, acting through her guardian (cf. line 18), made in her native tongue.

16 υἱῷ: om. *ed. pr.*

POSTSCRIPT

A preprint of the forthcoming article by H. J. Wolff (cf. above, note 5) became available to me after the preceding pages had been written. In that article—leaving aside here the extensive legal commentary—Wolff offers the following points of textual interest in document No. 1.

Line 20 (= 5–6): Wolff thinks that the end of line 20 can be read and restored as [μου τ]ὰ δέοντα [αὐτῷ], which gives excellent sense and fits the space well. Unfortunately, the vertical stroke that he takes as completing a nu is really the bottom of the rho of παρόντων in the line above.

Lines 6–7 (= 22): Wolff reads the visible end of line 6 as ἦν ηκου[, which may be right: the nu still remains troublesome (cf. above, note to line 6 [= 22]), but the eta, while not in its usual form, can be paralleled elsewhere in the document (e.g., in δηνάρια, line 7).

Wolff then restores ὁμειλίαν ἣν ἤκου[σα εἶχον ὑμῖν, translating "auf das Gespräch hin, das ich (zu euch) kommend mit euch hatte," and citing the "ähnliche Sprachwendung" τοὺς νόμους ἧκεν ἔχων of Demosthenes 37.45. Cf. also *P.Oxy.* 1588. 6–8, τὰ ἀργύρια περὶ ὧν πολλάκις σοι ἀπαντήσας ὠμείλισα. See now also Wolff's article in *RIDA* 23 (1976) 271–290.

The City University of New York

9

Some Roman Elements in Roman Egypt

J. F. GILLIAM

My purpose here is not to attempt a comprehensive survey of a large and often elusive subject. I will merely comment on a few texts that appear to deserve more attention, with larger questions in mind though they may not be stressed. No one would claim that in Egypt Roman influence was as penetrating and significant as in Gaul or Spain. Additions and changes that in some sense are specifically Roman may often seem as superficial and inconsequential as the inscriptions carved on the statue of "Memnon" or the graffiti of tourists of the Roman period in the nearby royal tombs. But even the seemingly superficial and ephemeral may prove to have some interest and significance, while what is basic and hardly changing through the centuries may often be taken for granted, once grasped. In any event, not everything Roman in Egypt was entirely superficial.

1. *P.Mich.* III 169 = *FIRA* III 4 = *CPL* 162

This diptych, found in Karanis and dated in A.D. 145, contains the birth certificate of illegitimate twins, *MM. Sempronii Sp(urii) filii Sarapio et Socratio*.[1] The choice of *cognomina* seems to reflect a concern for balance and shows more imagination than Gemellus and Geminus, for example, recorded in an inscription from Rome (*CIL* VI 19012). The twins are described as *ex incerto patre*. The mother, Sempronia Gemella, made the declaration, with the help of a *tutor*, C. Iulius Saturninus. Obviously, she was a Roman citizen and had this declaration prepared for that reason. Her sons' civic status, it will be seen, depended on hers. Gibbon remarked that among the "solid advantages" of Roman citizenship was "the benefit of the Roman laws, particularly in the interesting articles of marriage, testaments, and inheritances."[2] The advantages might involve troublesome

---

[1] First published by H. A. Sanders, *AJA* 32 (1928) 309–329.

[2] E. Gibbon, *The History of the Decline and Fall of the Roman Empire* (London, 1896) I 37 (ed. Bury).

complications for individuals. But though situations differed, at the time of this text citizenship often continued to have important consequences in everday life.

It will suffice to give the inner text of the diptych:[3]

II

Sempronia Gemella t(utore) a(uctore) C · Iulio Satur-
nino testata est eos qui signaturi
erant se enixam esse ex in-
certo patre · XII Kal · Aprel(es) q(uae) p(roximae) f(uerunt)
natos masculinos geminos eosque
vocetari M M Sempronios Sp · filios
Sarapionem et Socrationem
ideoque se has testationes in-
terposuisse dixit quia lex

III

Aelia Sentia et Papia Poppaea
spurios spuriasve in albo profiteri
vetat · d · e · r · e · e · b · t · ss ·
Actum Alex(andriae) ad Aeg(yptum) III · K · Maias Imp(era-
tore)
Caesare T · Aelio Hadriano Antonino
Aug(usto) Pio IIII M · Aurelio Caesare II cos ·
anno VIII Imp(eratoris) Caesare T. Aeli Hadriani
Antonini Aug(usti) Pii mense Pachon
die · IIII ·

The first editor of the diptych, H. A. Sanders, suggested that the *tutor* Saturninus was in fact the father of the twins and a soldier.[4] More recently H. C. Youtie has referred to this possibility with understandable interest in an article on illegitimacy, remarkable for its penetration and humanity.[5] Pertinent legal texts make it clear that the phrase *ex incerto patre* need not be taken literally. Herennius Modestinus states, *vulgo concepti dicuntur qui patrem demonstrare non possunt, vel qui possunt quidem, sed eum habent, quem habere non licet.*[6] A decision of Caracalla provides an example in the second category.[7] A woman found that she had unwittingly married a slave, named Eros, believing him to be free. The emperor ruled that she could recover her *dos* and whatever else Eros owed her, and adds regarding their children, *filii autem tui, ut ex libera nati incerto tamen patre, spurii ingenui*

---

[3] The numerals II and III are added by the editor in *P.Mich.*

[4] Specifically a legionary, *AJA* 32 (1928) 328.

[5] "*ΑΠΑΤΟΡΕΣ*: Law vs. Custom in Roman Egypt," *Le Monde Grec . . . Hommages à Claire Préaux* (Brussels, 1975) 723–740. For the diptych see 728–729, 736.

[6] *Dig.* I 5.23.

[7] *Cod. Iust.* V 18.3.

intelleguntur. It seems reasonable to conclude that the father of the twins was probably also illicit rather than unknown. At any rate, Gemella was not always careless and improvident, and she acted as a concerned but hopeful mother once her sons were born. The declaration was prepared to help protect a desirable civic status, and the copy we have was evidently thought worth keeping in the family records for a time.[8]

But should we assume that the father was probably a soldier? Such an assumption would not be unnatural in many periods.[9] More specifically, it is well known that till the time of Severus Roman soldiers could not marry, and that their illegitimate children were numerous.[10] Further, one may reasonably suspect that Sempronia Gemella's citizenship had been inherited from a father, or more remote ancestor, who had served in the army.[11] If so, she may have had family connections in military circles. Quite possibly, too, some or all of the men named in the text may have been soldiers or veterans.[12] But none is identified as such, and it seems necessary to consider the matter further.

The three other *testationes* that concern illegitimate children may prove instructive (*CPL* 159–161).[13] In date, they run from A.D. 127 to 138. All three were made by the fathers, who were soldiers serving in auxiliary cohorts; the mothers are merely named. The declarations were drawn up and signed in the *hiberna* of the soldiers' units.[14] In that prepared by Gemella one finds merely *Alex(andriae) ad Aeg(yptum)*, with no reference to a camp or unit.[15] In the only text in which the names of witnesses are

[8] It came from house B 7, "in which were found datable papyri of the second century A.D.," *AJA* 32 (1928) 309. Whether any may be connected with the diptych, I do not know.

[9] For the problem in France in the early eighteenth century, e.g., see A. Corvisier, *L'armée française de la fin du XVIIᵉ siècle . . .: Le Soldat* (Paris, 1964) II 885–886. A soldier found to be responsible might be imprisoned.

[10] See J. Lesquier, *L'armée romaine d'Égypte* (Cairo, 1918) 262–279; H. Nesselhauf, *CIL* XVI 154–155; G. R. Watson, *The Roman Soldier* (London, 1969) 133–140. The number of legionary recruits *ex castris* was considerable; for Egypt see Lesquier, 211, 214. H. C. Youtie discusses illegitimate children of soldiers, *loc. cit.* (n. 5) 737–740.

[11] R. Cavenaile lists 26 Sempronii in his "Prosopographie de l'armée romaine d'Égypte d'Auguste à Dioclétien," *Aegyptus* 50 (1970) 294–295. The name is common in Karanis, and Sempronii Gemelli are known there and in the army. The twins may have been given her father's *praenomen*. The fact that her *tutor* is not her father may mean that he had died.

[12] Sanders quite reasonably suggested legionaries, *AJA* 32 (1928) 328. There seems, however, to be no reason to think that Gemella was a freedwoman, as he does, pp. 327–328.

[13] For some comments on *CPL* 159 see J. F. Gilliam, *Hommages à Claire Préaux* 771–773.

[14] In *CPL* 161 *ad hib(erna)*. A town is also named in each.

[15] In *FIRA* III 47 = *CPL* 221 (A.D. 142) *in castris Aug(ustis) hibernis leg(ionis) II Tr(aianae) For(tis) et alae Mauretanae* is added. Cf. also *CPL* 102 (A.D. 92) and 189 (A.D. 153).

preserved, they identify themselves in the regular military fashion by their
century or *turma* and sometimes by rank (*CPL* 159). In all three *testationes*
those making the declarations explain their situation and thus the form of
the document (which is not the *professio* made for legitimate children) as
propter districtionem militarem. In one the father adds a specific reason for
preparing it: *ut possit post honestam missionem suam ad epicrisin suam adprobare
filium naturalem esse* (*CPL* 159). These *testationes* concerning children of
soldiers obviously differ from that of Gemella in significant ways. But the
most striking one is the role of the father in the former, and his complete
absence in the latter, made more emphatic by the substitution of *Spurius*
and *incertus pater*. The absence of any military titles and terminology has
already been stressed.

As has been noted, the fathers in *CPL* 159–161 were all auxiliaries. But
there is no reason to suppose that a legionary could not make use of such
a document. A well known letter of Hadrian, which was posted in the
camp of the two legions in Egypt in A.D. 119, specifically established the
right of children who were acknowledged during the period of military
service to succeed to their fathers' property.[16] A *testatio* would have been an
obvious way of acknowledging a child for this purpose or others. As regards
auxiliaries, after some date between A.D. 140 and 144 children were no
longer granted citizenship upon their father's discharge.[17] But this does not
seem to provide an adequate explanation of the absence or suppression of
the father's name in our text.

In considering a soldier's restrictions and especially his inability to have
a legal marriage, it should be kept in mind that he had a great deal of
freedom as regards relations with women and responsibilities to children.
No vow of celibacy was required. He could take an unofficial wife or
concubine, if he was not content with more casual connections, and
acknowledge children without concern about disciplinary action. A *testatio*
concerning illegitimate twins should not have caused trouble unless there
were other complications. The military *diplomata*, from the time of their
first appearance under Claudius, gave auxiliary soldiers *conubium* with the
informal *uxores* they might already have, when they approached or reached
the time of discharge.[18] The grant of citizenship to their children until

16 *BGU* 140 = Mitteis, *Chrest.* 373 = *FIRA* I 78. Cf. the fragmentary opening lines of
P.Oxy. XLII 3014 (a new text of the *Gnomon Id. Log.*).
17 As is evident from the *diplomata*; see e.g., G. Alföldy, *Historia* 17 (1968) 217, and now
esp. H. Wolff, *Chiron* 4 (1974) 479–510.
18 In the formula commonly used the emperor granted to those listed, *conubium cum
uxoribus, quas tunc habuissent, cum est civitas iis data, aut, siqui caelibes essent, cum iis, quas postea
duxissent dumtaxat singuli singulas.*

Antoninus Pius has already been mentioned. In *BGU* 140, as we have seen, Hadrian assumed that soldiers might formally recognize children and be interested in their welfare. Nevertheless, the wives of soldiers, to give them this courtesy title, were particularly dependent on the good will and sense of responsibility of their husbands. They had very little legal protection,[19] and whatever social pressures might be exerted on their behalf would depend on circumstances such as the unit's location and its movements, and on the proximity and importance of their relatives.[20]

Further, unlike peasants and villagers in Egypt or elsewhere, soldiers obviously did not need wives to share their work,[21] and though many nevertheless had and retained them, many others did not. Tacitus writes of some veterans settled in Italy in the time of Nero, *neque coniugiis suscipiendis neque alendis liberis sueti orbas sine posteris domos relinquebant* (*Ann.*, XIV 27.2). Gravestones of soldiers very often name *commilitones* or brothers as heirs, with no mention of wives or children. Of the auxiliary *diplomata* that are sufficiently preserved to settle the matter in the period from Claudius to 140, 28 include wives, children, or both, but in 38 neither wives nor children are found. At the end of this period, however, especially in a province as relatively quiet as Egypt, the proportion of soldiers having wives and children presumably became substantially higher.[22] But whatever the exact figure may have been, no doubt it was considerably lower than that of the same age group in the civilian population. On the other hand, one may suspect that the proportion of disappointed women and abandoned children was higher around military camps than in ordinary villages.

[19] They could not recover any money that had been given as a concealed *dos*; see *P.Cattaoui* = Mitteis, *Chrest.* 372. The state made no provision for soldiers' widows, though nearly half of auxiliary soldiers might be expected to die before they completed their twenty-five years term of service.

[20] Obviously daughters or sisters of soldiers in the unit might be expected to have an advantage.

[21] If soldiers had inherited or acquired property, wives might be useful, as any bride also might be who had land or money.

[22] Of the auxiliary *diplomata* from Claudius through Trajan 10 included wives and children, 4 children only, and 30 neither wives nor children. Of those from 117 to 140, 5 included wives and children, 8 children only, 1 a wife only, and 8 neither wives nor children. The figures are too small to allow one to reach any firm conclusions, but they suggest that more soldiers were forming families in the first part of the second century, which should be kept in mind in considering the withdrawal of grants of citizenship to children ca. 140. To judge from the figures we obtain from this source, sailors showed little interest in family life. Of their *diplomata* up to 140, 1 included a wife and a child, 2 children only, and 12 neither wives nor children. Inscriptions record more marriages and children, but it is hard to know how representative they are.

To return to the diptych, it seems to me very doubtful that the twins were born in a legally irregular but stable family of a soldier, and very doubtful too that Saturninus was their father. If he were, he would appear to be in effect disowning them, in direct contrast to the soldiers in *CPL* 159–161. Perhaps Gemella did not know or would not name the father. Or whoever she named may have felt uncertain and unwilling to accept responsibility. Perhaps the father was too closely related; e.g., Roman citizens could not marry sisters or aunts.[23] If the father was a *peregrinus*, Roman citizenship could not have been claimed for the twins if he were identified.[24] Or he may have been married to someone else or unmentionable for other reasons. The document simply does not provide enough information to settle the questions it raises.

Evidence from other sources would be welcome. As it happens, a C. Iulius Saturninus and a Sempronia Gemella are linked again in an entry in the great tax roll from Karanis of 171/172 and in another in the roll of 172/173.[25] The wax tablet of 145, it will be recalled, was found in Karanis. It is entirely possible that the two persons with these names in the tablet were still alive twenty-seven years or more later. Gemella was presumably quite young when her sons were born. Unfortunately, the tax rolls do not state the relationship of their Saturninus and Gemella. She merely pays some taxes for which Saturninus was responsible, as his agent or perhaps as a lessee. She did the same for other land owners, on what basis is also not recorded.[26] The combination of the names makes it tempting to conclude that the Saturninus and Gemella of the tablet and of the tax rolls were the same. If so, their relationship was evidently a continuing one, whether or not he remained her *tutor*. Further, in another papyrus from Karanis of 176/179 a Iulius Saturninus is described as a veteran and landowner, *P.Mich.* IX 535. It seems certain that he is the man found in the tax rolls.[27] If he was also Gemella's *tutor* in 145, which seems to me probable, he was no doubt at that time still a soldier on active service.[28] The most simple explanation of his role may be that he was a

[23] It seemed to be necessary to record the prohibition in *Gnomon Id. Log.* 23.

[24] In keeping with the *lex Minicia*. For instances of those affected see R. Taubenschlag, *The Law of Greco-Roman Egypt in the Light of the Papyri*[2] (Warsaw, 1955) 108, n. 18.

[25] *P.Mich.* IV 223, lines 3289–3291 and 224, lines 3901–3903.

[26] *P.Mich.* IV 223, lines 2144–2147 and 3292–3297 and 225, lines 2423–2425; cf. 223, lines 2906–2908, 224, lines 4913–4917, and 358 B, lines 19–21. But these entries require an expert's commentary. Close relatives (a brother and sister?) and a workman or lessee with an Egyptian name seem to be involved.

[27] This is the view of the editor, E. M. Husselman.

[28] If Saturninus had enlisted in a legion, ala, or cohort in 140, for example, he would have been discharged ca. 165 when about forty-five.

family friend from Karanis, who took the place of Gemella's deceased father in making arrangements for her *testatio*.

To turn to the witnesses, the names of several require revision or comments. The signatures are copied in this text, and it is helpful to have all of them in the same hand. But some are poorly preserved. They have been read as follows:[29]

> M. Vibi Pollionis
> M. Octavi Sereni
> L. Aemili Maximi
> L. Caponi Saturnini
> 5 C. Aebuti Saturnini
> C. Vibievi Crassi
> M. Holconi Ampiss[i]

In line 4 one should read *L. Aponi Saturnini*. This eliminates the name Caponius which, as Professor Sanders remarked, appears not to be attested. Nor does Ampissus in line 7 seem to be found elsewhere. Here I would suggest *Ampliati*. In line 6 the *gentilicium* appears not as yet to have been read satisfactorily. It may have ended -*usi*, but I have nothing to propose for the beginning.[30] *Crassi* is not right. *Carisi* is an attractive possibility, as Professor Youtie has observed.[31]

The seven names, considered as a group, have a correct, distinctly Latin aspect. Misleading or ambiguous as this may be, Holconius at least is a very rare *gentilicium*, otherwise known only in Pompeii.[32] L. Aponius

[29] I have depended on the plates published in Sanders' article (above n. 1), but H. C. and L. C. Youtie have most generously and helpfully examined the originals and checked my suggestions.

[30] Arangio-Ruiz' Vibieni is an emendation.

[31] He proposed this after I had suggested *Car-*   . The alternatives that I had not mentioned but had in mind were *Carisi* or *Carini*. The name is probably to be taken as *C(h)arisius* rather than the Latin *Carisius*. In regard to the *cognomen* in line 7 he writes "Your *Ampliati* is attractive, especially with respect to *l*, although *p* is hard to fix definitely on the photo."

[32] Sanders had noticed this, *AJA* 32 (1928) 320. The occurrences in texts published more recently, so far as I know, are all from Pompeii. For the family see M. della Corte, *Case ed abitanti di Pompei*[3] (Naples, 1965) 239–242. Ampliatus, which I read as Holconius' *cognomen*, is most often found as a name of slaves and freedmen. But it appears to be more widely used in towns of Central and Southern Italy, in the areas included in *CIL* IV, IX, X, and XI. In view of the *gentilicium* the occurrences in Pompeii are particularly interesting, e.g., L. Popidius L. f. Ampliatus and N. Popidius Ampliatus; for their family see della Corte, 151, n. 4. When and how this Holconius Ampliatus, or whoever first brought the name, came to Egypt is of course quite uncertain. Ampliatus himself may have been born there, needless to say. The fact that recruits from Italy, including one from Nuceria, were sent to the *legio II Traiana* in A.D. 132 or 133 illustrates the wide range of possibilities; see F. Gilliam, *AJP* 77 (1956) 363.

Saturninus has a name which, though much more common, also attracts one's attention. The senatorial Aponii Saturnini of the first century may have made the *cognomen* seem especially appropriate for an Aponius in a number of areas. A M. Aponius Saturninus was a conspicuous landowner in the Fayum in the time of Tiberius.[33]

C. Aebutius Saturninus raises particularly interesting possibilities. The *gentilicium* is familiar to students of the Republic and Roman Law,[34] but there were no conspicuous figures with this name in the second half of the first century B.C. or in the Early Empire who might have caused it to be assumed by large numbers of new citizens. It was widely if thinly spread, however, and in Egypt is found from the early first century.[35] In 142 an Aebutius (only his *gentilicium* is given) was a decurion in the *ala I Thracum Mauretana*, stationed in Alexandria in the same camp as the *legio II Traiana*.[36] This was of course only three years before the *testatio* of Gemella, also written in Alexandria. In view of the comparative rarity of the *gentilicium* and the coincidence in time and place, there seems to be a substantial possibility that C. Aebutius Saturninus was the decurion, and if so that all the witnesses as well as C. Iulius Saturninus were members of the *ala*.[37] The document in which the decurion was named was an elaborate

---

[33] For the senatorial Aponii Saturnini see *PIR*[2] A 936, 938. For the landowner, Rostovtzeff, *SEHRE*[2] 671. One part of his property was in the vicinity of Karanis. *P.Mich.* V 312 records him as sharing ownership of land with Ti. Claudius Balbillus, which indicates a high social standing however he is to be identified. The most recently published papyrus mentioning him is *P.Mich.* XII 633. Cavenaile (n. 11) lists three Aponii. The witness has a *praenomen* different from that of the landowner and the consul. For legionary Aponii Saturnini in Africa see *CIL* VIII 2554, 2564, 2810.

[34] Notably because of the fifth century consular Aebutii and the *lex Aebutia*. Others are listed in *R.E.* I cols. 442–443. See also *Th.L.L.* I cols. 905–906. Of the less conspicuous Aebutii one may note the three members of the *consilium* of Cn. Pompeius Strabo, each with a different *praenomen* and tribe, *CIL* I[2] 709 (B.C. 89).

[35] To those listed in the *Namenbuch* and Foraboschi, *Onomasticon*, one should add the early Latin text *PSI*. XIII 1321 = *CPL* 187; cf. my comments in *Hommages à Claire Préaux* 774.

[36] *FIRA* III 47 = *CPL* 221, cited above in n. 15. Published by O. Guéraud and P. Jouguet, *Études de Papyrologie* 6 (1940) 1–21, pls. I–VI. Because of the value of Cavenaile's "Prosopographie" (above, n. 11), it should be noted that the soldiers named in this text were omitted.

[37] To entertain such a possibility, after stressing the absence of military titles and terms, may seem to require some justification. The declaration was made by a civilian and otherwise concerns directly only her children. No question of military status or privileges is involved. The tutor and witnesses are acting simply as Roman citizens, not as *milites* or *commilitones*. The person who prepared the *testatio* may have felt that irrelevant terms and the like were out of place. Some other legal documents involving women of Roman citizenship with illegitimate children are equally concise, though the circumstances may

and carefully prepared *testamentum per aes et libram,* written on a well preserved polyptych and containing the will of an *eques* in the *ala.*[38] One conspicuous element which the will and the *testatio* have in common is that both are strictly Roman in form.

Whatever the circumstances of the *testatio* may be, in its language and content it reminds one that Roman law and status had real significance for tens of thousands of persons in Egypt at this time, even for an illiterate woman, new-born illegitimate children, and a *tutor* who wrote his *subscriptio* in Greek. Such important matters as marriage, testaments, and inheritances were involved, and in some cases a sense of identity, one may assume. The quite mixed group of resident Roman citizens was becoming larger, and its existence contributed to important developments that became much more apparent in the centuries that followed.[39]

2. *P.Oxy.* XXXI 2553

E. G. Turner has presented this important but fragmentary text with a careful and instructive commentary. He describes it, quite accurately, as a calendar of cult offerings and cites as a parallel *P.Oslo* III 77. A distinctive and conspicuous element, it should be added, is that the route and stopping places of the presiding magistrate[40] are included, as well as the prescribed sacrifices. The editor was inclined to conclude that Oxyrhynchus was the place concerned, but Alexandria is probably to be preferred, as others have suggested.[41] The hand is assigned to the end of the second or beginning of the third century. Emperors and even Antinous have a conspicuous role in the calendar. Professor Turner quite rightly remarks that "the text offers new evidence regarding the penetration of Roman cult in Egypt." But a Lageion is mentioned repeatedly as well as a Sebasteion. There are also

have been different in each case. In one the mother was a freedwoman, and one may suspect her *patronus* was the father, *SB* I 5217 = *FIRA* III 6 (A.D. 148). She had made the *testatio*, as had the mothers in *BGU* IV 1032 (A.D. 173) and *P.Oxy.* XII 1451 (A.D. 175).

[38] His heir was his son, a minor and presumably illegitimate. His citizenship was derived from his mother, Antonia Thermutha. She is described as *mater heredis mei.*

[39] In the third century a few began to receive equestrian posts which had been accessible much earlier to provincials elsewhere, and formed large estates. The evidence for one of them I have examined in *Mélanges d'histoire ancienne offerts à William Seston* (Paris, 1974) 217–225. In the fourth century administrative and other substantial careers became more common for natives of Egypt.

[40] It is not certain who the subject of the verbs is.

[41] C. Préaux, *Chron. d'Égypte* 42 (1967) 218 and P. M. Fraser, *Ptolemaic Alexandria* (Oxford, 1972) II: Notes, p. 101. The editor had recognized that Alexandria was a possibility. The suggestion presented in this note may make Alexandria seem more likely; cf. below, n. 44.

shrines or temples of Apollo and Heracles. One can assume some continuity with festivals of the Ptolemaic period, though nothing on the scale
of the great *pompe* of Ptolemy Philadelphus described by Callixeinus. Such
processions were of course common throughout the Greek and Roman
world, and from an early time in Egypt.

Despite the wide and varied interest of the text, I will confine myself to
comments on line 2 in the first entry:

Fr. i

[9/10].c τοῦ Διὸc καὶ ἐκθεώcι Ἀντινόο[υ
]ηcιον οἶκον τὸν Βρεταγικοῦ κ[
]ειο(ν) καὶ εἰc τὸ Τυχαῖο(ν) καὶ εἰc τὸ Ϲαραπ[
].[Ἀ]ντινόου θύει ἱππικ( ) αρ[.]...[

Who is Britannicus? The editor comments only that "after Claudius no
emperor till Commodus . . . took this title." But it seems unlikely that such
a title would be used by itself alone to identify either emperor or any of
their successors in this context. There was only one Britannicus, the ill-
fated son of Claudius, who could be so identified, just as there was only one
Germanicus. On some contemporary coins from Asia Minor, for instance,
he is called simply Βρεταννικός or Βρεταννικὸς Καῖcαρ.[42] At the end of
line 2 in the papyrus, incidentally, I believe that Κ[αίσαρος should be
restored.[43]

It may seem strange, and doubtless it is, that Britannicus should have an
oikos in Alexandria[44] and be mentioned in a religious calendar at the end
of the second century or later. The interval in time is not in itself extraordinary. Germanicus, for instance, is found in the *Feriale Duranum*. But
Britannicus was poisoned by Nero and brutally disposed of before his
fourteenth birthday, before he could distinguish himself in any way or
confirm the promise that some saw in him. He died too late for Seneca to
display his skills by including him in the *Apocolocyntosis*.

A partial explanation may be found in Suetonius, *Titus* 2. After telling
us that Titus was brought up at the court with Britannicus, he adds:

*erant autem adeo familiares, ut de potione, qua Britannicus hausta periit, Titus quoque
iuxta cubans gustasse credatur gravique morbo adflictatus diu. quorum omnium mox*

[42] For coins see F. Imhoof-Blumer, *Numismatische Zeitschrift* 48 (1915) 85–93; for the
second version of his name cited in the text, pp. 91–92. The use of Britannicus in the
authors is familiar; e.g., Cassius Dio LX 12.5; 22.2.

[43] Suggested by the editor with κ[αί as an alternative.

[44] Quite apart from other arguments, it seems more likely that something as unusual
as a shrine of Britannicus would be found in Alexandria rather than in Oxyrhynchus.
But for the point that I am discussing the location makes little difference.

memor statuam ei auream in Palatio posuit et alteram ex ebore equestrem, quae circensi pompa hodieque praefertur, dedicavit prosecutusque est.

To this may be added the *sestertius* bearing the portrait and name of Britannicus, which was struck under Titus in A.D. 80 in connection with his "restored" series of coins of honored predecessors.[45] They included Augustus, Agrippa, Tiberius, Drusus, Livia, Nero Drusus, Germanicus, Agrippina I, Claudius, and Galba. Caligula, Nero, Otho, and Vitellius are omitted. The series served to emphasize the continuity between the new dynasty and the old, but with careful discrimination.

The Alexandrians were not reluctant to grant honors to their rulers and members of their families, as the famous letter of Claudius, for example, and that of Nero more recently discovered show.[46] In giving an *oikos* to Britannicus they were doing no more or little more than Titus did in having the ivory statue included in the *pompa circensis*.[47] The *oikos* may well have been built or assigned during Titus' short reign, perhaps in 80 at the same time as the "restored" series of coins.[48] But quite possibly Titus arranged this, e.g., in 71, when he was in Alexandria, or earlier or later during his father's reign.[49]

It would be naively cynical to deny Titus any sense of shared experience, personal obligation, or pity, but, for those who remembered the connection at the time or were informed of it, gestures honoring Britannicus would bring to mind both Nero's crimes and a Flavian link with the Julio-Claudian prince whose place Nero had taken. For Alexandrians a hundred years or more later, Britannicus could have little or no personal significance. A certain number may have known that he was the son of one of the rulers of the empire of which Alexandria and Egypt were now a part. But not

[45] H. Mattingly, *Coins of the Roman Empire in the British Museum* II (London, 1930) lxxvii–viii, 293, no. 306. See also C. H. V. Sutherland, *Coinage in Roman Imperial Policy* 31 B.C.–A.D. 68 (London, 1951) 196.

[46] H. I. Bell, *Jews and Christians in Egypt* (London, 1924) = *Sel. Pap.* II 212. There is a reference to a *pompe* in lines 38–40. For the letter of Nero see O. Montevecchi, *Aegyptus* 50 (1970) 5–33.

[47] An honor given to *divi*. It was granted to Caesar in his life time. For Cicero's reaction see *ad Attic.* XIII 28.3; 44.1. Cf. Cassius Dio XLIII 45.2.

[48] It would be not be surprising if Alexandrian envoys came to Rome early in Titus' reign, with requests and prepared to do something that might please the emperor. For Titus and Alexandrians as represented in the fragmentary "Acta Hermiae" see C. H. Roberts *J.R.S.* 39 (1949) 79–80 and H. A. Musurillo, *The Acts of the Pagan Martyrs* (Oxford, 1954) 32.

[49] As is well known, the most direct and important contacts of Vespasian and Titus with Alexandria came soon after the former's proclamation. See A. Henrichs, *ZPE* 3 (1968) 51–80; C. P. Jones, *Historia* 22 (1973) 306–308.

much more would have been known, or needed to be known, about most of those formally and fully included in the imperial cult.

3. *PSI* XIV 1448

- - - - - - - - - - - -
```
   1   .... (traces) ...... [
            anno provinciae centesimo et tert[io
2d H.       Callistianus Aug ... [
            Nicostrati vicari mei (denarios) [
   5   [ - ca. 12 l. -]....ș Ruf[
```
- - - - - - - - - - - -

This scrap, of unknown provenance and incomplete on three sides, seems to have attracted little attention, not surprisingly perhaps. There are two hands. The second, in lines 3–5, is that of an Imperial slave, probably a *dispensator* or the holder of some other financial post to judge from the fact that he had a *vicarius*.[50] We may assume that from an early age he had been trained for a clerical career; quite possibly his hand may serve as an example of those in use in the great bureaux in Rome. The editor, V. Bartoletti, dated it in the second or third century.

The readings in lines 2–4 are certain except at the end of line 3. The plate suggests that *Augg* may be possible, but Professor Manfredi has kindly examined the original and confirms that there is only one *g*.[51] The traces that follow must be remnants of *ser[(vus)*.[52] Of the possibilities to be considered, they are compatible only with this; moreover, *vicari mei* in the next line clearly points to a slave, not a freedman.

Little remains to indicate the content or even the nature of the text. Following a suggestion of Arangio-Ruiz, the editor concludes that the text probably concerned the sale of the *vicarius*.[53] No sensible person is eager to differ with Arangio-Ruiz, but the *vicarius* of an Imperial slave was not simply his personal slave and merely part of his *peculium*. The *vicarius* was

[50] For *vicarius* see P. R. C. Weaver, *J.R.S.* 54 (1964) 117–128; *Familia Caesaris* (Cambridge, 1972) 199–206.

[51] In a letter of 2 December 1969. The reading is important for attempts to date the text. Thus in A.D. 208, a possibility if the era is that of the province of Arabia, *Augg* would be expected.

[52] In a note the editor comments, "*Aug(usti) ser[vus?* Ma le tracce sono incertissime." *Servus* is almost certainly abbreviated. For various designations of Imperial slaves, their forms, and dates see H. Chantraine, *Freigelassene und Sklaven im Dienst der römischen Kaiser* (Wiesbaden, 1967) 180–188.

[53] Accepted e.g., by R. Taubenschlag, *JJP* 11–12 (1957–1958) 356 and M. Amelotti, *Studia et Documenta Historiae et Iuris* 24 (1958) 386.

his deputy and in effect also a member of the civil service.[54] A sale such as is suggested was probably very unusual. It seems much more likely that the *vicarius* was somehow involved in the transaction, whether it was public or private in character, as the deputy or agent of Callistianus. I would suggest that the subscription that we have in lines 3–5 began something like this: *Callistianus Aug(usti) ṣẹṛ[(vus) accepi per personam] | Nicostrati vicari ṃei (denarios)* [.[55]

The writing runs across the fibres. One possibility to consider perhaps is a double document of the kind that those who were self-consciously Roman, or those who prepared legal papers for them, continued to use occasionally, even in Egypt after the form was generally abandoned there.[56] But too little remains of the text to make conjectures valuable.

As the editor remarked, the date in line 2 suggests that the document was not written in Egypt; at least, the date is not Egyptian.[57] In the Latin West a provincial era was in common use only in Mauretania Caesariensis. Inscriptions contain hundreds of examples of the formula found here, ordinarily abbreviated (*a. p.* or the like) but occasionally written out as in this papyrus.[58] Year 1 of the era was A.D. 40. In the East the only provincial era which might be considered here seems to be that of Arabia, in which year 1 = A.D. 106.[59] I am inclined to prefer the Mauretanian era, because it is so commonly used and because its form is so regular and fixed. Further, though Imperial slaves might use Latin anywhere, it is natural to assign a Latin document to Mauretania rather than Arabia. But caution is in order. If the Mauretanian era is that used, year 103 = A.D. 142; year 113, if one restores *tert[io decimo*, would be of course A.D. 152. The corresponding years in the Arabian era would give A.D. 208 or 218. The stereotyped official Latin hands are particularly difficult to date,[60] and I have no confidence in my ability to choose between the eras on the basis of the two hands we have here.

We do not know who the other party in the transaction was, to whom

---

[54] See Weaver, *Familia Caesaris* (above n. 50) 200–206.

[55] Without looking further, for *per personam* I may cite *P.Aberdeen* 61 = *FIRA* III 147 = *CPL* 186 = *ChLA* IV 224 (A.D. 48/49).

[56] For such a text recently published, and for a reference to one in another papyrus, see J. F. Gilliam, *Bonner Jahrb.* 167 (1967) 233–243; *JJP* 16–17 (1971) 63–70. In such a document the scrap discussed here would correspond roughly to lines 19–22 of *P.London* 229 = *ChLA* III 100.

[57] Conceivably the date is taken from another document being cited.

[58] See the index of *CIL* VIII, Suppl. V, pp. 179–180.

[59] For the day and year see G. W. Bowersock, *J.R.S.* 61 (1971) 231. I find that C. Préaux has suggested this era as a possibility in a review, *Chron. d'Égypte* 35 (1960) 303–304.

[60] Cf. R. Marichal, *Annuaire de l'École pratique des Hautes Études* 101 (1968–1969) 272.

Callistianus[61] acknowledges receipt of a sum in *denarii*.[62] Presumably it was he who brought the document to Egypt, rather than Callistianus. Nevertheless, it is not entirely out of place to remark that Imperial slaves and freedmen should not be overlooked when one is considering Latin and Latin influences in Egypt, for instance in official terms. Louis Robert has commented on their importance in this respect in the Greek East generally.[63] In Egypt the emperor's slaves and freedmen are comparatively unobtrusive, because of the nature of the administration of this province and because we have relatively few papyri from Alexandria. More might be found there than elsewhere. But it would be worth-while to collect the evidence. There are some striking texts as early as the time of Augustus.[64]

4. *A monastery library*

Two of the three texts that have been discussed in this paper are in Latin. It is well known that in the East the use of Latin never became common, despite the long continuation of Roman rule, the grants of citizenship and its consequences, and the penetration of much else that was Roman in origin and character.[65] As regards languages, for centuries Greek was the chief beneficiary, as well as one of the most important instruments, of processes we describe as Romanization. Descendants of Latin speaking immigrants or veterans seem as a rule to have been absorbed, within a few generations at most, into the Greek communities among which they lived. In Egypt, as elsewhere in the East, the appearance of Latin in any period requires an attempt at explanation.[66]

The papyrus and parchment codices acquired by the Bodmer Library some twenty-five years ago are among the most notable discoveries of their kind. Some are intact and others are preserved in large part. Those which have been published in the series P. Bodmer[67] include books of the Iliad,

---

[61] For names of slaves ending in *-ianus* in the second century see Weaver, *Familia Caesaris* (above, n. 50) 89–90.

[62] The *denarius* was used in Egypt in military accounts and in other formally Roman and administrative documents, but still it supports the assumption of a non-Egyptian origin.

[63] *L'Antiquité Classique* 37 (1968) 439–444.

[64] See e.g., W. Schubart, *Archiv. f. P.* 5 (1913) 41, 116–118. For restrictions on *Caesariani* and *vicarii* see *Gnomon Id. Log.* 109, 110.

[65] For one example see L. Robert, *Les gladiateurs dans l'Orient grec*[2] (Amsterdam, 1971).

[66] The admirable paper of U. Wilcken, "Ueber den Nutzen der lateinischen Papyri," *Atti del IV Congresso Internazionale di Papirologia* (Milan, 1936) 101–122 remains valuable.

[67] The first volume was published in 1954.

comedies of Menander, parts of the Old and New Testaments, and Christian texts of various kinds, in Greek and in Coptic. Considered individually, without regard to where they were found and in what context, many of the texts are highly important, some even unique. But it seems clear that they all come from the same source, and should be considered as a group, along with a few other parts of the find that are now in other collections.

What is most important here is the presence of Latin texts in the find. This was first recognized as a possibility when W. H. Willis published a scrap of the First Catilinarian, found between leaves of a Coptic codex, part of which is now in Mississippi, part in the Bodmer Library.[68] After R. Roca-Puig presented the Latin *Psalmus responsorius*,[69] a comparison of the hands immediately suggested a connection. Professor Roca-Puig soon confirmed that the fragment in Mississippi came from his papyrus codex in Barcelona, which contained in addition to the *Psalmus* the first two Catilinarians, as well as Greek texts.[70] There is other evidence, not yet published, for believing that the Barcelona codex and those in the Bodmer Library had once been together. In short, we have the remnants of a monastery library, from the Thebaid and more specifically, it appears, from the vicinity of Panopolis,[71] which in the fourth century contained at least three Latin texts.

It should be emphasized that the Barcelona codex does not appear to be a stray, brought from abroad perhaps by some ecclesiastic who found himself in this part of Egypt.[72] The ornamentation at the end of the *Samia*

[68] *TAPA* 94 (1963) 321–327. The two parts of the codex have been published in *P.Bodmer* XXII.

[69] *Himne a la Verge Maria 'Psalmus Responsorius': Papir Llatí del Segle IV*[2] (Barcelona, 1965).

[70] *Aegyptus* 46 (1966) 124. The "Anafora greca" included in the codex was described in the same volume of *Aegyptus*, pp. 91–92. More information about the Catilinarians, including their number, variant readings, and a good photograph of one leaf, was presented in a small but instructive publication, *Selecció de variants a les Catilinàries de Ciceró. P. Barc., I et II in Catilinam* (Barcelona, 1971). The Barcelona fragment of the Samia should be noted as confirming connections with the Bodmer codices; published by R. Roca-Puig, *Boletín de la Real Academia de Buenas Letras de Barcelona* 32 (1967–1968) 5–13. More recently he has described some Latin "Hexameters on Alcestis" also included in his Barcelona codex, *Proceedings of the XIV International Congress of Papyrologists*.

[71] Eric Turner, *Greek Papyri* (Oxford, 1968) 52–53.

[72] I have in mind Lucifer of Calaris, banished to the Thebaid in the mid-fourth century. Known to me through K. M. Setton, *Christian Attitude towards the Emperor in the Fourth Century* (New York, 1941) 92–93.

resembles that at the end of the First Catilinarian.[73] In general, it looks
like a local product rather than an import, whether from a Western
province or a good *scriptorium* in Alexandria. The combination in this small
codex of texts that are both Greek and Latin and at the same time
Christian and pagan may perhaps suggest local work. Ignorance, as well
as carelessness, seems required to explain errors in the *Psalmus*, though the
hand shows practice in writing Latin.

It is striking to find seemingly diverse elements brought together in this
setting: Greek classics, Coptic texts that represent a new literary language
and reflect the development of a distinctive form of Christianity, and both
Ciceronian and Christian Latin. To be sure, Homer and Menander were
not really out of place in an essentially Coptic monastery.[74] But Latin is
more unexpected, at least for one not at home in such establishments.
Diocletian's insistence on the use of Latin in administration and even on
coins struck in Alexandria should be recalled. Under the Tetrarchy too
Egypt became more fully integrated into the Empire. For a variety of
reasons, there came to be far wider opportunities for young men from
Egypt with talent, ambition, and education to have careers that had long
been open to others. In ecclesiastical matters, which might have wide
consequences, the opinions of Egyptian bishops and monks had to be taken
into account; in the second century no one in the capital cared much
about the views on large questions of Alexandrians and the population of
Egypt proper. For law and administrative posts in the fourth century the
study of Latin was necessary. Claudian of course was the most accom-
plished Latin poet of the Later Empire, quite extraordinary and exceptional but still the product of the study of Latin in Alexandria.[75] In his
case as in many others, conspicuous accomplishments in Greek or Latin

[73] See the photograph of the last leaf of the First Catilinarian mentioned above in n. 70.
This should be taken into account in dating the Menander codex. For the ornamentation
see C. Nordenfalk, *Die spätantiken Zierbuchstaben* (Stockholm, 1970) 116.

[74] Cf. H. G. Evelyn White, *The Metropolitan Museum of Art Egyptian Expedition. The
Monastery of Epiphanius at Thebes*, Part II (New York, 1926) 320–321, for school pieces
found on walls of cells including lines of the Iliad and *sententiae* from Menander (end of the
sixth/beginning of the seventh centuries). For a combination of the same three languages
as those found in the codices see W. Schubart, "Ein lateinisch-griechisch-koptisches
Gesprächbuch," *Klio* 13 (1913) 27–38 (fifth or sixth century).

[75] The whole of A. Cameron's *Claudian* (Oxford, 1970) should be read but see especially
pp. 19–21, and for his reading in Latin, pp. 315–321. The volume contains much information about the large number of Egyptian poets in this period and their wanderings,
e.g., pp. 22–29; see also Cameron's article in *Historia* 14 (1965) 470–509. For an Egyptian
member of the Museum who became *praefectus vigilum* in the early third century see my
article cited above, n. 39.

rhetoric had substantial rewards. Latin had become important enough that it might well be thought desirable to have it represented in a monastery in Upper Egypt. As a practical consideration, Latin might be useful or desirably ornamental in dealings with high authorities. The Catilinarians were a standard elementary text, then as now. The *Psalmus* is harder to explain, and reflects an interest without obviously practical ends.

The Institute for Advanced Study

10

Rules for Musical Contests

ORSAMUS PEARL

P.*Mich*.inv. 4682   i 11.3 × 5.5 cm.   ii 10.7 × 5.5 cm.   II–III A.D.
                    iii 2.9 × 4.5 cm.   iv 1.5 × 1 cm.

This fragmentary text was recovered during the University's excavations at Karanis in 1926. It survives on three small pieces, plus a scrap which bears only indecipherable traces. The papyrus was of poor quality, coarse and rough, and the writing is crabbed and irregular. Most features of the writing suggest the late second or early third century of our era as the date of our copy. Documents and coins found in the same area as this papyrus fall in the period A.D. 117–235.[1] The writing runs with the fibers.

No comparable text is at present known. Even so, the form and content suggest a tradition of specifications, both of requirements and prohibitions, which set the standards for the several categories of musical competition.[2] The opposition to innovation consistently maintained by conservatives, such as Aristophanes, the Spartan ephor, Plato, and a large section of the Athenian public, is well known.[3] The musical contests at the great games, to judge from the strict formalism imposed in such a genre as the Pythian

---

[1] A. E. R. Boak and Enoch Peterson, *Karanis: Topographical and Architectural Report, 1924–28,* 9.

[2] Emil Reisch, *De Musicis Graecorum Certaminibus* (Vienna, 1885), which collects and interprets the evidence to that date, is still useful. The documentation is mainly epigraphic, and usually identifies only the victors in the several categories of competition. It is principally valuable in showing the large number of contests throughout the Greek world and the wide variety of performances in many of them.

[3] Aristophanes: *Nub.* 961 ff., quoted with approval by Sextus Empiricus, *Adv. Mus.* 14–15, and paralleled in Pherecrates, quoted by Ps.-Plutarch, *De Mus.* 30 (1141C–1142). Sparta: Plutarch, *Inst. Lac.* 17 (238C). Terpander was fined and his lyre nailed to the wall because of one extra string. The ephor proposed to cut from Timotheos' lyre the strings beyond the traditional seven; Timotheos himself (*Pers.* 215 ff.) alludes to expulsion from Sparta and defends his "new songs." Plato: *Republic* 3.398–399. Athens: Plutarch, *An seni* 23 (745D); Satyros, *Vit. Eur.* (*P.Oxy.* IX 1176) col. 22.

nome,[4] must have been a stronghold of traditionalism. We judge that, to assure the perpetuation of tradition, requirements similar to those set forth in the Michigan text must have been imposed on the contestants. At what time the earliest rules were codified and set down, we do not know, and our text bears no evidence of its own antecedents or of its origin. Its presence and recovery in so provincial and undistinguished a village as Karanis is an oddity; yet even in the *chōra*, towns and villages featured musical contests at their major festivals.[5] Even for these, a written set of rules may have been required. The Museum at Alexandria may have been the source, and our copy was possibly commissioned from Alexandria by a local official or dignitary.

In our text, the rules are presented in a pattern clearly observable in the two sections which are substantially complete, lines 5–15 and 24–32. A heading specifies the genre of the performance—lines 5 and 24. Subspecies may be later indicated, as in lines 13 and 28. Following the heading, a sentence with a verb in the imperative prescribes what is to be done—lines 6 and 25–27. A further imperative—line 14—applies to the soloist of line 13. The several errors or blunders are described for which the contestant is disqualified—lines 6–10, 13–14, and 27. Certain permissible variations in personnel and performance are indicated—lines 10–13 and 29–32.

As is evident, it is throughout assumed that the contestants were well aware of the conventions which prescribed the form of the νόμοι and μέλη which were to be performed. Our imperfect knowledge of these matters offers a considerable obstacle to our comprehension. We meet with additional difficulties in the rare terms παρὰ θύραν, line 8, and μεσόχορ[ος, line 14. The choral, or choral–dramatic implication of these words, however, diminishes the surprise at the unanticipated indications of a dramatic or semi-dramatic performance. This feature is adumbrated by the presence of the *persona*, line 9, ἐξόδους, line 26, and κωμικ[ούς, line 12 and probably in the same form, line 32. The latter apparently refers to assisting citharists or to added actors or dancers. The piper's nome, as described in Pollux 4.84, suggests at least *mimēsis*, but by Greek concepts of music, music in itself had strong mimetic and depictive capabilities. At least in the earlier period, it is quite clear (e.g., from Strabo 9.3.10)

---

4 Described in Strabo, *Geog.* 9.3.10; a different account is given by Pollux 4.84.

5 H. I. Bell, "A Musical Competition in the 3rd Century B.C.," *Raccolto Lumbroso* 13–23; the occasion was perhaps the accession of Euergetes. See also Wilcken, *Chrest.* 491 (=*P.Giss.* 3), one column of a libretto for a pageant introducing a festival in which there will be athletic and musical exercises, probably competitive; the occasion was the accession of Hadrian.

that actors or dancers were not required or even permissible. Pollux[6] may be describing later elaborations of the performance, resembling pantomime, into which dramatic features had been introduced. Since the text here may reflect later practices and even derive from contemporary conventions, the evidence in Pollux need not be discounted.

It has proved impossible to establish with confidence the length of the lines and the extent of the loss at the right. Most suggestions for restoration can only be offered *exempli gratia*, and are presented in the notes.[7]

Fragment i

Column 1

$$]\epsilon\rho\alpha\sigma\mu\alpha \ (\quad)$$
$$].\alpha\lambda\eta.$$

Column 2

		$\tau\epsilon$-]
	$\lambda\epsilon\iota\omega\theta\hat{\eta}\nu\alpha\iota\ \mu\acute{\epsilon}\rho\sigma\varsigma\ \mu\epsilon\lambda\hat{\omega}\nu\ \pi\rho\sigma\sigma\pi\,\dot{}\,o[$	]
5	$\nu(\acute{\sigma}\mu\sigma\varsigma)\ a\mathring{v}\lambda\eta\tau\hat{\omega}\nu\ \overline{\kappa\upsilon\kappa\lambda}\,\dot{}\,\acute{\iota}\omega\nu\ [$	]
	$a\mathring{v}\lambda\eta\tau\grave{\eta}\varsigma\ \kappa\acute{\upsilon}\kappa\lambda\iota\sigma\varsigma\ a\mathring{v}\lambda\epsilon\acute{\iota}\tau\omega\ \tau\grave{\sigma}\nu\ \nu\acute{\sigma}\mu\sigma\,\overline{|\nu}.\ \dot{\epsilon}\grave{a}[\nu\ \delta\grave{\epsilon}$	]
	$\pi\alpha\rho\alpha\lambda\acute{\iota}\pi\eta\ \mu\acute{\epsilon}\rho\sigma\varsigma,\ \acute{\epsilon}\xi\alpha\theta\lambda(\acute{\sigma}\varsigma)\ \dot{\epsilon}\sigma\tau\iota.\ \overline{\dot{\epsilon}\grave{a}\nu}\ \overline{\delta\grave{\epsilon}}\ \overline{\mathring{\eta}\tau\tau\sigma}[\ ----$	]
	$[\epsilon\mathring{\iota}\sigma\alpha]\gamma\acute{a}\gamma\eta\ \mathring{\eta}\ \pi\alpha\rho\grave{a}\ \theta\acute{\upsilon}\rho\alpha\nu\ \epsilon\mathring{\iota}\sigma\acute{\epsilon}\lambda\theta\eta\ \mathring{\eta}\ \epsilon\mathring{\iota}\sigma\mu[$	]
	$[..]\ \epsilon\mathring{\iota}\sigma\kappa\sigma\mu\acute{\iota}\sigma\eta\ \tau\hat{\omega}\ \pi\rho\sigma\sigma\acute{\omega}\pi\omega\ \acute{\omega}\sigma\tau\epsilon\nu[$	]
10	$\tau\sigma\acute{\upsilon}\tau\omega\nu,\ \acute{\epsilon}\xi\alpha\theta\lambda(\acute{\sigma}\varsigma)\ \dot{\epsilon}\sigma\tau(\iota).\ \dot{\epsilon}\xi\acute{\epsilon}\sigma\tau\alpha\iota\ \delta\grave{\epsilon}\ \dot{\epsilon}\nu\ \tau\hat{\omega}\ [$	]
	$\tau\hat{\omega}\ \beta\sigma\upsilon\lambda\sigma\mu\acute{\epsilon}\nu\omega\ \sigma\upsilon\nu\epsilon\iota\sigma\acute{a}\gamma\epsilon\iota\nu\ \kappa\iota\theta\alpha\rho[\iota\sigma\tau$	$\sigma\mathring{\upsilon}\kappa$]
	$[\dot{\epsilon}\lambda]\acute{a}\tau\tau\sigma\upsilon\varsigma\ \tau\rho\iota\hat{\omega}\nu\ \mathring{\omega}\nu\ \tau\sigma\grave{\upsilon}\varsigma\ \bar{\beta}\ \kappa\omega\mu\iota\kappa[\sigma\grave{\upsilon}\varsigma$	]
	$[..]\mu\acute{\epsilon}\nu\sigma\upsilon\varsigma.\ \dot{\epsilon}\varphi'\ \acute{\sigma}\sigma\sigma\iota\varsigma\ \delta\grave{\epsilon}\ \dot{\epsilon}\tau\acute{\epsilon}\rho\sigma\iota\varsigma\ \acute{\sigma}\ \pi\upsilon\theta[\iota\kappa\grave{\sigma}\varsigma\ a\mathring{v}\lambda\eta\tau\grave{\eta}\varsigma$	$\acute{\epsilon}\xi$-]
	$[a\theta]\lambda\acute{\sigma}\varsigma\ \dot{\epsilon}\sigma\tau\iota\ \kappa\alpha\grave{\iota}\ a\mathring{\upsilon}\tau\grave{\sigma}\varsigma\ \acute{\epsilon}\sigma\tau\omega\ \mu\epsilon\sigma\acute{\sigma}\chi\sigma\rho[\sigma\varsigma$	]
15	$[.....\ \epsilon]\mathring{\iota}\sigma\acute{a}\gamma\omega\nu\ .[.]\sigma\sigma[..].. [$	]

Fragment ii

Column 1

$$].\varsigma$$

(In 17, 18 traces of two and one letter, respectively)

$$].\nu$$

20 (Trace of one letter)

$$]\kappa\alpha\varsigma$$

(in 22 trace of one letter)

[6] The terms used by Pollux are sufficiently ambiguous to suggest either the presentation by music alone of emotional states and even activities, or an accompanying dramatic miming of the action.

[7] For assistance in restoration and interpretation, I am especially grateful to J. J. Bateman, G. M. Browne, E. W. Handley, L. Koenen, G. M. Sifakis, and H. C. Youtie.

Column 2

[.] . . . . ọ . ειρα[. .]ạυτον βάλλων πληγ[ὰς   ]

    ν(όμος) κιθαριστ(ῶν) κυκλίῳ[ν   ]

25 κιθαριστὴς κύκλιος σκευὴν μὲν καὶ . . . .[   ]

    καὶ ἐξόδους κατὰ τὰ αὐτὰ τοῖς κυκλίοι[ς αὐληταῖς   ]

    ποιείσθω· κατὰ τὰ αὐτὰ δὲ [κ]α[ὶ] ἔξαθλός ἐστ[ι.   ὁ]

    ἐπὶ τῆς κιθάρας τοῖς πυθικοῖ[ς κι]θαρισταῖς ϵκ[   ]

    ηται καὶ ἐπὶ τῶν κυκλίων κιθ[α]ρ̣ιστῶν ἔ[σ]τω [ἐξ-]

30 ἔστω δὲ ἔχειν καὶ δύο τοὺς ὑ̣[πο]κιθαρ[ιστὰς   ]

    νον δ' ἐν τῷ τελευταίῳ μέρ[ει .]ονο[τελευ-]

    ταίῳ μέρει κωμικ[   ]

             ν'[   ]

.κξ[.] . .ρ̣αιο̣[

Fragment iii

35   ] .α̣χορευτω[

        ]νοικιαν διασκ̣[

        ]ι̣σται καθ' ἑκαστ[

        τελ]ε̣[υ]τ̣αίῳ μέρε[ι

        ] . . .ε̣λιον . η[

40   ] . . . .ως δε[

Fragment iv
(Traces of two letters)

TRANSLATION

Fragment i, Col. 2

. . . part of the melodies to have been completed.

Nome of the Cyclic Pipers

    Let the cyclic piper pipe the nome. But if . . . he omit a part, he is disqualified. And if he introduce (lead in ?) fewer (? –or less or worse) . . . or come in by the side door (wrong entrance ?), or bring in . . . for the actor . . . and so . . . of these, he is disqualified. And it shall be permitted in the (final part ?) for him who wishes to bring in with himself citharists (and actors ?) not less than three, of whom two (must be ?) comic . . . in order to (?) . . . And on as many counts as apply to the others, the Pythian piper is disqualified and let him be the chorus leader himself . . . bringing in . . .

Fragment ii, Col. 2

. . . raining blows.

Nome of the Cyclic Citharists

    Let the cyclic citharist, with gear (and garb ? and entrances ?) and exits perform on the same terms as the cyclic pipers. And on the same terms also he is disqualified. But if (?) . . . the one in charge of the cithara for the Pythian citharists . . ., let him also be in charge of the cyclic citharists . . . Let it be permitted for him to have also two accompanying citharists . . . and in the final part comic . . .

COMMENTARY

Traces of the ends of lines of preceding columns are preserved on both fragments i and ii. The intercolumnar space was only carelessly maintained. Where the first word of a section in column 2 is set to the left, there is no space. For example, the mark of abbreviation over alpha of line 1 extends over alpha beginning line 6; the doubtful sigma of line 16 is almost above the kappa of line 25.

1 ε̣ὐ̣ασμα( ): ε̣υ—possibly pi (Koenen). The dithyramb frequently figures in the contests, and would account for the presence of the Bacchic cry.

3–4 τε]λειωθῆναι: Youtie. An articular infinitive, one of result or purpose, or in temporal construction?

4–6 A small piece of papyrus, attached by two fibers, fell away and was lost after the first transcription, and the text it carried is marked off by dotted lines.

4 προσπο[: no compound verb offers a convincing supplement, and the possibilities for adjective or noun with the preposition are too numerous to be reckoned with.

5 αὐλητῶν κυκλίων: references to these are offered by Lucian, De salt. 2 and 26, "pipers who accompany cyclic dancers." They are cited with approval by Crato (section 2), who mentions that they are eligible to enter officially sponsored contests. We may conjecture that the music may have, on occasion, been performed as music, without dancers, as is much of our dance and ballet music.

5–6 As with μέλος, νόμος is a term of wide application. That it had specific meaning here is indicated by what follows; but we are in doubt as to precisely what the agonothetes and performers understood by it. A formalized sequence of musical patterns and action is envisaged with the assistance of a persona (an actor? or a dancer?).

7 The μέρος was either specified in the lacuna, or might have been any well-known and traditional section of the performance.

ἔξαθλ(ος): as in the scholion to Od. 21.76, explaining that the suitor is out of contention if the arrow he shoots fails to pass through the twelve axe-holes.

ἦττο[: the possibilities are: accusative neuter, singular or plural (adverbial?), or accusative masculine or feminine plural.

8 παρὰ θύραν: "beside the door," i.e., perhaps the central door; or παραθύραν, "through the side door." The opposition between κατὰ ("right") and παρὰ ("wrong") may give this the sense of "enter by the wrong door." Of interest is Demosthenes' complaint, *Against Meidias* 17, citing Meidias' harassment of Demosthenes as chorus-leader: "blocking the side-wings, a private citizen nailing up public property." (Bateman) The purpose appears to have been to force the chorus to come in by other than their normal entrance, the *paraskēnia*.

εἰσμ[: εἰς μ[έσον? (Handley). Perhaps it was followed by μή.

9 τῷ προσώπῳ: in nine instances elsewhere no iota adscript is indicated in the text, and the dual is extremely unlikely here.

ὥστεν[: ὥστε ν[or ὥστ' ἐν [.

At the end of the line perhaps καὶ ἀπὸ], ". . . *also because of* these . . .' (Sifakis).

10 τούτων: a partitive genitive, or after a preposition (cf. preceding note) or controlled by a verb?

ἐν τῷ [: cf. 31 ἐν τῷ τελευταίῳ μέρ[ει, and also 32.

12–13 [. .]μένους: context suggests a future participle, indicating the function of the ancillary performers; for the presence of added musicians, see line 30. An assumption that these were "comic" is startling, since the aulos was characteristically associated with comic dances and action. Conceivably the lacuna may have specified the number of citharists, followed by, e.g., (line 11) καὶ ὑποκριτὰς οὐκ [ἐλ]άττους with the participle modifying the latter, or κιθαρ[ιστὴν καὶ χορευτὰς οὐκ κτλ. Either conjecture would avoid the unexampled concept of "comic citharists."

13 ὁ πυθ[ικὸς: the Pythian nome was performed by pipers as well as by citharists: Strabo 9.3.10 and Pollux 4.84.

14 μεσόχορ[ος: the central position of the flute player in dithyrambic and cyclic choruses is attested very early; see Pickard-Cambridge, *Dithyramb, Tragedy, Comedy* (1962) 35: "The flute player . . . stood in the midst of the dancers," and footnote 2: "in circular choruses the flute player stood in the middle." The term present here came into use rather late, but is found in a Delphic inscription of the second century B.C.— *Fouilles de Delphes* 3 (1) No. 219, p. 126, and is regarded as equivalent to the πρωτόχορος noted by Foucart, *Rev. Phil.* 22 (1903) 223. The meaning is plainly *coryphaeus* ("chorus leader"), and even Pliny's use of the term (*Ep.* 2.14) is not as far from this meaning as the mention in *Fouilles* would indicate. The *Thes.Ling.Lat.* cites four instances much later than Pliny.

In Greek usage, D. M. Pippidi, "Album agonistique d'Istros," *BCH* 84 (1960) 434–458, notes several instances of the term and its companion verb in the mid-second and early third century of our era in inscriptions from the Koinon of the Pentapolis. Without specific evidence, Pippidi would regard the function of the dignitary as the recruitment and training of choruses, as well as directing the performances.

The dubious term μουσόχορος (see *LSJ*[9] s.v. and Addenda) is ruled out by the context here.

23 [. .]αυτον:]κλυτον is also possible.

βάλλων: may refer to percussion of the heavier (higher, in ancient terminology) strings (Bateman). Otherwise it might fit a comic context.

25 σκευήν: a term which covers any type of gear or equipment for a performance; καὶ στολήν may have been the second element. παρόδους, balancing ἐξόδους, probably stood at the end of the line. The sense might be "entrance and exit melodies." In the lacuna there may have been an intervening ἔχων, or ἐχόμενος, controlling the initial accusatives.

27 ὁ]: (Browne)—to accommodate the following prepositional phrase: "the one in charge of the cithara for the Pythian citharists." Otherwise, ἐπί with the genitive is extremely difficult to construe.

29 ηται: apparently reveals the subjunctive of another vivid future condition, as in 6–7 and following. Therefore, ἐὰν δέ probably stood in the lacuna, line 27.

καὶ ἐπὶ κτλ. : to indicate the extension of his supervision, or his judgment on conformity with the rules, to the cyclic performers? (Koenen)

30 ὑ[πο]κιθαρ[ιστάς: the noun has no parallel, but the verb (see *LSJ* s.v.) offers a firm base for the noun, which better accords with the structure here.

31–32 It is very difficult to determine whether or not a new section begins here. Uncertainty arises from the careless maintenance of line spacing and straightness, and the irregularity of intercolumnar space which is mentioned above at the beginning of the commentary. The nu of 33 is very doubtful, and the protrusion into the margin of the illegible letter and the kappa of 34 cannot be guaranteed. They may belong to the preceding column. In addition, the very dubious reading of 34 offers no discernible sense.

35 α: either the last letter of a numeral with "of dancers," or "of (performances) without dancers."

38 The reading is decisively influenced by 31 and 32.

University of Michigan

*P.Mich.*inv. 4682

11

Two Literary Papyri in an Archive from Panopolis

WILLIAM H. WILLIS

To the XIV International Congress of Papyrologists at Oxford in 1974 Professor G. M. Browne[1] and I in uncoordinated papers announced the separate acquisition by the University of Cologne and Duke University of papyri constituting an archive of documents deriving from an important family in Panopolis spanning the last decade of the third century and the first half of the fourth. Certain documents in fact were shared between the two collections. It was at once clear that the Cologne group and the Duke group derived from the same find, made apparently in Achmîm in the 1960's, though they traveled by separate routes through different dealers to their present homes. To Cologne had fallen some 30 papyri, mostly larger in size, while Duke's share comprised some 500 fragments, including a dozen texts of significant size, but mostly very small bits requiring reassembly, which by joins have now been reduced to about 150.

Through the statesmanship of Professor Ludwig Koenen it was arranged that the two collections would exchange lesser fragments in order that all parts of each divided document might be reunited in either of the two collections. This procedure is still in progress. But when Professors Koenen, Browne, John Oates and I spread the two groups side by side at the Duke Library during a memorable week in November 1975, it became clear that substantial parts of most of our documents are still missing, and are likely to have found their way elsewhere. We wish therefore to acquaint our papyrological colleagues everywhere with the existence and character of the archive and to enlist their aid in recognizing and reporting any other parts of it which may emerge.

So far as we have as yet ascertained, the new archive, though embracing

---

[1] G. M. Browne, "A Panegyrist from Panopolis," in *Proceedings of the XIV Int. Congress of Papyrologists* (E.E.S. Graeco-Roman Memoirs 61; London, 1975) 29–33.

the same period, has no connection with the Youtie–Hagedorn *Papyri from Panopolis*,[2] nor (except for sharing a few names) with *P.Panopolis-Beatty*[3] nor the Panopolite city register published by Martin[4] and Borkowski[5]; and the Panopolis documents at Vienna being edited by P. J. Sijpesteijn are of a quite different date, a century earlier. The Duke–Cologne archive comprises the papers of Aurelius Ammon son of Petearbeschinis, who styles himself "Scholasticus of Panopolis." They include some papers of his father Aurelius Petearbeschinis, son of Horós, priest of the first-ranked temples of Panopolis; of Petearbeschinis' first wife Senpasis, a priestess, and of his second wife, Senpetechensis, apparently not a priestess; of Ammon's older half-brother Horion, the *archiprophetes* of the Panopolite nome; and of other relatives and connections, perhaps including Ammon's full brother Harpocration, who has pursued an extended career abroad— in Greece, Rome and Constantinople—as panegyrist to the emperors and as an *epitropos* and *logistes* in Greece. The family was wealthy, educated and distinguished, apparently leading members of the pagan Thebaid metropolis at a time when Christianity was rising there.[6]

The earliest dated documents preserved in the archive are three concerning the sale of part of a house and land to Senpasis, which she registered with the *bibliotheke enkteseon* of Panopolis in A.D. 289; these three Cologne papyri (to which Duke contributed two fragments), have now been published by Professor Browne.[7] Next in sequence is a large but incomplete *apographe* at Duke filed by the *archiprophetes* Horion in 299 for his tithe of all temple properties in the nome, in response to the first census ordered by Diocletian in 297. This is followed, again in the Duke collection, by a fragmentary roll containing a series of six returns filed in 303 by Petearbeschinis and his second wife Senpetechensis. There is the merest fragment of one such return filed in 308, together with undatable small fragments of other returns. A receipt at Duke is dated 326. Duke possesses an extraordinarily long but incomplete and undatable letter, the last five columns

[2] L. C. Youtie, D. Hagedorn, H. C. Youtie, "Urkunden aus Panopolis," *ZPE* 7 (1971) 1–40, 8 (1971) 207–234, 10 (1973) 101–170.

[3] *Papyri from Panopolis in the Chester Beatty Library Dublin*, ed. T. C. Skeat (Dublin, 1964).

[4] V. Martin, "Relevé topographique des immeubles d'une métropole," *Recherches de Papyrologie* 2 (1962) 37–73.

[5] Z. Borkowski, *Une description topographique des immeubles à Panopolis* (Warsaw, 1975).

[6] For an illuminating account of Panopolitans of similar status in the following century see Alan Cameron, "Wandering Poets: a Literary Movement in Byzantine Egypt," *Historia* 14 (1965) 470–509.

[7] G. M. Browne, "Property Belonging to Aurelia Senpasis and Aurelius Petearbeschinis," in *Collectanea Papyrologica* (Festschrift Youtie) II (Pap. Texte u. Abh. 20; Bonn, 1976) 489–500 = *P. Coll. Youtie* 71–73.

of a rhetorically elaborate account written to his mother by one of the sons (probably Ammon but possibly Harpocration himself) reporting on his efforts to secure for his nephew the son of Horion, who is now dead, the *propheteia* of Panopolis, despite the opposition of the high priest. A number of other undatable fragmentary documents, especially petitions written by Ammon, must derive from the last two decades of the archive.

The latest dated document is an affidavit by Ammon on 9 December 348 addressed to the *catholicus* Flavius Sisinnius, edited by Professor Browne.[8] This is one of a series of petitions and drafts of petitions, some at Cologne, others at Duke, written in Ammon's own hand in preparation for his case before the *catholicus* asserting his right to inherit the slaves of his brother Harpocration, who has died abroad intestate, a right hotly contested by a certain Eugeneios son of Menoraphis. How the case was decided, and whether other fragmentary petitions by Ammon on behalf of his clients are to be dated later than 348, we do not know.

Among Ammon's papers at Duke are found two broken papyri of an altogether different sort, literary fragments each assembled from several smaller pieces but each remaining quite incomplete. It is these which I wish to present here, not because they may be as interesting as some of the documentary texts in the archive, but rather because in archives it is rare to find literary texts and unusual for literary papyri to have ascertainable provenience and context. Besides, their character may throw some additional light on the personality of their owner Ammon. And most importantly, each presents problems in need of solution.

The first of the two texts (*P.Duk.*inv. G 176; see Plate I) is a fragment of *Odyssey* 9, bearing on one side the ends of lines 298–309 and on the other the beginnings of lines 344–384. No literary papyrus was ever easier to identify, for the 4th and 22nd lines of the verso begin Κύκλωψ, and lines 24 and 27 name Οὖτις. As much text as survives offers no surprises, for, as the apparatus attests, it is a properly written copy of the vulgate, except that the scribe has added a *nu*-movable at the end of 9.301 and has written line 354 twice. At 9.302 our text reads ἔρ]υκε[ν], which modern editors prefer, against ἀνῆκεν given by a few MSS., the *Etymologicum Magnum* and some scholia. In the eight lines in which it overlaps the only other published papyrus containing this part of Book 9, it is in complete agreement with the Jouguet Papyrus[9] of the third century B.C. In line 370 apparently the scribe himself corrected his omission of *delta* by inserting it in place just

8 G. M. Browne, "Harpocration Panegyrista," *Illinois Classical Studies* 2 (1976) 184–196.

9 Pack² 1081 = O. Guéraud, "Un nouveau papyrus de l'Odyssée," *Revue de l'Égypte Ancienne* 1 (1927) 80–130. The text of Pack² 1082 (*P.Oxy.* XI 1396, now *P.Princ.* A.M. 9049) remains unpublished.

under the line; and the *iota* added to τῆ in line 347, though omitted by modern editors,[10] is commonplace in other Homeric papyri and manuscripts. Otherwise the text, as far as it goes, is unexceptionable.

1. *Odyssey* 9.298–309, 344–384

*P.Duk.*inv. G 176 (papyrus codex ca. 16.5 × 29.5 cm.) 4.8 × 22.0. Panopolis, III cent.

	recto ↓		verso →	
		1	cὺν [δ᾽ ὅ γε	
		2	καὶ τό[τ᾽ ἐγὼ	345
		3	κι[c]cύ[βιον μετὰ	
		4	Κύκλωψ, τῆι, π[ίε οἶνον	
		5	ὄφρ᾽ εἰδῆιc οἷόν [τι ποτὸν	
295	]..	6	ἡμετέρη· coὶ δ[᾽ αὖ λοιβὴν	
	]..	7	οἴκαδε πέμψεια[c· cὺ δὲ	350
	]..	8	cχέτλιε, πῶc κέ[ν τίc cε	
	μῆλ]ων	9	ἀνθρώπων πολ[έων;	
	μεγαλήτορ]α θυμὸν	10	ὡc ἐφάμην, ὁ δὲ [δέκτο	
300	παρὰ] μηροῦ	11	ἡδὺ ποτὸν πίν[ων καὶ	354
	ἧπα]ρ ἔχουcιν	12	ἡδὺ ποτὸν πίν[	354 bis
	ἔρ]υκε[ν]	13	δόc μοι ἔτι πρ[όφρων	355
	ὄλεθ]ρον	14	αὐτίκα νῦν, ἵνα [τοι δῶ	
	]..	15	καὶ γὰρ Κυκλώπ[εccι φέρει	
305	προcέθη]κεν	16	οἶνον ἐριcτάφυ[λον, καί cφιν	
	δῖ]αν	17	ἀλλὰ τό[δ᾽ ἀ]μβρ[οcίηc	
	]	18	[ὡc ἔφατ᾽· αὐτάρ	360
	]	19	τρὶc μ[ὲν] ἔδ[ωκα	
309	ἑκάcτ]ηι	20	αὐτὰρ ἐπεὶ Κύ[κλωπα	
		21	καὶ τότε δή μ[ιν ἔπεccι	
		22	Κύκλωψ, εἰρω[τᾷc μ᾽ ὄνομα	
		23	ἐξερέω· cὺ δ[έ μοι δὸc	365
		24	Οὖτιc ἐμοί γ[᾽] ὄ[νομα·	
		25	μήτηρ ἠδὲ [πατὴρ	
		26	ὡc ἐφάμην, [ὁ δέ μ᾽ αὐτίκ᾽	
		27	Οὖτιν ἐγὼ π[ύματον ἔδομαι	
		28	τοὺc ‚δ‚ ἄλλουc [πρόcθεν	370
		29	ἦ, κ[αὶ ἀνακλινθεὶc	
		30	κεῖ[τ᾽ ἀποδοχμώcαc	
		31	ἦρει π[ανδαμάτωρ·	
		32	ψωμ[οί τ᾽ ἀνδρόμεοι·	
		33	καὶ τό[τ᾽ ἐγὼ	375

301 ἔχουcι codd. 302 ἔρυκε(ν) codd. plur., schol. BT B 5, Z 524: ἀνῆκεν Paris. 2894, schol. AB A 173, Et.Mag. 458.15. 347 τῆ codd. nonnulli: τῇ codd. plur., Apoll.Soph., Herod., edd. 348 οφρ᾽ ειδηιc pap., ὄφρ᾽ εἰδῆιc codd., Ludwich: ὄφρα ἰδῇc Allen. 351 ἄν codd. pauci, Eust.: κέν codd. complur., edd. 353 δ᾽ ἔδεκτο codd. pauci: δὲ ἔδεκτο schol.: δὲ δέκτο codd. complur. 354 bis dittogr. 370 τοὺc δ᾽ ἄλλουc codd., edd.

[10] See the editions of A. Ludwich, T. W. Allen and P. Von der Mühll *ad loc.*, and LSJ *s.v.* τῆ at end.

34   εἴω[ς θερμαίνοιτο·
35   θάρςυ[νον, μή τίς μοι
36   ἀλ[λ’ ὅτε δὴ
37   ἄψε[ςθαι, χλωρός
38   καὶ τ[ότ’ ἐγὼν   380
39   ἵςτα[ντ’· αὐτὰρ
40   οἱ μ[ὲν μοχλὸν
41   ὀφθ[αλμῷ ἐνέρειςαν·
42   δίν[εον, ὡς ὅτε τις

- - - - - - - - - -   - - - - - - - - - - -

376 εἴως codd., Ludwich: εἶος, ἦος corr. edd. plur.   379 ἄψαςθαι codd. nonnulli: ἄψεςθαι P³¹
(Pack² 1081), codd. plur.

The format and date of the fragment are questions of some interest. On
the side bearing horizontal fibres the text preserved (Od. 9.344–84) is sharp
and clear, running from a top margin of 1.5 cm. down a left margin of
2.0 cm. (steadily increasing to 2.7 at the foot) along what appears to be
the original left edge of the papyrus; the fragment breaks off at the forty-
second line. The side with vertical fibres is badly abraded, preserving only
a few letters and scattered traces of ink near the middle of its height. The
discernible letters are of the same size and form, spaced at the same line-
intervals, as those of the text on the other side, thus suggesting a codex
rather than a roll. But only four consecutive letters are clear and certain—
YCIN. Within the hundred lines of Odyssey 9 immediately preceding and
following the text overleaf, the sequence -υςιν occurs only in the middle of
line 421 (εἴ τιν’ ἑταίροιςιν θανάτου λύςιν ἠδ’ ἐμοὶ αὐτῶι) and at the end
of line 301 (οὐτάμεναι πρὸς ςτῆθος, ὅθι φρένες ἧπαρ ἔχουςι) if the scribe’s
addition of an otiose nu-movable be allowed. Line 421 would require for
its last three words more space than the papyrus affords; and the traces of
ink above and below -υςιν do not conform to words in the lines immediately
preceding and following line 421. If we assume ἔχουςιν in line 301, however, all other traces of ink fall neatly into place in the surrounding passage,
and we are enabled to read with some confidence other words faintly
preserved.

We have, then, part of a codex leaf whose recto with vertical fibres
precedes its verso with horizontal fibres. The interval between corresponding points on recto and verso would accommodate 54 lines of text, a rather
large number per page. Extrapolating from the preserved height and
width and allowing for margins all round,[11] we may estimate an original

[11] I calculate the average length of line at slightly less than 12 cm. The preserved top
margin of the verso is 1.2 cm.; the left margin progresses from 2.0 to 2.7 cm. I assume a
bottom margin of 2 cm., a right margin averaging 2.5 cm. Forty preserved lines on the
verso occupy a height of 19.4 cm.; 54 lines would thus require 26.2 cm.

page size of ca. 16.5 × 29.5 cm.—a codex nearly twice as tall as wide. At 108 lines per leaf, Book 9 would have required only five leaves and a fractional page, and 112 such leaves would accommodate the entire *Odyssey*.

Other codices of similar dimensions are known, as Eric Turner has shown in his papers at the Marburg and Oxford congresses.[12] This format falls within his Marburg Group 6, most members of which are assigned by palaeography to the third and fourth centuries. Two of them, like ours, offer a large number of lines per page; both are *Iliads* (*PSI* II 140 [15 × 28 cm.] with 63 lines, *PSI* X 1169 [15 × 29 cm.] with 59 lines), written in a sloping hand characteristic of the third century. In his Oxford paper Turner has compiled a useful list of two dozen papyrus codices of tall format, all dated to the second and third centuries, most of which have 50 or more lines to the page; six contain the *Iliad*, two more Hesiod's *Theogony*. Of the thirteen of which photographs have been published, only one (*P.Mert.* I 3, an *Iliad* leaf 13.7 × [32.5] cm.) bears a hand at all resembling ours—a small, sharp, irregular capital, dated by Bell and Roberts to the third century; and it also has 54 lines to the page.

The hand of Ammon's *Odyssey* is written in tiny upright oval capitals, sharp and clear in black ink, nearly always bilinear, formal though irregular and occasionally ligatured. The only diacritical mark preserved is an apostrophe indicating elision at verso line 5; opposite verso lines 38–40 is the faint trace of a sort of coronis. I have not succeeded in finding a close parallel to the hand: that of the Merton *Iliad* is not bilinear and is even less regular, though none seems closer. Two noteworthy peculiarities of our hand, the tall narrow *omicron*, which sometimes forms a point at the bottom or even a chiasmus, and an occasionally exuberant *kappa* the lower oblique stroke of which swings below the line, are both paralleled in the Oxyrhynchus fragment of Menander's *Kolax* (*P.Oxy.* III 409; plates II and III), which Grenfell and Hunt assigned to the mid-second century. Regrettably, few photographs have been published of the early papyrus codices listed and classified by Turner, especially of the tall copies of Homer and Hesiod. Hesitantly, therefore, I should assign Ammon's *Odyssey* to the first half of the third century, and attribute to Ammon the possession of a copy written a century earlier than his own time.

Finally we come to the second of Ammon's two "literary" texts (*P.Duk.*inv. G 178; see Plate II). About it we can have hardly any question

---

[12] E. G. Turner, "Some Questions about the Typology of the Codex," in *Akten des XIII. Int. Papyrologenkongresses* (*Münchener Beiträge* 66 [1974]) 427–438; "Early Papyrus Codices of Large Size," in *Proceedings of the XIV Int. Congress of Papyrologists* (London, 1975) 309–312.

of date, for it is written in Ammon's own hand—the large rough informal hand, using dark brown ink, in which he wrote also the several drafts of petitions preserved in both the Cologne and Duke collections, not the more elegant hand he used in documents intended for eyes other than his own. Even without the dated record of his activities in the 340's, we should have assigned this hand to the mid-fourth century.

2. List of Philosophers

P.*Duk*.inv. G 178   9.7 × 18.1 cm.   Panopolis, IV cent.

col. i		col. ii	
1	].[ ]..[	1	Σπεύcιππ[ος Ἀθηναῖος
2	Ἀναξιμέ]νης Μιλήc(ιος)	2	Πλάτων[ος ἀδελφιδοῦς
3	Ἀναξαγόρα]ς ἐκ Κλαζο-	3	Ξενοκράτης [Χαλκηδόνιος
4	]μενῶν	4	Πολέμων 'Ạ[θηναῖος
5	Ἀρχέλαο]ς Ἀθηναῖος	5	Ἀρκεcίλαọς [ἐκ Πιτάνης
6	Φερεκύδ]ης Σύριος	6	Καρνεάδης [Κυρηναῖος
7	Παρμεν]ίδης 'Ελεά[τη]ς	7	Ἀκαδημ[ίας μέcης ?
8	Διογένης ἐξ Ἀπολλω]νίας	8	Κλιτόμαχο[ς Καρχηδόνιος
		9	Φίλ{ι}ων ẹ̓[κ Λαρίccης
		10	Ἀ]ṿτίοχ[ο]ς̣ [Ἀcκαλώνιος
		11	.φωṿαρχηγ[
		12	τρ[ί]της 'Ακαδ[ημίας
		13	Κυνικοί [
		14	Διογ]ένης ὁ Σ[ι]ṿωπ[εύ]ς
		15	Μό]νιμος ἀπὸ δουλίας
		16	Κ]ράτης Βοιώτιọς̣
		17	Περι]πατητικοί
		18	Ἀ]ρ̣ιστοτέḷης Σταγειρίτ(ης)
		19	Θεό]φ̣[ρ]ạστος "Ịων
		20	Στρά]των ἐκ Λαμψάκου
		21	Πραξιφ]άνης ['Ρ]όδιος
		22	Κριτόλ]αος Φα[c]ηλίτης
		23	Στωι]κοὶ μες.[]... Κυṿικ( )
		24	Ζ]ήνωṿ .[
			(Margin)

It is a list of Greek philosophers. Originally it must have contained three narrow columns, the first listing the Presocratics, the second the succession of Academics, Cynics and Peripatetics; and no doubt there was a third column, now missing, to list Stoics and Epicureans and perhaps others. While column ii retains part of its lower margin and most of its height, at least one line is lost at the top along with the top margin, and possibly two (or more) if Ammon inscribed a comprehensive title. If we assume two lines and a margin of a centimeter, and a third column but no more, the original sheet would have been approximately square, measuring about 21 × 21 cm. The sheet was folded vertically into six panels apparently, of which the top part of the second, most of the third, and the lower part of the fourth have survived.

So far as I have been able to ascertain, Ammon's *philosophorum index* is unique, in that its sole purpose appears to be to list the principal philosophers (each with his *polis*) in teacher-pupil sequence, and from the Academy onward by school, citing only those who were appointed heads of each school. The list of Academics ends with Antiochus, who died in 68 B.C.; of Cynics with Crates, to 285 B.C.; and of Peripatetics with Critolaus, in the second century B.C. The only other list of philosophers (and of physicians) among the papyri is *P.Vars.*inv. 5 (Pack² 2088) dated to the third century; but that is the catalogue of a library, and its purpose is to record the number of rolls by each author held. The two so-called *indices philosophorum* among the fragmentary Herculanean rolls[13] are doxographical histories of the Academy and the Stoa, respectively, in scope and detail somewhat resembling Diogenes Laertius; only at the ends of biographies of principal figures are found lists of names (with ethnics) of their minor students. Laertius remains our only extant full example of this genre, since the worthier predecessors whom he mentions as sources (e.g., the φιλοσόφων διαδοχαί of Hermippus, Hieronymus of Rhodes and Hippobotus of the third century B.C., Antisthenes of Rhodes, Sosicrates and Sotion of the second) all have perished. Sextus Empiricus in his more scholarly and extensive Πυρρώνειοι ὑποτυπώσεις and *Adversus Mathematicos* now and again mentions most of Ammon's philosophers but only to defend Skeptic doctrines against their own.

Somewhat closer in spirit to Ammon's index are the later doxographers collected by Hermann Diels in *Doxographi Graeci*. But these too were composed to summarize doctrines, *placita*, however briefly. Nevertheless they are useful in providing some parallels to the sequence of personalities in Ammon's list. None, however, presents the schools in precisely the same order, nor did Diogenes Laertius:

LAERTIUS	AETIUS	GALEN	HIPPOLYTUS	EPIPHANIUS	AMMON
Sages	Presocratics	Milesians	Presocratics	Presocratics	Presocratics
Milesians	Plato	Academy	Plato	Plato	?

[13] For *P.Herc.* 1018, often cited as "Index Stoicorum," see D. Comparetti, *Papiro Ercolanese inedito* (Turin, 1875); for *P.Herc.* 1021 see the edition of S. Mekler, *Academicorum Philosophorum Index Herculanensis* (Berlin, 1902).

Socratics	Aristotle	Cynics	Aristotle	Cyreneans	Academy
Academy	Zeno	Stoics	Stoics	Cynics	Cynics
Peripatetics		Socratics	Epicurus	Middle Academy	Peripatetics
Cynics		Peripatetics	Pyrrho	Peripatetics	Stoics?
Stoics		Presocratics		Stoics	?
Presocratics		Skeptics		Epicurus	
Epicurus		Epicureans			

Column i doubtless listed the Presocratics, beginning with Thales; our first line no doubt contained Ἀναξίμανδρος Μιλήσιος, within which the three surviving dots of ink could fit almost anywhere. The first three Milesian philosophers would have been given in the traditional order, then, followed by Anaxagoras, the only early candidate from Clazomenae, whom "some" named as a pupil of Anaximenes and the teacher of Archelaus of Athens, whom in turn some doxographers list as a teacher of Socrates.

In line 6 Pherecydes comes as a surprise, but as an early cosmogonist and as an alleged contemporary and possible "pupil" of Anaximander, he is the only candidate from Syros. We have no testimony that he taught Parmenides—rather Pythagoras or Heracleitus, depending on one's doxographer. At this point the list might have progressed in any one of several directions: the *De Placitis*[14] proceeded directly to Pythagoras, then Heracleitus, Xenophanes, the Atomists and Empedocles, omitting Parmenides since he was not concerned with material *archae*; the fragments of Galen's Περὶ φιλοσόφου ἱστορίας skip directly from Archelaus to Socrates and the Academy, returning separately to the Presocratics. But Hippolytus, who inserted Pythagoras, Empedocles and Heracleitus between Thales and Anaximander, gives Parmenides next after Anaximenes, Anaxagoras and Archelaus almost in our order, before going on to Leucippus. Closest to our list is the Ἑλλήνων διαφοραί of Epiphanius, the Palestinian Christian monk and bishop in the generation following Ammon, bitter foe of Hellenic education and so of Origen and John Chrysostom.[15] Through Parmenides his list of targets contains the same names in the same order as ours, except that he inserted Socrates after Archelaus and Pythagoras and Xenophanes after Pherecydes.

At any rate Elea and the traces of ink in line 7 seem to guarantee Parmenides, and I can find no other suitable candidate for line 8 from a city ending in -ία but Diogenes of Apollonia, whom "some" named as a

[14] For "Aetius," *De Placitis* see H. Diels, *Doxographi Graeci*[2] (Berlin & Leipzig, 1929) 276–289; for Galen, Περὶ φιλοσόφου ἱστορίας, pp. 599–601; for Hippolytus, *Refutatio omnium haeresium*, pp. 553–564.

[15] For Epiphanius' list see Diels, *Dox.Graec.* pp. 587–593; for his life see Jülicher in *RE* 6 (1907) 193 f., *s.n.* Epiphanius 3.

pupil of Anaximenes, a younger contemporary of Anaxagoras who shared his doctrine of *Nous*. In the remainder of column i there will have been room for other Eleatics, Pythagoras and some of his followers, Xenophanes, Empedocles and Heracleitus, the Atomists and Socrates. A minimal list of these would leave space for four or five others.

Presumably the line preceding the first preserved line of column ii contained the name of Plato as founder of the Academy. My supplements in this column are of course *exempli gratia*, after the analogy of column i. Nobody will object to Speusippus, Xenocrates and Polemon in the straight line of succession of *archegoi* in the Old Academy, though after Polemon, Krates of Athens is omitted; also omitted is Crantor of Soli, named by most doxographers though he was never *archegos*. Arcesilaus is credited by Galen and Laertius with founding the Middle Academy; and Carneades is said by Galen (Lacydes by Laertius) to have begun the New Academy. The only *paragraphus* interrupting the sequence of Academics in our text, however, separates Arcesilaus and Carneades, and the list of Academics ends at line 12 with clear reference to the "Third Academy," whose founder is not specified. There is no sign of recognizing Philo of Larissa as head of a "fourth Academy" or Antiochus of Ascalon of a "fifth," to which Sextus Empiricus (*Pyr.* 1.220–21) says that "some" authorities attributed them; of such authorities we possess only Galen (*Phil. Hist.* 3.227). Ammon seems to know only three Academies, so that in line 7 I suggest μέϲηϲ (or δευτέραϲ) for Carneades. In line 9 Ammon makes his only error by misspelling Philo *ΦΙΛΙΩΝ*: surely Philo of Larissa is meant.

Line 11 might be of great interest if it could be confidently read. Traces of ink protruding into the left margin may represent the final letter of a line lost in col. i (cf. col. i 8) or the first letter of the line in col. ii. If the latter, an apparent ligature curves downward as if from *sigma* or *upsilon*, very doubtfully *epsilon* or *alpha*. The descending hasta of the second letter is characteristic in this hand only of *iota, rho, phi* and *psi*, but not *tau*. Of the final letter the surviving stroke would conform to *gamma, eta, iota* or *nu*. Professor Jean Bingen astutely suggests as a possibility ἐφ' ὧν ἀρχὴ γ[ίνεται] τρ[ί]τηϲ Ἀκαδ[ημίαϲ], "in whose hands was the governance of the Third Academy." This may be right, but is open to the objection that nowhere else does the list offer a verb or syntactical clause.

After another *paragraphus* we begin the Cynics. Line 14 hasn't room for Antisthenes, but Diogenes would fit the traces. Monimos of Syracuse is a name rarely met, though he is mentioned by Menander (fr. 215 K.) and taken seriously by Sextus Empiricus (*adv. Math.* 7.48, 88; 8.5). He is remembered by none of the doxographers in Diels' collection, but Diogenes Laertius (6.82 f.) cites Sosicrates to the effect that he was a pupil of

Diogenes the Cynic, and was once in service to a Corinthian banker until he feigned madness and was dismissed—whence no doubt Ammon's phrase ἀπὸ δουλίας. He is credited with two books Περὶ ὁρμῶν and a *Protrepticus*. Of Diels' doxographers only Epiphanius mentions Crates, next after Diogenes, where he is styled ἀπὸ Θηβῶν. This Crates was a teacher of Zeno the Stoic (D.L. 7.4), one of whose books was entitled Κράτητος Ἀπομνημονεύματα.

To the Peripatetics Ammon gives rather short shrift. Theophrastus is identified not as 'Ερέcιοc from his home city on Lesbos but as "Ιων, if I have read the line correctly. If Ammon thought of all Aegean islands as Ionian, one might have expected the more ordinary 'Ιώνιοc. He has omitted such notables as Lycon and Ariston but has included the less well known Praxiphanes of Rhodes. Diogenes Laertius (10.13) quotes Apollodorus' *Chronica* as saying that Praxiphanes was one of the teachers of Epicurus, though Epicurus denied it. At any rate, the only one of Diels' doxographers who mentions him is again Epiphanius, who gives precisely the same list of five Peripatetics in precisely the same order. Immediately afterward Epiphanius goes on to list Ζήνων ὁ Κιτιεὺc ὁ Στωικόc, then a succession of seven other Stoics before arriving at Epicurus.

At line 23 we have a subtitle by which, with line 24, I am baffled. Zeno and the Stoics should come next, and only Στωι]κοὶ would seem to fit the space. But μεc .[seems to follow, and we might force the faint traces after that to yield a reading of the line as Στωι]κοὶ μέcο[ι] καὶ Κυνικ(οί)—but this cannot be right, for we are hardly ready for the Middle Stoa—which should begin with Ariston of Chios. The only convincing word is Κυνικ( ), and the Cynics are often associated with the Stoics; but we have had the Cynics already in lines 13–16. Moreover, the]ηνων of line 24 would seem to require Ζ]ήνων, although his name would be unexpectedly indented, like that of Plato (in line 2) who we assumed had already been mentioned two lines before. To be sure, Zeno followed Critolaus in Epiphanius' diatribe, but only there; and Zeno can hardly be called a "middle Stoic."

Ammon's index breaks off with a puzzle. Equally puzzling is the source from which he derived it. Clearly he is following a doxographical tradition, but one differing at points from all the traditions attested in earlier and contemporary sources. In selection and order of names Epiphanius offers the closest parallel, though he does not designate the schools. Epiphanius became bishop of Constantia in Cyprus in 367, some 20 years after Ammon's attested activity, and is believed to have composed his *Panarion* 10 years still later. If Ammon were still alive then, he would have been very old; and in any case we could hardly imagine the proud *scholasticus* of Panopolis, scion of the rich and educated family of priests of the old gods, to learn his Greek philosophers from a hostile Christian monk from Judaea. We may suspect that Ammon and Epiphanius drew their lists from a common source, one current in the third or early fourth century. While Epiphanius made use of his source to attack the Greek philosophical tradition, we may be sure that Ammon's sentiment in constructing and preserving his list was quite the opposite. It may, indeed, represent not an index extracted from a single contemporary doxography but rather his own effort to organize his recollections of the tradition he had acquired in a local school at Panopolis.

In the draft of a Cologne petition addressed to the *catholicus*,[16] Ammon the Scholasticus describes himself in the eloquent phrase ἡϲυχίαν τοίνυν ἀπράγμονα τοῖϲ ἐν φιλοϲοφίαι καὶ λόγοιϲ ἀνηγμένοιϲ πρέπειν καὶ αὐτὸϲ ἐπιϲτάμενοϲ—"since I myself too know that a quiet life free from intrigue befits those educated in philosophy and rhetoric." In a letter at Duke, Ammon introduces himself to the *catholicus* with the same phrase. The hypomnematic list before us at least attests his private concern to keep the philosophers straight, and may indicate that his interest in philosophy was something more than the gilded phrase in his letter.

Duke University

16 Browne, *op. cit.* (*supra* n. 8) 193 and n. 32.

P.Duk.inv. G 176

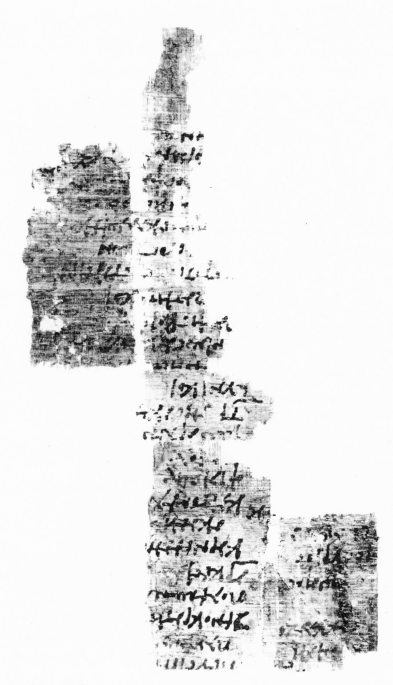

P.Duk.inv. G 178

12

Augustine and Manichaeism in Light of the Cologne Mani Codex[1]

LUDWIG KOENEN

I. The Importance of Augustine's Manichaean Period for his Discovery of the Greek Concept of Free Will

Man is the master of his fate. The thought is a cornerstone of the intellectual traditions which led to the development of western technology, civilization, and culture. Already in the Odyssey Zeus declares that, in addition to that assigned by the gods, man brings misery upon himself beyond fate.[2] Solon

---

[1] Paper read at the Papyrological Symposium in April 1976 at Urbana, Illinois. Earlier versions were read at the meeting of the Mommsengesellschaft at Bochum in 1972 (cf. K. Rudolph, *Mélanges d'hist. des rel. off. à H.-Ch.Puech* [Vendôme, 1974] 480 n. o and 483 n. 2) and at the Universities of Amsterdam (1973) and Cologne (1975). The texts quoted from the Cologne Mani Codex (*CMC*) are taken from the edition (pp. 1–72: A. Henrichs, L. Koenen, *ZPE* 19 [1975] 1–85; the next instalment [pp. 72–99] is scheduled to come out in 1977; the rest is in preparation; cf. *ZPE* 5 [1970] 97–216). I am particularly indebted to A. Henrichs, my editorial "twin," further to K. Rudolph and to R. W. Daniel; the latter improved the English of this version considerably.

[2] α 33. The passage marks a decisive change in human thought. In the rest of the Homeric epos we find the older view that fate and the gods are responsible for man's deeds and misery; the Homeric hero was not aware of man's freedom of decision and choice. Priamos, e.g., addresses Helena: οὔ τί μοι αἰτίη ἐσσί, θεοί νύ μοι αἴτιοί εἰσιν (Γ 164; cf. T 86 f. 409 f.; Φ 275 f.; α 347 ff.; λ 558 ff.; hymn to Dem. 77 ff.). See Ch. Voigt, *Überlegung und Entscheidung, Studien zur Selbstauffassung des Menschen bei Homer*, Beiträge z. klass. Phil. 48 (Meisenheim, 1972) (reprint of the dissertation [Hamburg, 1932]), particularly p. 104; D. Page, *The Homeric Odyssey* (Oxford², 1966) 168 f.; R. Merkelbach, *Untersuchungen zur Odyssee*, Zetemata 2 (München, 1951) 195; W. Pötscher, *Porphyrios ΠΡΟΣ ΜΑΡΚΕΛΛΑΝ* (Leiden, 1969) 79 f. (with more literatur); N. J. Richardson, *The Homeric Hymn to Demeter* (Oxford, 1974) 192 ff.; H. Erbse, *ZPE* 22 (1976) 4. A first step in the new direction is attested by the speech of Phoenix in I 496; see, e.g., M. Noé, *Phoinix, Ilias und Homer* (Leipzig, 1940); W. Theiler, *Festschrift E. Tièche* (Bern, 1947) 129 f.

blamed the citizens themselves, not Zeus and Athene, for ruining Athens;[3] and Hesiod formulated the idea that man must choose between κακότης and ἀρετή (*Erga* 286 ff.), a concept which Prodikos illustrated with the example of Herakles.[4] Although in Aischylos man's destiny is to suffer misfortune and ruin, he proceeds to this end on the basis of his free decisions.[5] In general, the Greeks sought to explain the human condition as situated between the poles of fate and self-determination. Plato formulated the theory thus: αἰτία ἑλομένου· θεὸς ἀναίτιος. The words were absorbed and transmitted by later Platonists as well as by Christian authors; according to Didymos of Alexandria, ἡμᾶς, οὐ γὰρ τὸν θεὸν αἰτιατέον.[6] Man is free in spite of all necessity.

The concept of free will lies at the basis of Aristotelian ethics: ἐφ᾽ ἡμῖν δὴ καὶ ἡ ἀρετή, ὁμοίως δὲ καὶ ἡ κακία.[7] Only on this assumption is it possible to impeach and punish a person. Thus Aristotle states that praise and blame are bestowed only on voluntary actions, whereas pardon is granted to involuntary offences (*Nic. Eth.* 3, 1, p. 1109b). Without free will morality is impossible.

The Greeks liberated man from almighty fate. Later, converted to Christianity, they had to reconcile their sense of human freedom with the experience of dependence on an almighty God. The philosophical concept of free will played a major role in the theology of the Christian writers of Alexandria. They were followed by others, especially the Cappadocians.

(*Untersuchungen zur antiken Literatur* [Berlin, 1970] 15 ff.); A. Dihle, *Homer-Probleme* (Opladen, 1970) 167 ff. For a different view see, e.g., E. Wüst, *Rh. Mus.* 101 (1958) 57 ff.; H. Lloyd-Jones, *The Justice of Zeus* (Sather Class. Lectures 41; Berkeley-Los Angeles-London, 1971) 9 ff. For the underlying psychology cf. also J. Russo, *JHI* 29 (1968) 483 ff.

[3] Fr. 4, 1 ff.W., cf. 11, 1 ff.; W. Jaeger, *SPAW* 1926, 69 ff. (*Scripta min.* I, 318 ff.); H. Fränkel, *Dichtung und Philosophie des frühen Griechentum* (New York, 1951) (*Early Greek Poetry and Philosophy*, transl. by M. Hadas and J. Willis [New York, 1975]) 293.

[4] Xen., *Mem.* 2, 1, 21 ff. (Diels-Kranz, *Vorsokratiker* II, 84 B 2); cf. E. Panofsky, *Hercules am Scheidewege* (Berlin–Leipzig, 1930) 42 ff.

[5] B. Snell, *Aischylos und das Handeln im Drama*, Philologus, Suppl. 20, 1 (Leipzig, 1928).

[6] Plato, *Rep.* 617E; cf. *Tim.* 42D. Corp. Herm. 4, 8 p. 52 Nock-Festugière; Hierocl., *In carm. aur.* 441B and 477A; Procl., *Ad Marc.* 12 p. 18 Pötscher (see also August., *Conf.* 2, 7, 15). The sentence of Didymos as quoted above is an amended version taken from the unpublished part of his commentary on Job (pp. 359, 29 ff.); the reading of the papyrus is: ο]ὺ γὰρ [[ἡμᾶς οὐ γὰρ]] τ[ὸ]ν θεὸν αἰτιατέο[ν]. Julian the Arian adopts Plato's phrase literally (p. 256, 16 Hagedorn). Cf. N. P. Williams, *The Ideas of the Fall and of the Original Sin*, Bampton Lectures, 1924 (London, 1927) 214.

[7] *N.E.* 3, 7 p. 1113b; cf. M. Wittmann, *Aristoteles über die Willensfreiheit* (Fulda, 1921) (*non vidi*); D. Amand, *Fatalisme et liberté dans l'antiquité grecque*, Recueil de Travaux, 3me série, 19 (Louvain, 1945) 35.

Not even God can force man to do what he does not desire to do; God offers grace, but man must accept it by free decisions.[8]

The belief in man's responsibility for his deeds and for the misery which can result from them would probably not have had the impact which made western culture possible, were it not that Augustine of Hippo made the concept of free will a central dogma of the Western Christian church; hence the insight passed through the Middle Ages to the present day.[9] Augustine's concept of free will was developed especially under the influence of Stoics, Neoplatonists and the Alexandrian church fathers.[10]

---

[8] See, for example, Orig., *hom. on Jer.* 20, 2 GCS 3, 178, 14 ff.; PG 12, 1511D; Did., *PsT* 198, 17 ff. (M. Gronewald in connection with A. Gesché, part III; the passage is directed against the Manichaeans). Cf. P. Mehlhorn, *ZKG* 2 (1878) 234; G. Teichtweier, *Die Sündenlehre des Origenes*, Studien zur Geschichte der kath. Moraltheologie 7 (Regensburg, 1958) 77 ff.; *idem, Das Sein des Menschen*, inaug. dissertation (Tübingen, 1951) (not printed), 381 ff.; H. Crouzel, *Théologie de l'image de Dieu chez Origène*, Théologie 34 (Paris, 1956) 132 f.; D. Amand, *loc. cit.* (see n. 7) 297 ff. For Didymos see A. Henrichs, *HiT* I, 27 n. 4 f.; J. Kramer, *EcclT* III, 23 n. 2 and IV, 27 n. 3; G. Bardy, *Didyme l'Aveugle* (Paris, 1910) 132 f.

[9] When in the Renaissance classical authors were read extensively, the concept of free will became tremendously important for life, art, and letters (see Panofsky, *loc. cit.* [n. 4]; Voigt, *loc. cit.* [n. 2]); but much of the background lies in the tradition of scholastic and other medieval teachings on the free will (cf. E. Cassirer, *Individuum und Kosmos in der Philosophie der Renaissance*, Studien der Bibliothek Warburg 10 [Leipzig and Berlin, 1927] chapt. 3 particularly on Pomponazzi's *De libero arbitrio* [= *The Individual and the Cosmos* . . ., transl. by M. Donandi (Philadelphia, 1963) 80 ff.]). "Augustine's study of Plotinus is one of the conditions which rendered Renaissance possible" (R. Dodds, *The Hibbert Journal* [1927–1928] 470).

[10] For Augustine's teaching on the free will see, e.g., J. Ball, *L'année théol. aug.* 6 (1945) 368 ff. and 7 (1946) 400 ff.; G. de Plinval, *Rev. des ét. Aug.* 1 (1955) 345 ff. and 5 (1959) 13 ff.; Fr. Sontag, *HTR* 60 (1967) 297 ff.; M. Huftier, "Libre arbitre, liberté et péché chez saint Augustin," *Recherches de théologie ancienne et médiévale* 33 [1966] 187 ff.); C. Andresen, *Bibliographia Augustiana* (Darmstadt, 1973) 124 ff. For the present purpose my documentation is mainly restricted to Augustine's antimanichaean writings. For the influence of the Neoplatonists on Augustine see, e.g., P. Courcelle, *Recherches sur les Confessions de S. Aug.* (Paris, 1950) 93 ff. (= *Zum Augustin-Gespräch der Gegenwart*, Wege der Forschung 5, ed. by C. Andresen [Darmstadt, 1962] 125 ff.); *idem, Les lettres grecques en Occident* (Paris, 1943) (2nd ed. 1948), 195 ff. (= *Late Latin Writers and their Greek Sources*, transl. by H. E. Wedeck [Cambridge, Mass., 1969] 208 ff.); H. Dörrie, *Miscellanea medievalia I: Antike und Orient im Mittelalter* (Berlin, 1962) 26 ff.; W. Theiler, *Porphyrios und Augustin*, Schriften der Königsberger Gelehrten Gesellschaft, Geistesw. Kl. 10 (1933) 1 ff. (= *Forschungen zum Neuplatonismus* [Berlin, 1966] 169 ff.); *idem* in: *Mullus, Festschrift Th. Klauser* (ed. by A. Stuiber and A. Hermann), Jahrb. Ant. u. Christ., Ergänzungsband 1 (1964) 352 ff.; Ch. Parma, *Pronoia und Providentia. Der Vorsehungsbegriff Plotins und Augustins*, Stud. zur Problemgeschichte der antiken und mittelalterlichen Philosophie 6 (1971); P. Brown, *Augustine of Hippo* (Berkeley–Los Angeles [Paperback] 1969) 88 ff.; A. Alfaric, *L'évolution intell. de S. Aug.* (Paris, 1918) 451 ff.; cf. C. Andresen's bibliography (above)

The latter taught that if one excludes human volition from moral actions, one eliminates the concept of virtue.[11] Augustine argues similarly: God bestowed free will upon the human mind to make moral acts possible.[12] Of course, Christian beliefs accounted for a slightly different phrasing and view of the old ideas. While Aristotle, for example, states that voluntary offences are punished and involuntary ones pardoned (see above), Augustine states that the very fact that man repents and is pardoned by God points to free decision: *"satis enim stultum est ignosci ei qui nihil mali fecit."*[13]

It was in the denial of free will that Didymos recognized the vulnerability of Manichaeism.[14] Underlying the quarrel was the question formulated by Plotinos: πόθεν τὸ κακόν; the Manichaeans had directed themselves against the Jewish faith; for to begin by accounting God the creator of all things easily led to assigning to him the ultimate cause of evil. To escape such a conclusion, the Manichaeans turned to gnostic ideas; instead of one God, they assumed two divine principles, the Good and the Evil, Light and Darkness which had fought each other since eternity. In the course of the struggle, the two substances partly mixed with each other; the Light was dispersed and imprisoned in the darkness, the *hyle*. The mind (*Noûs*), the soul of man and animals, and the vegetative power of plants, are particles of the Great *Noûs*, i.e., God's Light.[15] On the other hand, the spirits of

---

53 ff.; for Stoic influences, *ibidem* 97 ff.; on the problem of Augustine's knowledge of the Greek fathers, particularly of the Alexandrians, see P. Courcelle, *Les Lettres* (above), 183 ff. (= *Late Latin Writers*, 196 ff.); and several articles by B. Altaner, all reprinted in his *Kleine patristische Schriften* (ed. by G. Glockmann; Berlin–Darmstadt, 1967) particularly 154 ff. 224 ff. 297 ff. 316 ff.

11 Orig., *c. Cels.* 4, 3 GCS 1, 276, 18 f. ἀρετῆς μὲν ἐὰν ἀνέλῃς τὸ ἑκούσιον, ἀνεῖλες αὐτῆς καὶ τὴν οὐσίαν (cf. A. Miura-Stange, *Celsus und Origenes*, Beih. ZNW 4 [Gießen, 1926] 76); Did., *EcclT* 296, 6 (unpubl.) ἐάν, φησίν, περιέλῃς τῆς ἀρετῆς τὸ ἑκούσιον, οὐκέτι ἐστὶν ἀρε[τή, and *PsT* 199, 17 (M. Gronewald in connection with A. Gesché; part III).—*PsT* 67, 20 f. (Gronewald, part II) διὰ τοῦτο γὰρ τὸν λογικὸν πεποίηκεν, ἵνα δέχηται ἀρετὴν καὶ ἐνεργῇ αὐτήν.

12 *c. Fort.* 15 CSEL 25, 1, 92.5 ff.; cf., e.g., 16 p. 93, 26 ff.; 21 p. 100, 9 f.

13 *c. Fort.* 16 p. 94, 4 ff.; *c. Fel.* II, 17 p. 847, 11 ff. Cf. Did., *c. Manich.* 15 PG 39, 1103C f.

14 Did., *c. Man.* 10 ff. p. 1097C ff.; *EcclT* 88, 9 ff. (quoted by A. Henrichs in his edition of *HiT*, part I p. 29 n. 7); *PsT* 77, 25 ff. (Gronewald, part II; the passage reflects Aristotelian thought); *ZachT* II, 175 ff. p. 132, 28 (mainly against the Valentinians; cf. L. Doutreleau's introduction I, 93 f.). Cf. Orig., P.G. 14, 1305A.

15 G. Widengren, *The Great Vohu Manah*, Uppsala Universitets Årsskrift 1945, 5. H.-Ch. Puech, *Le manichéisme* (Paris, 1949) 74 ff.; H. J. Polotsky, *RE Suppl.* 6, 245 ff. (= *Collected Papers* [Jerusalem, 1971] 701 ff.; H. Jonas, *Gnosis und spätantiker Geist* (Göttingen³, 1964) 284 ff.; K. Rudolph, Mani, in: *Die Grossen der Weltgeschichte* (Enzyklopädie)

Darkness created, by copulation and cannibalism, the concupiscent body to fetter and retain the light of the soul.[16] Enmeshed in the physical creations of Evil, the soul or divine substance of man forgot its origin and became entirely powerless. With such a theodicy, not God, but the principle of Darkness is responsible for evil. In such a system, however, God is not almighty, but conditioned and limited by the power of evil. Exactly for this reason Augustine finally rejected the dualistic explanation of evil. Rather, in line with the scriptures and teachings of the Christian church, he accepted the principle that everything, even the human body, was created by God. But as God could not be the cause of the evil,[17] Augustine had to search for a different cause (cf. *Conf.* 7, 3, 4). He finally found the solution in a concept which was developed by interpreters of Plato and held by the Alexandrian fathers as well as by the Neoplatonists: evil is not a substance, but an accidence; as such it is a στέρησις τοῦ ἀγαθοῦ or a φθορά and μὴ ὄν. Thus as far as moral evil is concerned, it exists only in the bad intentions of the free will.[18] *discite non substantiam malum esse*, states Augustine expressly;[19] and elsewhere: *quid est autem aliud quod malum dicitur nisi privatio boni (ench.* 11). Or: *(malum) nihil aliud est quam corruptio,*[20] and: *exortum fuisse hominis malum ex libero voluntatis arbitrio.*[21] Occasionally he explains the existence of corruption and evil as due to

---

II, 545 ff., esp. 552 ff.; *idem*, Il manicheismo, in: *Storia delle religioni* (ed. by G. Castellani) IV, 775 ff., esp. 782 ff.; F. Decret, *Mani et la tradition manichéenne* (Paris, 1974) 79 ff.

[16] Therefore procreation is sinful for it causes the divine Light to be entrapped in another body. In the *CMC* the body is called μιαρώτατον καὶ διὰ μυσαρότητος πεπλασμένον, καὶ δι' αὐτῆς ἐτυρώθη καὶ οἰκοδομηθὲν ἔστη (85, 8 ff.).

[17] Aug., *De ut. credendi* 36 CSEL 25, 46, 24 ff.; *De div. quaest.*, PL 40, 21E. It is significant that Augustine began his first book on free will (CSEL 74) with the question whether God is the cause of evil. For the arguments by which evil was connected with God see, e.g., *de duab. anim.* 10 p. 63, 15 ff. The wrong answer to the question *unde malum et qua re* was regarded as the source of gnosticism (Tert., *de praescr.* 7; *adv. Marc.* 1, 2; cf. Ps.Clem., *rec.* 3, 75, 6). Cf. H. J. Schoeps, *Das Judenchristentum* (Bern and Munich, 1964) 99 (= *Jewish Christianity*, transl. by D. R. A. Hare [Philadelphia, 1964] 121 ff.); *idem*, *ZRGG* 11 (1959) 93 (= *idem*, *Studien zur unbekannten Religionsgeschichte*, Veröffentlichungen der Gesellschaft f.Geistesgesch. [Göttingen, 1963] 93).

[18] U. and D. Hagedorn and L. Koenen in their edition of Didymos, *HiT*, part III (Bonn, 1968), pp. 229 ff. n. 22.

[19] *c. ep. fund.* 27 CSEL 25, 227, 10 f.; cf. *c. Fel.* II, 4 p. 831, 26 ff.

[20] *de nat. boni* 4 p. 857, 3 ff.; *c. ep. fund.* 35 p. 239, 18 ff. Didymos used the priority of the good as evidence for the preexistence of the soul; see *PsT* 259, 16 ff. (M. Gronewald, part IV); 129, 6 ff. (Gronewald in connection with A. Gesché, part III) = 1, 5 ff. Kehl; *HiT* 260, 20 ff. (Hagedorn-Koenen, part III).

[21] *retr.* 1, 15 (*contra Fort.*) CSEL 36, 82,10. Sin is defined as follows (*de duab. an.* 15 CSEL 25, 70, 15 ff.): *peccatum est voluntas retinendi vel consequendi quod iustitia vetat et unde liberum est abstinere. quamquam si liberum non sit, non est voluntas.* Cf. *ibidem* 71, 4 ff.

God's creation *de nihilo*. This is slightly different from the Greek explanation of evil as μὴ ὄν.[22] Without Augustine's being aware of it, his *nihil* becomes an *aliquid* and assumes the negative qualities of the Manichaean *hyle*.

Because no creator of evil is required in this philosophy, Augustine succeeded in overcoming the dualistic notions of the Manichaeans. This was important for his spiritual development and thus for his teachings and writings, which came to influence the formation of the Western Church. The mere presence of the Manichaeans forced Augustine to react; consequently, the idea of free will and of man's responsibility for himself prevailed against fatalistic conceptions.

Nevertheless Augustine's notion of the free will was colored by Manichaean thoughts. He once stated that free will existed only in Adam and Eve, and another time that free will was lost with sin.[23] The concept of original sin was not invented by Augustine; rather the notion is inherent in the structure of the human mind and can be traced to the behavior of primitive man.[24] Among Christian authors, it was particularly the

[22] *c. ep. fund.* 36 p. 241, 23 ff. explains the corruption *ex eo quod hae naturae quae corrumpi possunt non de deo genitae* (the Manichaean explanation), *sed ab illo de nihilo factae sunt*. This is repeated in 38 p. 244, 1 ff., then 244, 15 ff.: *cum enim dicitur "natura corruptibilis," non unum, sed duo nomina dicuntur; item cum dicitur "deus fecit de nihilo," non unum, sed duo nomina audimus. redde ergo istis singulis illa singula, ut cum audis "naturam," ad "deum" pertineat, cum audis "corruptibilem," ad "nihilum," ita tamen, ut ipsae corruptiones, quamvis non sint ex dei arte, in eius tamen potestate sint disponendae pro rerum ordine et meritis animarum.* The *nihil* assumes almost the quality of being, just as, on the next level, the *hyle* becomes *paene nihil* and a *paene nulla res* which God created *de nulla re* (*Conf.* 12, 8, 8; cf. Ch. Parma, *loc. cit.* [see n. 10], 79). W. Theiler compares the Christian term *de nihilo* with Porphyry's concept of the demiurge who brings the sensible things into existence by the very act of thinking, ἀύλως ⟨παράγων⟩ τὸ ἔνυλον (Porph. ap. Procl., *in Tim.* 1, 396, 5; W. Theiler, *loc. cit.* [see n. 10] 14 f. = 177).

[23] *c. Fort.* 22 CSEL 25, 103, 26 ff. *liberum voluntatis arbitrium in illo homine fuisse dico qui primus formatus est. ille sic factus est ut nihil omnino voluntati eius resisteret si vellet dei praecepta servare. postquam autem libera ipse voluntate peccavit, nos in necessitatem praecipitati sumus qui ab eius stirpe descendimus. Ench.* 30 p. 68 Barbel *libero arbitrio male utens homo et se perdidit et ipsum . . . cum libero peccaretur arbitrio, victore peccato amissum est liberum arbitrium* (the argument is aimed at the necessity of grace). Cf. *c. Fort.* 25 p. 108, 18 ff. Elsewhere and later Augustine distinguishes clearly between the freedom of paradise which has been lost in consequence of sin and the free will without which man could not even sin (*c. duas epist. Pel.* 1, 2, 5 CSEL 60, 425, 24 ff.—The aspects of necessity, providence, and grace, though essential for Augustine's concept of the free will, can be neglected in the present context. For the persistence of Manichaean ideas in Augustine's thought see A. Adam, *ZKG* 69 (1958) 16 ff.

[24] W. Burkert, *Homo Necans*, RGVV 32 (Berlin–New York, 1972). For the history of the idea of original sin in the church and in Judaism see, e.g., J. Gross, *Entstehungsgeschichte des Erbsündendogmas* (München–Basel, 1960); N. P. Williams, *loc. cit.* (see n. 6); F. R. Tennant, *The Sources of the Doctrine of the Fall and Original Sin* (Cambridge, 1903); cf. n. 8.

Alexandrians who incorporated the sin of Adam in their theological system, though quite differently from what became a dogma of the church. They assumed two original sins; one explains the state of man's soul, the other the state of his body. The first sin is connected with the belief that all souls once lived with God in the happiness of preexistent life. There they turned towards the *hyle*, i.e., they sinned, and as a consequence they were incorporated in human bodies. The other sin is that of Adam and Eve. Their bodies were of light, or rather, spiritual *hyle* which suited the condition of paradise; as they were created by God, they were good. But with their sin Adam and Eve had turned towards the *hyle* and, by that, they lost paradise. For the new material world they needed new bodies of more solid *hyle*. God thus had to create the "garment of skin," the mortal body as we know it (*Gen.* 3, 21). This body again suits its purpose. It is good, as created by God; but as made of solid *hyle*, it is mortal, hinders the intellectual abilities of the mind and reduces the capacity to recognize right and wrong. Thus man is bound to commit sins without knowing it. This applies particularly to the sins of youth. Consequently man is ἐν ῥύπῳ, before he is redeemed by Christ. Because this second body is that transmitted in procreation, the sin of Adam and Eve and its consequences are inherited. Nevertheless nobody is punished for the sin of his forefathers. For when a soul falls from heaven, it gets exactly the body which corresponds to its state of mind and disposition. Each gets the body it deserves due to the sin committed in the preexistent life. No person is held responsible and punished for sins which he did not commit himself.[25]

---

[25] This account is based on Didymos the Blind's lectures and writings preserved by the Toura papyri; in Origen, enough of the essential details can be found so that I feel confident that he had already had the same system. The main passages in Didymos are as follows: *HiT* 260, 23 ff. (Hagedorn-Koenen; part III); 365, 7 ff. (unpubl.): see particularly 366, 2 ff., where *Job* 14, 4 (τίς γὰρ καθαρός ἐστιν ἀπὸ ῥύπου; οὐδὲ εἶς, ἐὰν καὶ μία ἡμέρα ὁ βίος αὐτοῦ ἐπὶ τῆς γῆς), according to one of two possible explanations, refers to ὁ νῦν ἂν γεννώμενος ὁ [κα]τὰ διαδοχὴν ἔχων τοῦ Ἀδ[ὰ]μ τὸ ἁμάρτημα; 282, 23 ff. and 283, 15 f. (both in part III); 66, 5 ff. (Henrichs, part I), where the essential sentence may be reconstructed thus: εἰ γὰρ μὴ ἦν αὕ[τη ἡ οἴξ]ασα (*sc.* ἡ νύξ, i.e., the state of the soul, when it sinned before it was born and consequently was on its way into life), | οὐδ' ἂν ἠνοίγοντο π[ύλαι γασ]τρ[ὸς] μητρός (*Job* 3, 10), ὅ ἐστιν· οὐκ [ἄν μοι ἦν ὁ ἐπώ]|δυνος οὗτος βίος, [εἰ μὴ δι' ἀμ]|αρτίαν τοιαύτης ν[υκτὸς (the sin of the preexistent soul) ἐποι]|εῖτο (*sc.* this miserable life) τοῦ γένους ἀμ[άρτοντος (*sc.* the mankind in Adam). μὴ] | τούτου δ' ὑπάρχον[τος οὐκ ἂν] | οὐδ' ὁ κατ' οἰκονομίαν κ[ατὰ τὴν γῆν] | διάγων διὰ ταύτης [τ]ῆς [καταστά]|σεως παρετείνετο (the saints did not commit the sin of the preexistent souls, but were sent by God into the world to serve as models for others; as members of the human race, however, they were subject to the consequences of Adam's sin); *PsT* 129, 10 f. (M. Gronewald in connection with A. Gesché; part III) = p. 1, 10 ff. Kehl. Cf. Hagedorn-Koenen, *HiT* III p. 246 ff. n. 70 f.; 257 ff. n. 101; A. Henrichs, *HiT* I p. 311 ff.

Free will and self-responsibility are fully retained in this system. In it, original sin does not result in compulsion which virtually eliminates the freedom of will; original sin is not yet the antipole of free will, as it became with Augustine. It was Augustine's personal recognition of his own concupiscense and his Manichaean past which led him to regard free will in human nature only as severely conditioned by the consequences of original sin; human nature is spoiled and extremely weak. Augustine thought of concupiscense as one of the main results of original sin. It seems that he did not forget that according to the Manichaeans the body is created out of concupiscense and sexual excess. But he saw clearly that, as a creation of God, human nature and human body had to be good. Consequently they were spoiled by the original sin of Adam's free will.

As a powerful influence on Augustine and thus as a significant, though indirect influence on the formation of our culture, the Manichaeans command attention. Augustine's victory over the Manichaeans[26] became the victory of the occident over fatalism.[27]

II. Mani's Relationship to Christianity and Gnosticism

Central for the understanding of the growth,[28] influence, and religious nature of Manichaeism is its relationship to Christianity and Gnosticism. The *Cologne Mani Codex* (*CMC*) has confirmed that Mani was brought up among the Elchasaites in ancient Syria. This baptist movement originally sprang from heretical Judaism and was christianized with a Christianity which was or became Gnostic.[29] With Gnosticism travelled old Iranian

[26] This victory became possible when Augustine learned allegorical interpretation from the Alexandrian theologians. Significantly he concludes his *Confessions* with three books which explain the first lines of *Genesis*. Certainty on the interpretation of the creation account was necessary for him to overcome the Manichaean myths and theology. Thus the three final books are an integral part of the whole. On the importance of different methods of interpretation of the Old Testament see, e.g., *de util. cred.* 5 ff. CSEL 25, 7, 26 ff.: *secundum historiam, secundum aetiologiam, secundum analogiam, secundum allegoriam.*

[27] Mani's own activities were certainly not hindered by fatalism. But ordinary people could not do much for the redemption of the divine Light within them.

[28] Cf. P. Brown, *JRS* 59 (1969) 92 ff. (= *Religion and Society in the Age of Saint Augustine* [London, 1972] 94 ff.).

[29] Cf. now *ZPE* 5 (1970) 133 ff.; A. Henrichs, *HSCP* 77 (1973) 23 ff.; K. Rudolph, *Mélanges* (see n. 1) 475 ff. The name of Elchasaios has recently also been found in a Parthian text ('*lxs*'; see W. Sundermann, *Acta Or.* 36 [1974] 130 and 148 f.; on the meaning of the name cf. Henrichs, 45 n. 77). For Jewish Christianity see H. J. Schoeps, *Theologie und Geschichte des Judenchristentums* (Tübingen, 1949); *idem, Das Judenchristentum* (= *Jewish Christianity*; see n. 17); *idem, ZRGG* 10 (1958) 1 ff. (= *idem, Studien* [see n. 17] 80 ff.); J. Daniélou, *Théologie du Judéo-Christianisme* (Tournai-Paris, 1958). For Jewish Christian Gnosticism see G. Strecker, *Das Judenchristentum in den Pseudo-Klementinen*, T.u.U.

ideas, notably an extreme dualism. From such various traditions in the
baptist movement Mani developed his religious system by eliminating
what he regarded as contradictions and innovations. This meant an
elimination of the Jewish Law; for Mani fervidly departed from the
Jewish heritage of the Elchasaites. He started as their reformer, but he
did not restrict himself to their teachings. Already the Elchasaites thought
that the True Prophet had come and would continue to come into the
world in a series of incarnations. Thus the revelation was spread and had
to be recollected from all places and times. Under these premisses it is not
astonishing that Mani's reform of the Elchasaites turned into a syncretism
in which all people, except the Jews, could recognize their own traditions.

The details should become clearer in the following pages. Our chief
concern shall be the Christian elements in Manichaeism. Scholars tend to
see them as superficial additions which were either part of the missionary
activity of the Manichaeans beginning already in the lifetime of Mani or
part of defensive propaganda in times of persecution, particularly in the
4th century in North Africa and Rome.[30] But Christian elements which

---

70 (Berlin, 1958); cf., however H. J. Schoeps, *ZRGG* 11 (1959) 72 ff. (= *Studien*, 91 ff.).
Schoeps' distinction between Jewish Christianity as a belief in the salvation of a God of
revelation, and gnosticism as belief in self-salvation of man is theologically useful and,
concerning the Ebionites and Ps. Clement, probably correct; nevertheless, as Schoeps well
knows, it cannot be applied to the Elchasaites, and in terms of history it is helpful to refer
to Jewish Christian gnosticism (see H. J. Schoeps, *Urgemeinde-Judenchristentum-Gnosis*
[Tübingen, 1956]). The concept of the True Prophet marks the difference between the
Ebionites and the Elchasaites; according to the latter, the series of incarnations of the
prophet did not stop with Christ, but continued afterwards in the person of Elchasaios.
Again, in terms of theology, this marks the departure of what can be called Christianity;
but for historical purposes I shall continue to refer to Christianity in connection with the
Elchasaites and Manichaeism. For the concept of the True Prophet see G. Strecker,
loc. cit., 145; H. J. Schoeps, *Judenchristentum* 20; 25; 33; 57; 68 ff.; 96; 100 f.; 108 (*Jewish
Christ.* 16; 23; 35; 66; 68 ff.; 120; 126 f.; 138); *idem, ZRGG* 11 (1959) 72 ff. = *Studien*, 94;
idem, Numen 4 (1957) 229 f. (= *Studien*, 118). Cf. also n. 59.

30 Christianity so obviously affected even the Iranian texts (see n. 34) that G. Widengren
accepted Christian influences on Mani for the last period of his life (*Mani und der Manichäismus* [Stuttgart, 1961] 158 = *Mani and Manichaeism* [London, 1965] 157 f.). For the
Christian roots of Manichaeism see particularly A. Böhlig, *BSAC* 15 (1960) 41 ff.
(= *Mysterium und Wahrheit* [Leiden, 1968] 202 ff.); E. Rose, *Die Christologie des Manichäismus nach den Quellen dargestellt* (Diss. Marburg, 1941; cf. S. Schulz, *Theol. Rundschau*,
N.F. 26 [1960] 230 ff.); M. Boyce, *Indo-Iranian Journ.* 7 (1963) 75; G. Quispel, *Eranos Jb.*
36 (1967) 20 ff.; J. Ries, *Augustiniana* 14 (1964) 437 ff.; P. Nagel in: K. W. Tröger, *Gnosis
und N.T.* (Berlin, 1973) 149 ff. ("bescheidenes christliches Erbe"); see also E. Waldschmidt
and W. Lentz, *Die Stellung Jesu im Manichäismus, APAW* 1926, 4; according to H.-Ch.
Puech's well balanced description of Manichaeism (p. 69; see above, n. 15), Christian as
well as Indian and Iranian elements were for the most part later and superficial; this view
now needs the modification given above. For the western branch of Manichaeism see
F. Decret, *Aspects du Manichéisme dans l'Afrique Romaine* (Paris, 1970).

were hitherto considered peculiarities of the western branch of Manichaeism belong in fact to the oldest strata and are an integral part of the
system. They should not be taken merely as an indication that the western
branch departed from its Iranian origins.

(A) The Manichaeans' Identification of themselves as Christians, according to Augustine

According to the picture given in Augustine's polemic treatises, the
Manichaeans regarded themselves as *christiani* and *veri christiani*, whereas
they thought the *catholici* to be *semichristiani*.[31] Felix signed the protocol of
the first proceedings against him: *Felix christianus, cultor legis Manichaei*
(CSEL 25, 827, 3 f.). According to Faustus, the Manichaean bishop, his
church considered itself in terms of the *sponsa Christi*; he regarded himself
as a *rationabile Dei templum*.[32] He distinguishes between three churches:
Jewish, Christian, and pagan, and in this distinction the Manichaeans are
represented as Christians.[33] Consequently these Manichaeans spoke of the
Old Testament as the work of the demons; yet they accepted the New
Testament in general.[34] Paul was of the highest authority for them.

[31] For example, *de util. cred.* 30 CSEL 37, 21; 36 p. 47, 27 ff.; *c. Faust.* 26, 2 p. 730, 9 f.;
1, 2 p. 251, 23 f. and 3 p. 252, 13 ff.; cf. 15, 1 p. 415, 26 ff.; 26, 2 p. 730, 9 ff. Cf. E.
Haenchen in: *Christentum und Gnosis*, ed. by W. Eltester. Beih. ZNW, 37 (Berlin, 1969) 38.

[32] *sponsa c.*: *Faust.* 15, 1 p. 416, 8; 3 p. 419, 15 ff. *templum*: *c. Faust.* 20, 3 p. 537, 17
(cf. now *CMC* 15, 10 ff.: Manis body as ἱερὸν πρὸς εὔκλειαν τοῦ νοῦ and as ἁγιώτατος νεὼς
πρὸς ἀποκάλυψιν τῆς αὐτοῦ σοφίας).

[33] *c. Faust.* 31, 2 p. 757, 18 ff.; the Catholic church and the Jews were regarded as
schismata gentilitatis with the result that only the Manichaeans remained the true Christians
(*ibidem*, 20, 3 f. p. 537, 3 ff.; cf. F. Ch. Baur, *Das manichäische Religionssystem* [Tübingen,
1831; repr. Hildesheim, 1973] 334 ff.). Faustus reports that once he thought that in order
to be a true Christian he would have to obey the Jewish Law and to become first a Jew;
but he was taught by his Manichaean teacher that this would be a wrong interpretation of
Matth. 5, 17. Thanks to this teacher, Faustus is *hodie christianus*, not *Iudaeus* (19, 5 p. 501,
1 ff.).

[34] F. Decret, *loc. cit.* (see n. 30), 123 ff., 151 ff.; for quotations from the gospels (most
probably from Tatian, see below p. 193 f.) in Parthian texts see O. Klíma, *Manis Zeit und
Leben* (Prague, 1962) 468 ff. (M 18; M 132; M 475); W. Sundermann, *MIO* 14 (1968)
389 ff. (M 4570; cf. J. P. Asmussen, *Manichaean Literature* [Delmar, New York, 1975] 101;
Sundermann, *loc. cit.* [n. 29], 139); idem, *Mittelpersische und parthische kosmogonische und
Parabeltexte der Manichäer*, Berliner Turfantexte IV (Berlin, 1973) 106 f. (M 6005) and 108
(M 338). The Coptic texts and now the *CMC* frequently refer to and cite the *NT* (cf. here
p. 193; I was unable to consult A. Böhlig, *Die Bibel bei den Manichäern* [inaug. dissert.
Münster, 1947]). In spite of their rejection of the Old Testament, they imitated the
Psalms; a whole group is directed to Jesus (C. R. C. Allberry, *A Manichaean Psalm-Book*,
Manichaean Manuscripts in the Chester Beatty Collection II [Stuttgart, 1938]). For Paul

(B) The Manichaean Church as *Corpus Manichaei* or *Corpus Christi*,
according to the *CMC*

Though traces of Christianity are left in the Iranian texts (see nn. 30
and 34), they are especially obvious in the Coptic texts and the new Greek
CMC. Both show the typical Christian abbreviations of holy names.[35]
Moreover, the theological language of the new codex is partly influenced
by Paul.[36] A good example is provided by its title: περὶ τῆς γέννης τοῦ
σώματος αὐτοῦ, "On the Birth of His Body." In fact, the Coptic Manichaean codex, which was unfortunately lost in the Second World War,
seemingly showed the same literary structure and probably was part of
the same work.[37] The Coptic part dealt with the history of the Mani-

---

see now the reference to a *martyrium Pauli* in a middle Persian homily: W. Sundermann in:
Hommages et opera minora, monumentum H. S. Nyberg, II. Acta Iranica (Leiden, 1975) 297 ff.;
cf. 310 f., a homily on Paul. Also for Paul, cf. C. Colpe, *Ex orbe religionum, Studia G.
Widengren*, Suppl. Numen 21 [Leiden, 1972] 401 f. The *NT* was regarded as interpolated
by Jews and Catholics; cf., e.g., *de haeres.* 46 PL 42, 38 (= A. Adam, *Texte zum Mani-
chaeismus*, Kleine Texte 175, no. 49); *c. Faust.* 8, 5 p. 383, 2 ff.; 11, 1 p. 313, 1 ff.; 16, 2
p. 441, 6 ff.; 18, 3 p. 491, 27 ff. (cf. 7 p. 495, 16 ff.); 23, 2 p. 707, 23 ff.; 24, 2 p. 724, 5 ff.;
31, 1 ff. p. 756, 2 ff.; 32, 7 p. 766, 15 ff. (list of refuted teachings of the *NT*); 32, 16 p. 776,
12 ff.; 33, 3 p. 788, 14 ff. The critical approach of the Manichaeans to the text is illustrated
by Faustus in *c. Faust.* 17, 1 p. 483, 3 ff. The Manichaeans could judge the authenticity of
the *NT* by the tenets of their faith; for Mani was regarded as *apostolos* and *paraclete* (see
below); the *paraclete* told the Manichaeans *quid accipere ex eodem* (sc. *ex novo testamento*)
debeamus et quid repudiare (*c. Faust.* 32, 6 p. 765, 19 f.).

35 Cf. *ZPE* 19 (1975) 2.

36 *ZPE* 19 (1975) 1 ff. n. 33, 74, 76, 78, 80, 96, 109, 111–114, 117, 119, 121, 122, 129,
134; *ZPE* 5 (1970) index p. 208 and 215 f.

37 In their first description of the Coptic codex C. Schmidt and H. J. Polotsky (*SPAW*
phil. hist. Kl. 1 [1933] 29) wrote: "Unser historisches Werk war offensichtlich nicht aus
der Feder eines einzigen Schriftstellers geflossen, sondern ein Sammelband aus ver-
schiedenen kleineren Aufsätzen und Berichten, die unter den Namen der betreffenden
Autoren hier zusammengestellt sind." This description suits the *CMC* perfectly. Headings
in the Coptic Codex furnish the names of Ammos, Salmaios, and Kustaios as authors of
the articles and reports. Having the same function, the names of Salmaios and Kustaios
occur in the headings of the *CMC*. The Iranian biographical fragments seem not to come
from the same historical work (W. Sundermann, *loc. cit.* [see n. 29] 146 f.); however some
fragments quote the reports of older authorities in a similar way. A section of M 4575
begins: "(Es berichten) die Geliebten" (Sundermann, *Acta Or.* 24 [1971] 87); this recalls
the heading of *CMC* 26, 6 οἱ διδάσκαλοι λέγουσιν; but in the Iranian text the introductory
phrase is not written as a heading. To the same Parthian codex belong M 6033 and 6031
(Sundermann, *loc. cit.* [see n. 29], 141), which seem to rely on information going back to
Pattikios: ["Further, Pate]cius thus relates" (M 6033 col. A 3 f.; W. B. Henning, *BSOAS*
10 [1942] 942 ff.; L. J. R. Ort, *Mani. A Religio-Historical Description of his Personality*
[Leiden, 1967] 55 ff.); cf. also M 6031, recto II, 1 (*ibidem*; also in Asmussen's collection
[see n. 34], p. 55). Other information comes from Nūḥzādag, the interpreter (M 3;

chaeans after the death of Mani up to c. 300 A.D. The whole work was a history of the Manichaean church, and it consisted of several codices.[38] It was translated from Syriac into Greek, then from Greek into Coptic. If this is correct, the title found in the *CMC* may be the title of the whole work. In this case it cannot refer to the real body of Mani. In addition, from the Manichaean point of view, it is hard to see why they were interested in the real body of Mani which, according to their teaching, was no better than the body of other men and which could not be redeemed.[39]

The title must have broader theological significance.[40] In the Manichaean tradition it stems from a phrase used by Baraies, a Manichaean apologist of the first generation after Mani.[41] It can, however, be traced further back to the language of the Pauline formulation of the church as the body of Christ.[42] Thus the title of the codex should be understood as "On the Birth of the Manichaean Church." In the Coptic *Kephalaia*, Mani addresses his pupils as "my brothers and my limbs" (213, 3). This shows that in the same way as the Christian church thinks of itself as the mystical body and as the limbs of Jesus Christ, the Manichaean church was regarded as the body and limbs of Mani. The conformity of ideas is even greater. According to the *Kephalaia*, both the Christian and the Manichaean church are the body of the heavenly spirit whom they called the "Apostle of Light." He invests himself in a series of bodies which are identified as the churches.[43] Thus the Manichaean church is the body of the "Apostle of Light," as the Christian church was previously. The Manichaean and the Christian churches were incarnations of the same heavenly spirit; as such they had the same essence.

Henning, *ibidem* 948 ff.; Ort, *ibidem* 52; Asmussen, *ibidem* 54). Cf. also *ZPE* 5 (1970) 110 ff.; K. Rudolph, *Mélanges* [see n. 1] 472 n. 7.

38 To judge from the space which the *CMC* needed to deal with the early years of Mani, it seems that the history originally was comprised of several volumes.

39 In *ZPE* 5 (1970) 104 our assumption that the title referred only to the physical body of Mani led us astray in our explanation of its meaning.

40 See *ZPE* 8 (1971) 249 f.; A. Henrichs, *HSCP* 77 (1973) 40 f.; K. Rudolph, *Mélanges* (see n. 1) 471.

41 *CMC* 46, 8 f.; see p. 170 §2. In this damaged passage σῶμα might refer to Mani's physical body. For Baraies see *ZPE* 5 (1970) 110 ff.; *ZPE* 19 (1975) 16 n. 28; 78 n. 40; 80 f. n. 80.

42 *Rom.* 12, 5; *1 Cor.* 10, 17; 12, 13 f. and 27; *Eph.* 1, 23; 2, 16; 4, 12 and 16; 5, 23 and 30; *Col.* 1, 18 and 24; 2, 19; 3, 15; cf. Bauer, *s.v.* σῶμα 5. C. Colpe in: *Judentum, Christentum Kirche. Festschrift für J. Jeremias*, edit. by W. Eltester, Beih. ZNW 26 (Berlin, 1960) 172 f.

43 *Keph.* 36, 3 ff. "Die erste Kraft (sc. des Licht-*Noῦs*) ist der Apostel des Lichtes, der jeweils zu seiner Zeit kommt und sich bekleidet mit der Kirche des Fleisches der Menschheit und Oberhaupt wird innerhalb der Gerechtigkeit" (Polotsky).

The same conclusion is suggested by the Manichaean chain of emanation of the five heavenly fathers. "Jesus the Splendor," the third father, emanated the "Light—*Noûs*"; the latter emanated the "Apostle of Light," who has just been mentioned as embodied in the churches. Moreover, the "Light—*Noûs*" himself is the "Father of all Apostles, the First of all Churches whom Jesus (*sc.* 'Jesus the Splendor') has installed in the holy church after our likeness."[44] Thus "Jesus the Splendor" is the divine essence of the Christian church as well as of the Manichaean church. The Manichaean church is the church of Jesus in the time of Mani.

This brings us back to the title of the *CMC*. "On the Birth of His Body" refers to the birth of the Manichaean church. "His Body" could be understood on different levels: the mystical body (1) of Mani, (2) of the "Apostle of Light," (3) of the "Light—*Noûs*" and (4) of Jesus. Theologically all these were interchangeable.[45] The "birth of the church" began with the physical birth of Mani;[46] thus the history of the Manichaean church as the mystical body of the divine emanations had to begin with the biography of Mani. Finally, within this broad context, the "birth of His body" includes also his physical body.

The title of the new codex and its theological connotations show that the early Manichaeans thought of themselves in much the same way that they did in the time of Augustine.[47] They claimed that after the Christian church turned away from the genuine teaching of Christ, the Manichaean church was sent into this world. Consequently, Faustus thought of his church as the fulfillment of the Christian church just as the Christian church understood itself as the fulfillment of the synagogue.

---

[44] *Keph.* 35, 18 ff.; cf. 36, 1 ff.: "Der vierte Vater ist der Licht-*Noûs*, der erwählt alle Kirchen" (Polotsky); 245, 8 ff.: ". . . der Licht–*Noûs*, der sie (sc. the church) erlöst, gerettet und gesammelt hat aus allen Orten" (Böhlig); 256, 6 f.: "Der Licht-*Noûs*, der in den Electi wohnt" (Böhlig). For the system of emanations see H. J. Polotsky in: Schmidt–Polotsky (see n. 37), 64 ff. (= Polotsky, *loc. cit.* [see n. 15], 674 ff.); also *ZPE* 5 (1970) 183 ff.

[45] The church was also (5) the body of the Perfect Man who was emanated by the Messenger, as Jesus the Splendor was; see Cod. Joung 122, 27 ff., a passage which is regarded as Manichaean (see J.-E. Ménard in: *Christentum und Gnosis* [n. 31], 55). He is τὸ πᾶν καὶ τὰ πάντα, i.e., a kind of Jesus (cf. *Col.* 3, 11; *Rom.* 11, 36; *Eph.* 1, 10) and the Cross of Light (see below pp. 184 ff.). Thus the church is the body of the Perfect Man who, in essence, is identical with Jesus and the Cross of Light: it is the *ecclesia patiens*.

[46] *Keph.* 14, 3 f.: "[Als?] die Kirche des Heilands sich zur Höhe erhoben hatte, da geschah mein Apostelamt (sc. Mani's), nach dem ihr mich gefragt habt ---," 24 ff.: "Als aber die Kirche das Fleisch angelegt hatte, da war die Zeit gekommen, die Seelen zu erlösen --- In dieser selben Zeit [bildete?] er mein Bild, welches ich trage ---" (Polotsky).

[47] Faustus regarded himself as *rationabile Dei templum*; see p. 163.

(C) Mani as the "Apostle of Jesus Christ" and as the "*Paraclete*"

The Manichaean claim to be the genuine Christian church and to decide what is authentic in the New Testament was theologically based on the concept that Mani was the "Apostle of Jesus Christ." Mani claimed this himself just as Paul did in the opening formula of his letters: Παῦλος ἀπόστολος Χριστοῦ 'Ιησοῦ διὰ θελήματος θεοῦ.[48]

The main evidence for Mani is as follows:

1. *Gospel*: ἐγὼ Μαννιχαῖος 'Ιησοῦ Χριστοῦ ἀπόστολος διὰ θελήματος θεοῦ πατρὸς τῆς ἀληθείας. Middle Persian version: "Ich, Mani, (der) Gesandte Jesu (des) Freundes durch (den) Willen (des) Vaters, (des) wahrhaftigen Gottes."[49]

2. *ep. fund.*: *Manichaeus apostolus Iesu Christi providentia dei patris.*[50]

3. *exordia* of Mani's other *letters*: Μανιχαῖος ἀπόστολος 'Ιησοῦ Χριστοῦ. *Manes apostolus Iesu Christi.*[51] Cf. the imitations in a fictitious letter and an oration in the *Acta Arch.*: *ego, viri fratres, Christi quidem sum discipulus, apostolus vero Iesu.*[52]

4. The longer *Formula of abjuration*: ἐτόλμησεν ἑαυτὸν παράκλητον ὀνομάζειν καὶ ἀπόστολον 'Ιησοῦ Χριστοῦ.[53]

[48] *2 Cor.* 1, 1; *Col.* 1, 1; *Eph.* 1, 1; *2 Tim.* 1, 1; cf. *1 Cor.* 1, 1.

[49] *CMC* 66, 4 ff.; M 17; cf. *ZPE* 5 (1970) 189 ff. For (πατρὸς) τῆς ἀληθείας, an unparalleled addition to the Formula, see, e.g., *2 Clem.* 3, 1 and 20, 5. "Jesus the friend" of the Iranian version is the redeemer who awakened and saved Adam, the first (and divine) man, after the latter was defeated by the Darkness (Theodor bar Kōnai, *Liber scholiorum* XI, CSCO 66, 317, 20 = A. Adam, *Texte* [see n. 34] no. 7, p. 22, 180). The expression occurs in Iranian and Chinese texts (Waldschmidt-Lentz, *loc. cit.* [see n. 30] 38 and 106 n. 2; *ZPE* 5 [1970] 193; cf. also H.-Ch. Puech, *L'annaire du College de France* 71, *résumé des cours de 1970–1971*, 264). It is peculiar that the Iranian Manichaeans avoided the Jewish and Christian term of Christ in their *Gospel*. This may well be a later reaction to theological discussions of the kind attested by Augustine in *c. Faust.* 13, 4 p. 381, 6 ff.: --- *quemnam testem vobis sui apostolatus adduxit? nomenque ipsum Christi quod non scimus nisi in regno Iudaeorum in sacerdotibus et regibus institutum --- cur iste invasit, cur usurpavit qui prophetis Hebraeis vos vetat credere, ut vos falsi Christi fallaces discipulos falsus et fallax apostolus faciat?*

[50] August., *c. ep. fund.* 5, p. 197, 10; 6 p. 199, 10 f.; *c. Fel.* 1 p. 801, 16; cf. 16, p. 819, 18; below, p. 176.

[51] C. Schmidt and H. J. Polotsky, *loc. cit.* (see n. 37), 26 who reconstructed the Greek from the Coptic. August., *Op. imperf.* 3 PL 45, 1318 = Adam, *Kl. Texte* (s. n. 34), no. 12 (from Mani's *epist. ad Menoch.*); cf. August., *c. Faust.* 13, 4, p. 381, 4 f.: *omnes tamen eius epistulae exordiuntur: Manichaeus apostolus Iesu Christi*; idem, *de haer.* 46 PL 42, 38 (see n. 34): *promissionem Domini Jesu Christi de paracleto Spiritu sancto in suo haeresiarcha Manichaeo dicunt esse completam. unde se in suis litteris Iesu Christi apostolum dicit eo quod Iesus Christus se missurum esse promiserit atque in illo miserit spiritum sanctum*; cf. G. Quispel, Mani the Apostle of Jesus Christ, in: *Epektasis, Mélanges patristiques offerts au Cardinal Jean Daniélou* (Paris, 1972) 667 ff.; E. Rose, *loc. cit.* (see n. 30).

[52] 15 p. 23, 17 Beeson; cf. the letter, *ibidem*, p. 5, 22.

[53] PG 1, 1461C = Adam, *Texte* (s.n. 34), no. 64; cf. the shorter *Formula of abjuration*, PG 100, 1324C (= Adam, *loc. cit.*, no. 63).

Augustine argued against this claim of Mani. He said that Mani is not mentioned as an apostle in the New Testament and that he was not called by God as Paul was. The alternative would be that he was the apostle of the Holy Spirit, but, as Augustine stressed, this is not what Mani claimed to be.[54] Obviously Augustine did not understand or did not want to understand what the Manichaeans meant by Mani's apostleship. We have already followed the chain of emanation from "Jesus the Splendor" through the "Light—$No\hat{u}s$" to the "Apostle of Light." The latter elects the churches (see n. 45) and sends the apostle into this world. Hence, for the Manichaeans, Mani was the Apostle of "Jesus the Splendor"; he was not the apostle of the historical Jesus, as Augustine thought.[55] In terms of Manichaean theology Mani's apostleship made sense. Paul's apostleship was based on the call he received from Jesus in the apparition at Damascus after the lifetime of Jesus. Mani could understand this as a call by Jesus, the heavenly Father. Hence Mani could feel entitled to call himself an apostle of Jesus in the *exordia* of his letters as Paul did. In fact, Baraies quotes Paul's allusion to his vocation (*2 Cor.* 12, 1–5) in order to illuminate Mani's call.[56] In Mani's interpretation the initial formula of his letters referred to the relationship of the apostle to "Jesus the Splendor." The same phrase frequently meant different things to Christians and Manichaeans. This fact made the Manichaeism embarrassing to Christians.[57]

Mani's claim went further than one might suspect from his use of the Pauline formula. He was the apostle of Christ, because he was the *Paraclete*, i.e., the "Spirit of Truth" whom Jesus had promised to send (*John* 16, 17; cf. 14, 16).[58] For the Christians the *Paraclete* came into the world at

[54] *c. Fel.* 1,1 p. 802, 1 ff.; *c. epist. fund.* 6 p. 199, 10 ff. See also Augustine's arguments against Mani's claim to be the *Paraclete* (below).

[55] Augustine was, however, fully aware that the Manichaean Jesus was essentially different from the Christ of the Christian church; see, e.g., *c. Faust.* 2, 4 p. 257, 2 f., where Jesus Christ is the son of the First Man, that is to say that Jesus the Splendor is the son of the Messenger (the second Father). This belief enabled Faustus to confess *Jesum esse Christum filium dei vivi* (*ibidem*, 5, 3 p. 274, 14; cf. 20, 18 f.). For several Jesuses see n. 143.

[56] *CMC* 61, 4 ff.; cf. *ZPE* 5 (1970) 114 ff. The *Epistle to the Galatians* in which Paul also alludes to his vocation was also known to Baraies (*CMC* 60, 16 ff.). The quarrels about the apostleship of Mani reflect earlier discussions among Jewish Christians on the apostleship of Paul. The latter was refused as based on ὅραμα ἢ ὀπτασία (Ps. Clem., *Hom.* 17, 13 f.; cf. H. J. Schoeps, *Judentum* [see n. 17], 42 ff. = *Jewish Christ.*, 47 ff.). In the *CMC* Mani's mission proceeds from ὀπτασίαι (3, 8 f.) and the vision of the Twin.

[57] That the vocation was brought to Mani by his Twin who acted as mediator between the Father and Mani is discussed below p. 170.

[58] Felix uses *1 Cor.* 13, 9 (*ex parte scimus et ex parte prophetamus; cum venerit autem quod perfectum est, abolebuntur ea quae ex parte dicta sunt*) in order to demonstrate that Paul was not yet the *Paraclete*, but that somebody greater was to be expected, sc. Mani (*in Fel.* 1, 9 p. 811, 4 ff.).

Pentecost. In the Manichaean system, however, the concept was that the Spirit of Truth was sent into the world on several occasions, and that different generations had their own apostle.[59] Mani was the final fulfillment of this spirit, and for this reason he called himself *paraclete*. As he was this spirit of Truth, his revelation was true. According to Baraies, Mani reported his mission to his pupils in order that they could not doubt the truth of the revelation given to him (*CMC* 47, 1 ff. and note).

The chief passages for Mani's claim to be the *Paraclete* are the following:

1. *Gospel:* "––– daß er der Paraklet sei, den der Messias angekündigt habe –––."[60]

2. Baraies, *CMC* 17, 1 ff. [ἵνα ––– (*sc.* the νοῦς of Mani who descended into his body) –––] –––, ἐλευθερώσηι δὲ τὰς ψυχὰς τῆς ἀγνοίας γινόμενος παράκλητος καὶ κορυφαῖος τῆς κατὰ τήνδε τὴν γενεὰν ἀποστολῆς. *ibidem*, 45, 1 ff. γνῶτε ––– καὶ περὶ τοῦ τρόπου καθ᾽ ὃν ἀπεστάλη ἤδε ἡ ἀποστολὴ ἡ κατὰ τήνδε τὴν γενεὰν –––, ἔτι δὲ καὶ περὶ τοῦ [σώ]ματος [αὐτοῦ –––] [new paragraph:] τ[αῦτα δὲ γέγραπται ἵνα μηδεὶς πιστεύσηι τοῖς βλασφημοῦσί τι περὶ] τῆς ἀποστολῆς ταύτης τοῦ πνεύματος τοῦ παρακλήτου –––. πάλιν δὲ καὶ περὶ τῆς γέν[νη]ς τοῦ σώματος αὐτοῦ[. *ibidem*, 63, 1 ff. ––– τοῦ πανευφημοτάτου ἀποστόλου ––– ἀκόλουθόν ἐστιν ἡμῖν γράψαι ––– τοῖς μεταγενεστέροις πᾶσι ––– ὡς ἂν γνωσθῇ αὐτοῖς ἥ τε ἁρπαγὴ αὐτοῦ καὶ ἀποκάλυψις. ἐπιστάμεθα γάρ, ὦ ἀδελφοί, τὸ ὑ[περ]βάλλον τῆς σοφίας [ὅ]σον τυγχάνει τὸ μ[έγε]θος πρὸς ἡμᾶς κα[τὰ ταύ]την τὴν ἄφιξ[ιν τοῦ πα]ρακλήτου τῆ[ς ἀληθεί]ας. *ibidem* 70, 10 ff. πλεῖσται δὲ ὑπερβολαὶ ––– ὑπ[ά]ρχουσιν ἐν ταῖς βίβλοις τοῦ πατρὸς ἡμῶν αἳ δεικνύουσι τήν τε ἀποκάλυψιν αὐτοῦ καὶ ἁρπαγὴν τῆς αὐτοῦ ἀποστολῆς. μεγί[στ]η γὰρ τυγχάνει ἤδε ἡ [ὑ]περβολὴ τῆς ἀφίξεως [τ]αύτης τῆς διὰ τοῦ πα[ρακλή]του πνεύματος[61] τῆς ἀλη[θείας ἀφ]ικομένης πρὸς [ἡμᾶς].

3. *Keph.* 16, 28 ff.: "Wir [aber] haben es ausführlich angenommen und geglaubt, daß du bist der [Paraklet], der aus dem Vater (kommt), der Offenbarer aller Geheimnisse." (Polotsky).

4. In the Coptic *Psalm-Book* Mani is frequently invoked as *Paraclete*.[62]

---

[59] This Manichaean doctrine is based on the Elchasaite concept of cyclic incarnations of the "True Prophet"; see above p. 4 and n. 29; *ZPE* 5 (1970) 139; A. Henrichs, *HSCP* 77 (1973) 54 f.; *ZPE* 19 (1975) 76 n. 39 and 81 n 80. From the Christian point of view nobody could be "Apostle of Christ" and *Paraclete* at the same time (cf. A. Böhlig, in *Synkretismus im syrisch-persischen Kulturgebiet*, ed. A. Dietrich, *Abh. Göttingen*, Phil.-hist. Kl., 3. Folge, 96 [Göttingen, 1975] 157). For the Manichaeans, however, both titles expressed the belief that Mani had been sent by Jesus the heavenly father.

[60] Al-Bīrūnī 207, 18 f. Sachau = Adam, Texte (see n. 34) no. 1b.

[61] The addition of πνεύματος does not point to the Twin. According to *John*, the Paraclete is τὸ πνεῦμα τῆς ἀληθείας or τὸ πνεῦμα τὸ ἅγιον (14, 17 and 26; 15, 26); the *Liber graduum* (3, 11 p. 69 f.: D. M. Kmosko, Patr. Syr. 3 [Paris, 1926]) renders the Old Syrian text of the *Diatessaron* as: *ecce ego mitto vobis Spiritum Paraclitum*.—For the interpretation of the Νοῦς in *CMC* 17, 1 see *ZPE* 19 (1975) 17 n. 30.

[62] Cf. K. Rudolph, *Mélanges* (see n. 1) 479 n. 1. For the Psalm-Book see above n. 34.

5. August., *c. Faust.* 13, 17 p. 398, 25 f.: *hunc paracletum dicentes esse Manichaeum vel in Manichaeo* ---. 15, 4 p. 423, 1 --- *qui se paracletum dicit* ---.[63]

Baraies clearly considered Mani to be the *Paraclete*. This confirms the other assertions of the faith of Manichaean communities. Moreover it would be unreasonable still to doubt the information Albīrūnī gives on Mani's gospel; there Mani declared himself the *paraclete*. In one passage (*CMC* 17, 1 ff.), Baraies expresses the doctrine more exactly: it is Mani's *Νοῦς* that is the *paraclete*. His *Νοῦς*, like that of all men, descended from the heavenly realm of Light and was imprisoned in the body. The real Mani was the *Νοῦς* of Mani.

According to other evidence, however, neither Mani nor his *Νοῦς* were identified with the *paraclete*, but rather his *alter ego* who brought him the revelation. This is the σύζυγος, the "Twin," a gnostic term which may have been consciously reminiscent of *Phil.* 4, 3.[64] The main evidence is the following:

1. *Keph.* 14, 4 ff. (Polotsky): "Von jener Zeit an (*sc.* the beginning of Mani's apostleship) wurde der *Paraklet*, der Geist der Wahrheit, entsandt, der zu euch gekommen ist in dieser letzten Generation, wie der Heiland gesagt hat: 'Wenn ich gehen werde, werde ich euch den Parakleten schicken.'[65] ---;" 32 ff.: "--- da kam der lebendige Paraklet herab [zu mir und] redete mit mir. Er offenbarte mir das verborgene Mysterium, das verborgen ist vor den Welten und den Generationen, das Mysterium der Tiefe und Höhe ---;" 15, 19 ff. "Auf diese Weise ist alles, was geschehen ist, mir durch den Parakleten offenbart worden ---;" 16, 19 "[Denn der] Geist des Parakleten ist es, der zu mir gesandt worden ist von [dem Vater der Größe (?). ---];" Latin *Formula of abjuration* 18: *qui credit Manem sive Manichaeum --- spiritum sanctum habuisse paracletum, cum ea omnia non potuerit spiritus veritatis, sed spiritus falsitatis, anathema sit.*[66] In the *CMC*, however, and in Iranian and Arabic texts it is the Twin that brings Mani the revelation (*ZPE* 5 [1970] 161 ff. and below §2). The *Paraclete* and the Twin have the same function and are identical.

2. According to the report of Baraies in the *CMC*, Mani said several times that the heavenly Father sent the Twin to Mani in order to bring him the

[63] See also the following passages quoted from Augustine, particularly n. 82; further *Acta Archel.* 15, 3 *GCS* 24, 3 *sum quidem ego paracletus* ---; 31, 6 p. 44, 15 f.; 42, 2 p. 62, 3 f.; the two Greek *Formulas of abjuration* (see n. 53). For attestations in Arabic literature see C. Klíma, *loc. cit.* (see n. 34).

[64] For the gnostic term see below p. 174; I thank Mrs. J. Kenney for referring me to *Phil.* 4, 3.

[65] *John* 16, 7. The quotation is continued in the *Keph.*; see P. Nagel, *Festschrift zum 150 jährigen Bestehen des Berliner Ägyptischen Museums*, Staatliche Museen zu Berlin, Mitteilungen aus der Ägyptischen Sammlung VIII (Berlin, 1974) 303 ff.

[66] PL 65, 26 = Adam, *Texte* (see n. 34) no. 62; cf. M. de Beausobre, *Hist. crit. de Mani.* (Amsterdam, 1784) I, 267. For another relevant passage see below, §3 and n. 82.

revelation.[67] Because in the Kephalaia the Twin is identified with the *Paraclete*, one may wonder whether Baraies' phrasing refers to the words by which, according to *John*, Jesus promised to send the *Paraclete*. In this case Baraies' words reflect the assumption that the Twin was identified with the *Paraclete*. But before this conclusion can be reached (section D) we shall review (A) the relevant passages from Baraies, (B) the promises of the *Paraclete* according to the Syriac versions of *John*, and (C) the phrasing of these promises in other Manichaean writings.

A. Baraies on the mission of the Twin: *CMC* 18, 14 ff. ἀπέστειλέν μοι [ἐκεῖθεν ε]ὐθὺς σύζυγόν [μου (*sc.* ὁ μακαριώτατος πατήρ). 19, 16 ff. ἀπ[έ]στειλέ[ν μοι τὸν σύζυ]γό[ν μου. 54, 5 ff. (The Twin tells Mani:) ὁ ἰσχυρότατος τὴν ὑπεροχὴν ἀπέστειλέ με πρὸς σέ. 69, 13. ἐξαπέστειλεν ἐκεῖθεν σύζυγόν μου τὸν ἀσφαλέστατον.[68]

B. The promises to send the *Paraclete* according to the Old Syriac texts:[69]
   a. *John* 14, 16 κἀγὼ ἐρωτήσω τὸν πατέρα καὶ ἄλλον παράκλητον δώσει ὑμῖν (*sc.* ὁ πατήρ).

[67] Baraies does not specify which of the Fathers sends the Twin; one may think of the Light-*Νοῦς* (4th Father), Jesus the Splendor (3rd Father) or of the Father of Greatness (1st Father). It will become clear that the phrasing depends on *John* 16, 7 where Jesus sends the *Paraclete*; this he does also in the Syriac version of *John* 14, 16 (see below, sections B and D). Hence Mani or Baraies probably thought of Jesus the Splendor. Superlatives like ὁ ἰσχυρότατος τὴν ὑπεροχήν (*CMC* 54, 5 f.; see section A) suit him; they do not necessarily denote the first Father (see also n. 101). Besides, the Manichaeans did not always distinguish between the powers of the heavenly Fathers. On the other hand, it is not very likely that Mani and the early Manichaeans knew the *Separate Gospels* (see p. 193) in which, according to *John* 14, 16, the "Father" is supposed to send the *Paraclete* (p. 171, text a).

[68] Cf. Epiph., *Pan.* 65, 6, 8 GCS 3, 9, 14 ἄλλον παράκλητον ὑμῖν ἀποστελῶ. 48, 11, 5 GCS 2, 234, 12 f. τὸ πνεῦμα τὸ παράκλητον ἀποστέλλω ὑμῖν. Naturally Baraies uses the same verb for Mani's mission: *CMC* 72, 15 ff. γνῶμεν τὴν [παρου]σίαν αὐτοῦ πνευ[ματο]-ειδῶς, ὡς ἀπεστά[λη] ἐξ ἐντολῆς τοῦ πατρὸς [αὐτοῦ] καὶ ποίωι τρό[πωι ἐγ]εννήθη κατὰ τὸ [σῶμα κα]ὶ ὡς ἦλθεν (cf. *John* 15, 26; 16, 7) αὐτῶι σύζυγος αὐτοῦ ὁ σεμνότατος ——— (cf. *ZPE* 5 [1970] 117 f.). 22, 4 f. ποίωι τρόπωι διαστὰς αὐτοῦ (*sc.* τοῦ πατρός) ἀπεστάλην (says Mani according to Baraies). Cf. 45, 4 ff. (Baraies) καθ᾽ ὃν (*sc.* τρόπον) ἀπεστάλη ἥδε ἡ ἀποστολὴ ἡ κατὰ τήνδε τὴν γενεάν. Timotheos, *CMC* 104, 12 ff. (The Twin tells Mani:) οὐκ εἰς τοῦτο μόνον τὸ δόγμα (*sc.* the baptists of Jewish origin) ἀπεστάλης, ἀλλ[ὰ᾽] εἰς πᾶν ἔθνος καὶ διδασκαλείαν καὶ εἰς πᾶσαν πόλιν καὶ τόπον. Similarly regarding the Manichaean missionaries *CMC* 124, 7 ff. (Timotheos?) ἀποσταλή[σονται] πρεσβευταὶ καὶ [ἀπόστο]λοι εἰς πάντα τό[πον] (cf. Tat., *Diatessaron Arab.* 55, 5 f. p. 239 Preuschen-Pott: "Und wie mich gesandt hat mein Vater, ebenso sende auch ich euch [*John* 20, 21]. Geht nun in die ganze Welt und predigt das Evangelium bei allem Geschöpf [*Marc.* 16, 15]. Und lehrt alle Völker und tauft sie ——— [*Matth.* 28, 19]." *Act. ap.* 28, 28; Paul is ἐθνῶν ἀπόστολος, *Rom.* 11, 13. In the *NT* ἀποστέλλειν is frequently used for the mission of the apostles and disciples). In the *apoc. Enoch* quoted by Baraies the verb is applied to Michael: τούτου χάριν πρὸς σὲ ἀπεστάλην (*CMC* 59, 6 ff.). For the *Keph.* see, e.g., 9, 19.25; 10, 10; 12, 3; 16, 4.10.

[69] For the following discussion see P. Nagel, *loc. cit.* (n. 65) and G. Quispel, *RSR* 60 (1972) 143 ff.; *idem, loc. cit.* (n. 51).

α) *Sy^c* (*Separate Gospels*): "Und ich werde erbitten von meinem
Vater, daß er euch einen *anderen* Parakleten *sende* ---."[70]

β) Tatian's *Diatessaron*: "--- I further send you another *Paraclete*.[71]

b. *John* 16, 7 ἐὰν δὲ πορευθῶ, πέμψω αὐτὸν (*sc.* τὸν παράκλητον)
πρὸς ὑμᾶς.

γ) *Sy^s* (*Separate Gospels*): "Wenn ich aber gehe, sende ich euch den
Parakleten."[72]

δ) Tatian's *Diatessaron*: --- "Behold! I send you the *Paraclete*."[73]
The distinctive pattern of the old Syriac versions is that they always
use a verb for sending[74] and add *"Paraclete"* as object. In the version
of *John* 14, 16 according to the *Diatessaron* (text β) it is Christ who sends
the *Paraclete* as in *John* 16, 7 (b). But the significant difference is that
John 14, 16 has the addition of the word "another."

C. The promises of the *Paraclete* in the Manichaean writings: *Keph.* 14, 7 ff.
(in the part quoted above in §1) follows the old Syriac version of
John 16, 7 f. (b), either in the version of the separate *gospels* (above
text γ) or in the version of the *Diatessaron* (text δ). The same is the case
with Felix; August., *c.Fel.* 1, 2 p. 802, 10 ff. *vado ad patrem et mitto vobis
spiritum sanctum paracletum*;[75] cf. 811, 10 *mitto vobis spiritum sanctum*.

---

[70] Translated by P. Nagel, *loc. cit.* (n. 65), 309; *Sy^p* (*Pešitta*) literally follows the Greek
text: "Und ich werde erbitten von meinem Vater, und er wird euch einen anderen
Parakleten geben" (Nagel). *Sy^c* (*Curetonian*): F. C. Burkitt, *Evangelion damepharreshe*
(Cambridge, 1904); cf. A. Smith Lewis, *The Old Syriac Gospels* (London, 1910).

[71] Ephraem Syrus: "Je vous envoie encore quelqu'un d'autre qui profère de bonnes
paroles" (L. Leloir, *Ephrem de Nisibe, Comm. de l'évang. concordant ou Diatessaron*, Sources
Chrét. 121 [Paris, 1966] 338; *idem* [Latin translation], CSCO 145 [Louvain, 1954] 197).
The passage is extant only in Armenian.

[72] *Sy^s* = Sinai palimpsest; see Nagel, *loc. cit.* (n. 65), 308.

[73] Cf. n. 71. Ephraem Syrus: "Voici que je vous envoie celui qui profère de bonnes
paroles." Titus from Bostra, *Adv. Manich.* Syr. 4, 13 p. 135, 26 Lagarde: "Siehe, ich sende
euch den Parakleten" (Nagel). See also *Liber graduum* 3, 11 (quoted in n. 61). The addition
of *ecce* is the only difference between *Sy^s* and the *Diatessaron*.

[74] Cf. also *John* 15, 26 ὁ παράκλητος ὃν ἐγὼ πέμψω ὑμῖν παρὰ τοῦ πατρός. The same
verb is used for Christ's mission and that of John's himself.

[75] *vado ad patrem et* cannot be traced to any version of *John* 16, 7, though there is a vague
possibility that it corresponds to the Syriac *Diatessaron* of which only the second part of
the sentence is extant. It seems that Felix for his convenience combined three quotations
into one sentence. *John* 16, 16 *vulg.*: (a) *quia vado ad patrem;* or 28 *vulg.: et vado ad patrem*
(see also 16, 5 and 7); (b) *John* 16, 7 (see above); (c) The quotation is continued with a
version of *John* 16, 13 *qui vos inducat in veritatem* (for these combinations see Fr. Decret,
loc. cit. [see n. 30], 161, who, however, did not take the *Diatessaron* into account). To
combine several quotations from the Bible into one sentence was a standard practice of
the ancient theologians. Hence Felix' combination does not discredit the textual form of
the quotation of *John* 16, 7 (*mitto --- paracletum*). General reasons lead to the assumption
that he rather quotes the *Diatessaron* (above, text δ) than the *Separate Gospels* (text γ).
Cf. G. Quispel, *loc. cit.* (see n. 69); for traces of the *Diatessaron* in the *Keph.* see A. Böhlig,
BSAC 18 (1965/6) 5 ff. = *Mysterium und Wahrheit* (see n. 30) 252 ff., particularly p. 261

Cf. also *De haer*. 46 (*Christus*) *in illo miserit spiritum sanctum* (see n. 51). Augustine himself, however, once followed the Syriac version of the *Diatessaron* corresponding to *John* 14, 16 which he obviously knew from his Manichaean days (see above text β): *c.epist.fund*. 6, p. 199, 16 *et alium paracletum mittam vobis*.[76]

D. Conclusion: The Manichaeans followed the Syriac versions of *John* 16, 7. They differ from the Greek text in that they have "I send you the *Paraclete*." This corresponds to Mani's words in the *CMC*: "He sent me the Twin." The phrasing suggests indeed that Mani thought of his Twin as the promised *Paraclete*.

3. According to Augustine and the Latin *Formula of abjuration*, the *Paraclete* was thought to be *in* Mani. Hence he is different from Mani. But the phrase "*in* Mani" does not suit the concept of the Twin; therefore we shall deal with it below separately.

To sum up, Mani identified (1) himself or rather his *Noûs* and (2) his "Twin" with the *paraclete* of *John*. The seeming contradiction causes scholars difficulties. They tend to attribute the identification of Mani with the *Paraclete* to the later development of the Manichaean church.[77] If so, Al-Bīrūnī's report on the gospel of Mani must be wrong (cf. p. 169, §1). Such a conclusion would be valid only if the two identifications of the *paraclete* were really opposite. The contradiction, however, disappears upon consideration of the gnostic concept of the Twin. When Mani, i.e., the *Noûs* of Mani, was sent into the world, a mirror image of the *Noûs*, i.e., his *alter ego*, remained in heaven. The one ego, the *Noûs*, was imprisoned in the body and, consequently, forgot his mission. Then the Twin, the *alter ego*, was sent to him from heaven. He brought Mani the revelation by reminding him of his divine nature and mission and, like an angel, protected him. The *Noûs* of Mani and his Twin are the two complementary aspects of Mani's identity. The first represents him as incorporated in the body; the second represents his being as it is outside the body. Together they are the one complete Mani.[78] When Mani looked into

---

n. 3; A. Baumstark, *OC*, 3rd ser. 12 (1937) 169 ff.; *Keph.* 7, 21 ff. reports that Christ's disciples recorded his parables and miracles and were ordered to compose a book (not books); see A. Baumstark, *OC*, 3rd ser. 8 (1933) 94 f. For the influence of the *Diatessaron* on Faustus see L. Leloir, *Ephrem de Nisibe* (see n. 71), p. 21; on Adamantus see Quispel, *loc. cit.* (*RSR*; see n. 69); for the *Acta Arch.* see G. C. Hansen, *St. Patr.* 7 (Berlin, 1966) 473 ff. But see also the sceptical remarks of P. Nagel regarding the use of the *Diatessaron* in the *Keph.* (*loc. cit.*; see n. 65).

[76] G. Quispel, *loc. cit.* (*RSR*; see n. 69) 145 f. For *c. epist. fund.* 6 p. 200, 12 ff. see below.

[77] See particularly O. Klíma, *loc. cit.* (n. 63) 237 ff.; K. Rudolph, *Mélanges* (n. 1) 478 n. 3; P. Nagel, *loc. cit.* (n. 65); cf., however, *ZPE* 19 (1975) 75 f. n. 39.

[78] Perhaps a misunderstanding of this concept prompted a disciple of Mani to assume the possibility of duplicating Mani on earth so that one Mani could stay with them, while

himself, he found his Twin approaching him from heaven; or, *vice versa*, when he looked at his Twin, he found himself. The story of the Twin bringing him the revelation relates what in abstract terms may be called the rediscovery of his identity and mission.

A similar gnostic structure is known from the Valentinians. They believed that each person has his *syzygos*. The latter is an angel who protects him and brings him the *gnosis* during his lifetime; after the person's death his *syzygos* leads him to the *pleroma* where, with the help of Christ, the two are finally united in a wedding.[79] Perhaps one may go a step farther. According to the Valentinians Christ and the Holy Ghost form a *syzygy*. They stay mainly in the *pleroma*.[80] Nevertheless this concept may have further inspired Mani to speak of a *syzygy* between himself and the *Paraclete* (the Holy Spirit).

In any case, Mani and his Twin were regarded as the same entity and as identical. Thus, if one of them is the *Paraclete*, so also is the other.[81]

This view of Mani and his Twin is illustrated in the *Kephalaia*. There Mani teaches his pupils that the *Paraclete* was sent to him in fulfillment of the Savior's promise (p. 170, §1); in these passages the *Paraclete* is identified with the Twin. Mani's pupils immediately reply with a confession of faith and they call Mani himself the *Paraclete* (p. 169, §3). As the *Νοῦς* of Mani and the Twin share the same identity, Mani's statement and the reply of his pupils are not contradictory. Rather, they express the same belief from different points of view.

---

the other was going to king Shapur. The disciple might also have thought of the Manichaean concept of several Jesuses (see n. 143 and 55). The answer he got from his master was this: "Siehe, ich ein einziger Mani, bin in die Welt gekommen ———" (*Keph.* 184, 3; cf. A. Henrichs, *HSCP* 77 (1973) 23 ff.).

[79] Cf. H.-Ch. Puech, *L'annuaire* (see n. 49), 258; G. Quispel in *Eranos-Jahrb.* 15 (1947) 263 ff.; 36, 1967, 9 ff. J.-E. Ménard in: *Christentum und Gnosis* (see n. 31), 49 f. See particularly the fragment of Herakleon which is quoted by Origen, *In Joh.* 13, 11, 67 ff. (GCS 4, 235, 16 ff.; *Die Gnosis* I, by W. Foerster, edited by C. Andresen [Zürich and Stuttgart, 1969] 222 f = W. Foerster, *Gnosis, A Selection of Texts*, Engl. transl. edit. by R. McL. Wilson [Oxford, 1972] I *Patristic Texts*, p. 169 f.). For the gnostic origins of the concept of the Twin see further *ZPE* 5 (1970) 161 ff.; for the Valentinians see n. 124.

[80] Iren., *Adv. haer.* 1, 2, 5 ff. (= Epiphanios, *Pan.* 31, 13, 1 ff. *GCS* 1, 404, 23 ff.); Hipp. 6, 31, 7; *Die Gnosis* (see n. 79), 174 and 247. (Engl. transl. p. 129 f. and 188). The concept of the syzygies was Jewish (cf. H. J. Schoeps, *Judenchristentum* 73 ff. = *Jewish Christ.* 88 ff.; G. Strecker, *loc. cit.* [see n. 29], 188 ff.); the Manichaean concept, however, due to its gnostic connotations of mirror image and self-knowledge, was entirely different. Although it grew out through amalgamation of Elchasaite and gnostic concepts of syzygies; this will be shown in a forthcoming article in *ZPE*.

[81] Euodius, *De fide Manich.* 24 CSEL 25, 961, 16 f. on Mani (continuing the quotation in n. 85): *et utique si geminus est spiritus sancti, et ipse spiritus sanctus est ———.*

Augustine did not understand the gnostic concept. He left it undecided whether the Manichaeans claimed that Mani was the *Paraclete* or that the *Paraclete* was in Mani.[82] The latter position, however, does not fully account for the Manichaean identification of the σύζυγος with the *Paraclete*.[83] Augustine knew that the Manichaeans believed that Jesus appeared *in* the flesh.[84] In addition they held the anthropological view that the *Noûs* descends from the heavenly realm into a body (see above, p. 169, §2); thus the *Noûs* of Mani was incorporated *in* his body (Baraies in *CMC* 14, 4 ff.). But this is not what Augustine meant when he said that the Manichaeans believe in the *paraclete* as being in Mani. Trying to understand what he learned from the Manichaeans of his time, he insinuated that Mani equated the relationship between himself and the *Paraclete* with the relationship between Christ as the second person of the Trinity and Christ son of Mary. On the question as to why Mani called himself "Apostle of Christ" and not "Apostle of the *Paraclete*," he argues:

> What other reason do we assume than this: arrogance, the mother of all heretics, brought it about that this man did not want to appear as sent by the *Paraclete*, but as taken on by him in such a way that he himself be called *Paraclete*. As Jesus Christ the Man has not been sent by the Son of God, i.e., the Power and Wisdom of God by which all things have been created, but as, according to the catholic faith, Christ the Man has been taken on by the Son in such a way that he himself be the Son of God, i.e., that the Wisdom of God appear in him in order to heal the sinners, thus Mani wanted to appear as taken on by the Holy Ghost whom Christ had promised, in order that as soon as we hear of Mani as the Holy Ghost we may understand that he is the Apostle of Christ, i.e., the Apostle sent by Jesus Christ who promised to send him.[85]

[82] See p. 170, §5, cf. August., *Conf.* 5, 5, 8: *non enim parvi se aestimari voluit, sed spiritum sanctum, consolatorem et ditatorem fidelium tuorum, auctoritate plenaria personaliter in se esse persuadere conatus est.* c. Faust. 7, 2 p. 305, 2 f.; Felix in August., *c. Fel.* II, 22 p. 852, 10 f. *sed sic anathema ut spiritum ipsum qui in Manichaeo fuit et per eum ista locutus est, anathemes.* Similarly in the Latin *Formula of abjuration* (see n. 66), 10: *quicumque adventum spiritus paracleti ––– in Mane vel in Adimanto discipulo eius venisse credit, anathema sit*; cf. also p. 172, §2, sect. c and nn. 51 and 85. *per Manichaeum:* August., *de ut. cred.* 7, p. 10, 6 ff. *nosti enim, quod auctoris sui Manichaei personam in apostolorum numerum inducere molientes dicunt spiritum sanctum quem dominus discipulis se missurum esse promisit, per ipsum ad nos venisse.*

[83] According to K. Rudolph, Augustine's wording reflects his knowledge of the inconsistency of the Manichaean tradition regarding the identification of the *Paraclete* (K. Rudolph, *loc. cit.* [see n. 1], 480 n. 0).

[84] *Keph.* 37, 14: "––– ist er gekommen und erschienen im Fleische" (Polotsky).

[85] August., *c. ep. fund.* 6 p. 200, 2 ff. *quid hoc esse causae arbitramur, nisi quia illa superbia, mater omnium haereticorum, impulit hominem ut non missum se ab paracleto vellet videri, sed ita susceptum ut ipse paracletus diceretur? sicut Iesus Christus homo non a filio dei, id est virtute et sapientia dei per quam facta sunt omnia, missus est, sed ita susceptus secundum catholicam fidem ut ipse esset dei filius, id est in illo ipso dei sapientia sanandis peccatoribus adpareret, sic se ille voluit ab*

Augustine tried hard to understand the Manichaean concept, but he interpreted their terms as used in the dogma of his church. Consequently he was baffled by the use the gnostics made of the same terms. Nevertheless, his approach was justified by what was probably a later development of the Manichaean theology in the West. When Felix abjured the Manichaean faith, he accepted Augustine's opinion that the *Paraclete* was *in* Mani (see n. 82). The Psalms of the Coptic Manichaeans praised the Trinity: "Glory, victory to the Father, the God of the Truth, and his beloved Son Christ, and the Holy Spirit, the *Paraclete.*"[86] These Manichaeans understood the Christian Trinity as embracing the Father of Greatness, Jesus the Splendor, and Mani the *Paraclete*. Thus, Augustine could easily interpret Mani's introductory phrase as a trinitarian formula: *Manichaeus apostolus Iesu Christi providentia patris*, i.e., the Holy Ghost sent by Jesus Christ through providence of the Father.[87] Augustine was correct when he reports that the identification of Mani with the *Paraclete* goes back to Mani. But Augustine's theological interpretation is directed against the beliefs of the Manichaeans of his time, and it is colored by his misunderstanding of Manichaean theological terms.

(D) *Jesus Patibilis* and *Crux Lucis*

Mani's identification with the *paraclete* has been attributed to the later development of the western Manichaean church. The same was done with the doctrine for which Augustine's Manichaeans used the terms *Jesus patibilis* and *crux lucis*. Manichaean myths describe how particles of the divine Light, Augustine's *substantia vitalis*, fell to the earth and were tied up and kept captive in plants and trees.[88] It was the duty of the Manichaean

---

spiritu sancto quem Christus promisit videri esse susceptum, ut iam cum audimus Manichaeum spiritum sanctum, intellegamus apostolum Iesu Christi, id est missum a Iesu Christo qui eum se missurum esse promisit. Cf. Euodius, *De fide Manich.* 24 CSEL 25, 961, 14 f. *qui se mira superbia adsumptum a gemino suo, hoc est spiritu sancto, esse gloriatur* (quotation continued in n. 81).

[86] *Psalm-Book* 49, 29 ff. (see n. 34). This is one of the typical endings of Manichaean psalms directed to Jesus. Cf., e.g., 57, 31 ff.; 87, 11 ff.; K. Rudolph, *Mélanges* (see n. 1) 479 n. 1.

[87] *c. epist. fund.* 8 p. 201, 20 ff.: regarding why the Holy Spirit is not mentioned in the initial formula, *respondetis utique Manichaeo apostolo nominato sanctum spiritum paracletum nominari, quia in ipso venire dignatus est.*

[88] Mani, *Thes.* 7 *apud* August., *De nat. boni* 44 CSEL 25, 881, 24 ff. = Adam, *Texte* (see n. 34), no. 2: *tunc beatus ille pater* (i.e., Jesus the Splendor) *qui lucidas naves ⟨seu magnitudines⟩* (i.e., the sun and moon) *habet diversoria et habitacula {seu magnitudines}* (transposui) *pro insita sibi clementia fert opem qua exuitur et liberatur ab inpiis retinaculis et angustiis atque*

elect to liberate the divine substance and to make it possible for it to return to the realm of Light. According to Augustine's vivid phrasing, the *elect* separate the spiritual gold from the ordure in which it is mixed.[89] The divine substance is called Christ; it is the *Christus salvandus* whom the *elect* liberate by the sighings of their prayers and burping and digestion.[90] According to Baraies, Mani talked about food as being turned into blood, bile, farts, and ordure.[91] The particles of the divine Light are separated from these in the stomach of the *elect*, but not completely. Parts of it, i.e., parts of Jesus, remain in the ordure and cannot be released even in the long and repeated processes of becoming compost, nourishing fruits and vegetables which, in turn, will—it is hoped—be eaten by the *elect*.[92] Christ dies daily, suffers daily, and is born daily in pumpkins, leeks, purslane, and other plants.[93] Cutting, cooking, chewing and digestion cause pain to the divine substance, to the limbs of God. Such suffering was symbolized by the cross and interpreted as *crucis eius* (*sc. Christi*) *mystica fixio* or as

---

angoribus sua vitalis substantia (*sua* conieci: *suae* codd. | *vitalis* GMAL: *vitali* SPV). Augustine explains (*ibidem*, line 17 f.): *vitalis substantia, hoc est dei natura quam dicunt in eorum* (*sc. principum tenebrarum*) *corporibus ligatam teneri.* Cf. 45 p. 884, 18 f.; *c. Faust.* 6, 6 p. 292, 12 f. and 294, 1 f.; *de haer.* 46 PL 42, 35 ff. (Adam, *Texte*, no. 34, 4 p. 66 ff.). See also W. Henning, *Ein manichäisches Bet- und Beichtbuch*, APAW 1936, 10 (Berlin, 1937) 31 f., line 482 ff. Cf. H.-Ch. Puech, *loc. cit.* (see n. 15), 154 n. 275.

[89] Augustine calls the stomach of the *elect* a *fornacem in qua spiritale aurum de stercoris commixtione purgatur et a miserandis nexibus divina membra solvuntur* (*c. Faust.* 6, 4 p. 290, 17 f.). Cf. *ibidem* 2, 5 p. 258, 19 ff.

[90] August., *c. Faust.* 2, 5 p. 258, 11 ff.: *unde ista sacrilega deliramenta vos cogunt non solum in caelo atque in omnibus stellis, sed etiam in terra atque in omnibus quae nascuntur in ea confixum et conligatum atque concretum Christum dicere, non iam salvatorem vestrum sed a vobis salvandum, cum ea manducatis atque ructatis. nam et ista inpia vanitate seducti seducitis auditores vestros ut vos cibos adferant quo possit ligato in eis Christo subveniri per vestros dentes et ventres.* Cf. p. 259, 9 f.; *ibidem* 20, 13 p. 553, 4 ff. *vobis autem per fabulam vestram in escis omnibus Christus ligatus adponitur adhuc ligandus vestris visceribus solvendusque ructatibus. nam et cum manducatis, dei vestri defectione vos reficitis, et cum digeritis, illius refectione deficitis.* 6, 6 p. 292, 12 f.; *Conf.* 3, 10, 18 (*gemendo in oratione atque ructando*).

[91] *CMC* 81, 5 ff. (Mani argues against the ritual ablution of food which was practiced by the baptists) ὁρᾶτε δὲ ὡς ἐπάν τις καθαρίσῃ ἑαυτοῦ τὴν ἐδωδὴν καὶ ταύτης μεταλάβῃ ἤδη βεβαπτισμένης, φαίνεται ἡμῖν ὅτι καὶ ἐξ αὐτῆς γίνεται αἷμα καὶ χολὴ καὶ πνεύματα καὶ σκύβαλα τῆς αἰσχύνης καὶ τοῦ σώματος μιαρότης.

[92] August., *c. Faust.* 2, 5 p. 258, 19 ff.; 2, 6 p. 261, 2 ff.; *de haer.* 46 PL 42, 34 = Adam, *Texte* (see n. 34), n. 49, 1 p. 66; F. Decret, *Mélanges* (see n. 1), 487 ff.

[93] Euodius, *De fide* 34 CSEL 25, 965, 31 ff. The Manichaeans believed in *metempsychosis*; however, what was once purified by the digestion of the *elect* did not have to return into a body. For the whole context see F. C. Baur, *loc. cit.* (n. 33), 73 ff. and 395 ff.; Fr. Decret, *loc. cit.* (n. 30), 283 ff., 291 f., 302 f.; H.-Ch. Puech, *Le Manich.* (see n. 15) 82 f.; *ZPE* 5 (1970) 150 ff.

crux lucis and *cruciatus*.[94] Thus in the Coptic *Kephalaia* the Manichaean should avoid stepping on the "Cross of Light" and causing damage to a plant. He must keep his hands off the "Cross of Light," i.e., he should not cut plants and fruits. It is through this "Cross of Light," the invisible presence and consummation of salvation, that the "Life of the Vivid Soul" ascends to the sun and moon and further to the realm of heaven.[95] In suffering and redemption, the divine substance becomes the *Jesus patibilis*.[96] Both *Jesus patibilis* and Jesus the Splendor form a kind of gnostic *syzygy* such as that discussed earlier.

A passage of Faustus on the *Jesus patibilis* reveals through an interesting textual detail how the Manichaeans continued to change Christian Scripture to suit their own beliefs. Faustus praises *Christus patibilis* thus (see n. 96):

> *qui est vita ac salus hominum omni suspensus ex ligno.*

vita ac salus is a Christian phrase; according to Ignatius, the cross is σωτηρία καὶ ζωὴ αἰώνιος.[97] The second part of the sentence is based on Paul. In *Gal.* 3, 13 he argues that Christ redeemed us from the curse of the Law by becoming a curse for us; to support this, Paul quotes *Deut.* 21, 23.

---

[94] Faustus *ap.* August., *c. Faust.* 32, 7 p. 766, 20 ff. *crux lucis: en. in Ps.* 140, 12 PL 37, 1823 = Adam, *Texte* (see n. 34), no. 48. *qui enim in usuram — — — dat pecuniam, non laedit crucem lucis. — — — qui autem — — — agricola est, multum laedit crucem luminis. quaeris, quam crucem luminis. membra, inquiunt, illa dei quae capta sunt in illo proelio, mixta sunt universa mundo et sunt in arboribus, in herbis, in pomis, in fructibus.* Cf. *c. Faust.* 20, 11 p. 550, 4 f. *cruciatus:* August., *de haeres.* 46 PL 42, 37 = Adam, *Texte,* no. 49, 4 *herbas enim atque arbores sic putant vivere, ut vitam quae illis inest et sentire credant et dolere, cum laeduntur; nec aliquid inde sine cruciatu eorum quemquam posse vellere aut carpere. c. Faust.* 2, 6 p. 261, 7 *labores atque cruciatus.* 6, 4 p. 290, 7 f.; 6 p. 292, 17 f.; *c. Fort. 1,* 2 p. 88, 1 ff.; Alexander Lycop., *c. Manich. opin.* 4 p. 7, 19 Brinkmann = Adam, *Texte,* no. 36, about Christ being identified with the Νοῦς: ἐνεσταυρῶσθαι τῇ ὕλῃ.

[95] *Keph.* 208, 12 ff.; 192, 8; 124, 1 ff. (and note); 213, 3 ff. Cf. *Acta Arch.* 10, 8 GCS 17, 9 f.

[96] August., *c. Faust.* 20, 2 p. 536, 9 f. *igitur nos Patris quidem dei omnipotentis et Christi Filii eius et Spiritus Sancti unum idemque sub triplici apellatione colimus numen; sed Patrem quidem ipsum lucem incolere credimus summam ac principalem, quam Paulus alias inaccessibilem vocat* (cf. *Tim.* 6, 16), *Filium vero in hac secunda ac visibili luce consistere; qui quoniam sit et ipse geminus, ut eum apostolus novit Christum dicens esse dei virtutem et dei sapientiam* (cf. *1 Cor.* 1, 24), *virtutem quidem eius in sole habitare credimus* (cf. n. 88), *sapientiam vero in luna; necnon et Spiritus Sancti, qui est maiestas tertia, aeris hunc omnem ambitum sedem fatemur ac diversorium; cuius ex viribus ac spiritali profusione terram quoque concipientem gignere Patibilem Iesum, qui est vita ac salus hominum, omni suspensus ex ligno* (cf. *Gal.* 3, 13 and Deut. 21, 23; see below). *quapropter et nobis circa universa et vobis similiter erga panem et calicem par religio est, quamvis eorum acerrime oderitis auctores.*

[97] *Ephes.* 18, 1; *2 Clem.* 19, 1 offers the connection σωτηρίαν καὶ ζωήν. Cf. *John* 11, 25 and 14, 6 ἐγώ εἰμι — — — ἡ ζωή, also *Col.* 3, 4; *Hebr.* 2, 10 Jesus as ἀρχηγὸς τῆς σωτηρίας.

The Greek text and the Latin translation of Marcion's text[98] come closer
to Faustus' text than does the *Vulgate*:

1. Faustus: *omni suspensus ex ligno*
2. Marcion: *maledictus omnis ligno suspensus*
3. Greek: ἐπικατάρατος πᾶς ὁ κρεμάμενος ἐπὶ ξύλου
4. Vulg.:   *maledictus omnis qui pendet in ligno*

In the Manichaean tradition, *omnis* was changed into *omni* rather than
πᾶς into παντός. By the omission of one letter in the Latin text,[99] the
sentence taken from Paul and *Deuteronomy* came to express the sufferings
of Christ in every tree and plant. Probably the change was made before
the time of Faustus. For elsewhere Faustus and the contemporary Manichaeans quote *Gal.* 3, 13, as does Augustine, according to the Vulgate:
maledictus qui pendet in ligno.[100] Moreover, Faustus and Felix use the sentence
for their polemic against Moses and, in doing so, they are not aware of the
slight change which could give to the sentence a Manichaean meaning.
Whenever the change was made, the Manichaean phrase *omni suspensus
ex ligno* demonstrates the habit of the Manichaean church to take advantage
of the Christian Scriptures. The practice was established by Mani, and in
this he was followed by his successors.[101]

The term *Jesus patibilis* is illustrated by Augustine in several passages
where he vividly refers to the pains a plant suffers when it is torn, cooked
and eaten.[102] A fig and its tree weep when the fruit is plucked.[103] Elsewhere

[98] Tert., *Adv. Marc.* 5, 3, 10 Moreschini (*ligno* MFX: *in ligno* R. Evans). Cf. A.v.
Harnack, *Marcion*, Leipzig[2] 1924, 73*.

[99] However, it cannot be entirely excluded that the change was made on the basis of
the Greek text.

[100] *c. Faust.* 14, 1 p. 401, 21 ff.; cf. 16, 5 p. 443, 21 ff.; 32, 5 p. 764, 22 ff.; 32, 14 p. 773,
11 f. Felix, in *c. Fel.* 2, 10 p. 839, 17 ff.; cf. *c. Adim.* 21 p. 179, 21 ff. [*saepe a Manichaeis ista
quaestio ventilata* (*est*)]; cf. Fr. Decret, *loc. cit.* (n. 30), 128 f. and 166 n. o. See also *Psalm-
Book* (see n. 34) 155, 24 ι]ⲏⲥ ⲉⲧⲁϣⲉ ⲁⲡϣⲉ ("Jesus that hangs to the tree"), but there the
use of the relative clause is due to Coptic grammar.

[101] Mani took advantage of another part of the Pauline phrase. According to Baraies,
he said (*CMC* 69, 10 ff.) that his father sent the Twin to him ὡς ἂν οὗτος ἐξαγοράσῃ[ι] με
καὶ λυτρώσαιτο [ἐκ] τῆς πλάνης τῶν τοῦ [νό]μου ἐκείνου. This reflects Paul's Χριστὸς
ἡμᾶς ἐξηγόρασεν ἐκ τῆς κατάρας τοῦ νόμου (*Gal.* 3, 13: ZPE 19 [1975] 85 n. 134). In other
words, Mani tells us that he was redeemed by Jesus the Splendor through the mediation
of his Twin. Thus he became the apostle of Jesus and the *Paraclete* (cf. p. 167 ff. and
nn. 67 f.).

[102] August., *c. Faust.* 6, 4 p. 288, 29 ff. *accipitis ergo viventes cucurbitas quas, si possitis,
degluttire deberetis, ut post illud unum vulnus, in quo eas cum decerpsit vester auditor reus factus est vestra
indulgentia liberandus, saltem deinceps ad officinam aqualiculi vestri, ubi deum vestrum illo proelio
confractum reformare possitis, inlaesae atque integrae pervenirent. nunc autem antequam eis conterendis
dentes incumbant, minutatim, si hoc palato placuerit, conciduntur a vobis; quibus tam crebris vulneribus
earum quomodo vos non estis rei?* --- (p. 289, 18 ff.) *dicitis enim dolorem sentire fructum cum de*

he mocks the *electus* who is not permitted to harvest his own food; rather, he waits for a layman to turn up in the garden with a knife to murder a pumpkin and to deliver the miraculously living corpse to him. Thereupon the layman is accused of murder, but gets forgiveness due to the prayers of the *electus*. This comedy of innocence is well known from Greek texts, and the *Kephalaia* talk about the "murdered soul."[104] Strikingly similar stories are now found in the *CMC*. What seemed to be Augustinian irony turns out to have been told by the Manichaeans as educational stories which expressed their beliefs. A palm tree defends its branches and calls its pruner a murderer. Vegetables literally weep and cry with human voices, and they bleed when they are cut with a sickle.[105] The young Mani was thought to have told such stories to the Elchasaites. For they ate only what they themselves grew in their gardens in order to guarantee the ritual cleanness of their food, and they wanted Mani to obey their regulations. Mani's stories, however, demonstrated to them that ritual cleanness was not the issue; rather, the particles of Light imprisoned in trees and vegetables should not suffer at the hands of the pious *elect*. Therefore Mani refused in one of the stories to go into the garden for his own food, but asked somebody else to pick it and bring it to him as an exercise of piety.[106]

---

arbore carpitur, sentire cum conciditur, cum teritur, cum coquitur, cum manducatur. --- (290, 9 f.) *at enim plorat arbor, cum fructus carpitur. De haer.* 46 (see n. 94); *c. Adim.* 17, p. 172, 2 *panem plorare;* 22 p. 181, 27 f. *talem animam arboris esse cred(u)nt qualem hominis. En. in Ps.* 140, 12 (see n. 94): *dei membra vexat qui terram sulco discindit; dei membra vexat qui herbam de terra vellit; dei membra vexat qui pomum carpit de arbore.* Cf. *ZPE* 19 (1975) 7 n. 10 and 13 n. 21.

[103] August., *Conf.* 3, 10, 18 --- *ficum plorare cum decerpitur et matrem eius arborem lacrimis lacteis.*

[104] August., *c. Faust.* 6, 4 p. 288, 22 ff. *vos autem* --- *expectatis, quis auditorum vestrorum propter vos pascendos cultello vel falcicula armatus in hortum prosiliat, homicida cucurbitarum quarum vobis adferat, mirum dictu, viva cadavera.* Cf. n. 102 (*reus factus est vestra indulgentia liberandus*). *De haer.* 46 PL 42, 37 = Adam, *Texte* (see n. 34), no. 49, 4 p. 68 f. --- *agriculturam* --- *tanquam plurium homicidiorum ream dementer accusant: suisque auditoribus ideo haec arbitrantur ignosci, quia praebent inde alimenta electis suis, ut divina illa substantia in eorum ventre purgata impetret eis veniam quorum traditur oblatione purganda. Acta Archel.* 10, 6 GCS 16, 14 ff. = Adam, *Texte* (see n. 34), no. 38); Kyril. from Jerusalem, *Catach.* 6 (*de uno deo*), 32 PG 33, 596B (= Adam, *Texte*, no. 39); P.Ryl. 469 (Adam, *Texte*, no. 35), 25 ff. *Keph.* 178, 5 ff.: "Die man 'geschlachtete, getötete, bedrängte, gemordete Seele' genannt hat, ist die Kraft der Früchte, der Gurken und Samen, die geschlagen, gepflückt und zerrissen werden und den Welten des Fleisches Nahrung geben. Auch das Holz, wenn es trocken wird, und das Kleid, wenn es alt wird, werden vergehen. Es ist auch [ein] Teil der ganzen 'getöteten, geschlachteten Seele'" (Böhlig). Cf. *ibidem*, 191, 16 ff. Regarding the "comedy of innocence," see *ZPE* 5 (1970) 153 f.

[105] *CMC* 6, 2 ff.; 9, 1 ff. *ZPE* 5 (1970) 145 ff. For the Jewish background of such stories see *ZPE* 19 (1975) 8 f. n. 14.

[106] *CMC* 9, 8 f. ἐν λόγωι εὐσεβείας. Cf. *ZPE* 19 (1975) 11 n. 20.

The Mani of these stories acts as the later *elect* and endorses the concept of the *anima patibilis*.

The same holds true in stories which Mani told a synod of the Elchasaites. There he was accused of schismatic heresies and tried to defend his behavior and beliefs by arguing that he adhered to the teachings of Elchasaios and religious authorities like Sabbaios[107] and Aianos, whereas the present community deserted the traditional faith. Thus these stories have a double meaning. On one level they should express Elchasaite beliefs, on the other, however, they should justify Mani's own religion and express his theology.[107a] For example, according to an authority whose name is lost in the *CMC*, he reports that the Baptist Sabbaios was addressed by a vegetable; it asked him not to sell it to the officials of a city. This suits exactly the beliefs of the baptists and explains their regulations which forbade the sale of agricultural products to pagans. But in Mani's mind, the same story proved that his personal refusal of agricultural work and, consequently, his corresponding prohibitions for the *elect*[108] are Elchasaite.

In the same situation and according to the same authority, he reminds the Elchasaites that their founder once saw some of his disciples baking bread. Then the bread talked to Elchasaios, and he prohibited further bread-baking.[109] In the *CMC*, the story is shortened to the extent that its religious implications hardly make sense. But light is shed on them by Baraies' report on Mani's account of the same synod. There Mani leaves no doubt that the Elchasaites did eat bread, though not wheaten bread. They were particularly offended because Mani ate such bread against

---

[107] For this typical name see *ZPE* 5 (1970) 133 n. 89.

[107a] The interpretation of such stories on both levels is essential. If they did not express Manichaean belief in some way, it would have been pointless to transmit them in Manichaean devotional literature. If, on the other hand, the stories were not known to the Elchasaites of Mani's youth, he could not have used them for his defense, and we would have to conclude that they were later inventions by Mani or by Manichaean authorities. But this assumption is equally difficult. As long as the Elchasaites were living in Ancient Syria, the Manichaeans could not risk the authority of Mani by attributing obvious falsifications to him. They would hardly have endangered their missionary efforts by declaring as Elchasaite stories which were not.

[108] August., *en. in Ps.* 140, 12 (see n. 94 and 102) and *de haer.* 46 (see n. 94 and 104). For the story (*CMC* 97, 18 ff.) see *ZPE* 5 (1970) 148. The Manichaean interpretation would be forced since the *elect* was prevented from all farming activities, not only from selling agricultural products. Thus it is most unlikely that the story is a Manichaean invention.

[109] *CMC* 97, 11 ff. ἔφη δ' αὖ πάλιν (*sc.* Mani) ὅτι εὗρεν τοὺς μαθητὰς αὐτοῦ Ἀλχασαῖος πέπτοντας ἄρτους ὡς καὶ λαλῆσαι τὸν ἄρτον πρὸς τὸν [Ἀλ]χασαῖον· ὃς δὲ ἐνετε[ίλα]το μηκέτι πέπτει[ν]. This prohibition precludes interpretation as a simple devotional story without precise religious meaning.

what they thought were the commands of Christ.[110] Mani considered this accusation serious.[111] His reactions are revealing. First he refers to Christ celebrating the Eucharist with his disciples and asks rhetorically whether this was not wheaten bread. Then he interprets Christ's visit to the house of Martha and Maria: "Therefore, observe that also the disciples of the savior accepted bread from women and idol-worshippers and ate it, and that they did not distinguish between different kinds of bread."[112] Finally Mani stresses that, when Jesus commissioned the apostles, he told them not to take unnecessary equipment with them, including ovens for baking.[113] Mani actually responds to two accusations: (1) that he eats wheaten bread, and (2) that he eats it together with other people, even with idol-worshippers. The story of Elchasaios' prohibition to bake bread cannot mean that baking wheaten bread was forbidden.[114] The second accusation, however, illuminates the story. As every Elchasaite had to grow his own food, he may also have had to bake his own bread; this would mean he had to do it privately, not in a bakery and not with other people, certainly not with pagans, but probably not even with other

110 One of the standard accusations was (91, 11 ff.) βούλει δὲ καὶ ἄρτον σίτινον ἐσθίειν καὶ λάχανα ἅπερ ἡμεῖς οὐκ ἐσθίομεν. The latter seems to imply that certain vegetables were prohibited. The ἄρτος σίτινος, one of the main provisions of the Manichaeans (cf. K. Rudolph, Mani [see n. 15], 557) is also called by the Elchasaites Ἑλληνικὸς ἄρτος (87, 20 ff.). It may have been difficult to grow wheat or any other grain for the personal use of a single man. A. Henrichs drew my attention to Strabo, who mentions that in Babylonia meal and bread are gotten from the palm tree (16, 1, 14; 742). Palm trees were cultivated by the Elchasaites; thus they may have produced this kind of bread. Deut. 16, 3 calls unleavened bread a "bread of misery," which shall be eaten in memory of the misery of the Exodus. Our passage is not concerned with unleavened bread but with daily food. However, it still may have been regarded as a bread of poverty by which the misery of the Exodus was renewed daily. Later, under different economical conditions, the Karaites, a Jewish ascetic movement originating in 8th-century Persia, admitted only barley for the Passover bread; for barley bread was regarded by them as the bread of poverty (as pointed out to me by J. Maier, my former colleague in Cologne).

111 Cf., e.g., CMC 91, 20 ff. (Mani to the Elchasaites) μὴ γένοιτό μο[ι τὰς ἐν]τολὰς τοῦ σωτῆρος [καταλύ]ειν.

112 93, 3 ff. σκοπεῖτε τοίνυν ὡς καὶ οἱ μαθηταὶ τοῦ σωτῆρος ἄρτον ἀπὸ γυναικῶν καὶ εἰδ[ω]λολατρῶν ἤσθιον καὶ οὐ διεχώρησαν ἄρτον ἄρτου, ἀλλ' οὐδὲ λάχανον λαχάνου ---. For the whole section see A. Henrichs, HSCP 77 (1973) 50 f.; however, he points to the celebration of the Eucharist with unleavened bread.

113 93, 14 ff. ὁμοίως δὲ ὁπηνίκα ἀ[πέ]στειλεν αὐτοῦ τοὺ[ς μα]θητὰς ὁ σωτὴρ καθ' ἕκ[αστον] τόπον κηρύξαι, [οὔτε] μύλον οὔτε κλί[βανον] συνεπεφέρο γ[το με]τ' αὐτῶν ---. Cf. Luke 9, 3 and Mark 6, 8 f.

114 It would mean that the bread of the pagans talks to Elchasaios and asks him not to be baked.

disciples.[115] This guaranteed the cleanness requisite for the holy act of eating. For Mani, however, the story indicated the *anima patiens* in bread,[116] and it justified his refusal to bake his own bread.

A further consideration leads from the *anima patibilis*, as attested by such stories in the *CMC*, to *Jesus patibilis* and to the theology of the *crux lucis*. Once Mani appealed to the authority of Elchasaios and related how Elchasaios one day went to get his ploughs from storage. But the earth addressed him:

"Why do you make your living from me?" Then Elchasaios took dust from that earth which had spoken to him, wept, kissed it, placed it in his lap, and began to talk: "This is the flesh and the blood of my Lord."[117]

This story also fits into the pattern we met before. On the Elchasaite level it prohibits agriculture for business: perhaps for this reason ploughs are mentioned in the plural number.[118] At first, Elchasaios, it seems, is spoken of as a professional farmer; but through the miracle he learns that he has to change his profession and life. The story is Elchasaite. If so, it was the Elchasaites who combined their regulation with the concept of Christ's flesh and blood as present in matter. The presence of Christ in matter, i.e., the presence of a soul or divine particles, resulted in the abilities of

[115] One wonders whether the Elchasaites were so consistent that they ate in privacy and did not have their meals together in the community of the baptists; for the Jewish and Jewish-Christian meals of the community, see G. Strecker, *loc. cit.* (see n. 29), 209 ff. The Manichaeans had one common meal each day; see K. Rudolph, Mani (n. 15), 557.

[116] It was also forbidden to give bread to a hungry man: August., *c. Faust.* 15, 7 p. 430, 11 *non das esurienti panem, hic formidans homicidium falsum, illic perpetras verum.* Cf. n. 102 and *Acta Archel.* 10, 6 p. 16, 15 f. Beeson: οὔτε εἰς κλίβανον ἔβαλον (τὸν ἄρτον).

[117] *CMC* 96, 18 ff. (the name of the author from whom this section is taken is broken off): [πάλιν δ]είκνυσιν ὅτι εἶ[χεν ἄρ]οτρα ὁ Ἀλχασαῖος [ἀποκείμ]ενα καὶ ἐπορεύ[θη εἰς α]ὐτά. ἐφθέγξα[το δ' ἡ γῆ λ]έγουσα αὐτ[ῷ]· "[τί] πράττ[ε]τε ἐξ ἐμοῦ [τ]ὴν ἐργασίαν ὑμῶν;" [ὁ δ]ὲ Ἀλχασαῖος δεξάμενος χοῦν ἐκ τῆς γῆς ἐκείνης τῆς λαλησάσης πρὸς αὐτὸν κλαίων κατεφίλησε καὶ ἐπέθηκε τῶι κόλπωι καὶ ἤρξα[το] λέγειν· "αὕτη ἐστὶν ἡ σάρξ καὶ αἷμα τοῦ κυρίου μου." Cf. *ZPE* 5 (1970) 147. For the prohibition against ploughing see n. 102.

[118] They are stored away. An explanation is not given. The compilor of the *CMC* may have taken the story out of a fuller context, which in itself was probably already an abbreviation of Mani's report. Originally, the earth may have addressed Elchasaios on two different occasions; after the first time, he may have stored the ploughs away, but later he may have tried to plough again. The latter part may have become our extant story. Similarly, the water had to address Elchasaios at least on two occasions before he abolished bathing (*CMC* 94, 10 ff.; cf. *ZPE* 5 [1970] 143 f. and here below p. 188). These two stories are taken from the author of the story about the ploughs; his name is lost; see n. 117.

trees, vegetables, bread, earth, and water to talk and to express their pain. Thus the strange rituals assuring the cleanness of food become understandable: eating was a celebration of the Eucharist.[118a]

We now come to the point at which the story underwent a new Manichaean interpretation. The concept of Christ's flesh and blood is attested as Manichaean in Iranian and Chinese sources.[119] It expresses the idea of the *Christus patiens*. Our story attests this doctrine already for the early Mani. The basic beliefs of the Elchasaites and the Manichaeans seem not to have differed too much in this point.[120] They became much more elaborate, however, as they were theoretically and systematically explored by the Manichaeans; and the rituals which followed from their religious conceptions became totally different. In the history of religion, rituals are normally more permanent than beliefs. But the case is different with Manichaeism, because Mani radically turned from the Elchasaite predominance of ritual to the *Gnosis*.[121] In the case of the *Christus patiens*, the later Manichaeans thought of the meals of their *elect* in terms of the Holy Supper of the Christians. Faustus states: "Therefore we have the same piety, we concerning the universe, and you in a similar way concerning the bread and cup" (see n. 96). Needless to say, the underlying theologies of the Christian and Manichaean churches were different. The stories in the *CMC*, however, show that the Christian elements were a part of the central ideas developed by Mani when living with the Elchasaites.

In later Manichaeism, the concept of *Christus patiens* is connected with the idea of the *Crux lucis*. The Cross, of course, is a symbol of suffering. Now that we know that Mani developed his doctrine of *Christus patiens* from the Elchasaite heritage, the same should be expected of the *Crux lucis*. The concept occurs also in the *Acta Johannis* which were known by the Manichaeans and had their origin probably in encratitic sects of Syria and

---

[118a] The Elchasaites regarded the earth as an element and kind of divine power. From this thought, speculation led easily to the belief in the presence of Christ's flesh and blood in earth. This will be shown in a forthcoming article to appear in *ZPE*. Compare also the *Gospel according to Thomas*, logion 77.

[119] W. Henning, *loc. cit.* (see n. 88), p. 48 line 762 f. (cf. J. P. Asmussen, *loc. cit.* [see n. 34], 59). The electus confessed that before the meal he did not meditate on the question: "Whose flesh and blood is this?" *Chinese Roll of Hymns*, str. 253 f. (Tsui Chi, *BSOAS* 11 [1943] 198: "All the wonderful offerings which are received, as said by the Law, are restored to the original Law, dignified and solemn, clean and pure. And these are exactly the flesh and blood of Jesus.") Cf. *ZPE* 5 (1970) 150.

[120] In this respect K. Kessler's remark that the Elchasaites were pre-Manichaean Manichaeans (*Mani, Forschungen über die manichäische Religion* [Berlin, 1889] 8 n. 3) is not far off the mark. Cf. A. Henrichs, *HSCP* 77 (1973) 58 and below n. 154.

[121] *CMC* 84, 9 ff.; *ZPE* 5 (1970) 137.

Asia Minor.[122] There the "Cross of Light," so that it can be understood by man, is identified with terms such as *Logos, Nus,* Jesus, Christ, Door, Way, Bread, Seed, Resurrection, Son, Father, Spirit, Life and Truth; in itself, however, it is the "boundary of everything, is, further, the firm elevation of the unsteady which has become solid and the harmony of wisdom. On its right and left side are Powers, Mighty Angels, Rulers and Daemons, Forces, Threats, Angers, Devils, Satan and the Root in the Depth from which the Nature of created things came forward." This cross has fixed (διαπηξάμενος) everything by means of the Logos. On the other hand, it separates the world of created things from heaven (διορίσας); then, however, it integrates them in itself.[123] On the one hand, this cross is the boundary between the two worlds; on the other, it is the bridge between them by which salvation becomes possible. It is the salvation of unsteady things, i.e., of what has been connected with matter; these will become steady in the cross. Finally everything will be integrated in it and thus saved by Christ. It is bread and seed. This concept is not much different from the Manichaean Cross of Light. It can, however, be traced back to the century before Mani. For in Valentinian gnosticism, the Cross divides the *pleroma* from the world, and on this cross Christ reaches the *Sophia* who had been thrown out of the *pleroma* into this world, and thus he initiates her salvation. The double function of the Cross is to separate

---

122 Cf. H.-Ch. Puech, *loc. cit.* (see n. 15), 176 n. 343. He refers also to the φωτεινὸς σταυρός of *Acta Phil.* 138 and 141, which reaches from the depth to the height, resembles a ladder and enables those in Hades to ascend. For the *Acta Johannis,* their origin and their influence on the Manichaeans, see W. Schneemelcher and K. Schäferdiek, in Hennecke-Schneemelcher, *Neutestamentliche Apokryphen* (Tübingen³, 1964) II, 110 ff., particularly 117 ff. and 143. Compare also P. Nagel, *loc. cit.* (see n. 30) 165 ff. These *Acta* are as relevant for the formation of the Manichaeism as are the *Acta Thomae* (*pace* P. Nagel, *loc. cit.* 171).

123 98 p. 200, 5 ff. Bonnet (the text is badly distorted) ὁ σταυρὸς οὗτος ὁ τοῦ φωτὸς ποτὲ μὲν Λόγος καλεῖται ὑπ' ἐμοῦ δι' ὑμᾶς, ποτὲ δὲ Νοῦς, ποτὲ Ἰησοῦς, ποτὲ Χριστός, ποτὲ Θύρα, ποτὲ Ὁδός, ποτὲ Ἄρτος, ποτὲ Σπόρος, ποτὲ Ἀνάστασις, ποτὲ Υἱός, ποτὲ Πατήρ, ποτὲ Πνεῦμα, ποτὲ Ζωή, ποτὲ Ἀλήθεια, ποτὲ Πίστις, ποτὲ Χάρις. τὰ{ι} (τὰ scripsi) μὲν πρὸς ἀνθρώπους· ὁ δὲ ὄντως ἐστὶν αὐτὸς πρὸς αὐτὸν νοούμενος καὶ εἰς ἡμᾶς λεγόμενος διορισμὸς πάντων, ἔστιν (sic interpunxi) καὶ τῶν πεπηγμένων ἐξ ἀνεδράστων ἀναγ⟨ω⟩γὴ β⟨ε⟩β⟨αί⟩α καὶ ἁρμονία σοφίας {σοφία δὲ οὖσα ἐν ἁρμονίᾳ} (glossam delevi)· ὑπάρχουσιν δεξιοὶ καὶ ἀριστεροὶ (post ἀριστεροὶ interpunxit Bonnet) δυνάμεις, ἐξουσίαι, ἀρχαὶ καὶ δαίμονες, ἐνέργειαι, ἀπειλαί, θυμοί, διάβολοι, Σατανᾶς καὶ ἡ κατωτικὴ ῥίζα ἀφ' ἧς τῶν γενομένων προῆλθεν φύσις. 99 οὗτος οὖν ὁ σταυρὸς ὁ διαπηξάμενος τὰ πάντα Λόγῳ καὶ διορίσας τὰ ἀπὸ γενέσεως καὶ κατωτέρω, εἶτα καὶ εἰς πάντα πή⟨ξ⟩ας. The vision took place on Good-Friday (Hilgenfeld; cf. Hennecke-Schneemelcher, *loc. cit.* [see n. 122], 157 n. 4 and 143) and depicted what really happened; the Cross of Light is the real cross of Christ, not the wooden cross. In the vision the Cross of Light is described as πεπηγμένος, surrounded by a crowd consisting of many shapes, whereas the cross has one shape.

(μερίζει καὶ διορίζει) and to make steady (ἑδράζει καὶ στηρίζει). Such also is the function of the Cross in the *Acta Johannis*. The second Christ of the Valentinians who continues the salvation after the first Christ returned into the *pleroma*, is made out of everything and is everything; in the same way the Cross of Light in the *Acta* absorbs and fixes all things.[124] It should be noted, however, that the *Acta* employ the concept with much more straightforward dualism than does Valentinian gnosticism; and it cannot be said that the *Acta* are Valentinian. Nevertheless, the idea of the Cross of Light has its origin in gnostic circles which were influenced by some form of Valentinianism.

This conclusion is confirmed by the report of Mose bar Kepha on the cosmogony of Bardesanes. When the Darkness assaulted the "pure beings" and tried to mingle with them, Christ, sent by the Highest God, separated the Darkness from the "pure beings." He fixed each being to its proper place "according to the mystery of the Cross." Thus this cross has one of the two essential functions of the Cross of Light. Hence it is the Cross of Light to which the phrase "Mystery of the Cross' alludes. In addition, we have only to remember that according to the ancient tradition Bardesanes was Valentinian before he converted to Christianity; allegedly he never escaped the heretic influence entirely. It seems clear that the Cross of Light was Valentinian.[125]

[124] Irenaeus, *Adv. haer.* 1, 2, 4; 3, 4 f. (Epiphanios, *Pan.* 31, 12, 4 ff. GCS 1, 404, 11 ff.; 31, 12 ff. GCS 1, 408, 3 ff.). Cf. *Die Gnosis* (see n. 79) I, 162 ff. (Engl. transl. 121 ff.); H. Jonas, *loc. cit.* (see n. 15), 362 ff.; E. de Faye, *Les gnostiques et le gnosticisme* (Paris², 1925); W. Foerster, *Von Valentin zu Herakleon*, Beih. ZNW 7 (Berlin, 1929); H. Langerbeck, *Aufsätze zur Gnosis*, AAWG, 3. Folge 69 (Göttingen, 1967) 38 ff.; K. Rudolph in: *Koptologische Studien in der DDR*, Sonderh. der Wiss. Zeitschr. der M.-Luther-Universität (Halle–Wittenberg, 1965) 162. For the relationship between the *Acta Johannis* and Valentinian gnosticism, see particularly H. Schlier, *Religionsgeschichtliche Untersuchungen zu den Ignatiusbriefen*, Beih. ZNW 1929, 102 ff. and 175; cf. C. L. Stuhrhahn, *Die Christologie der ältesten apokryphen Apostelakten* (Heidelberg, 1951) 26 n. 4 (*non vidi*; cf. K. Schäferdiek [see n. 122], 143. Cf. also above n. 79.

The relationship between the "Cross of Light" of the *Acts of John* and the Valentinian Cross has been stressed particularly by A. Orbe ("La teología del Espíritu Santo," *Analecta Greg.* 158 [Rome, 1966] 270 ff.; cf. *idem*, "Los primeros herejes ante la persecución," *Analecta Greg.* 83 [1956] 161 ff.; J. Baggarly has brought these studies to my attention). The idea of the cross and Christ as "everything" is, of course, derived from *Col.* 3, 17 (cf. n. 45). Similar Pauline language was used by Mani for the "Tree of Life," as will be shown in a forthcoming article in *ZPE*.

[125] For the cosmogony see H. H. Schaeder, *ZKG* 3. Folge, 51 (1932) 52 (= *idem*, *Studien zur orientalischen Religionsgeschichte*, edit. by C. Colpe [Darmstadt, 1968] 138); cf. H.-Ch. Puech, *loc. cit.* (see n. 122). Bardesanes is attested as a former Valentinian by Didymos the Blind, *PsT* 181, 8 ff. (M. Gronewald in connection with A. Gesché, part III); Eusebios, *h.e.* 4, 30, 3 (οὐ μὴν καὶ παντελῶς γε ἀπερρύψατο τὸν τῆς παλαιᾶς αἱρέσεως

It is now an obvious guess that these gnostic circles affected the thoughts of the community of Elchasaites in which Mani lived. There he became acquainted with the concept of the Cross of Light and developed the related concept of the *Christus patiens*. Thus it seems safe to assume that at least some groups of the Elchasaites were open to gnostic speculation. It was in these groups that Mani found the gnostic idea of the *syzygos* (see p. 174).

(E) The Authenticity of the Elchasaite Stories

When Mani was confronted with the synod of the Elchasaites, he surely had tactical motives to quote Elchasaios. Nevertheless, I think, he originally thought of himself as a reformer who wanted to free Elchasaite teachings from Jewish influences and to restore the true Christian beliefs.[126] To be sure, Mani's point of view was not correct historically. The Elchasaites had Jewish roots, and the Christianity Mani experienced was gnosticized. Similarly, Manichaeans later thought that they were adhering to the true teachings of Christ when they eliminated the Old Testament.

In spite of Mani's bias, one can for the most part believe his claim that the stories which he reported were Elchasaite.[127] This is the implication of what was said in the previous section. By selling his own inventions as Elchasaite stories, Mani could never have hoped to impress an Elchasaite audience. Occasionally the stories expressed Mani's own views so poorly that neither he nor any Manichaean could have invented them (see already n. 108). For example, he told the synod that once upon a time dates were stolen from a palm tree. The tree then asked Ajanos the Baptist to serve as interpreter so that it could talk to its owner and the thief. To the owner it promised to replace the stolen fruits in the same year and also to

---

ῥύπον); Hieron., *De vir. ill.* 33. Cf. D. Amand, *loc. cit.* (see n. 7) 228 and A. Henrichs, *HSCP* 77 (1973) 52 n. 110 (with literature on Bardesanes). See now H. J. W. Drijvers in: *Synkretismus* (see n. 59) 107 ff. B. Aland argues that Mani had adopted and transformed the gnostic cosmogony myth as extant in the version of Bardesanes (*ididem*, 123 ff.).

126 Cf. K. Rudolph, *loc. cit.* (see n. 1), 477 and above p. 161. Felix says: *Manichaeus autem in nulla fide fuit a qua recesserit, sed in qua fuit in ea permansit* (August., *c. Fel.* 1, 8 p. 810, 13 ff.). Nevertheless Mani talks about ὁ νόμος ὑμῶν (not ἡμῶν); see, e.g., n. 129. In the *CMC* Timotheos reports a vision in which Mani was instructed to set aside Sita, the leader of the Elchasaites (77, 4 ff.). In *Keph.* 258, 27 ff. the Father awarded Mani the privilege of having the Manichaeans named after him; Mani and the Manichaeans are clearly understood as different from the Christians (cf. A. Böhlig, *Mysterium und Wahrheit* [see n. 30], 243). However, even in this passage Christ and Mani are still understood as propagating the same religion.

127 For the authenticity of passages in *CMC* ascribed to Mani, cf. the argument in *ZPE* 8 (1971) 249 n. 2 and *ZPE* 19 (1975) 77 n. 40. Cf. also n. 107a.

produce fruits in future years as long as the owner would not fell it. Then it threatened the thief that it would throw him down the next time.[128] Such stories of talking trees were and are told by many peoples, among others by the ancient Jews. The present story is supposed to demonstrate (1) how dangerous it is to steal fruit from a neighbor's tree and (2) that one should not fell a tree after its fruit has been stolen. Who would do the latter? Which society would regard this as a desirable practice? Only a community which prohibits sales to unclean people might question whether it is sinful to provide fruits for stealing and whether the lawful owner should not rather fell the tree, so that the sin will not be repeated. So understood, the story accords exactly with the religious provisions of the baptists. But when Mani quotes the story in order to justify his refusal to work in the garden, his interpretation is that it is forbidden to fell a tree because of the divine Light in it. In itself, the story does not suggest such an idea. Hence, the fact that Mani's interpretation is so forced demonstrates that it is not his invention. Rather, it is what he said it was: an Elchasaite tradition.

(F) The Elchasaites of Mani: A Community in Change

As I have tried to argue, Mani's idea of the Light which fell from heaven into plants and trees, and which, as the suffering redeemer, had to be liberated, grew out of Christianized Judaism which was or came to be under the influence of gnosticism. At least some groups of the Elchasaites were open to influences which were, in fact, not consistent with their historical background and with the essence of their religion: the baptism. This can be demonstrated by two other stories which, according to the above-mentioned author whose name is lost, were also used by Mani for his defense before the synod of the Elchasaites. In the first story, the spirit of a fountain prevents Elchasaios from washing himself and polluting the water.[129] In the second story, Elchasaios, after the intervention of the

---

128 Baraies in *CMC* 98, 9 ff. [π]άλιν δείκνυσιν ὡς μετὰ Ἀϊανοῦ τοῦ βαπτιστοῦ τοῦ ἀπὸ Κώχης φοῖνιξ συνελάλησεν καὶ ἐνετείλατο αὐτῶι εἰπεῖν τῷ κυρίωι μου· "μὴ [δ]ὴ ἐκκόψῃς διὰ τὸ κλέ[π]τεσθαί μου τοὺς καρ[π]ούς, ἀλλ' ἔασόν με τὸ [ἔτο]ς τοῦτο. καὶ τούτωι [τῶι] ἐνιαυτῶι δώσω σοι [καρπ]οὺς ἀναλογοῦν[τας το]ῖς κλαπεῖσιν, ἔ[τι δὲ ἐ]ν π[ᾶσ]ι τοῖς ἑτέ[ροις ἔτεσιν]." ἐνετείλα[το] δὲ κἀκείνωι τῶι ἀνθρώπωι τῷ κλέπτοντι τοὺς καρποὺς αὐτοῦ εἰπεῖν· "μὴ ἔλθῃς τῶδε τῶι καιρῶι ἀποκλέψα[ι] μου τοὺς καρπούς. ε[ἰ] δὲ ἔλθοις, ἐκρίπτω σε ἐκ τοῦ ὕψους μου καὶ ἀποθανεῖσαι." Cf. *ZPE* 19 (1975) 8 f. n. 14; the reconstruction and interpretation of details of the text have been changed since the publication; thus our report there is not quite correct.

129 *CMC* 94, 2 ff. εἰ τοίνυν περὶ τοῦ βαπτίσματος κατηγορεῖτέ μου, ἰδοὺ πάλιν ἐκ τοῦ νόμου ὑμῶν δείκνυμι ὑμῖν καὶ ἐξ ἐκείνων τῶν ἀποκαλυφθέντων τοῖς μείζοσιν ὑμῶν ὅτι οὐ δέον ἐστὶ βαπτίζεσθαι. δείκνυσι γὰρ Ἀλχασαῖος ὁ ἀρχηγὸς τοῦ νόμου ὑμῶν· πορευομένου γὰρ αὐτοῦ

spirit, preferred to let the dirt dry on his head rather than pollute and upset water.[130] Mani concludes that the repeated ceremonies of purification and baptism contradict the original teaching of Elchasaios. Indeed, it is hard to reconcile the stories with baptismal rites. Are they Mani's invention? Our interpretation of other stories does not suggest this. Quite telling is the first story which refers to Elchasaios with a most characteristically Jewish term: the righteous one.[131] But if the stories are Elchasaite, they can be accounted for by a kind of antibaptismal mood which seemingly began to develop even among baptists.

The second story accepts as a general practice of the Elchasaites that one should not baptize in the sea. This conforms to Jewish as opposed to Greek custom;[132] such a restriction can be expected of the Elchasaites. The same story says that Elchasaios wanted to bathe in what seems to have been a shallow body of water. This was against Jewish regulations.[133] But the spirit of the water objects to the pollution and it argues that it and the water of the sea are identical.[134] If so, the shallowness of the water cannot

λούσασθαι εἰς ὕδατα εἰκὼν ἀνδρὸς ὤφθη αὐτῶι ἐκ τῆς πη[γ]ῆς τῶν ὑδάτων λέγου[σα] πρὸς αὐτόν· "οὐκ αὐ[τάρ]κως ἔχει τὰ ζῷα σου [πλή]ττειν με, ἀλλὰ καὶ [αὐτὸς] σὺ καταπονεῖς [με...].[..]ον καὶ τὰ ὔ[δατά] μου ἀ]σεβεῖς;" ὥσ[τε θαυμάσ]αι τὸν Ἀλχα[σαῖον καὶ ε]ἰπεῖν πρὸς αὐτήν· "[ἡ] πορνεία καὶ ἡ μιαρότης καὶ ἡ ἀκαθαρσία τοῦ κόσμου ἐπιρίπτεταί σοι καὶ οὐκ ἀπαυδᾷς, ἐπ' ἐμοὶ δὲ λυπῇ;" ἔφη πρὸς αὐτόν· "εἰ καὶ οὗτοι πάντες οὐκ ἔγνωσάν με τίς τυγχάνω, σὺ ὁ φάσκων λάτρης εἶναι καὶ δίκαιος διὰ τί οὐκ ἐφύλαξάς μου τὴν τιμήν;" καὶ τότε κινηθε[ὶς ὁ] Ἀλχασαῖος οὐκ ἐλούσ[α]το εἰς τὰ ὕδατα. Cf. ΖPE 5 (1970) 135 n. 97.

130 CMC 95, 14 ff. (text continued from n. 129) καὶ π[ά]λιν μετὰ πολὺν ἐβου[λή]θη λούσασθαι εἰς τ[ὰ ὕδα]τα καὶ ἐνετείλατ[ο τοῖς] μαθηταῖς αὐτ[οῦ ἐπιτη]ρῆσαι τόπον ἔχ[οντα] ὕδατα μὴ συ[χνὰ(?)] ἵνα λούσηται· ε[ὗρον δὲ οἱ] μαθηταὶ α[ὐτοῦ τὸν τό]πον αὐτῶι. μέ[λλον]τος δὲ αὐτοῦ λού[σασθαι] πάλιν ἐκ δευτέρου ὤφθη αὐτῷ εἰκὼν ἀνδρὸς ἐκ τῆς πηγῆς ἐκείνης λέγουσα αὐτῷ· "ἡμεῖς κἀκεῖνα τὰ ὕδατα τὰ ἐν τῇ θαλάσσῃ ἐν τυγχάνομεν· ἦλθες οὖν καὶ ἐνταῦθα ἁμαρτῆσαι καὶ πλῆξαι ἡμᾶς." πάνυ δὲ τρομάσας καὶ κινηθεὶς ὁ Ἀλχασαῖος τὸν πη[λ]ὸν τὸν ἐπὶ τῆς κεφα[λῆ]ς αὐτοῦ εἴασεν ξηραν[θῆ]ναι καὶ οὕτως ἀπέ[δε]ιξεν.

131 The Jewish and Christian term of "the righteous one" was adopted by the Manichaeans; see A. Henrichs, HSCP 77 (1973) 46 n. 84 and K. Rudolph, loc. cit. [n. 1], 484 n. 2.

132 See ΖPE 5 (1970) 143 n. 120.

133 Qumran, CD 10, 10 ff.: "Niemand soll sich waschen in Wasser, das schmutzig ist oder nicht ausreicht, um einen Mann ganz zu bedecken. Nicht darf man darin ein Gefäß reinigen. Und was jede Lache in einem Fels betrifft, in der nicht genügend Wasser ist, um ganz zu bedecken, (so gilt:) wenn es ein Unreiner berührt hat, so wird sein Wasser unrein sein wie das Wasser eines Gefäßes" (E. Lohse, Die Texte aus Qumran, Hebräisch und Deutsch, [Darmstadt, 1964] 86 f.).

134 This argument comes as a surprise. Thus one wonders whether the story originally was preceded by another one in which Elchasaios tried to bathe in the sea; cf. n. 118.

The equation of ὕδατα in which Elchasaios wanted to wash himself with θάλασσα is easy to understand from the point of view which, among others, caused the Mandaeans to regard as Jordan every water they used for baptism. For the word θάλασσα denoted

have been the main point.[135] We know, however, of a Persian restriction against washing one's hands in a river, thus preventing pollution of the water (Herod. 1, 138). It seems that the Jewish and the Persian restriction were combined and generalized. Thus there resulted a ban on bathing in all open water, and this is reflected in the two stories.[136]

If our interpretation is correct, we can see how some Elchasaites let themselves be influenced by an old Persian custom and adapted it to suit their rigorism. This was probably possible as a consequence of growing gnostic influence. Iranian influence on gnosticism cannot be denied (see n. 156), though it is almost impossible to isolate the different sources. At any rate, Mani became the exponent of those Elchasaites who were influenced by gnosticism to such an extent that a schism seemed unavoidable. When it came to the break, however, only three Elchasaites followed Mani, one of whom was his father.

The first story requires one additional remark. The water is aware that it is polluted by the adultery, foulness, and impurity of this world. Since this cannot be prevented, it objects only to being polluted by the righteous one who should know better. From others it must suffer. This foreshadows, as it seems, the type of Manichaeism according to which the *elect* were not permitted to do agricultural work or to collect their own food, but had to ask the layman to do these things for them.

(G) Marcion and the Docetism of Mani

The Jewish Christian background of the Elchasaites exposed them to the different currents in a Christianity which still lacked the embankments of official dogma. When living among the Elchasaites, Mani must have been exposed to the teaching of Marcion and Bardesanes. Each of them,

---

also the lake of Gennesaret (*ZPE* 5 [1970] 143 n. 120). If so, then the prohibition may have been transferred from the sea to this lake and then extended to other bodies of water. Some restrictions are attested for the original Elchasaites. They did not baptize on unlucky days, particularly not on a Sabbath or a Wednesday; this too conforms to Jewish custom (W. Brandt, *Elchasai* [Leipzig, 1912] 12 ff. and 26 f.).

[135] The shallowness of the water is not stressed in the first story; in itself this could be an intentional omission on the part of Mani. But, as is shown above, this explanation is not sufficient.

[136] The prohibition made sense from the Manichaean point of view; see W. Henning, *loc. cit.* (see n. 88), p. 31 f. line 482 ff.: "Und ich quäle und verletze zu jeder Zeit die fünf Elemente, das gefesselte Licht – – –, wenn (ich zulasse, daß) der schwere Körper, der quälerische Leib, mit dem ich bekleidet bin, – – – in die Wässer hineingeht, im Schlamm, Schnee, Regenwasser oder Tau des Weges geht." Therefore A. Henrichs thought that the factual background of the stories interpreted above is almost nil (*HSCP* 77 [1973] 47).

though opposed to each other, influenced him in a different way, as has been said frequently. We already dealt with the influence of Bardesanes and the Valentinians on the Elchasaites and on Mani.[137]

Similarly, the asceticism of the Marcionites must have impressed already the encratitic Elchasaites. But they could not follow Marcion's anti-Jewish teachings. He refused the Old Testament and preferred Paul; for Mani this opened the road to the Greeks and Greek philosophy. Furthermore, Marcion believed in the existence of two gods, the good God of salvation and the evil God of the Old Testament and the cosmogony; in addition he saw the *hyle* as the eternal principle of evil. Man is the creation of the evil god, and his body is made of *hyle*. These ideas became elements in Mani's dualism. Such teachings, however, prompted his break with the Elchasaites, their adherence to the "Law" and their rites of baptism and the Sabbath. The Manichaean prayer by which the *electus* requests remission of the sin of eating the *Christus patiens* still reflects Marcion's belief that eating in general is a sin and a crime. The Manichaean *elect* had a position in his church which was similar to the position of the ascetics in the Marcionite church. In both churches those who were not of the *elect* or who were not ascetics could not hold a rank higher than catechumens; they were not part of the church in the proper sense.[138]

For Marcion as well as for Mani, the dualistic concept of the *hyle* left no space for a belief in a resurrection of the body. Consequently, the body could not be cleaned by means of ablutions. Cleanness through baptism had to become Mani's cleanness of the soul by means of *gnosis* (see n. 121). The keeping of the Sabbath rest became the rest of the *elect* who waited for the layman to bring them the food from which they released the Divine parts for their return into the eternal rest of the Divine Light.[139] The Manichaean and Christian interpretation of the Sabbath was still discussed by Faustus and Augustine.[140]

Marcion's teachings were particularly responsible for Mani's docetism. Both Marcion and Mani did not doubt that Jesus really came into this world, but they thought that his body was not of flesh. It was only similar

137 See pp. 184 ff. A good summary of the influence of Marcion, Valentinian, Tatian, and Bardesanes is given by O. Klíma, *loc. cit.* (see n. 34), 127 ff.

138 See A. Vööbus, *History of Asceticism in the Syrian Orient*, CSCO 184, Subsidia 14 (Louvain, 1958) 45 ff.

139 It has been said of Marcion that his reaction against Judaism was the result of a resentment which stemmed from his youth (A. v. Harnack, *Marcion* [see n. 98] 22 f.); the same was true of Mani.

140 August., *c. Faust.* 6, 1 p. 284, 14; 4 p. 288, 12 ff. (cf. A. Henrichs, *HSCP* 77 [1973] 48 ff.); 16, 28 p. 473, 5 ff.; 18, 5 p. 493, 18 ff.; 20, 13 p. 553, 15 ff.

to flesh.[141] Thus, it was not born by Mary and did not feel pain the way the body of flesh does. Still, the Manichaeans could have interpreted Jesus' death on the cross as a historical concretization of the *crux lucis*. Mani was not crucified, but his suffering was understood as crucifixion, because it made visible the suffering of the divine Light as incorporated in bodies like plants, trees, and other things. But it is precisely this which leads to a problem. The suffering of the divine Light is the suffering in a body. Jesus, however, was supposed not to have such a body. Therefore, the crucifixion of Jesus lost its theological relevance. Consequently, it played almost no role in Manichaean rites. However, the Manichaeans celebrated the passion of Mani at the *Bema* Feast. The reactions of the Manichaean church to the death of Jesus and the death of Mani were different; Augustine felt that they were contradictory.[142]

Mani knew several Jesuses, particularly Jesus the Splendor and *Jesus Patiens*.[143] There would have been place for a Jesus who as an apostle of the divine Father and as *paraclete* could have been incorporated in a human body. Mani's *Noûs*, a manifestation of the divine Apostle of Light, was sent into a real body, as was the case, for example, with Buddha. Mani's system is not responsible for his belief that the historical Jesus did not have a body of flesh; the convictions of his youth led to this view. It is true that in Mani's system there was no room for a sinless body of Christ; all bodies were the work of the powers of Darkness. Since Mani, by virtue of his Elchasaite education, knew that such a body was not fitting for Christ, he simply adopted the docetism of Marcion and of Christian gnostics.

[141] A. Böhlig, *Mysterium und Wahrheit* (see n. 30), 208; H. J. Polotsky, *loc. cit.* (see n. 15) 269 = 713. J. P. Asmussen, *loc. cit.* (see n. 34), 98. For Marcion see A. v. Harnack, *loc. cit* (see n. 98) 125. The docetism of the *Acta Joh.* is similar.

[142] When Augustine asked for reasons he was told (*c. ep. fund.* 8 p. 202, 15 ff.) *eius diem passionis celebrandum esse qui vere passus est; Christum autem, qui natus non esset, neque veram, sed simulatam carnem humanis oculis ostendisset, non pertulisse, sed finxisse passionem.* However, the phrase *finxisse passionem* does not quite correctly express the Manichaean doctrine. Cf. *c. Faust.* 5, 5 p. 277, 8 ff.; 14, 2 p. 404, 14 ff.; 10 p. 410, 28 ff. Mani, like other gnostics, had difficulties in dealing with the passion of Christ; cf. A. Böhlig in: *Christentum und Gnosis* (see n. 31), 11 n. 63.

[143] August., *c. Faust.* 20, 11 p. 550, 14 ff. *postremo dicite nobis, quot Christos esse dicatis: aliusne est quem de Spiritu Sancto concipiens terra patibilem gignit, omni non solum suspensus ex ligno* (see p. 178 f.), *sed etiam iacens in herba, et alius ille quem Iudaei crucifixerunt sub Pontio Pilato, et tertius ille per solem lunamque distentus.* Cf. F. Ch. Baur, *loc. cit.* (see n. 33), 72 f.; above n. 55 and 78; cf. also the distinction between Jesus and Christ in the *Acta Arch.* (p. 167, § 3). In addition, there was also Jesus the Boy (J. P. Asmussen, *loc. cit.* [see n. 34], 110 ff.; K. Rudolph, *loc. cit.* [see n. 1], 173. Mani encountered the concept of several Christs among the Elchasaites; see W. Brandt, *Elchasai, ein Religionsstifter und sein Werk* (Leipzig, 1912) 79 ff.

(H) Tatian

The Elchasaites had their own holy book.[144] Nevertheless one may assume that they were familiar with Tatian's *Diatessaron*, particularly as Tatian's asceticism cannot have failed to impress them.[145] General reasons make it probable that Mani also knew the contents of the four Gospels from the *Diatessaron*. But this is hard to prove; detailed studies will be necessary. For the *Kephalaia* the problem is still being discussed, though I think the answer should be in favor of knowledge of Tatian (see n. 75). Lately traces of the *Diatessaron* have been found in a Parthian text.[146]

The difficulties are numerous. We still know too little of the original *Diatessaron*. Texts written and translated into different languages have to be compared. The *CMC* was originally written in Syriac; this means that the passages from the Greek gospels in the course of the tradition were translated into Syriac and then retranslated into Greek, a procedure which led to divergences. Furthermore Mani and the Manichaean authors allude to passages and coined words of the New Testament, but they feel perfectly free to arrange the allusions as they wish. Thus mixtures of the formulations of *Matthew*, *Mark*, and *Luke* may raise the suspicion that the *Diatessaron* is quoted; but this is not conclusive.[147]

An example of the problems involved is offered by *CMC* 107, 1 ff.:

προῆλθον τοίνυν βουλ[ή]σει τοῦ ἡμετέρου δεσ[πό]του ἐκ τοῦ νόμου ἐκείνου
πρὸς τὸ κατασπε[ῖ]ραι τὸ κάλλιστον αὐ[τοῦ] σπέρμα———καὶ πρὸς τὸ
ἐνπεριπ[ατῆ]σαι τῶι κόσμωι κατ[᾿ εἰ]κόνα κυρίου ἡμῶν Ἰησοῦ [ξί]φος
τε βαλεῖν κα[ὶ αἵ]ρεσιν καὶ μάχαι[ραν] τοῦ πνεύματος ἐπὶ τῆς [γῆς.][148]

Mani begins with a revealing reference to *Matth.* 13, 37: ὁ σπείρων τὸ καλὸν σπέρμα ἐστὶν ὁ υἱὸς τοῦ ἀνθρώπου, and by this he identifies himself with Jesus. The Manichaeans liked the metaphor of the Sower.[149] Here it is followed by typical Manichaean phrases which we may pass over (see n. 148). Then the Christological concept is resumed: *2 Cor.* 6, 16 = *Lev.* 26, 12) ἐνοικήσω ἐν αὐτοῖς καὶ ἐμπεριπατήσω καὶ ἔσομαι αὐτῶν θεός. Jesus is *expressis verbis* mentioned as precedent. Then follows a contamination of *Matth.* 10, 34 (οὐκ ἦλθον βαλεῖν εἰρήνην, ἀλλὰ μάχαιραν) and *Luke*

---

[144] J. Irmscher in Hennecke-Schneemelcher, *Neut. Apokr.* (see n. 122) II, 529 ff.

[145] A. Vööbus, *loc. cit.* (see n. 138), 31 ff.

[146] M 4570, M 6005, and M 338; cf. also the remarks of O. Klíma, *loc. cit.* (see n. 34) and H. H. Schaeder, Urformen und Fortbildungen des manichäischen Systems, *Vorträge der Bibliothek Warburg*, 4, 1924/5 (Leipzig, 1927) 72 (= *idem*, *Studien* [see n. 125], 22).

[147] As, for example, *CMC* 92, 3 ff.; see A. Henrichs, *HSCP* 77 (1973) 50. Cf. also n. 68.

[148] The section is attributed to Timotheos.—Cf. *ZPE* 5 (1970) 180 n. 208.

[149] See, for example, *Keph.* 258, 29 ff.; M 6005 (see n. 34) and W. Sundermann's introduction (p. 107; with parallels).

12, 51 (δοκεῖτε ὅτι εἰρήνην παρεγενόμην δοῦναι ἐν τῇ γῇ; οὐχί, λέγω ὑμῖν, ἀλλ' ἢ διαμερισμόν). In this the translator first replaced μάχαιρα with ξίφος. He did this either to save μάχαιρα for the continuation of his phrase (see below) or because he did not know which word the Greek original had. Second, he replaced διαμερισμός with αἵρεσις, again either unaware of the original phrasing or under the influence of another logion.[150] The combination of *Matth.* 10, 34 and *Luke* 12, 51 is also attested by the *Gospel according to Thomas*, in which the sentence became even more expanded: "Men possibly think that I have come to throw peace upon the world and they do not know that I have come to throw divisions upon the earth, fire, sword, war."[151]

It is not likely that Mani depended directly on this longer list and shortened it in order to make space for an addition of his own: μάχαιρα τοῦ πνεύματος (see below). But it might well be that he followed Tatian in combining *Matthew* and *Luke*;[152] at his time, however, Tatian may have known longer lists which were current in Jewish Christian communities.[153] Though Mani probably depends here on Tatian, he found Tatian's list insufficient. Thus he further combined it with *Eph.* 6, 17, καὶ τὴν μάχαιραν τοῦ πνεύματος (δέξασθε), ὅ ἐστιν ῥῆμα θεοῦ. The additional allusion fits excellently into the context. Mani appears once more as the new Christ; however, μάχαιρα τοῦ πνεύματος after the preceding ξίφος sounds odd.

To sum up, we have found that the Christian elements belong to the heritage which Mani adopted from the Elchasaites.[154] The *CMC* makes it

---

[150] Justin, *Dial. cum Tryph.* 35 ἔσονται σχίσματα καὶ αἱρέσεις; Syr. *Didask.* 6, 5 "Wie auch unser Herr und Heiland sagte: Es wird Parteihader geben und Spaltungen;" Ps. Clem., *Hom.* 2, 17 and 16, 21 (cf. J. Jeremias in Hennecke-Schneemelcher, *Neutest. Apokr.* [see n. 122], I, 54). The *Logion* is eschatological; cf. *2 Petr.* 2, 1 (*1 Cor.* 11, 19; *Gal.* 5, 20). Thus the context is different from that of our passage, and one might doubt if the translator of the *CMC* thought of this *Logion*.

[151] *Logion* 16 (A. Guillaumont, H.-Ch. Puech, G. Quispel, W. Till and Yassah 'Abd al Masîh, *The Gospel according to Thomas* [Leiden–New York, 1959]; J. Leipoldt, *Das Evangelium nach Thomas*, T.u.U. 101 [Berlin, 1967]).

[152] I could not, however, find any evidence for this text in the tradition of Tatian.

[153] I do not think that this *Logion* depends on Tatian; cf. G. Quispel, *Vig. Christ.* 25 (1971) 131 ff.

[154] Cf. n. 120. For a list of teachings which Mani inherited from the Elchasaites and other Elchasaite teachings which he refused, see K. Rudolph, *loc. cit.* (n. 1) 485 n. 1. Before the *CMC* had been found, K. Rudolph thought that the Christian elements in Mani's teachings were transmitted to him through the filter of gnosticism (*loc. cit.* [n. 124], 157). This statement needs only slight modification. Mani became familiar with Jewish Christianity already as a child, when he was educated by the Elchasaites, and with Christian gnosticism at the same time.

easier to understand the complex development of Manichaeism from a Christianized Judaism which was subject to the growing influence of gnosticism. The stream of Christian influence, however, continued in the later history of Manichaeism and led to the incorporation of topics which came up in the history of the dogma of the Christian church. Thus the Manichaeans adopted the conception of the trinity; they did so in the form of subordinationism.

The picture Augustine gives is basically correct,[155] though he did not always understand the underlying gnostic theology. This does not, however, mean that scholars were ill-advised when they searched for relationships between Manichaeism and the religion of Ancient Iran.[156] Still, Mani did not begin his life in a community which stood in the Iranian tradition. Iranian influence came first with gnosticism and then with the needs of the missionary praxis.

University of Michigan

155 Augustine's form of the name of Mani's father (*Patticius*) has been confirmed by the *CMC* (Παττίκιος). It seems that it is an Aramaic name which is derived from puttāḵa and means "host." This is a perfect description of the function of Mani's father according to the gnostic ideas in the *Song of the Pearl* (new translation with notes: R. Köbert, *Orientalia* 38 [1969] 447 ff.): Pattikios was the host of the inn (the world and Mani's body) into which Mani was sent (see R. Köbert and L. Koenen, *ZPE* 8 [1971] 243 ff.). The name can perhaps also be traced back to the Valentinians. puttāḵa itself is derived from Greek πανδοκεῖον (Brockelmann, *Lex. Syr.*[2] 618b; cf. Köbert in *ZPE*); and Valentinus used πανδοκεῖον as a metaphor for the heart which is exposed to the demons (Clem. of Alex., *Strom.* 2, 114, 3 ff. p. 174, 31 ff.). However, K. Rudolph doubts the explanation of the name for linguistic reasons (*loc. cit.* [see n. 1] 474 n. 2).

156 Cf. K. Rudolph, *loc. cit.* (see n. 1), n. 2. I do not think one should entirely deny the influence of Iranian ideas on gnosticism (cf. n. 29 and p. 190), as G. Quispel does (*Eranos Jahrb.* 22 [1952] 195 ff.); but it was less strong than most scholars assumed (see also J.-E. Ménard in: *Christentum und Gnosis* [n. 31], 55 f.).

13

The Sahidic Version of Kingdoms IV*

GERALD M. BROWNE

In contrast to other parts of the Old Testament, the four books of Kingdoms do not seem to have enjoyed a high degree of popularity with the Copts of early Christian Egypt. Thanks to a single manuscript from the Pierpont Morgan Library, we have a nearly complete text of the Sahidic version of Kingdoms I and II;[1] but only fragments survive of Kingdoms III and IV.[2] It is therefore particularly welcome whenever papyri or parchment leaves of these books appear with portions of text not previously attested in Coptic translation. Hence the importance of *P.Mich.*inv. 607, of which I here present the editio princeps:[3] this papyrus contains parts of the Sahidic version of Kingdoms IV not hitherto known in Coptic.

*P.Mich.*inv. 607 was briefly described, without transcription, by E. M. Husselman in W. H. Worrell, *Coptic Texts in the University of Michigan*

---

* A version of this paper was presented as a public lecture at the University of Illinois (Urbana-Champaign) on 30 April 1976, during the International Papyrological Symposium. In revised form, it was delivered on 13 December 1976, at the First International Congress of Coptology (Cairo, Egypt).

[1] James Drescher, *The Coptic (Sahidic) Version of Kingdoms I, II (Samuel I, II)*, CSCO 313/Copt.35 (Textus), 314/Copt.36 (Versio) (Louvain, 1970).

[2] For the fragments of Kingdoms III and IV, see A. Vaschalde, "Ce qui a été publié des versions coptes de la Bible," *RBibl* 16 (1919) 242 f.; W. Till, "Coptic Biblical Texts Published After Vaschalde's Lists," *BullRyl* 41 (1959) 225. To these lists should be added the following: P. Kahle, *Bala'izah* (Oxford, 1954) I 6A (3 Kgs. 1.51–2.5), appendix to 6A (3 Kgs. 21.4 and 2.1–4), 6B (3 Kgs. 22.39–54), 7 (4 Kgs. 14.17–22, 24, 25, 27–29; 17.13–23); T. Orlandi, *Koptische Papyri theologischen Inhalts*, MPER, N.S. 9 (Vienna, 1974), I (K 7549a–h, containing portions of 4 Kgs. 1.6–17.15). See further P. Bellet, "Un fragmento de la versión sahídica de 3 Reyes 4,11–13.15–19," *StudPapyrol* 3 (1964) 69–78, who identifies a fragment left unattributed by Kahle; and for improved readings in Orlandi's text, see G. M. Browne, "The Vienna Papyrus of Kingdoms IV," *BASP* 12 (1975) 145–150.

[3] I am grateful to Professor H. C. Youtie for permission to publish this text. Professor and Mrs. Youtie also very kindly checked my transcript against the papyrus.

Collection (Ann Arbor, 1942) 9. It consists of two consecutive leaves of a
papyrus codex. Originally, each page contained two columns of writing,
and the text they preserve may be tabulated as follows:

Folio 1 Recto Col. i: 1.18d–2.2 (19 lines)
        Col. ii: 2.3–2.4 (2 lines)
   Verso Col. i: 2.6 (5 lines)
        Col. ii: 2.8–2.10 (20 lines)
Folio 2 Recto Col. i: 2.11–2.14 (19 lines)
        Col. ii: lost
   Verso Col. i: lost
        Col. ii: 2.19–2.21 (18 lines)

Until the appearance of the Michigan papyrus, we had the Sahidic
version of only a portion of the text tabulated above: a parchment codex
published by G. Maspero in 1892 contained the beginning of Chapter 2
up to the first part of verse 8, and in 1939 W. Till edited a small fragment
from a lectionary with a portion of 2.6.[4] Now, thanks to the Michigan
papyrus, we have the end of Chapter 1, and a large amount of the material
from 2.8 to 2.14, and 2.19 to 2.21.

Both sheets of *P.Mich.*inv. 607 are broken off at the top, but we may
establish the original number of lines with some degree of certainty. A tentative reconstruction of the Coptic, based upon Maspero's text, suggests
that four lines have been lost at the beginning of Folio 1 Verso Col. ii,
which would therefore have originally contained 24 lines. Only a small
amount of text is missing between the end of Folio 1 Verso Col. ii and the
beginning of Folio 2 Recto Col. i; as a likely reconstruction of the Coptic
indicates,[5] no more than five lines have vanished from the beginning of
this column, and thus, like the preceding, when complete it would have
held 24 lines of writing.

On paleographical grounds, the text should probably be assigned to the
ninth century of our era, perhaps to the second half: the hand is somewhat
similar to that of a Vienna papyrus of Kingdoms IV, recently edited by
T. Orlandi and dated by G. Cavallo "forse alla seconda metà del secolo
IX."[6] Despite the affinity of subject matter, it is clear that the Michigan

4 G. Maspero, "Fragments de la version thébaine de l'Ancien Testament," *Mémoires
publiés par les membres de la mission archéologique française au Caire* 6 (1892) 174; W. Till,
"Kleine koptische Bibelfragmente," *Biblica* 20 (1939) 245.

5 See below, note to 2 R i 1.

6 For the Vienna papyrus, see above, footnote 2; Cavallo's opinion about the date is
from the introduction to the text, p. 25.

and Vienna papyri do not come from the same codex: the writing styles, though similar, are obviously the work of different scribes, and the line lengths of the Vienna text are characteristically shorter than those of the Michigan piece.

The provenance of *P.Mich*.inv. 607 cannot be fixed with certainty, but it is possible that it came from the White Monastery in Upper Egypt, the source of many of the Coptic papyri in the Michigan collection; for further information on this subject, see T. Orlandi, "Un projet milanais concernant les manuscrits coptes du Monastère Blanc," *Le Muséon* 85 (1972) 405.

As lectional aids, the scribe employs both the supralinear stroke and the point, and although he prefers the latter, he often uses both without apparent distinction: e.g., I V ii 6f ελῑcλῑoc and 11 ελιcλιoc; 8 ν̄λκ and 11 ν̇λϥ. At times the stroke is considerably shortened, so that it is hardly distinguishable from a point. The latter usually appears slightly to the right of the letter, while the stroke is often extended to cover the left side of the letter following. For convenience of typesetting, in this edition I have centered the supralineation. Diaeresis occurs only once: 1 R i 8 εϩρλῑ; elsewhere it is replaced by the stroke (e.g., 1 V ii 12 εϩρλῑ) or the point (e.g., 2 R i 4 εϩρλι̇). The treatment of nomina sacra varies: once a grave-shaped sign is used (1 V ii 12 πεκπνλ̀), and once a bar (2 R i 8 πῑηλ̄). The end of a sentence is often, though not invariably, indicated by a medium punctum. A sign shaped like a 7 signals the beginning of a new section, and a coronis marks the inception of Chapter 2. (For the Coptic text, see below, pp. 204 f.)

Translation

Folio 1 R i: (1.18d) And the Lord was enraged in anger at the house of Nachaab (*sic*). (2.1) And it happened, when the Lord was about to take up Helias the prophet in an earthquake up to heaven, Helias proceeded with Elisaios out of Galgalon. (2.2) Helias said to Elissaios (*sic*), "Sit here, because it is to Baithel that the Lord has ordered me to go." Elisaios said to him, "The Lord lives, and your soul lives . . ."

R ii: (2.3) . . . "I also know. Be silent." (2.4) Helias . . .

V i: (2.6) . . . "Sit here, because it is to the Iordanes that the Lord has told me to go." And Elisaios said to him . . .

V ii: (2.8) . . . [He] struck the water with it; the water separated on this side and that, and they crossed the dry sea together. (2.9) And when they had crossed, Helias said to Elisaios, "Ask me for a thing, and I shall do it for you before I am taken up from your sight." Elisaios said to him, "Let your spirit become doubled upon me." (2.10) Helias said to him, "You have exceeded the measure for requesting. If you see me being taken up from your sight, this shall happen to you. But if I am not taken up, this thing shall not happen to you."

Folio 2 R i: (2.11) . . . They separated them from one another. Immediately Helias was taken up in an earthquake up to heaven. (2.12) And Elisaios saw, and he cried out, saying, "My father, charioteer of Israel and its horseman!" And he no longer saw him. Immediately he laid his hands upon his clothes; he tore them; he made them two broken pieces. (2.13) And he raised up the sheepskin of Helias, the one which had fallen upon Elisaios. And he turned; he stood by the bank of the Iordanes. (2.14) He took the sheepskin . . .

V ii: (2.19) ". . . [The situation of] the city is good, just as the Lord sees it. But the waters are bad, and the land does not produce." (2.20) Elisaios said to them, "Bring me a new little pitcher, and throw salt into it." They got it; they brought it to him. (2.21) And Elisaios arose; he came forth to the channels of the waters; he threw the salt there, saying, "This it is that the Lord says: 'these waters I have cured, and I . . .'"

COMMENTARY

1 R i

3 f. ṆNAXAAB: read NAXAAB (Gr.[7] *Αχααβ*). Gemination of N is not unusual with proper names: e.g., 2 Kgs. 15.19[8] NNETϨI (*Εθθι*). Cf. also Drescher, *Kingdoms, Versio* 64 n. 1; G. M. Browne, "The Martyrdom of Paese and Thecla (*P.Mich.*inv. 548)," *Cd'E* 49 (1974) 205 (ad 83 R ii 17–19).

5 ΔЄ: here, below in line 9, and in 1 V ii 6, 19; 2 R i 5; 2 V ii 4, *καί* of the original is replaced by ΔЄ; cf. Drescher, *Kingdoms, Versio* vi: "δέ is very rare in the Greek of Kgs., much more so than, for example, in the Greek Genesis, but ΔЄ is very common in the Coptic. Perhaps it was introduced to provide a change from the monotony of the perpetual ΑΥⲰ (*καί*)." Other instances where the Coptic uses one Greek word to render another will be discussed in the commentary; see on 1 R i 6, 2 R i 7, 2 V ii 1, and 2 V ii 7.

6 ΑΝΑΛΑΜΒΑΝЄ: here the Greek has *ἀνάγειν*. Elsewhere in the

---

[7] For the Greek text, I have throughout used A. Rahlfs, *Septuaginta, id est Vetus Testamentum graece iuxta LXX interpretes* (Stuttgart, 1935); whenever necessary, I have consulted A. E. Brooke, N. McLean, H. St. J. Thackeray, *The Old Testament in Greek . . .*, Vol. 2; *The Later Historical Books*, Part II: *I and II Kings* (Cambridge, 1930).

[8] All citations from 1 and 2 Kgs. are from Drescher's edition (see above, footnote 1). I shall refer to the text volume as *Kingdoms, Textus*, and to the translation volume as *Kingdoms, Versio*.

portion of text covered by the Michigan papyrus, the Greek uses ἀναλαμ-βάνειν to refer to the ascension of Elijah, and this is reflected by the appearance of ANAΛAMBANE in the Coptic: 1 V ii 9, 16, (cf. 18 f.), 2 R i 2 f. It is perhaps a desire on the translator's part to be consistent that explains the presence of ANAΛAMBANE in the present passage. Cf. further Drescher, *Kingdoms, Textus* 192.

7 ΠΕΠΡΟΦΗΤΗC: not in Gr. or in M.[9]

9 ϨΗΛΙΑC ΔΕ ΑϤΜΟΟϢΕ: Α ϨΗΛΙΑC ΜΟΟϢΕ M.

11 ΠΕϪΕ: cf. Drescher, *Kingdoms, Versio* vi: "The conjunction 'and' is regularly omitted in sequences of verbs . . .; nor is 'and' usually found before ΠΕϪΕ, '(he) said,' for καὶ εἶπεν, whether in sequence or not." The conjunction before ΠΕϪΕ is also omitted in 1 R i 16; 1 V ii 10 f., 13; 2 V ii 5. Note that in M, ΔΕ is added after ϨΗΛΙΑC, in the section corresponding to 1 R i 11 f.

12 ΕΛΙCCΑΙΟC: elsewhere in this papyrus, the name is spelled ΕΛΙCΑΙΟC; the Greek original varies between Ἐλισαιε and Ἐλισσαιε; see Rahlfs' apparatus ad 2.1.

13–16 ΕΒ[Ο]Λ . . . ΒΑΙΘ[ΗΛ: "because it is to Baithel that the Lord has ordered me to go." The restoration is modeled upon Maspero's text, as is the corresponding section below, 1 V i 8–10. Here the Greek has ὅτι κύριος ἀπέσταλκέν με ἕως Βαιθηλ. For a similar expansion of the Greek original, also employing a Second Tense, see 1 Kgs. 10.14, where in response to the question ΝΤΑΤΕΤΝΒⲰΚ ΕΤⲰΝ (ποῦ ἐπορεύθητε;), the Coptic has ΝΤΑΝΒⲰΚ ΕΚⲰΤΕ ΝCΑ ΝΕΟΟΥ (ζητεῖν τὰς ὄνους). Cf. also 1 Kgs. 27.10.

16–19 The restorations are modeled upon M.

16 f. ΠΕϪΕ ΕΛΙ]CΑΙΟC Ν̣[ΑϤ: the Greek has καὶ εἶπεν Ἐλισαιε. When translating such phrases, the Coptic often adds ΝΑ-; cf. 1 V i 11; 1 V ii 11, 14; 2 V ii 6. For the omission of the conjunction, see above, n. to line 11.

1 R ii (the line numbers refer to col. i)

7 f. Despite the scant remnants, a tentative reconstruction, based upon M, suggests that these lines come from the end of 2.3 and the beginning of 2.4. Note especially the verse mark in the margin, signaling the start of a new section. M has served as the model for restoring the two lines.

1 V i (the line numbers refer to col. ii)

7–11 The restoration of this badly damaged section is modeled upon M. Instead of ΑΥⲰ ΕΛΙCΑΙΟC ΠΕϪΑϤ ΝΑϤ, Till's lectionary[10] has ΠΕϪΑ[Ϥ ΝΑϤ.

---

[9] M designates Maspero's text (see above, footnote 4).
[10] See above, footnote 4.

1 V ii

1 ⲣⲱϩⲧ: i.e., ⲁϥ]ⲣⲱϩⲧ (Gr. ἐπάταξεν). In Classical Sahidic we expect either ⲁϥⲣⲉϩⲧ ⲡⲙⲟⲟⲩ (the reading of M) or ⲁϥⲣⲱϩⲧ ⲙⲡⲙⲟⲟⲩ. The use of the status absolutus for status nominalis, if not simply a mistake, suggests Achmimic influence; see H. Quecke, *Das Markusevangelium saïdisch* (Barcelona, 1972) 45 and n. 4.

ⲛϩⲏⲧ[ⲥ: after this word the text of M breaks off.

3 ⲁⲩⲭⲓⲟⲣ: read ⲁⲩⲭⲓⲟⲟⲣ; cf. line 5, where the classical spelling is found. Reduction of a double vowel occurs elsewhere in this papyrus only in line 8 of this column; in each case we are probably dealing with a mistake, not a legitimate orthographic variant; cf. Quecke, *Markusevangelium* 32.

8 ⲛⲧⲁⲁϥ: read ⲛⲧⲁⲁⲁϥ and cf. preceding note.

9 ⲙⲡⲁⲧⲟⲩ-: i.e., ⲉⲙⲡⲁⲧⲟⲩ- (Till, *Koptische Grammatik²* §328).

14 f. ⲁⲕⲣ ϩⲟⲩⲟ ⲉⲡϣⲓ [ⲉⲁⲓⲧⲉⲓ]: here the Greek has ἐσκλήρυνας τοῦ αἰτήσασθαι. A verbal reminiscence of the Coptic version appears in T. Orlandi, *Constantini Episcopi urbis Siout encomia in Athanasium duo*, CSCO 349/Copt. 37 (Louvain, 1974) 36.6 f. ⲕⲁⲛ ⲉⲁⲛⲣ ϩⲟⲩⲟ ⲉⲡϣⲓ ⲉⲁⲓⲧⲉⲓ ("etiamsi . . . modum petitionis superavimus"—editor's translation in CSCO 350/Copt. 38.22). Orlandi's text suggests the restoration [ⲉⲁⲓⲧⲉⲓ] in the Michigan papyrus.

15–20 The Greek here has ἐὰν ἴδῃς με ἀναλαμβανόμενον ἀπὸ σοῦ, καὶ ἔσται σοι οὕτως· καὶ ἐὰν μή, οὐ μὴ γένηται. For the phrases ⲉⲣⲉ ⲡ]ⲁⲓ ϣⲱ[ⲡⲉ ⲛⲁⲕ and ⲛⲛⲉ [ⲡⲉⲓϩⲱⲃ ϣⲱⲡⲉ] ⲛⲁⲕ, cf. e.g., 1 Kgs. 28.22 (text in Drescher's apparatus) ⲉⲣⲉ ⲟⲩϭⲟⲙ ⲛⲁϣⲱⲡⲉ ⲛⲁⲕ, 2 Kgs. 22.42 ⲛⲧⲉⲧⲙ ⲃⲟⲏⲑⲓⲁ ϣⲱⲡⲉ ⲛⲁⲩ. The Coptic translator has expanded καὶ ἐὰν μή to ⲉⲩ]ⲧⲙⲁⲛⲁ[ⲗⲁⲙⲃⲁⲛⲉ ⲇⲉ] ⲙⲙⲟⲓ; similar expansions occur in 1 Kgs. 2.16, where, for καὶ ἐὰν μή, we find ⲉⲕϣⲁⲛⲧⲉⲙⲧ ⲇⲉ; and in 6.9, where ⲉⲥⲧⲙⲧⲁⲁⲥ ⲇⲉ ⲉⲡⲥⲁ ⲉⲧⲙⲙⲁⲩ renders καὶ ἐὰν μή.

2 R i

1 The beginning of verse 11 reads in the Greek: καὶ ἐγένετο αὐτῶν πορευομένων ἐπορεύοντο καὶ ἐλάλουν, καὶ ἰδοὺ ἅρμα πυρὸς καὶ ἵπποι[11] πυρὸς καὶ διέστειλαν[12] ἀνὰ μέσον ἀμφοτέρων, κτλ. This suggests the following exempli-gratia restoration for the lost beginning of this column (for the number of lines, see above, p. 197):

[ⲁⲥϣⲱⲡⲉ ⲇⲉ ⲛⲧⲟⲟⲩ]
[ⲉⲩⲙⲟⲟϣⲉ ⲛⲉⲩⲙⲟⲟϣⲉ]

---

11 ἵππος: Vaticanus and s (a late ms.).

12 διέστειλεν: Vaticanus. (The Cambridge Septuagint lists other variants, from late mss., which need not be reported here.)

[ⲁⲩⲱ ⲛⲉⲩϣⲁⲭⲉ ⲁⲩⲱ ⲉⲓⲥ]
[ⲟⲩϩⲁⲣⲙⲁ ⲛⲕⲱϩⲧ ⲙⲛ]
[ϩⲉⲛϩⲧⲱⲱⲣ ⲛⲕⲱϩⲧ ⲁⲩⲱ]
[ⲁⲩⲡ]ⲟⲣⲭⲟⲩ ⲉⲃⲟⲗ, etc.

For parallels, cf. the following passages: 1 Kgs. 9.11 ⲛⲧⲟⲟⲩ ⲉⲩⲙⲟⲟϣⲉ; 14.26 ⲛⲉⲣⲉ ⲡⲗⲁⲟⲥ ⲇⲉ ⲙⲟⲟϣⲉ ⲉϥϣⲁⲭⲉ. Although only the present Michigan papyrus contains this part of Kingdoms IV in Coptic translation, there is an unmistakable reference to the ascent of Elijah in the Encomium of Stephanus, Bishop of Hnes, on Saint Helias (ed. Sobhy[13]) 72: ⲉⲓⲛⲁⲧⲛⲧⲱⲛⲅ ⲉⲡⲉⲧⲟ ⲛϩⲩⲙⲟⲛⲟⲙⲟⲥⲩⲕⲏ ⲛⲡⲁ ⲡⲓⲣⲁⲛ ⲛⲟⲩⲱⲧ ⲛⲙⲙⲁⲕ ϩⲏⲗⲓⲁⲥ ⲡⲉⲛⲧⲁⲩⲁⲛⲁⲗⲁⲙⲃⲁⲛⲉ ⲙⲙⲟϥ ϩⲓⲧⲛ ϩⲛϩⲧⲱⲱⲣ ⲙⲛ ϩⲛϩⲁⲣⲙⲁ ⲛⲕⲱϩⲧ ("je te comparerai à ton homonyme,[14] à celui qui porte le même nom que toi, Hélias, qui fut emporté par des chevaux et un char de feu"—editor's translation, 114 f.). It is these last few words, ϩⲛϩⲧⲱⲱⲣ ⲙⲛ ϩⲛϩⲁⲣⲙⲁⲛⲕⲱϩⲧ, which are clearly derived from this portion of the Coptic version of Kingdoms IV, and which may therefore be used for its partial reconstruction. Note that ϩⲛϩⲧⲱⲱⲣ suggests that the Coptic translator had ἵπποι, not ἵππος, in the text he used (see above, footnote 11).

[ⲁⲩⲡ]ⲟⲣⲭⲟⲩ: i.e., διέστειλαν. If ϩⲉⲛϩⲧⲱⲱⲣ originally stood in the text (see preceding paragraph), [ⲁⲩⲡ]ⲟⲣⲭⲟⲩ is more likely than [ⲁϥⲡ]ⲟⲣⲭⲟⲩ, i.e., διέστειλεν (see footnote 12).

1 f. [ⲛⲛⲉⲩⲉ]ⲣⲏⲩ: also possible is [ⲉⲛⲉⲩⲉ]ⲣⲏⲩ; cf. 2 Kgs. 1.23 ⲙⲡⲟⲩⲡⲱⲣϫ ⲉⲃⲟⲗ ⲛⲛⲉⲩⲉⲣⲏⲩ (var. ⲉⲛⲉⲩⲉⲣⲏⲩ).

7 ⲡⲉⲛⲓⲟⲭⲟⲥ: (i.e., ἡνίοχος). Here the Greek has ἅρμα, and it is likely that we have another example of the tendency of the Coptic translators to substitute one Greek word for another (see above, n. to 1 R i 5). Confronted with ἅρμα, and interpreting it as a vocative, the translator may have decided not to refer to Elijah as a chariot but to be more logical—if less poetic—and to call him a charioteer. We should, however, note that the Old Latin version has *agitator*, as opposed to *currus* of the Vulgate,[15] and it is therefore possible that ἡνίοχος is a legitimate variant within the Greek recension. The Massoretic text here has רֶכֶב "chariot," but the Hebrew word for "charioteer" is רַכָּב. In an unpointed text, both

---

[13] G. P. G. Sobhy, *Le Martyre de saint Hélias et l'encomium de l'évêque Stéphanos de Hnès sur saint Hélias* (Cairo, 1919).

[14] "Homonyme" translates ϩⲩⲙⲟⲛⲟⲙⲟⲥⲩⲕⲏ, a corruption, perhaps, of ϩⲟⲙⲱⲛⲩⲙⲟⲥ ⲉⲩⲭⲏ, i.e., ὁμώνυμος εὐχή.

[15] Cf. R. S. Haupert, *The Relation of Codex Vaticanus and the Lucianic Text in the Books of the Kings from the Viewpoint of the Old Latin and the Ethiopic Versions* (Philadelphia, 1930) 13 and n. 4.

would be spelled the same, thereby allowing for the possibility of ἅρμα and ἡνίοχος as variant readings in the Greek text.

9 ⲁⲩⲱ ⲟ̄ⲉ: for the phrase, see Crum, *Dictionary* 802b, and cf. 1 Kgs. 20.2.

ⲁⲩⲗⲟ: read ⲁϥⲗⲟ (for the interchange of ϥ and ⲩ, see Quecke, *Markusevangelium* 21 f.).

14 ⲙⲉⲗⲱⲧⲏ: i.e., μηλωτή.

19 After ⲛⲧⲙⲉⲗⲱ[ⲧⲏ begins the parchment manuscript of 4 Kgs. 2.14–15, ed. J. Schleifer, *SBWien* 164.6 (1911) 25.

2 V ii

1 ⲛⲁⲛⲟⲩϥ: the Greek text here reads ἰδοὺ ἡ κατοίκησις τῆς πόλεως ἀγαθή, and the suffix in ⲛⲁⲛⲟⲩϥ refers to a masculine noun, the equivalent of κατοίκησις, in the preceding line: e.g., ⲙⲁ ⲛⲟⲩⲱϩ (Crum 508a) or ⲙⲁ ⲛⲟ̄ⲟⲉⲓⲗⲉ (808b).

[ⲕⲁⲧ]ⲁ: the Greek has καθώς; see Drescher, *Kingdoms*, *Textus* 192: "ⲕⲁⲧⲁ takes the place of καθώς often."

7 ⲛⲟⲩⲕⲟⲩⲓ ⲛϩⲩⲇⲣⲓⲁ: here the Greek reads ὑδρίσκην. W. Till, "Die koptischen Versionen der Sapientia Salomonis," *Biblica* 36 (1955) 61, gives some instances of "Ausdrücke . . . deren Übersetzung aus einer Kombination eines koptischen Wortes mit einem griechischen besteht, das vom selben Stamm ist, wie das übersetzte Wort." The examples he cites parallel the use of ⲟⲩⲕⲟⲩⲓ ⲛϩⲩⲇⲣⲓⲁ to render ὑδρίσκη; they include: ⲁⲭⲛ ϩⲩⲡⲟⲕⲣⲓⲥⲓⲥ (ἀνυπόκριτος), ⲙⲛⲧⲁⲅⲁⲑⲟⲥ (ἀγαθότης), and ϯ ⲙⲡⲟⲗⲓⲥ (πεντάπολις).

9 ⲁⲩⲭⲓⲧⲥ ⲁⲩⲉⲓⲛⲉ: καὶ ἔλαβον Vaticanus, Lucianic, Hexaplaric; the rest of the tradition adds καὶ ἤνεγκον.

11 ⲁϥⲧⲱⲟⲩⲛ: intrusive ⲧⲱⲟⲩⲛ, with no equivalent in the Greek, characterizes the Coptic of Kgs. See Drescher, *Kingdoms*, *Textus* xv.

17 ⲛⲉⲓⲙⲟⲟⲩⲉ: this short form of the plural of ⲙⲟⲟⲩ is not known to me elsewhere, although it finds an analogue in the use of ⲙⲟⲩⲓⲉ alongside of ⲙⲟⲩⲓⲉⲩⲉ in Subachmimic (see Kasser, *Compléments* s.v. ⲙⲟⲟⲩ). Also possible is ⲛⲉⲓⲙⲟⲟⲩ ⲉ[ⲁ]ⲓⲧⲁⲗϭⲟⲟⲩ, with ⲉⲁⲓⲧⲁⲗϭⲟⲟⲩ as Second Perfect (cf. H. J. Polotsky, *Etudes de syntaxe copte* [Cairo 1944] 48 f. = *Collected Papers* [Jerusalem, 1971] 152 f.). But both the Greek (ἴαμαι τὰ ὕδατα ταῦτα) and the following First Perfect make this interpretation unlikely.

18 ⲁⲩⲱ ⲁⲓ: Gr. οὐκ ἔσται ἔτι ἐκεῖθεν θάνατος. Here again the Coptic translator has resorted to paraphrase, e.g., ⲁⲓ[ϥⲓ ⲙⲡⲙⲟⲩ ⲉⲃⲟⲗ ⲛϩⲏⲧⲟⲩ, vel sim.

Folio 1 (15.3 × 18 cm.)

Recto

Col. i

Col. ii

↑   Faint traces of one line

– – – – – – – –

ⲁⲅⲱ ⲡⲭⲟⲉⲓⲥ ⲁϥϭⲱⲛⲧ   1.18d
ϩⲛ̄ ⲟⲩⲟⲣⲅⲏ ⲉϫⲙ ⲡⲏⲓ ⲛ̣
ⲛⲁ̄ⲭⲁⲁⲃ

5   ⲁⲥϣⲱⲡⲉ ⲇⲉ ⲉⲣⲉ ⲡⲭⲟ̄   2.1
    ⲉⲓⲥ ⲛ̄ⲁⲁⲛ̄ⲁⲗⲁⲙⲃⲁ̄ⲛⲉ ⲛ
    ϩⲏⲗⲓ̄ⲁⲥ ⲡⲉⲡⲣⲟⲫⲏⲧⲏⲥ   ⲁ̣[ⲓⲉⲓⲙⲉ ϩⲱ ⲕⲁⲣⲱⲧⲛ·]   2.3
    ϩⲛ ⲟⲩⲕⲙⲧⲟ ⲉϩⲣⲁⲓ̈ ⲉⲧⲡⲉ   7 ϩ̣[ⲏⲗⲓⲁⲥ   2.4
  7 ϩⲏⲗⲓⲁⲥ ⲇⲉ ⲁϥⲙⲟⲟϣⲉ   – – – – – – – –
10 ⲙⲛ̄ ⲉⲗⲓⲥⲁⲓⲟⲥ ⲉⲃⲟⲗ ϩⲛ
    ⲅⲁⲗⲅⲁⲗⲱⲛ· ⲡⲉϫⲉ ϩⲏ   2.2
    ⲗⲓⲁⲥ ⲛ̄ⲉⲗⲓⲥⲥⲁⲓⲟⲥ ϫⲉ ϩ[ⲙⲟ]
    ⲟⲥ ⲛⲁⲕ ⲙⲡⲓⲙⲁ ⲉⲃ[ⲟⲗ ϫⲉ]
    ⲛ̄ⲧⲁ ⲡϫⲟⲉⲓⲥ ⲟⲩ[ⲉϩ ⲥⲁϩ]
15 ⲛⲉ ⲛⲁ̣[ⲓ ⲉⲧⲣⲁⲃⲱⲕ ϣⲁ]
    ⲃⲁⲓⲑ[ⲏⲗ· ⲡⲉϫⲉ ⲉⲗⲓ]
    ⲥⲁⲓⲟⲥ ⲛ̣[ⲁϥ ϫⲉ ϥⲟⲛϩ ⲛ]
    ϭⲓ ⲡⲭⲟ[ⲉⲓⲥ ⲁⲩⲱ ⲥⲟⲛϩ]
    ⲛ̄ϭⲓ ⲧ[ⲉⲕⲯⲩⲭⲏ

Verso

Col. i

Col. ii

– – – – – – – –

→   ⲣⲱϩⲧ ⲡⲙⲟⲟⲩ ⲛϩⲏⲧ[ⲥ]   2.8
                                    ⲁⲡⲙⲟⲟⲩ ⲡⲱⲣⲝ̄ ⲉⲡⲓⲥⲁ
                                    ⲙⲛ̄ ⲡⲁⲓ· ⲁⲩⲱ ⲁⲩϫⲓ̄ⲟⲣ
                                    ϩⲓ ⲟⲩⲥⲟⲡ ⲙⲡⲡⲉⲧϣⲟ̄ⲩ
                              5   ϣⲟ̄ⲩ· ⲛ̄ⲧⲉⲣⲟⲩϫⲓⲟⲟⲣ   2.9
                                  7 ⲇⲉ ⲡⲉϫⲉ ϩⲏⲗⲓⲁⲥ ⲛ̄ⲉⲗⲓ̄
                                    ⲥⲁⲓⲟⲥ ϫⲉ ⲁⲓⲧⲉⲓ ⲙⲙⲟⲓ̄
                                    ⲛ̄ⲟⲩϩⲱⲃ ⲛ̄ⲧⲁⲁϥ ⲛ̄ⲁⲕ
                                    ⲙⲡⲁⲧⲟⲩⲁⲛ̄ⲁⲗⲁⲙⲃⲁⲛⲉ
                              10   ⲙⲙⲟⲓ̄ ϩⲁ ⲡⲉⲕϩⲟ· ⲡⲉ
                  – – – – – – –   7 ϫⲉ ⲉⲗⲓⲥⲁⲓⲟⲥ ⲛ̄ⲁϥ ϫⲉ ⲙⲁ
              ϩⲙⲟ]ⲟⲥ̣   2.6   ⲣⲉ ⲡⲉⲕⲡⲛ̄ⲁ ⲕⲱⲃ ⲉϩⲣⲁⲓ̄
[ⲛⲁⲕ ⲙⲡⲓⲙⲁ ϫⲉ ⲛⲧⲁ ⲡ]ϫⲟⲉⲓⲥ   ⲉϫⲱⲓ̄· ⲡⲉϫⲉ ϩⲏⲗⲓⲁⲥ   2.10
[ϫⲟⲟⲥ ⲛⲁⲓ ⲉⲧⲣⲁⲃⲱⲕ] ϣⲁ   [ⲛⲁ]ϥ ϫⲉ ⲁⲕⲣ ϩⲟⲩⲟ ⲉⲡϣⲓ̄
[ⲡⲓⲟⲣⲇⲁⲁⲛⲏⲥ· ⲁⲩⲱ] ⲉⲗⲓ̄   15   [ⲉⲁⲓⲧⲉⲓ] ⲉ̣ⲕϣⲁⲛⲛⲁⲩ ⲉⲣⲟⲓ̄
[ⲥⲁⲓⲟⲥ ⲡⲉϫⲁϥ ⲛⲁϥ] ϫⲉ̣   [ⲉⲩⲁⲛⲁⲗⲁⲙⲃⲁ]ⲛ̣ⲉ ⲙⲙⲟⲓ̄
– – – – – – –   [ϩⲁ ⲡⲉⲕϩⲟ ⲉⲣⲉ ⲡ]ⲁⲓ ϣⲱ
                                   [ⲡⲉ ⲛⲁⲕ· ⲉⲩ]ⲧ̣ⲙⲁⲛ̄ⲁ
                                   [ⲗⲁⲙⲃⲁⲛⲉ ⲇⲉ ⲙ]ⲙⲟⲓ̄ ⲛ̄ⲛⲉ
                              20   [ⲡⲉⲓϩⲱⲃ ϣⲱⲡⲉ] ⲛⲁⲕ

Folio 2 (13.5 × 21 cm.)

Recto—Col. i

- - - - - - - -

→ [ⲁⲩⲡ]ⲟⲣⲭⲟⲩ ⲉⲃⲟⲗ [ⲛⲛⲉⲩⲉ]   2.11
ⲣⲏⲩ ⲛ̇ⲧⲉⲩⲛⲟⲩ ⲁⲩⲁⲛⲁⲗ[ⲁⲙ]
ⲃⲁⲛⲉ ⲛⲟⲏⲗⲓⲁⲥ ⲟⲛ ⲟⲩⲕⲙ̄
ⲧⲟ ⲉⲟⲣⲁⲓ̇ ⲉⲧⲡⲉ· ⲉⲗⲓ̄   2.12
5 7 ⲥⲁⲓⲟⲥ ⲇⲉ ⲛ̇ⲉϥⲛⲁⲩ ⲁⲩⲱ ⲁϥ
ⲱϣ ⲉⲃⲟⲗ ⲉϥⲭⲱ ⲙ̇ⲙ̇ⲟⲥ
ⲭⲉ ⲡⲁⲉⲓ̇ⲱⲧ ⲡⲉⲛⲓ̇ⲟⲭⲟⲥ
ⲙ̇ⲡⲓ̄ⲏ̄ⲗ̄ ⲁⲩⲱ ⲡⲉϥⲟⲓ̄ⲡ
ⲡⲉⲩⲅ̄· ⲁⲩⲱ ⲟⲉ ⲁⲩⲗⲟ ⲉϥ
10 ⲛ̇ⲁⲩ ⲉⲣⲟϥ· ⲛ̇ⲧⲉⲩⲛⲟⲩ ⲁϥⲧ̇
7 ⲧⲟⲟⲧϥ ⲛ̇ⲛ̇ⲉϥⲟⲟⲓ̇ⲧⲉ ⲁϥ
ⲡⲁⲟⲟⲩ ⲁϥⲁⲁⲩ ⲙ̇ⲡⲟϭ[ⲉ ⲥⲛ]
ⲧⲉ· ⲁⲩⲱ ⲁϥⲧⲱⲟⲩ[ⲛ ⲉ]   2.13
ⲟⲣⲁⲓ̄ ⲛⲧⲙⲉⲗⲱⲧⲏ ⲛ̇
15 ⲟⲏⲗⲓ̇ⲁⲥ ⲧⲁⲓ ⲛ̇ⲧⲁⲥⲟⲉ ⲉ
ⲭⲛ̇ [ⲉ]ⲗⲓ̇ⲥⲁⲓ̄ⲟⲥ· ⲁⲩⲱ ⲁ[ϥ]
ⲕⲧⲟϥ ⲁϥⲁⲟⲉⲣⲁⲧϥ ⲟⲓⲧ[ⲙ]
ⲡⲉⲥⲡⲟⲧⲟⲩ ⲙ̇ⲡⲓⲟ[ⲣⲇⲁⲛⲏⲥ]
ⲁϥⲭⲓ̇ ⲛⲧⲙⲉⲗⲱ[ⲧⲏ   2.14

Verso—Col. ii

- - - - - - -

↑ ⲧⲡ[ⲟ]ⲗⲓⲥ ⲛ̇ⲁⲛⲟⲩϥ [ⲕⲁⲧ]ⲁ   2.19
ⲑⲉ ⲉⲧⲉⲣⲉ ⲡⲭⲟⲉⲓ̄ⲥ ⲛⲁⲩ ⲉ
ⲣⲟϥ· ⲙⲙⲟⲩⲛⲉⲓ̇ⲟⲟⲩⲉ
7 ⲇⲉ ⲥⲉⲟⲟⲟⲩ ⲁⲩⲱ ⲡⲕⲁⲟ ⲛϥ̄
5 ⲧ̇ ⲟⲩⲱ ⲁⲛ ⲉⲟⲣⲁⲓ̄ ⲡⲉⲭⲉ ⲉ   2.20
ⲗⲓ̇ⲥⲁⲓⲟⲥ ⲛ̇ⲁⲩ ⲭⲉ ⲭⲓ ⲛⲁⲓ̄
ⲛⲟⲩⲕⲟⲩⲓ̇ ⲛ̇ⲟⲩⲁⲣⲓ̇ⲁ ⲛⲃⲣ
ⲣⲉ̄ ⲛ̇ⲧⲉⲧⲛ̇ⲛⲉⲭ ⲟⲙⲟⲩ ⲉⲟⲣⲁⲓ̄
ⲉⲣ[ⲟ]ⲥ ⲁⲩⲭⲓ̇ⲧⲥ ⲁⲩⲉⲓ̇ⲛⲉ ⲙ
10 ⲙⲟⲥ ⲛ̇ⲁϥ· ⲁⲩⲱ ⲉⲗⲓ̇ⲥⲁⲓⲟⲥ   2.21
ⲁϥⲧⲱⲟⲩⲛ̇ ⲁϥⲉⲓ̇ ⲉⲃⲟⲗ ⲉⲙ
ⲙⲁ ⲛ̇ⲟⲁⲧⲉ ⲛ̇ⲙⲙⲟⲩⲛⲉⲓ̄ⲟ̄
ⲟⲩⲉ· ⲁϥⲛ̇ⲟⲩⲭⲉ ⲙⲡⲉ
7 ⲟⲙⲟⲩ ⲉⲡⲙⲁ ⲉⲧⲙⲙⲁⲩ
15 ⲉϥⲭⲱ ⲙⲙ[ⲟⲥ] ⲭⲉ ⲛ̇ⲁⲓ
ⲛⲉⲧⲉⲣ[ⲉ] ⲡⲭⲟⲉⲓⲥ ⲭⲱ ⲙ
ⲙⲟⲟⲩ ⲭⲉ ⲛⲉⲓ̇ⲙⲟⲟⲩⲉ
[ⲁ]ⲓ̇ⲧⲁⲗϭⲟⲟⲩ· ⲁⲩⲱ ⲁⲓ̇

*P.Mich.*inv. 607, Folio 2 Verso

14

The Role of the Papyri in Etymological Reconstruction

HENRY AND RENÉE KAHANE

I. INTRODUCTION

The papyri can contribute in many and varied ways to etymological reconstruction. The total cultural background behind the papyri is, after all, far broader than the framework in which papyrological investigation usually operates. The following word histories illustrate the multiple benefits that can be derived from diachronic papyrological lexicology. The derivational hypotheses to be presented are assumed to be correct—certainly a risky assumption as anyone knows who is familiar with the slippery field of etymology. No one is more aware of this than the authors themselves of the propositions. But the chance of error seems to us less grave than the demonstration of the methodological impact of the papyri on etymological research.

II. WORD HISTORIES

1. *Torta* "Egyptian bread" (*Revue de Linguistique Romane* 31 [1967] 127–129)

The origin of *torte*, that widespread name of a cake or pastry, has been an etymological puzzle. The word occurs in the Vulgate as *torta* (Exod. 29:23) and *tortula* (Num. 11:8); its modern congeners, Ital. *tọrta* and Rum. *turtă* require a Latin base with close *ọ*. Two principal solutions have been proposed: **tōrta* "the twisted one" and **tŏrta* "the toasted one" but neither is a viable reconstruction. Some help comes from a first-century Hellenistic grammarian, Erotianus; he comments on the Hippocratean term ἄρτος ἐγκρυφίας: it is a bread used by the Attics, consisting of oily dates, flour, and water, is baked covered in hot ashes, and is usually called τούρτα. Now, fourth-century papyri, contemporary with the word's first

appearance in Latin, contain, within various lists of victuals, nine occurrences of the suffixed variant τουρτίον (P.Ryl. IV, p. 202, s.v.; with
penultimate stress as in I. Kalleris, 'Ἐπετηρὶς 'Ἑταιρείας Βυζαντινῶν
Σπουδῶν 23 [1953] 694). The provenience of these papyri and the
additional testimony of the grammarian's remark that the τούρτα is
prepared with dates, indicate the area of the term's origin: Egypt. The
Egyptian designation of the bread must have been borrowed by the
Romans in Egypt, not later than the fourth century. The Egyptian bi-
morphemic base, we suggest, was t-rth "baked bread," consisting of the
constituents t "bread" and rth, a participle, "baked" (the vocalization is
unknown). The Egypt. bread t-rth had been, for a long time, part of ritual
offerings, and was recorded as such up to Roman times. In various rustic
areas of Italy, above all Umbria and the Trentino, torta is still, as in its
distant origins, a cake baked under hot ashes.

2. *Bernicarium* "nitrum, glass, vessel" (*Romance Philology* 14 [1960–1961]
   289–294)
   Νιτρία, famed center of Egyptian nitrum production, was located near
Naucratis. It was also known as Βερενίκη in Greek and as *Pernoudj* in
Coptic. The product was called βερενίκιον/βερ(ε)νικάριον. The latter
derivative is used for Egyptian nitrum in Galen, and it recurs in an
alchemistic third-century papyrus as νίτρον βερνικάριον (*P.Leid.* II,
pap. 10, pag. 13.16–17 [= p. 239]). The derivative survives but changes
its referent: from the chemical it shifts to glass, from glass to a medieval
receptacle, widely used in the Catalan-Provençal-North Italian area; it
appears at times with the inherited suffix -*ariu* (Catal. *berniguier*), at times
with the secondary suffixes -*ale* (Fr. *vernigal*) or -*atu* (Ital. *vernicato*).

3. *Gulf* (*Romance Philology* 27 [1973–1974] 46–49)
   Gulf, the geographical term, is clearly related to synonymous Gr. κόλπος,
yet the phonological bridge, *p* → *f*, i.e., stop → spirant, long remained a
puzzle. The papyri shed light on the problem: κόλφος is the Egyptian
form of the lexeme. Thus, the papyri document κόλφος "bay" in the
third century, in Alexandria (*P.Mich.* VIII 514.30) and its semantic
variant κόλφος "bosom" since the third century (Pap. from Karanis 2.20,
ap. A. E. R. Boak and H. C. Youtie, *Aegyptus* 31 [1951] 324), most
strikingly in the characteristically Egyptian sepulchral formula εἰς κόρφον
τοῦ 'Ἀβραάμ "in Abraham's bosom," found in Upper Egypt in the sixth
century (*P.Oxy.* XVI 1874.16). The change reflects a vagueness of
boundaries between stops and aspirates, which is a typical feature of the
Egyptian dialect within the Greek koine: either π or φ may appear,

e.g., where the opposite member is historically justified. The neutralization of the contrast was probably caused by the Coptic substratum. The Egyptian variant spread through the Hellenic world and beyond. The geographical term κόλφος is still the demotic form in Modern Greek and survives in Old Venetian and Dalmatian; *golfus, the international pattern, spreading in early Byzantine times, shows sonorization of the initial. The sepulchral formula εἰς κόλφον τοῦ Ἀβραάμ was also exported from Egypt: it reached Sicily in pre-Muslim times, between the fourth and the middle of the seventh century, as indicated by a Christian inscription, containing the Egyptian variant κόλφος, in the Catacombs of San Giovanni in Syracuse. In this Graeco-Egyptian expression, Judeo-Christian sepulchral traditions had blended with the indigenous Egyptian funerary cult.

4. *Dardanus' Sword* (*Romance Philology* 12 [1958–1959] 216–218)

In Western medieval civilization Roland's *Durendart* is the earliest occurrence of a sword's name. Many derivations have been attempted, none of which relates it to any tradition. Yet, its magic power directs attention to the old magic practice of naming swords, and this practice comes impressively to life in the *Grosse Pariser Zauberpapyrus*, of the fourth century. It contains a section entitled Ξίφος Δαρδάνου, the Sword of Dardanus (*P.Graec. Mag.* IV.1716 [= Preisendanz I 126]), a set of bizarre magic prescriptions, and precisely this name *Dardanus* may represent the base of *Durendart*. *Dardanus*, as a magician's name, is the focus of a long tradition: the diffusion of the mysteries was attributed to Dardanus, the mythical ancestor of the Trojans, and Columella described magic as *Dardaniae artes*. Dardanus was incorporated into both Jewish magic legend and Arabic alchemy. The association of his name with a sword is based on his eminence as a magician and on the significance of the sword in magic tradition. The sword symbolizes the magician's wand, a metaphor best-known through Moses' wand, which turns into Moses' sword, *Harba-de-Mosheh* in medieval Jewish lore. A Coptic papyrus, from Edfu and probably of the tenth century (E. Drioton, *Muséon* 59 [1946] 479–489), cut in the form of a sword and decorated with letters and magic designs, testifies to the perpetuation of the pagan magic symbol into the Christian era. Syntactically, *Dardanus' Sword* has simply become *Dardanus* or, possibly, an adjectival *spatha dardana*. As to the form of the word (whether referred to magician or to sword), such medieval variants as Grk.-Lat. *Durdanus*, Ital.-Span. *Dur(l)indana*, and above all Arab. *Dardaris* indicate the pattern underlying OFr. *Durendart*: it must have been somewhat like *Durdaris* or *Durindaris*. The explanation fits the tradition: Roland's Sword is just another of the sundry Gnostic and magic elements in the *Song of Roland*.

5. *Calamita*, the Lodestone (*Romance Philology* 13 [1959–1960] 269–278, and 26 [1972–1973] 435–437)

In the Middle Ages, both the mineral magnetite and the technical device in which it played its dominant role, the compass, were called *calamita*. The origin of the term, debated for a long time, is cleared up by records in the Hellenistic magic literature of Egypt: a Hermetic treatise (third century?) mentions a λίθος κεραμίτης "lodestone" and so does the magic *Papyrus Mimaut* (written after 300). This papyrus lists for each two-hour period of the day one animal in the sky, one animal on earth, one bird, one plant, and one stone, and the sun-god Helios takes on or begets their shapes and through them the magician can exert influence on the god. The stone of the second hour is the κεραμίτης (*P.Graec.Mag.* III 505–506 [= Preisendanz I 54]). The name was taken over, not later than the ninth century, by Arabic, as *qaramiṭ*. It spread from Arabic to the West, first still with the original *r* in the Catalan-Provençal-Genoese area, then, with hypercorrect *l* for Genoese *r*, as *calamita*, in wide distribution. The magic meaning of the papyri was retained with the term in Catalan; but in medieval nautical parlance, its referent shifted from the lodestone to the needle it magnetized and from the needle to the compass.

6. The Stone *peridot* (*Romance Philology* 14 [1960–1961] 287–289)

A semiprecious stone called *peridot* turns up frequently in the medieval lapidaries of the West. The origin of the term, illuminated through the papyri, reflects its Hellenistic-Egyptian magic heritage. For the fourth two-hour period the magic *Papyrus Mimaut* includes a tree and stone both known as boylove, παιδέρως (*P.Graec.Mag.* III 510 [= Preisendanz I 54 f.]); and the *Grosse Pariser Zauberpapyrus*, of the fourth century, lists among weird objects, of often sexual connotation, symbolizing Hecate's magic power, the same stone παιδέρως, helpful in dealing with those in authority, in averting evil, in alleviating fear of Hecate, and, of course, in meeting pederastic adventures (*P.Graec.Mag.* IV 2309 [= Preisendanz I 144]). The stone recurs in various medieval Latin lapidaries as *pederotes*, preserving the original form; then, from the eleventh century on, in the metathetic variant *peredot-*. While the stone retained its magic powers, all feeling for the original constituents of the word, *paid-* "boy" and *erot-* "love," had disappeared.

7. *Cotrophium*, from "cranium" to "receptacle" (*Studia Hispanica in honorem R. Lapesa* I [Madrid, 1972] 331–333)

The widespread medieval name of a receptacle, Byz. κουτρούβι with Mod.Grk. κουτρούφι, South Ital. *cutrufo* with MHG *kuterolf*, OProv. *cotofle* with Span. *cotofre*, has given rise to various explanations. The most convincing, by Ph. Koukoules, relates the Byz. term to Anc.Grk. κρόταφος "temple," via an intermediate stage "nape, cranium," preserved in Mod.Grk. κούτρουφας/κουτρούφι. The papyri fill the two gaps of intervening changes, metathesis and assimilation. The metathesis, κότραφος (instead of κρόταφος), is first recorded in a fourth-century papyrus (*P.Osl.* I *Magical Papyri* 1.152); the assimilation, κότροφος (instead of κότραφος), in a Coptic papyrus of the sixth century (H. I. Bell and W. F. Crum, *Aegyptus* 6 [1925], Index, p. 221, s.v. κρόταφος). This latter form in its diminutive variant, *κοτρόφιον, applied to a receptacle and Latinized as *cotrophium, spread in the West, as the distribution shows, from probably both Southern-Italian and Massaliotic Greek.

8. Grk.-Egypt. λάνκος "pit" (*Italia linguistica nuova ed antica: Studi linguistici in memoria di Oronzo Parlangèli* [Galatina, 1976] 327–329)

A medieval and modern Greek morpheme *lank-* "valley" is realized as λάγκος in Graecanic (the Greek dialects of Southern Italy). Essentially, two explanations have been suggested: either it is related to a pre-Romance (Gallic or Illyrian) relic, *lanka* "river, bed," widely spread in Northern Italy, or it is considered a nasalized variant of Grk. λάκκος "pit," of IE stock. The papyri favor a separation of *lank-* from the Western relic word and an acceptance of a Hellenistic-Egyptian origin of the nasalized form, i.e., a polygenetic over a monogenetic explanation. An unorganic nasal is typical, after all, of the Greek of Hellenistic Egypt. The first record of *lank-* appears, indeed, in an Egyptian papyrus of the second century (*P.Lond.* II 335.22 [= p. 192]): it contains the compound κοππόρανκος, emendated as κοπρόρανκος and identified as *κοπρόλανκος "cesspit," consisting of κόπρο- "ordure" and λάνκος "pit." Medieval and Modern Greek dialects preserve both the non-nasalized and the nasalized doublets.

9. Graecanic τρακλός "bent" (*Studi . . . Parlangèli* 333–335)

Graecanic τρακλή "bend in a road," a member of a large Greek word family, has been associated with the Anc.Grk. verb κατακλάω "to bend down." Phonologically, this derivation implies a succession of two stages: first, *katakl-* → *takl-*, confirmed by the marginal dialect of Pontus, and second, *takl-* → *trakl-*, confirmed by the marginal dialect of Laconia. The Pontic variant, however, means "somersault," the Laconian "to stagger, to trip." (The feature underlying these semantic shades must have been the bent posture of the body.) Corroboration of this derivational hypothesis comes from still another marginal dialect area, Egypt: A second-century papyrus, from Tebtuni in Upper Egypt, contains the noun κατακλή "bend made by a swampy ground" (*P.Mil.Vogl.* II 105.20), combining the base form *katakl-* with the same topographical application as in Southern-Italian Greek.

10. *Algalía* "catheter" (*Romance Philology* 20 [1966–1967] 427; *Homenaje a Antonio Tovar* [Madrid, 1972] 213)

The general Greek name for a tool, ἐργαλεῖον, plur. ἐργαλεῖα, survives in Romance as a technical medical term "tool for rinsing; catheter," thus Ital. *algalía*, Fr. *algalie*, Span. *algalia*. Three changes are involved, semantic, morphologic, and phonologic. The term, as *argalia*, spread probably in the eleventh century from Southern Italy, with the medical specialization inherited from Byzantine Greek and transmitted through the School of Salerno, the famous polyethnic center of medical studies. Morphologically, the Western feminine continues a Greek neuter plural. Phonologically, a change of initial *e-* to *a-* is presupposed by the Western form; and indeed, the new form ἀργαλεῖον due to assimilatory sandhi (τὰ ἐργαλεῖα → τὰ ἀργαλεῖα) is recorded several times in the papyri, possibly as early as the third century B.C. (*P.Enteux.* 78.3), then since the first century (*P.Lond.* II 280.10), thus confirming the colloquial use of this variant in the koine.

11. *Sambata/sambatum* (*Romance Philology* 20 [1966–1967] 433; *Reallexikon der Byzantinistik* I [Amsterdam, 1970] 366)

Sabbath, a Graeco-Hebrew borrowing, appears widely with an epenthetic nasal, so Rum. *sâmbăta*, Ladin *samda*, SGerm. *Samstag*, Fr. *samedi*. The spread of the nasal has been puzzling; but the papyri provide a missing link. Whether of Syriac or of Greek origin, the vulgar nasalized variant, σάμβαθον, appears in a fourth-century papyrus (*P.Oxy.* VI, 903.19): ἐν σαμβάθῳ "on the Sabbath." In terms of linguistic geography, this Hellenistic-Byzantine *m*-form occurred in the marginal areas of Egyptian Greek and Palestinian Greek (sixth century) just as it survives in the marginal areas of Greek, Cappadocian, the Tsakonian dialect, and South Ital. Graecanic: an indication of its age and popularity in Vulgar Greek. The early presence of the nasal in Judeo-Latin is again revealed by a papyrological record: a letter, written by a Jew, in a second-century papyrus from Egypt mentions *sambatha* (*P.Ryl.* IV 613.4). The geographical distribution of the *m*-form in the Western languages, with either final *-a* or final *-um*, supports a spread, in part through Gothic channels, from the Balkanic area to the Danube and the Rhine.

12. Mozarab. *feriwel* "cloak" (*Romance Philology* 21 [1967–1968] 509–510)

A kind of cloak going back to the sixteenth century is called *ferreruelo* in Spanish, *ferragoulo* in Portuguese, and *ferraiolo* in Italian. It reached the

Western world via Mozarabic, the Arabized Romance dialect of the Christians living under Islam. A document of 1161, from Toledo, records *f-r-w-y-l*, which could be transcribed alternatively *fir(i)wil* [fir-/fer- (i)wél]. The vocalization points to Grk. περιβόλαιον "wrapper" occurring in the Septuagint (e.g., De. 22:12) and in the papyri, first until the third century (*P.Stras.* II 91.9; the dim. in *-άδιον, BGU* VIII 1848.13 and *P.Oxy.* VI 921.2), then in the Byzantine period (*P.Bon.* 46.10). The documentation identifies Egypt as the area in which Arabic borrowed the Greek term. In Byzantine times, περιβόλαιον designated preeminently a cloak worn by Syrian monks, later, the town dweller's typical garment.

13. Mozarab. *corachón*, a medical plant (*Polychronion: Festschrift F. Dölger* [Heidelberg, 1966] 308–309)

In Mozarabic, between the tenth and the twelfth century, Saint-John's-wort, a medical plant, was called (*yerba*) *corichnera/corochón/corachón*. The origin of the term has been obscure. A hint to its provenience is hidden behind the fact that in Provençal-Catalan the element -*iĕ* renders Grk. -*ίδιον*; and indeed, two seventh-century papyri list a plant called κορίδιον (*SB* 4483.12 and 4485.3). The latter is clearly a derivative of ancient κόρις (gen. κόριδος) "Saint-John's-wort," the base form of the scattered word family. Two branches seem to evolve: *koris-*, probably reflected in Pliny's Grecism *corisson/corissum*, and *korid-*, surviving in Mod.Grk. σκορδίτσα and in the Mozarabic forms. The borrowing took place within the pharmacological terminology. The isolated morpheme, as shown by Mozarab. *corachón*/Catal. *corassonillo*, was secondarily drawn into the orbit of Span. *corazón* "heart."

14. *trulla*, from "ladle" to "cupola" (*Homenaje Tovar* 222–223)

The complex history of *trulla* is twice illuminated by records in the papyri. Lat. *trulla* "ladle" was borrowed by Hellenistic Greek, as shown by two papyri, which, within their vocabulary of everyday life, record as "receptacle, measure" the two diminutive variants τρύλλιον (*Stud.Pal.* XX 67.10 [second to third century]) and τρούλι(ο)ν (thus corrected by the scribe *BGU* 814.10 [third century]). The metaphorical use of vessels is common, and τρούλλα "receptacle" turned into "cupola." The semantic change is dated by the masculine offshoot τρούλλος, found in a sixth-century description of Saint Sophia in Constantinople. Τρούλλα, the Hellenism of Latin provenience, was then reborrowed by two Italian dialects rich in Byzantinisms, Venetian and Apulian. The masculine form was also reborrowed and became the name of the Apulian farmhouse, the *trullo*, with its characteristic conic roof. There is a third, metathetic form of the morpheme, τουρλ-, recorded, as his colloquial variant, by the scribe of the third-century papyrus (*BGU* 814.10), and this variant spread through the Balkanic area into Northern Italy: Alb. *turlɛ* "tower," Serbo-Croatian *turla*, Rum. *turlă* "cupola," North Ital. *turlo* "spire of a church" and in Old Venetian specifically the "cupola of the Campanile."

15. *Baneum* for *balneum* (*Romance Philology* 17 [1963–1964] 313–314)

The Romance congeners of Lat. *balneum* "bath," such as Ital. *bagno*/Fr. *bain*/Span. *baño*, presuppose a VL base *baneum*. The phonological hypothesis is confirmed by a Pompeian inscription (*CIL*, IV 3878; M. Niedermann, *Archivum Romanicum* 5 [1921] 441). The extent of its use is indicated by records in Greek papyri: βανιάτωρ "bath attendant," i.e., the morpheme [banj-] plus agent suffix, appears in papyri of the sixth (*P.Kl.Form.* II 980.2) and the early eighth century (*P.Apoll.* 97A.12). The secondary stem [banj-] survived also in Byz. βανιάριν "bath," which in conjunction with Slav. *banja* corroborates the variant's wide popularity as indicated by the papyri: The Latin colloquialism had taken root even in the margins of the Empire, in Egyptian Latinity as well as in the Graeco-Latin *Mischkultur* of the Balkanic area.

16. *Calefactor* "one who heats (pitch)" (*Lingua Franca in the Levant: Turkish Nautical Terms of Italian and Greek Origin* [Urbana, 1958] ##775 and 776; *Reallexikon der Byzantinistik* I 410 f.)

The Mediterranean name of the caulker, Ital. *calafato*/Fr. *calfat*/Span. *calafate* has been derived either from Arabic or from Latin. The term's early appearance in the papyri weakens any Arabic hypothesis. The noun καλαφάτης is found in two sixth-century papyri: the one, a papyrus of 565–566, from Oxyrhynchus (*P.Oxy.* XXVII, 2480.33), the other from Syene, of the second half of the sixth century (*P.Lond.* V 1852). The Greek term is based on Lat. *calefactor* "the one who heats"; the verb *calefactare* was used in reference to pitch in the fourth century (Pertinax 8.5, in D. Magie, ed., *Scriptores Historiae Augustae* I). Morphologically, Lat. *-tor* was replaced by the equivalent Grk. *-της*; specialization to the nautical occupation may have taken place in Greece. By the tenth century, καλαφάτης is to Liutprand of Cremona, the shrewd observer of the Byzantine scene, a typically Byzantine expression. From Greek it spread to Arabic and the West.

17. *Calamarium*, from "pen case" to "inkwell" (*Homenaje Tovar* 223)

The adjectival element in the Lat. expression *calamaria theca* "pen case" was borrowed by Greek, as an elliptical neuter, with the meaning of the

entire phrase: καλαμάριον appears in this use in a sixth-century papyrus
(*P.Lond.* III 1007.5 and 27 [pp. 262 f.]). Then, in Greek, the term
broadens to include not only the receptacle where the pen was kept but
also the one into which it was dipped, the "inkwell"; as such, it is mentioned, explicitly as a Greek word, by St. Jerome as well as in bilingual
glosses. It is reborrowed by the West, not later than the eighth century,
when it appears in the *Ordines Romani*; it survives in Ital. *calamaio*/OProv.
OCatal. Span. *calamar*.

18. *Codicus* for *codex* (*Studia Lapesa* I 323–324)

Lat. *cōdex*, a third-declension noun, survives not only in the regular
pattern, say Ital. *codice*, but also in a variant representing the *-us* declension,
i.e., **codicus*, as in OItal. *còdico*, Catal. *còdic*, Span.Portug. *código*. The
impact of the *Codex Iustinianus*, with its Graeco-Latin blending, suggests a
Byzantine role in the history of the word, and, indeed, Lat. *cōdex* was
borrowed by Greek, at times with secondary adaptation to the morpho-
logical system: The neuter κώδικον "register of taxes" is found, as a
variant of synonymous κῶδιξ, in Egyptian papyri of the seventh to the
eighth century (*Stud.Pal.* X 63.9 [with erroneous emendation] and *SB*
4790.1); a masculine subvariant, Κώδικος, with reference to the *Codex
Iustinianus*, occurs much later, in the eleventh century, in Michael Psellus.
The Byzantine Latinism was reborrowed by the Romance languages.

19. The *Magarites* (*Zeitschrift für romanische Philologie* 76 [1960] 185–204)

In medieval French epics the morpheme *Margariz* is used various times
to characterize noble Saracens. The word has traditionally been identified
as Grk. μαγαρίτης "renegade," an explanation which fits morphologically,
but requires a more convincing semantic base. In the early period after
the Islamic conquest, when papyri were still written in Greek, the language
of the conquered, the Aphrodito Papyri, of the beginning of the eighth
century, contain over fifty records of a term μωαγαρίται rendering Arab.
Muhādžirūn (*P.Lond.* IV, p. 630, Index s.v. Μωαγαρίτης; furthermore,
P.Apoll. 2.3 and 3.1). The *Muhādžirūn* "emigrants," were the first adherents
of the new faith who followed the Prophet into exile in Medina. *Muhādžir*
became a title of honor, applied, by the middle of the seventh century, to
the true Arabic settlers in Egypt. They and their offspring represented the
aristocracy in the conquered areas.

Grk. μωαγαρίτης, then, spread in its Byzantine short form, μαγαρίτης.
This appears in the earliest Islamic documentation, two papyri of 642 and
643 (*P.Erzherzog Rainer* 558 vo. ap. A. Grohmann, *Et. de Papyrologie* 1
[1932] 41 f., and *P.Erz. Rainer* 564.10 ap. Grohmann, *ibid.* 8 [1957] 28 f.).

The lexeme, a reflection of the Arabo-Byzantine cultural fusion, radiated far, probably from Southern Italy, the common habitat of both civilizations. In its uses it reflects three main aspects of Islam in Christian eyes: (*a*) The first aspect is the political. *Margariz de Sibilie*, in the *Song of Roland*, continues the tradition of the *Muhādžirūn*; in his beauty and his chivalric virtues he typifies the Noble Heathen. Later, in various twelfth-century epics, the term is extended to the Saracen in general. (*b*) The second aspect is the military. The Aphrodito Papyri, within descriptions of the Egyptian fleet of the Arabs, mention marines recruited from among the early settlers: the μωαγαρίται of the dromonds, of the raiding fleet of the Orient, of the castellated ships (*P.Lond.* IV 1449.42, 49, 63) and of the city of Fustat preparing for their expeditions (*P.Lond.* IV 1394.8). *Margariz* "pirate" in a thirteenth-century French chronicle shows the survival of this semantic shade. (*c*) The third aspect is the religious, where the non-Arabic convert to Islam is seen by Christians as the renegade. One of numerous records: in 876, Pope John VIII feared for the fate of Rome, where the fifth column of the *Margaritae* would support the Saracens attacking from the outside. The religious view is the only one which survives into the present, in the much discussed Byz. and Mod.Grk. verb μαγαρίζω with its three semantic phases: from "convert to Mohammedanism" → "break the rules of fasting" → "soil."

20. *Risk* (*Verba et Vocabula: Ernst Gamillscheg Festschrift*, ed. H. Stimm and J. Wilhelm [München, 1968] 275–283)

The history of *risk*, the Western expression, is closely tied to the papyrological documentation. Pers. *rogik* "daily ration, maintenance" is borrowed by Arabic as a technical term of Islam's military government in Egypt, referring to the maintenance of the Arabic overlords and their requisition of provision. Muslim government officials in the conquered areas depended on what they could get from the country itself. The Arabo-Persian term recurs in Greek papyri since the late seventh century, i.e., since early Islam, in the Hellenized form ρουζικόν, thus, in the Nessana Papyri (*P.Ness.* III 69.1 and 92 passim), the Aphrodito Papyri (*P.Lond.* IV 1335.5, 1404.7, 1407.2, 1434.165, 1435.122), and the papyri of Apollonopolis (*P.Apoll.* 94.6, 95B.2, 49.5). In Arabic, *rogik* developed to *rizq*; thus *rizq* "maintenance of a farmer of taxes" occurs in an Arabic papyrus of 917 from Upper Egypt (*P.Hamb.* III 11.5). This second variant, *rizq*, was also borrowed by Greek, as ριζικόν. It was still a military term, but shifted meaning from the soldier's right to requisition to his luck, good or bad, in finding maintenance. The background of the record in question is the siege of Salonica by the Normans, in 1185: The ἄνδρες τοῦ ριζικοῦ "men of risk" (as they are called in Eustathius of Salonica's report) made their fortune "by chance," ἐκ τῆς τύχης. Here we are dealing with the beginnings of the Western mercenary soldatesca. A second use of the Byzantine Arabism evolved in sea law, *risicum maris et gentium*, an insurance term first recorded in 1158, in a Venetian document from Constantinople, and followed in the thirteenth century by the short form *riscum*. In a diachronic view, then, our modern *risk* has two semantic roots, "danger met with in an enterprise," spreading to the West with the terminology of the Mediterranean sea law; and "good or bad luck," perpetuating the military tradition of Islamic Egypt.

21. Admiral (*Romance Philology* 17 [1963–1964] 311–313; *Reallexikon der Byzantinistik* I 405)

The derivation of Western *admiral* from Arab. *'amīr* "commander, governor" is generally accepted; yet, the details of the development, in particular the suffix patterning, shades of meaning, and stages of borrowing, can hardly be cleared up without the papyrological data. The root morpheme appears, still as a crude and unsuffixed Arabism, ἀμίρ, first probably by the late seventh century (*P.Ness.* 92.18 and passim, 93.34), most assuredly by the eighth (*PSI* XII 1266.4; *P.Apoll.* 1.1). The dominant variant of the papyri, however, is the Byzantinized form ἀμιρᾶς (R. Rémondon, *P.Apoll.*, p. 8). This *amiras* form abounds also in the Western documentation, from the ninth to the eleventh century, and marks the Western term as a Byzantinism. The suffixal variant ἀμιράτος, occurring in two papyri of the Arabic period, of the seventh or eighth century, from Hermoupolis (*P.Lips.* 103.12; *P.Wurz.* 20.9), moved likewise via Greek to the West, with a first appearance as *amiratus* in 801 in Eginhard. The primary suffix string of *-as* and *-atus* produced, through suffix change or hypercorrection, a secondary string including *-alis*, i.e., *admiral*. Some of the Western semantic shades of the lexeme were prefigured in the papyri. The Arabic papyri written in Greek used the term as "dux or governor" (*P.Ness.* 92.18; *P.Apoll.* 9.5 and 14), reflected in OSpan. *almirante* and OFr. *amiral* "commander"; they also used it as "subaltern official" (e.g., *P.Kl.Form.* 447.3; *Stud.Pal.* X 118, 120, 204), recurring in tenth-century Span. *amirate*. The final semantic phase, "nautical commander," developed in the eleventh century, in the Arabic-Byzantine-Norman *Mischkultur* of Sicily.

III. Contribution of the Papyri to Etymology

The foregoing twenty-one word histories centering around papyrological documentation should suffice to reveal the contours of a particular subfield of etymological reconstruction. The Greek papyri of Egypt, one should not forget, are both Greek and Egyptian, and this fact determines their contribution: on the one hand, they share much with contemporary Greek materials unrelated to Egypt; on the other hand, they represent a specific subculture, Egyptian Grecism in Hellenistic and Byzantine times. The dichotomy is not always clear-cut, but it must be kept in mind.

1. *Methodology*. The papyri fulfil, first of all, a methodological function in linguistic reconstruction since they reveal either the missing link in a grammatical chain or the underlying concept in a semantic string.

(*a*) *Missing Links*. The papyri frequently fill in a phonologic or morphologic gap in an etymological hypothesis. Thus, κότραφος and κότροφος bridge the gaps of metathesis and assimilation between κρόταφος, the base form, and *κοτρόφιον, required by the Western offshoot (7); the variant κόλφος leads from standard κόλπος to Western *gulf* (3); ρουζικόν preserves the backvowel of Pers. *roğik*, precursor of Arab. *rizq*, the base of Grk. ριζικόν (20). Morphologically, κορίδιον establishes the bridge from *corachón* to κόρις (13); κατακλή ties together the various congeners of Graecanic τρακλή (9); suffixed patterns such as ἀμιρᾶς/ἀμιράτος unite 'amīr with *admiral* (21); καλαμάριον evidences the transition from a noun modifier, *theca calamaria*, to an autonomous noun (17).

(*b*) *Underlying Concepts*. Morpheme identifications based on papyrological materials may reveal hidden semantic bases from which there evolve later uses of a lexeme. In this way they illustrate the process of semantic change.

The change may result from metaphorical vision: the temple or cranium is viewed as a receptacle (7 *cotrophium*), the receptacle as a cupola (14 *trulla*). The change may be based on the isolation of a single characteristic aspect of the concept: for the physician the general designation of tool becomes the specialized name of the catheter (10 *algalia*); for the seaman lodestone turns into the designation of its primary application, the needle it magnetizes, and via the needle, of the compass (5 *calamita*); for the glassmaker the name of the chemical which he uses in the manufacture of glass develops into the name of yellow glass, and the name of glass into that of the finished receptacle (2 *bernicarium*); for the soldier the search for maintenance becomes an undertaking involving chance (20 *risk*). The change may reflect bias: the convert from one's own faith to an alien one is viewed as a renegade (19 *Magarites*). The change may be due to a mystic perception of objects: a stone used in the Middle Ages to ward off nervous sufferings derives its name, *boylove*, from its original force: to be helpful in pederastic pursuances (6 *peridot*); a sword believed to have magic power is named for the sword or wand of a famed magician (4 *Dardanus*).

2. *Koine Features*. The papyri represent essentially the level of Vulgar Greek, the koine; and the word histories under discussion corroborate the fact. In this respect three features are characteristic: phonologic and morphologic informality, adaptation, and borrowing.

(a) *Non-standard forms*. The nasalized variant λάνκος, as distinct from standard λάκκος (8), occurs in a papyrus explicitly described (*P.Lond*. II, p. 191) as "extraordinarily illiterate." The epenthetic nasal in Judeo-Greek σάμβαθον may likewise render a colloquialism (11). Similar phonological exceptions are the metathetic variant τουρλ- for τρουλλ- (14) and change of the initial through sandhi in ἀργαλεῖον for ἐργαλεῖον (10). The Greek variant βανιάτωρ of Lat. *balneator*, with simplification of the cluster *ln* (15), indicates borrowing of a substandard form. Morphologically κώδικον for κῶδιξ (18) shows the effect of regularization.

(b) *Hybridization*. The adaptation of a borrowed lexeme to the target language is sometimes fostered by the technique of suffixal hybridization: an indigenous derivational suffix attached to a foreign root morpheme functions as a bridge to its naturalization. Examples: καλαφάτης, with -της for Lat. *-tor* (16); ἀμιρᾶς/ἀμιράτος, adaptations of the crude Arabism ἀμίρ (21); μαγαρίτης, the Hellenizing of Arab. *Muhāǧir* through the agent suffix -ίτης (19); ρουζικόν, the transformation of the ending of Arabo-Pers. *rogik* by the Greek suffix -ικόν (20).

(c) *Contacts*. Greek, the dominant language of the Eastern Mediterranean, is in a continuous exchange, both giving and absorbing, with the languages and dialects with which it is in contact. From Latin we have τρουλλ- (14), βανιάτωρ (15), καλαφάτης (16), καλαμάριον (17), and κώδικον (18). Most of these go back, earlier or later, to the Latin West. Greek lexemes expanding to the West are ἀργαλεῖον (10), *κοτρόφιον (7), τουρτ- (1), παιδέρως (6), and βερνικάριον (2). Byzantine Greek transmits much to Arabic, e.g., Δάρδανος (4), κεραμίτης (5), περιβόλαιον (12), κορίδιον (13), and καλαφάτης (16). The Balkanic borderland between the Greek and the Latin spheres of influence shares [banj-] (15) and [sambat-] (11) with Egyptian Greek; and the marginal area of Egyptian Greek shares lexemes or phonological features with that other marginal area, the Greek of Southern Italy: κατακλή (9), λάνκος (8), and, in Sicily, κόλφος (3).

3. *Egyptian Hellenism*. Several of the word histories based on the papyri are specifically Egyptian stories. They evidence the survival of relics from the indigenous Egyptian substratum or the impact of the Islamic superstratum, heralding the end of Egyptian Hellenism.

(a) *The Egyptian substratum*. Old Egyptian customs of baking, with ritual undertones, survive in τούρτ- (1). Indigenous funerary traditions blended with Judeo-Christian ones underlie the expression κόλφος τοῦ Ἀβραάμ, Abraham's bosom (3); the phonological shape ƒ for standard p in κόλφος may reflect Coptic speech habits (3). The typically Egyptian nitrum production is echoed in the name of several medieval vessels, such as Catal. *berniguier*; the term goes back to a toponym marking one of the Egyptian nitrum centers: Βερενίκη in Greek, with the Coptic equivalent *Pernoudj* (2).

(b) *The Arabic superstratum.* Just as Latin survived in the West during the Middle Ages as the standard form of bureaucratic communication, so did Greek in the East. In the early stages of the Arabic administration in Egypt, Greek was the vehicle of officialdom. In other words, the Greek papyri of the Arabic period often express Arabic reality in Greek guise. Three Arabic keywords testify to this situation: Μαγαρῖται, the honorary name of the early settlers (19); ρουζικόν, the technical term for the soldier's search for maintenance (20); and ἀμιρᾶς, the title of officials (21). All three reached the West through Byzantine channels and in Byzantine reinterpretation.

University of Illinois at Urbana

15

Juvenal, Satire 12: On Friendship
True and False

EDWIN S. RAMAGE

The twelfth satire is both the shortest and, along with the ninth, perhaps the most neglected of Juvenal's satires. One of the main reasons for its being all but ignored is the fact that it is generally considered to be inferior to the rest of the collection. The poem has been described as one of the weakest, if not the weakest, of Juvenal's satires[1] and as a surprising piece that a person would not willingly read a second time.[2] One scholar has gone so far as to call the poem "one of the strangest productions in Latin literature" which "seems to be a joke, and not a very good one."[3]

The criticism stems mainly from the form of the satire and from the way in which Juvenal develops his argument. Some have felt a certain discontinuity in style and content, while others find frequent digressions and repeated banalities that leave them distressed. And the satire has also been criticized for being harsh, obscure, confused, confusing, and ambiguous.[4] It is no wonder, then, that Otto Ribbeck questioned the authenticity of this poem when he rejected a number of the later satires in the Juvenalian corpus.[5] But Ribbeck's ideas have never found general acceptance—and

---

[1] L. Friedlaender, *D. Junii Juvenalis saturarum libri V* (Leipzig, 1895) 511; U. Knoche, *Die römische Satire*[3] (Göttingen, 1971) 92 (trans. E. S. Ramage, *Roman Satire* [Bloomington, 1975] 149).

[2] P. de Labriolle, *Les satires de Juvénal* (Paris, 1932) 293, 298.

[3] W. C. Helmbold, "Juvenal's Twelfth Satire," *Classical Philology* 51 (1956) 15, 16.

[4] J. A. Gylling, *De argumenti dispositione in satiris IX–XVI Juvenalis* (Lund, 1889) 78, 79, 81; H. L. Wilson, *D. Iuni Iuvenalis saturarum libri V* (Boston, 1908) 120; J. de Decker, *Juvenalis declamans* (Ghent, 1913) 81; de Labriolle (above, note 2) 298.

[5] O. Ribbeck, *Der echte und der unechte Juvenal* (Berlin, 1865).

rightly so—and scholars have tended to accept this piece as being Juvenal's, some with more enthusiasm than others.[6]

The satire has attracted a little attention, then, but thus far there has been no detailed analysis of the poem to determine precisely what Juvenal was trying to do and how he carried out his purposes.[7] What follows is an attempt to make up for this lack, though it will have to be left to the individual reader to decide for himself whether the poet is successful or not.

There is nothing in the satire that suggests a date. But if Satire 13 can be confidently placed in or shortly after 127 after Christ, then this satire should fall a little earlier.[8] It is clear from the address to Corvinus in the first line, which is repeated later in the poem (93), that the satire is meant to have the loose epistolary form that other satires of Juvenal also show.[9] There is no way of knowing who Corvinus was, and it probably does not matter. He does have an important function in the poem, however, since he provides a specific dramatic target for the very personal feelings and observations that Juvenal is about to put forward. The whole thing would be weakened if the satirist unburdened himself to the world at large. Corvinus is a friend to whom the poet is talking with a certain intimacy about friendship.

But a closer look at Satire 12 reveals that it is really a fusion of forms from prose and poetry. It begins as a poem of thanksgiving for the return of a friend and in this respect recalls two poetic types—the speech of welcome that is found in epic, lyric, tragic, and elegiac poetry, and the

[6] For a recent, quite sympathetic treatment of the satire see G. Highet, *Juvenal the Satirist* (Oxford, 1954) 134–137. Some appreciation of individual passages in the poem has been expressed. Lines 83–92, for example, are praised by D. Nisard, *Études des moeurs et de critique sur les poètes latins de la décadence*[5] (Paris, 1888) 67–69; de Decker (above, note 4) 94, note 3; E. Malcovati, *Giovenale* (Rome, 1935) 117; A. Serafini, *Studio sulla satira di Giovenale* (Florence, 1957) 192–193. Gylling (above, note 4) 78–82, discusses the problems that the satire presented for himself and for his predecessors.

[7] There has been a tendency to deal with separate aspects of Satire 12 and to ignore the satire as a whole (e.g., Helmbold [above, note 3]; R. E. Colton, "Echoes of Martial in Juvenal's Twelfth Satire," *Latomus* 31 [1972] 164–173). W. S. Anderson in his article, "The Programs of Juvenal's Later Books" (*Classical Philology* 57 [1962] 145–160) all but omits the twelfth satire from consideration. E. E. Burriss ("The Religious Element in the Satires of Juvenal," *Classical World* 20 [1926] 19–21) makes one reference to the last three lines (p. 20), while ignoring completely the longer passages of religious thanksgiving (lines 1–16; 83–92) and the religious travesty making up the last scene (lines 93–127). Most recently, L. I. Lindo ("The Evolution of Juvenal's Later Satires," *Classical Philology* 69 [1974] 17–27) has skirted Satire 12 almost completely while taking into account both Satire 11 and Satire 13 and most of the later satires.

[8] E. S. Ramage, D. L. Sigsbee, S. C. Fredericks, *Roman Satirists and Their Satire* (Park Ridge, N.J., 1974) 155, 160. Cf. Highet (above, note 6) 14–15.

[9] On Juvenal's use of the epistolary form see Lindo (above, note 7).

expression of thanksgiving which was especially popular with the Roman elegists.[10] The last section of the poem, on the other hand, is out-and-out satire (93–130), actually a satire in miniature. At the same time, the whole piece is a study of friendship in which the extremes of altruism and utility are contrasted. As will be noted later, this reminds us of philosophical essays like Cicero's *De amicitia* or a number of Seneca's *Epistulae morales* in which the subject is discussed, at least in part, from a similar point of view. In this satire, then, Juvenal seems to be exploiting a number of forms or types.

There are different ways of viewing the arrangement of the poem, but it is probably simplest and easiest to take it as dividing into four main parts.[11] In the first sixteen lines the poet describes a sacrifice of public thanksgiving that he is undertaking for his friend, Catullus, who has returned safely after narrowly escaping disaster at sea. This is followed by a lengthy account of the near shipwreck which Juvenal's friend experienced (17–82). Then comes further description of the poet's sacrifices which includes completion of the public service and his intention to perform a similar ceremony in private at home (83–92). Finally, there is a surprising and sudden hyperbolic attack on legacy-hunters and their motives (93–130). While each of these sections is a clearly delineated unit, a fair reading of the satire shows that they follow naturally from one another and that the poem is a coherent whole.

The satire begins with a surprise, for Juvenal tells Corvinus that this is the happiest day of his life—"sweeter to me than my birthday" (1). This is a little startling, since nowhere else does the satirist begin one of his

10 Other examples of poems or passages of welcome in Latin literature are Catullus 9; Horace, *Odes* 1.36; Ovid, *Amores* 2.11.37–56; Statius, *Silvae* 3.2.127–143. Poems of thanksgiving include Catullus 44; Horace, *Odes* 2.17 and 3.8; Propertius 2.28.59–62; Tibullus 3.10; Ovid, *Amores* 2.13; Statius, *Silvae* 1.4. In the last 9 lines of the latter poem mention is made of the fates, birthday, Nestor, Clitumnus, bulls, gods, turf altar, and grain (*farra*), all of which are also present in Juvenal 12. F. Cairns, *Generic Composition in Greek and Roman Poetry* (Edinburgh, 1972) 20–23, includes Satire 12 in his genre prosphonetikon ("speech of welcomer") and lists fourteen other examples from Greek and Latin literature. However we may feel about the ideas expressed in this book, the number of examples suggests that welcoming was a recognized convention in the proper literary context. A little later (pp. 73–75) Cairns mentions the genre soteria ("thanksgiving"), but does not include this satire among the examples (p. 73), probably because of his rather rigid system of classification. It does seem to belong here as well. See also the introductory note on Horace, *Odes* 1.36 in R. G. M. Nisbet and M. Hubbard, *A Commentary on Horace: Odes Book I* (Oxford, 1970) 401–402. I am indebted to B. R. Fredericks, S. C. Fredericks, and J. W. Halporn for drawing my attention to both modern references.

11 This is the arrangement that de Decker finds (above, note 4, p. 80) and the one that Highet follows (above, note 6, p. 280).

poems in such a positive, lyrical way.[12] For that matter, such expressions of joy are rare anywhere in Juvenal. The fact that the thought is complete in the first line also catches the reader's eye; this happens only in one other satire (7.1), and there the statement is relatively neutral in tone.

The first line stands out, then, as an attention-getting topic sentence for the satire, and the subordinate clause which follows (2–3) reinforces this mood and point of view. A festal altar of turf is waiting to receive the sacrifices that the poet has vowed to the gods. The meter also helps provide this reinforcement, for it is identical in the two lines, and three of the four caesuras of the first line have direct parallels in the second line. As if this is not enough, Juvenal has placed *die* at the metrical center of the one line and *deis* at the metrical center of the other. The play on sounds is obvious and draws our attention to "a day for the gods."

But Juvenal provides the seeds of imbalance as well to make the parallels all the more effective. The verb is missing from both lines. In the first it would have been a colorless *est* anyhow, but in the case of the subordinate clause, the sense runs on into the third line where the verb suddenly appears (*expectat*) after an eye-catching enjambment. At the same time this word takes on a special color from the fact that it provides a mild personification for the altar of turf. It should also be noticed that the fourth caesura appears in the last foot of the first line and in the first foot of the second line. The word order is also quite different between lines, though in both cases there are clear intralinear parallels involving nouns and adjectives.

What does Juvenal accomplish with all of this? He certainly catches the attention of the reader with the metrical parallels, diction, and the statement of joy followed immediately by an idyllic picture of religious activity motivated by piety and happiness. No other satire in the Juvenalian corpus begins this way. The satirist also uses these lines to begin creating a suspense. The reader is surprised, and part of this surprise is a curiosity as to why the poet is happy, why the animals have been promised to the gods (2: *promissa deis*), and why the altar "expects" the offerings (3: *expectat*). Something has happened to cause all of this and the reader's appetite is whetted. But Juvenal is just beginning to build the suspense and gives no indication of the reasons for his happiness for another twelve lines.

Instead, he elaborates the religious activities that he has already alluded to. He is going to sacrifice a white lamb to Juno (3) and another to

---

[12] There may be some significance in the fact that all three occurrences of *dulcis* thus far in the satires (5.139, 6.38, 9.88) resemble this one in that they involve a context of legacy-hunting. There is only one other instance (13.185) where the word is used, appropriately enough, to describe Mount Hymettus.

Minerva (4). Jupiter, however, will get a lively heifer (5–9) which shakes and pulls on his rope and tosses his head. He is ready for sacrifice; he has given up mother's milk and attacks oak trees with the horns that are just beginning to grow on his head. The poet insists that, if his resources matched his feelings, he would be sacrificing a fine bull fattened not on the grass that grows close to town, but on that which is found in the lush fields in the valley of the Clitumnus—a bull so large that only a tall priest could perform the sacrifice (10–14).

Throughout these lines the positive, idyllic atmosphere is maintained, and as the picture develops we are reminded of similar passages elsewhere in Juvenal's satires. In the satire immediately preceding this one, for example, the poet had already associated himself with the simple country life that was typical of Rome and Italy in the good old days before gluttony and extravagance had invaded society (11.65–116; esp. 65–76).

Parallels for the words and pictures that Juvenal conjures up in the first fourteen lines of Satire 12 are to be found in Horace's *Odes*, Vergil's *Georgics*, and the *Fasti* of Ovid.[13] White lambs, frisky heifers, fine bulls fattened by the Clitumnus are all commonplace elements of the ideally and serenely simple life. The passage actually divides into two parts—a description of the animals that are being led to sacrifice (3–9) and an account of what the sacrifice would be if the poet had ampler means (10–14). Here Juvenal helps to increase the suspense by directly mentioning the positive feelings (10: *affectibus*) which make him wish that he could present a more elaborate offering.

In these lines we also have the first hint of satire as Juvenal mentions Hispulla in passing (11): the poet's ideal bull is to be fatter than this fat woman. But it is only a touch and may be meant as a gentle reminder that, in spite of the picture presented, the poem is a satire.

At last Juvenal gives the reason for all of this celebration—a friend has been saved (15–16). Important and climactic as this is, it is tacked on to the lines which precede it as a simple subordinate prepositional phrase (*ob reditum*). This in turn has a rather elaborate genitive combination subordinate to it which also conveys crucial information. But even in these two lines the poet maintains his sense of climax. The reason for rejoicing is the return of someone who is still trembling after having such a terrible experience that he wonders that he has survived. Only at the very end of the line, the period, and the section of the poem does the reader learn the

13 The following parallels and echoes have been noticed: line 1 = Horace, *Odes* 4.11.17–18; lines 7–9 = Horace, *Odes* 4.2.53–56; line 9 = Vergil, *Georgics* 3.232–33 (cf. *Eclogues* 3.86–87); lines 11–14 = Vergil, *Georgics* 2.146–148; line 13 = Horace, *Odes* 4.4.13; line 14 = Ovid, *Fasti* 4.415. Cf. Horace *Odes*, 2.17.30–32; 3.23.9–20.

identity of this person—he is "a friend" (16: *amici*). The poet makes
certain, then, that the word *amicus* is not overlooked. Not only is it in a
climactic position, but the satirist still puts off naming his friend. This is
Juvenal's way of drawing attention to the fact that friends and friendship
are an important part of the subject matter of this satire.[14]

The poet has still not provided complete information. Who is this
person? What terrible disaster has he avoided? The identity of the friend
has to remain a mystery for another thirteen lines, but in the second
section of the satire (17–82) Juvenal immediately provides the answer to
the second question as he begins the account of the storm and the near
shipwreck of Catullus. In places this episode is as full of action as the
passages that precede and follow it are peaceful and idyllic. It should also
be noticed that, with the exception of the odd aside and digression, the
account proceeds systematically from the clouding of the sky through the
trials and tribulations caused by lightning, high seas, and high winds to
the final safe landing of the ship at Ostia.

The narrative begins with a topic sentence: Juvenal's friend has
survived the dangers of the sea and even a lightning stroke (17–18). The
conjunction *nam* (17) placed at the beginning of the line provides a clear
causal relationship between what has preceded and the account of the
storm which follows.

The satirist now goes on to deal with both aspects of the storm—first the
lightning (18–22) and then the perils of the sea (24–61). The sky becomes
quickly overcast with one huge cloud and the ship is suddenly struck by
lightning. The elisions and the spondees which predominate in these lines
(18–20) contribute to the threatening aspect of the passage. Juvenal makes
the picture more vivid by describing the reaction of the sailors to what is
going on (20–22) rather than concentrating on the burning ship. Once
again the sequence is the natural one: everyone thinks he has been struck
by lightning and soon (*mox*) is horrified at the prospect of experiencing fire
and shipwreck. Fire at sea, of course, has haunted mariners from earliest
times to the present. But there is an unexpected light touch here when
Juvenal describes each sailor as being "thunderstruck" by it all (21:
attonitus).

---

[14] The poetry of lines 15 and 16 is worth noticing in passing. The dactyls in line 15
combine with the hard and explosive consonants *b*, *d* (4 times), *t* (3 times), and *p* (2 times)
to reinforce the fear and apprehension. The combination of vowel sounds, the repetition
of the *h*'s, and the *r* and *n* sounds in *adhuc horrendaque* together suggest the awe that is present
in the mind of the person having these experiences. In line 16 there is continuing agitation
in the dactyls, but these are soon replaced by spondees which combine with the long vowels
and the *n* (3 times), *m* (4 times), and *s* (3 times) sounds to produce the sounds and sighs
of relief that the friend felt when he found himself safe (*incolumem sese*).

Now the satirist indulges in an editorial comment: everything happened just as terribly as when a storm arises in a poem (22–24). This has been interpreted in various ways. Some have taken the words to be a serious criticism of the methods of contemporary poets, paralleling and extending the comments at the beginning of the first satire, while at the other extreme it has been interpreted as Juvenal's comment on the exaggerated story that Catullus gave him.[15] But such subtle interpretation is probably unnecessary, since the comment can be viewed simply as a gentle reminder that this is not an epic poem, but a satire. It provides a mock-heroic touch to this account of a near shipwreck,[16] performing much the same function as the reference to Hispulla (11) mentioned earlier.

Maintaining his systematic approach, the satirist now draws his reader's attention to the second aspect of the shipwreck (24: *genus ecce aliud discriminis audi*), the problems with wind and sea. But before he begins this part of his account, he points out the fact that, terrible as the experience was, it was not unique; many had undergone shipwreck, as the great numbers of votive tablets in the temples prove. "And who doesn't know that painters are supported by Isis?" (24–28). The sequence of thought is quite Juvenalian—the generalization, proof of this, and satiric comment on the proof. There is satire here, of course, and it serves to remind us once again that this poem is not an epic. But even though the painters may be fed like slaves or animals (28: *pasci*), the satire is hardly biting. Actually, it anticipates the stronger criticism of people who take to the sea that comes a little later (57–61).

A similar misfortune befell Catullus, says Juvenal (29), at long last providing us with his friend's name and at the same time underlining the fact of their friendship as he refers to the other man as "my Catullus" (*nostro . . . Catullo*). The story of the near disaster now begins in earnest, and the reader is plunged *in medias res*. The hold is half full of water; the waves are beating now one side and now the other side of the ship; the mast is tottering; the situation has reached the point where even the helmsman with all his years of experience cannot help the situation. The next logical step, then, is to throw things overboard to lighten the ship (30–36). There is a lot packed into these lines and the pile-up of language reflects the mounting problems. The comparison with the beaver who in a crisis jettisons his valuable testicles as Catullus is going to jettison his priceless cargo provides mild satire on a number of levels. There is the obvious and

15 The latter is J. D. Duff's idea (*D. Iunii Iuvenalis saturae XIV. Fourteen Satires of Juvenal*, [Cambridge, 1898; rev. 1970], note on line 23, p. 382).

16 The situation is not quite as simple and straightforward as I. G. Scott describes it (*The Grand Style in the Satires of Juvenal* [Northampton, Mass., 1927] 83–87). The parodic and mock-heroic elements in the shipwreck scene are not as all-pervading as she suggests.

grotesque comparison that is to be made between what the beaver is forced
to do and what Catullus has to do. Juvenal increases the humor and the
irony of the whole thing by first pointing to the fact that the beaver
personally makes himself a eunuch to avoid the loss of his testicles and then
endowing the animal with an almost human intelligence (36: *intellegit*).[17]
The whole story helps contribute to the mock-heroic atmosphere, though
once again it is not violently irreverent.

At this point the poet heightens the drama by quoting Catullus directly
(37): "Throw my things overboard—all of them!" And overboard they go,
one after another for the next ten lines (38–47). Once again Juvenal's
methodical approach is obvious. For the first five lines various garments
disappear overboard and these are followed by five lines of plates and pots.
The garments, in turn, are of two kinds—fine purple clothing destined for
fops like Maecenas and also the best wool from Spain. The catalogue of
vases is marked by an interesting variety. There are Roman silver plates
(43: *lances*) and a Greek urn, also presumably of silver (44: *cratera*), as well
as British food baskets (46: *bascaudas*), a thousand food dishes (46: *mille
escaria*), and a great deal of engraved or embossed ware (46–47: *multum
caelati*). It is impossible to miss the satire here, all of it centering around
luxury and excess. The name of Maecenas was by now synonymous with
foppish luxury, while the wife of Fuscus, for whom the mixing bowl is
destined, was probably a notable inebriate of the time, since she is coupled
with the centaur Pholus (45) to suggest excess in drinking. Finally there
is an oblique reference to Philip of Macedon who is described as "the clever
purchaser of Olynthus" because he managed to capture that city in
347 B.C. by buying off its leaders. But once again, while the whole passage
is an ironic treatment of the luxury trade and the people to whom it
catered, the satire is telescoped and hardly biting. Much of it, moreover,
is implied.

On the other hand, the four lines following the catalogue of objects
thrown overboard are pointedly satiric, for they contain clear moral
commentary on the situation. What other man is there and where is he
who dares to value his life more than his silver and his safety more than his
possessions? For there is a certain element of humanity whose purpose is
not to make fortunes for living, but to live for making fortunes (48–51).[18]

---

[17] The hiatus in *testiculi* is striking, since this is the only time that it occurs in Juvenal
in this position in the line. It may be designed to contribute to the humor with the poetic
"gap" reflecting the anatomical "gap" that the beaver has just created.

[18] Lines 50–51 were rejected by Bentley and, though Friedlaender retains them,
modern scholars like Knoche and Clausen tend to bracket them. Retention or rejection of
them does not seriously affect the interpretation of the passage.

This kind of moral satire that is so obvious and so typical of Juvenal has been completely missing from the poem thus far. And so it is almost with a sense of relief that the reader at last comes upon it. But it is not quite the straightforward satire that we might expect from Juvenal, since he does not proceed to criticize Catullus directly, but actually compliments him (and of course criticizes the others) by implying a contrast between these people and his friend who has decided to throw his valuables overboard. In a way it is a backhanded compliment, since Catullus did this only when the state of the emergency was extreme and for all intent and purposes he still belongs to this group of money-seekers. It is only a few lines later that Juvenal indulges in extended criticism of people like Catullus who have to go trading on the high seas (57–61).

In the meantime, however, Juvenal completes his description of the attempts to avoid shipwreck. Neither jettisoning the luxury items nor getting rid of most of the stores and gear ("the useful things") relieves the situation, so that as a last resort (55: *discriminis ultima*) the mast has to be cut down (52–56). Once again Juvenal keeps the events in sequence and even stresses the fact that cutting down the mast was the last step.[19]

At this point in the satire, with Catullus on the brink of drowning, Juvenal chooses to develop the aside already mentioned as containing criticism of those who entrust their lives to sailing ships (57–61). Even though he uses an imperative singular (57: *i nunc . . . committe*), it is a rhetorical and satiric formula directed at a person *like* Catullus rather than at him directly. In its obliqueness it resembles the criticism of the money-seekers (48–51) mentioned earlier where Catullus could be included in the criticism. Juvenal does not criticize his friend directly anywhere in the satire, in spite of the fact that his vocation does make him vulnerable to attack. But the reader is left in no doubt as to how Juvenal feels about the sailing and trading that men like Catullus do. They rely on a plank of wood that puts a quarter of an inch between them and death. And so Juvenal tells them not only to take the usual provisions but also to supply themselves with axes to be used when the storm comes. This is the most pointed satire thus far in the poem and it is the last until the legacy-hunter makes his appearance.

Now the storm abates, and it takes Juvenal nearly ten lines to describe what happens (62–70). He has been criticized for dwelling on this description,[20] and the three clauses introduced by *postquam* (62, 64) might indeed

[19] This part of the near shipwreck began with *genus . . . aliud discriminis* (24) and *discriminis ultima* ends it. *Damna* (53) also recalls the ablative *damno* used earlier (35) to describe the beaver's loss. The ship is "self-castrated," then, just as the beaver was.

[20] Gylling (above, note 4) 83, 90.

be considered redundant and repetitious. Certainly it is wrong to blindly defend a poet like Juvenal at every juncture, and it may be that this is not a particularly good part of the satire. But it is at least possible that the repetition, disproportion, and disorder that are evident here reflect an attempt on Juvenal's part to portray the sudden, confused, unrestrained relief that Catullus and his fellow travelers felt as they came to realize that the storm was subsiding.[21] The scene had begun with the sky clouding over (18–19) and it now ends with the sun coming out as the winds die down (69–70).

The happy return is now described in a relatively few lines to end this part of the satire (70–82). Once again Juvenal is careful to keep strictly to the sequence of events. After the sun has appeared, the travelers "next" (70: *tum*) catch sight of the Alban height, and this brings thoughts of Iulus, Lavinia, and the experiences of the Trojans (70–74). The connection is obvious. Just as Aeneas and his happy crew finally arrived at their destination in Italy allotted by fate after sailing through many trials and tribulations, so Catullus and his happy fellow travelers finally arrive in Italy with the help of fate (64–66) after experiencing their share of troubles. The happiness that Catullus and his companions feel is not only brought out by the mention of the Trojans, but it is also mirrored in the language that the satirist uses. Everything is "pleasing," "lofty," "white and shining," "happy," "marvelous," and the like.[22]

Finally (75: *tandem*) they arrive at Ostia, and the travelers' reactions once again are made clear in Juvenal's description. All the protective aspects of the harbor are carefully noted—breakwater, lighthouse, and piers. The latter are "arms that run out in the middle of the sea and leave Italy far behind" (76–78). They reach out, then, to embrace the survivors. The aside at this point (78–79) in which Juvenal says that no natural harbor is as marvelous as this one may serve as a compliment to Trajan for his reconstruction of the harbor at Ostia, but it can be taken as well as a reflection of the feelings that the survivors would naturally have as they at last entered the safe harbor.

[21] The passage is not without its merits. Meter and sound combine in the first two lines (62–63) to reinforce the calm and quiet that is described. The line immediately preceding (61) is full of harsh consonants (especially *c*'s, *t*'s, and *s*'s) and clipped vowels (especially *e*). In these lines by contrast soft consonants (*m, n, l, r*) and more open vowels (*o, a, u*) predominate and combine with a careful choice of diction throughout the passage (*iacuit, planum, prospera, fatumque, valentius, meliora, benigna, hilares, albi, modica, aura*) to leave an impression of smoothness, serenity, and relief.

[22] The adjectives in this passage carry these connotations: 70: *gratus* = pleasing; 71: *praelata* = preferred; 72: *sublimis* = lofty; *candida* = white and shining; 73: *laetis* = happy; *mirabile* = marvelous; 74: *numquam visis* = unique; *clara* = famous, outstanding.

It should also be noted that the captain "seeks out" (80: *petit*) the innermost part of the harbor (80: *interiora*), which is described as a "pond in a safe bay" (81: *tuti stagna sinus*), where even small pleasure craft are safe.

The final touch is a pleasant and natural cap to the whole episode: now safe, the sailors have their heads shaved to fulfil their vows and then start chattering about the troubles they have just been through. This is a thoroughly human reaction and a far cry from the equally human stupefaction and fear that they all felt as the storm began (20–22).

At this point, Juvenal shifts the scene back to himself and the religious celebration of thanksgiving (83–92), and as he does so, he adds a new dramatic element by addressing his slaves who are to prepare the sacrifices mentioned at the beginning of the poem. Once again the relationship between this new scene and the one preceding it is carefully made clear in the use of the postpositive *igitur* (83: "and so") which reinforces the causal relationship between the sacrifice and the near shipwreck. The atmosphere here returns to what it had been in the opening scene—happy and idyllic. As Juvenal turns to tell his reader that he is also going to make offerings at home, the meter suddenly becomes predominantly dactylic (87–88), apparently to reflect the poet's eagerness and enthusiasm. Just as he is going to perform his public sacrifices in the proper way (86: *sacro . . . rite peracto*), so at home all the necessary trappings will be arranged and all the rites duly performed—wreaths, incense, flowers, the decorated house door, lamps. In its own way, then, this is going to be just as festive an occasion as the sacrifice to Jupiter, Juno, and Minerva. And just as that began from a "festal altar of turf" (2: *festus . . . caespes*), so this ends with a "festal doorway" (91–92: *ianua . . . festa*). Each is symbolic. The altar stands for public sacrifice, while the poet goes through the doorway and into his house to perform the private ceremony.

It is important to notice first that Juvenal carries out both kinds of religious services and secondly that, except for the rather mild reference to Hispulla, there is no hint of satire in either religious scene. Both help to underscore the sincerity of Juvenal's feelings and his close attachment to his friend. He depicts himself, then, as observing all due process, and at the same time he avoids the irreverence of satire. It is all part of a contrast, for his activities here are the diametrical opposite of the legacy-hunter's as he is described in the next and final scene of the satire.

Thus far the poet has presented a poem of thanksgiving, and for all intents and purposes the piece could easily end at this point (92). Juvenal, however, is not an epic, lyric, or dramatic poet, but a satirist with his own purposes, and it is not long until these satiric intentions become clear.

The satire suddenly bursts upon us, though not before Juvenal has given his reason for going on with the subject (93–98): he wants to allay any suspicion Corvinus (and the world at large) might have about his motives in offering thanks. The simple fact of the matter is that Catullus has three heirs, and all young ones, so that the poet cannot expect to profit from his show of thanksgiving. His motives, then, are thoroughly honest; people just do not waste money on friends with heirs.

The apparent discontinuity between this last scene and the one that precedes it may be a little bothersome at first sight, but even a quick reading of the first two lines (93–94) shows that there is no reason for this. Not only does the question of motives arise naturally from the preceding narrative, but Juvenal also provides a connection in the language he uses. The first word, whether it be *neu* or *nec*, is clearly transitional and linking, and so is the poet's use of *haec* (93: "these things") to refer to what has gone before. Juvenal even goes so far as to summarize the action to this point as he speaks of "Catullus for whose return I am setting up so many altars" (93–94).

His mention of Corvinus in the first line of this last scene serves a number of purposes. It, of course, reminds the reader of the immediate dramatic situation in which the satire is being presented. The vocative *Corvine* also recalls the same form as it appears in the first line of the poem and so provides a connection. But it also serves a disjunctive function, since it suggests a new beginning. It signals a new scene and subject, then, but one that follows logically from what has gone before.

With mention of the person who would not spend money on a dying chicken for a friend who has heirs and, even more extreme, the person who would not sacrifice a cheap pheasant for a man who is a father (95–98), Juvenal has moved in two steps from himself as a friend to legacy-hunters as friends, and the hyperbolic description now begins. The subject is not new; it was a commonplace of satire and a favorite subject for Juvenal's attack, as we shall see. What is important here is not the fact of his satirizing legacy-hunters, but the way in which he develops his attack and its relationship to the theme of the satire.

Juvenal has begun with what is in essence a negative topic sentence. No one ever courts a person who has heirs. But he develops his argument against legacy-hunters by showing what they really do and what success they really have (98–130). Not only is this natural, but it also makes the comparison with *his* feelings and activities that have been described more direct. In typical satiric fashion he names his names, preferring to deal with examples rather than with the type. First it is a case of two-on-two, with Gallitta and Pacius being the hunted (99) and Novius and Pacuvius

Hister the hunters (111–112). Pacius, however, disappears immediately and Novius also fades away, perhaps shouldered aside by Pacuvius (115). Soon, too, Gallitta's presence is barely felt as she becomes a typical invalid (122: *aeger*), and Pacuvius holds the center stage. And so the reader's attention is concentrated on Pacuvius as it was earlier on Juvenal, and Gallitta is the same shadowy, but necessary, character that Catullus was.

The antithesis between the actions of the legacy-hunter and those of Juvenal, the sincerely thankful friend, is implicit throughout the account of Pacuvius' activities. Gallitta and Pacius just have to begin to feel a little hot (98–99: *sentire calorem/ si coepit locuples Gallitta et Pacius orbi*) and the legacy-hunter goes to work with his insincere show of friendship. By contrast, it was a terrible experience of a friend that motivated Juvenal's sacrifices. The offerings made for Gallitta and Pacius grow from mere extravagance to the ultimate in folly—from a whole portico filled with votive tablets (100–101) through a hecatomb (101) and sacrifices of elephants (102–114) and slaves (115–118) to a ceremony in which a daughter is the victim (118–120). Juvenal's offerings, on the other hand, are unpretentious to begin with and become even less elaborate. In fact, everything about the poet's show of thanksgiving is simple and idyllic, while the legacy-hunter's position becomes increasingly more grotesque and the hyperbole grows. It is difficult enough to visualize a "whole portico" covered with tablets, but this is just the beginning. A hecatomb is not only gross, it is Greek! Elephants are in themselves grotesque, but Juvenal also dwells on other unnatural aspects of these animals: they are not native to Latium and will not breed there (103–104); they are foreign (104) and were used by foreigners like Hannibal and Pyrrhus (107–108); they served as unnatural towers of war moving into battle (110). The contrast between the Emperor's elephants grazing in the Rutulian forest and the country of Turnus (105–106) and the poet's ideal sacrificial bull fattened in the field by the Clitumnus (11–13) leaps to mind.[23]

We should also notice that in these lines Juvenal plays on the theme of past and present that was so popular in the rhetorical and satiric traditions. Turnus and the Rutulians of the ideal and heroic past are balanced

[23] A kind of tribrach antithesis between what is Italian and what is foreign is carefully maintained throughout these lines: Latium (103)—the "dark tribe" (104)—the Rutulian forest and the land of Turnus (105); Caesar (106)—Hannibal and Pyrrhus (108)—"our [i.e., Roman] leaders" (108).

This contrast between what is Roman and what is foreign appears frequently in Latin literature. Cf. Juvenal, *Sat.* 3.58–125; E. S. Ramage, *Urbanitas: Ancient Sophistication and Refinement* (Norman, Okla., 1973) 72–76; 98–100; 116–118.

against Caesar of the luxury-ridden present. Then come Hannibal, Pyrrhus, and earlier Romans from the practical past. As if to underline this contrast, Juvenal speaks of the "herd of Caesar" (106) in contemporary Italy and of the "ancestors" of these elephants (109: *horum maiores*) and their part in earlier wars. Roman ancestral tradition, then, has been transferred to the elephants with a delightfully grotesque touch which suits the mood of the passage perfectly.[24]

But Juvenal saves the most striking irony for the end of the period as he wrenches his reader back to the present (113–114). The elephant—or more probably elephants—would fall as a sacrificial victim before Gallitta's *household gods*. Here the antithesis with his own actions is made clear by the language Juvenal uses. The poet had performed a private ceremony before the household gods of his ancestors (89: *Laribus paternis*), while Pacuvius indulges in a grotesque, relatively public ceremony before someone else's household gods (113: *Lares Gallittae*). Juvenal's motives are sincere and personal; Pacuvius' ulterior motives lead him to a thoroughly unnatural display designed to catch Gallitta's eye.

The grotesqueness and hyperbole increase as Juvenal suggests that, if it were allowed (115: *si concedas*), a man like Pacuvius would even sacrifice a slave or two or actually go so far as to sacrifice his own daughter (115–120). This is the ultimate folly, the supreme tragedy, and the most extravagant perversion, since there is no hope for a secret substitution such as the gods made for Iphigenia (120).

And with this Juvenal passes on to the rewards for legacy-hunting. In a passage full of irony he praises his fellow citizen, since offering sacrifice for a successful expedition to Troy is not at all to be compared with sacrificing to obtain a place in a will (121–122). For if the hunted person escapes death, he will be caught like a fish in a net.[25] Pacuvius will perhaps get everything and will then strut proudly among his vanquished rivals. "And so you see," says the satirist, "how well worthwhile it was to slaughter the girl at Mycenae" (126–127). The world is upside down! Whole expeditions are worth less than a single will; because a "pigeon" escapes, it is caught; the undeserving are rewarded; we should all go out and sacrifice a daughter. The ultimate folly has become the ultimate irony.

It has been pointed out often enough that legacy-hunting comes up fairly frequently in Juvenal's satires. But nowhere else is it treated in such

---

[24] On the contrast between past and present see Juvenal, *Sat.* 6.286–300; 11.77–127. Cf. Ramage, Sigsbee, Fredericks (above, note 8) 61 for the "then-now dichotomy" in Varro's Menippean satires.

[25] Cf. Horace, *Satires* 2.5.44.

detail or, for that matter, even from the same point of view as it is in the twelfth satire. Usually it is part of a broader theme. In Juvenal's programmatic satire, for example, it is just one element that contributes to a perverted world (1.37–44), while in his satire on Rome it is brought up as an example of the kind of thing to which people holding the highest offices in the city have prostrated themselves (3.128–130). Again, Juvenal uses the theme to make points about selfishness (4.18–19), gluttony (5.97–98), old age (10.202), the military (16.54–56), or a gallant taking a wife (6.38–40).

But in Satire 5, as the satirist turns to describe Virro's treatment of his clients, there is a brief passage on legacy-hunting (137–140) which has overtones similar to those in this passage of the twelfth satire. The poet says that, if a person wants to be courted by Virro, he should be without a son or daughter and have a barren wife, for "a sterile wife makes [Virro] a dear and close friend" (*iucundum et carum sterilis facit uxor amicum*). Friendship and legacy-hunting, then, come together in the fifth satire as they do in Satire Twelve. But even in the earlier poem the description is brief and is part of a larger context.

Juvenal's treatment of Pacuvius is different from these other occurrences in another respect: it is really only the climactic part of such an attack. The actions described are extreme, and there is no buildup to them through the use of realistic activity. Juvenal begins with a whole portico full of votive tablets and moves on up to the most extreme human sacrifice. This is effective criticism, of course, but it serves another purpose as well. It contributes to the violent antithesis that Juvenal is trying to develop between his concept of friendship and the legacy-hunter's idea of what it should be. He has already portrayed himself at the one extreme as engaged in the simplest and purest act of friendship possible. The legacy-hunter is portrayed as falling at the opposite extreme, since he engages in the grossest and most grotesque acts under the guise of friendship. To put it another way, it is a case of pure sincerity balanced against extreme hypocrisy.

But Juvenal is not finished. He has caricatured Pacuvius' motives and actions and has ridiculed his "success," and now he adds a final editorial comment (128–130): may this creature have a life as long as Nestor's, a fortune as great as all the wealth that Nero stole—gold piled as high as mountains—and may he have a complete lack of friends. The ending is bold, to say the least. It may not be surprising to find this kind of thought following the exaggerated attack on Pacuvius and his cohorts, but within the context of the poem as a whole, the last three lines represent a complete reversal of form. For as we finish reading them we suddenly realize that this poem which began as a happy statement of thanksgiving has ended at the opposite extreme with a curse. There is an analogy to be drawn with Satire 13 where the poet leads the reader to expect a poem of consolation and instead produces what has been called a "false consolation."[26] The process is a little different in Satire 12, but here as in 13 Juvenal raises certain literary expectations for the reader and then produces something quite different. What results is not a poem of consolation or a poem of thanksgiving, but a satire.[27]

And there can be no doubt that old age, wealth, and a lack of friends are curses. In a long and vivid passage of Satire 10, the first satire in this book, Juvenal speaks at length about the distasteful aspects of old age. While people think this is something to wish for, it is actually a bane (10.188–288). And Nestor is mentioned there, too, as the proverbial example of a man who has lived a long life (10.246–255). In the tenth satire Juvenal also dwells on wealth and the problems it brings (10.12–53), where once again Nero is introduced as the type that is to be rejected (15). When we consider the negative role that wealth and extravagance play in the eleventh satire and the statement made there that luxury and old age do not mix (45), it is tempting to imagine that the poet has purposely picked up the two topics of old age and wealth at the end of Satire 12 and added friendship, the subject of this satire, to them. This is just the kind of clever twist that can be expected of Juvenal—to wish for Pacuvius two "blessings" that he has shown to be curses and to deny him what has just been shown to be a real blessing.[28]

The last line serves to remind the reader of the point that Juvenal wants to make in this satire. There are two kinds of friendship, sincere and insincere. Or, to put it another way, friendships are based either on altruism or on what can be gained from them. This was really a philosophical commonplace, and it is quite likely that Juvenal had Cicero's

[26] A. D. Pryor, "Juvenal's False Consolation," *AUMLA, Journal of the Australasian Universities Language and Literature Association* 18 (1962) 167–180; S. C. Fredericks, "Calvinus in Juvenal's Thirteenth Satire," *Arethusa* 4 (1971) 219–231. Cf. M. Morford, "Juvenal's Thirteenth Satire," *American Journal of Philology* 94 (1973) 26–36.

[27] Cf. Persius' Satire 2 which begins ostensibly as a birthday poem, but soon becomes a satire on right and wrong prayers. Similarly, Persius 5 starts out as a tribute to Cornutus, but ends on a far different note.

[28] The connections between Satires 10, 11, and 12 outlined here are hardly fortuitous. It is also significant that elephants appear in all three of these satires (10.150; 11.126) and that in all three contexts they are referred to as *belua* (10.158; 11.126; 12.104). The parallels between these three satires suggest that Juvenal had a fairly clear concept of the unity of this book.

De amicitia in mind as he wrote, for there (52) Cicero says quite emphatically:

> Gods above and men below! Who is there who would want to abound in all material things and live amid an abundance of everything, though he love no one and is himself loved by no one?[29]

In spite of the fact that Juvenal has substituted subjunctive forms of *amo* for the corresponding forms of *diligo* that Cicero uses, the wording of the last line of the satire and of the concessive clause in the passage from the *De amicitia* are so similar that it is difficult not to believe that the satirist was drawing on his predecessor.

And so perhaps we can see a little more clearly what Juvenal was attempting to do in the twelfth satire. Writing in a loose epistolary manner, he actually produced a blend of forms—the poem of thanksgiving, the poem celebrating the safe return of a hero or loved one, straightforward satire, and the philosophic essay. Corresponding to each of these forms is a thematic element—the poet's worship of the gods, the near-shipwreck, criticism of legacy-hunters, the essence of true friendship, with the latter uniting the poem thematically. If we remember that Roman satire began as a medley and could still be called a *farrago* or hotch-potch by Juvenal (1.86), we can see in the structure and subject matter of Satire 12 the continuing importance of the miscellaneous element. But it is worth making the point once again that Juvenal carefully binds all of these elements together to produce a cohesive, coherent study of friendship, true or false.[30]

Indiana University

---

[29] Cicero's words are *Nam quis est . . . qui velit, ut neque diligat quemquam nec ipse ab ullo diligatur, circumfluere omnibus copiis atque in omnium rerum abundantia vivere?* Cicero spends some time discussing the problem (27–55) and says, among other things, that hope of gain is not the proper basis for friendship, even though the majority of men believe that its essence lies in a desire for wealth. He deals with flattery a little later (97–98). The theme of expediency and friendship appears in other philosophic contexts as well (Horace, *Satires* 2.6.75; Seneca, *Moral Epistles* 3, 9, and 35).

[30] It should be pointed out that Juvenal is not finished with his examination of friendship, for he goes on in Satire 13 to look at an example of a false friend who has refused to pay back a deposit of money left with him.

16

Tacitean *Nobilitas*

REVILO P. OLIVER

In 1912, Matthias Gelzer, in his fundamental *Die Nobilität der römischen Republik*, demonstrated that Cicero, following the accepted usage of his time, employed the words *nobilis* and *nobilitas* in socio-political contexts with a restricted and specific meaning to designate the hereditary status of descendants of men who had held the consulship. This brilliant demonstration is now almost universally accepted and without significant dissent.

In 1915, in a comparatively short article in *Hermes*, Gelzer extended the scope of his definition and argued that during the Principate, and particularly in Tacitus, the words in socio-political contexts designated only the descendants of men who had held the consulship during the Republic, so that the *nobiles* formed a closed caste, to which it was no longer possible for *novi homines* to gain admission.[1] This view has been accepted as authoritative in standard works of reference,[2] despite vehement opposition that has continued to the present time and has perhaps become

[1] *Hermes*, L (1915), 395–415, reprinted in Gelzer's *Kleine Schriften*, Wiesbaden, 1962, Band I, 136–153. This article was combined with Gelzer's earlier book in Robin Seager's excellent translation, *The Roman Nobility*, Oxford, 1969. Since Seager's notes report Gelzer's latest opinions, presumably expressed when he reviewed the translation, I refer below to the translation except at the two points at which the wording of the German may be important for its implications.

[2] Gelzer's thesis that the *nobiles* formed a closed caste is accepted, for example, in such recent reference works as the *Oxford Classical Dictionary*, 2d ed. (1970), s.v. "nobilitas," and *Der kleine Pauly* (IV, 1972), s.v. "nobiles," where Volkmann condenses and reaffirms the conclusions of H. Strassburger in his article in Pauly-Wissowa-Kroll (Halbband XXXIII, 1936), s.v. "nobiles" (p. 790). Given the great and deserved prestige of Ronald Syme, his *Tacitus*, Oxford, 1958 (= 1963), 654, is virtually a work of reference on all matters pertaining to the early Empire. One would suppose that the definition in the new *Oxford Latin Dictionary*, s.v. "nobilis," ¶5a, was intended to apply only to the Republic, but the citation of Tacitus extends it to the Principate, and the citation of Curtius Rufus destroys our confidence in the editors' judgement.

even sharper in recent years.[3] A reexamination of the problem is therefore in order.

Gelzer's article had two glaring defects, to which we shall return later, but these have only incidentally entered into the debate, which has been centered on his major thesis that under the Principate the *nobiles* formed a closed caste to which the only admission was by birth. That thesis has been attacked, sometimes passionately, by scholars who hold that the *nobilitas* of the Principate must have been analogous to the nobility of modern Europe, which has never been a closed caste, since noble rank could be conferred by a reigning monarch, not only for services to the state, but even for personal services of the kind that made Barbara Villiers the Duchess of Cleveland and elevated Louise de Kéroualle to the rank of Duchess of Portsmouth.[4] It is contended that the successors of Augustus must have had, and did in fact use, the power to make any favorite a *nobilis* by having him hold a consulship and perhaps in other ways.

I

Before we undertake a reconsideration of the problem, we must clarify and delimit it by stating explicitly certain considerations which should be obvious, but have been neglected or obfuscated in the heat of debate.

1. We are dealing with a highly specialized and quasi-technical use of the words in a specific context. The adjective *nobilis* simply means "noteworthy, distinguished, eminent," and it never lost that primary meaning. Obviously, when Cicero calls Xenocrates a *nobilis philosophus* and Nico a *nobilissimus pirata*, he does not imply that the ancestors of either ever held office at Rome or elsewhere. Even when he speaks of non-Romans who were probably politically prominent among their own people, Cicero

---

[3] I see no reason for devoting a dozen pages to a history of the debate. The major challengers will be identified below. The most complete attempt to refute Gelzer was made by H. Hill, *Historia*, XVIII (1969), 230–250. The latest, at the time I write, is by T. D. Barnes in *Phoenix*, XXVIII (1974), 444–449.

[4] The creation of nobility by the reigning monarch was a practice common to all the nations of Western Europe, although there were very considerable differences in the details of the procedure, especially in connection with the possession or purchase of landed estates, which need not concern us here, but we should note that the willingness of the older aristocracy to accept new creations naturally varied with the circumstances and the character of the individuals ennobled, and also with the extent to which that aristocracy had been demoralized by the social preponderance of mere wealth. The most instructive modern analogy to Rome in the period in which we are interested, involving very significant contrasts, is the Republic of Venice, on which see James C. Davis, *The Decline of the Venetian Nobility as a Ruiling Class*, Baltmore, 1962.

intends no analogy: the *nobiles Poeni* who were held captive in Rome during the First Punic War had not all been *sufetes*, and a *nobilis Ferentinus* or a *nobilis Aeduus* is merely a man who comes from a leading family among his own people. It is only when he is speaking of Romans that Cicero uses the adjective in its specialized and restricted sense, and we can be confident that he intends that specific meaning only when the word occurs in passages in which we can assume that so careful a stylist would have avoided possible ambiguity. When he called T. Roscius a *nobilis gladiator*, he could be certain that no member of his audience would suppose that he was attributing consular ancestry to that man, but he called Oppianicus an *eques Romanus in municipio suo nobilis*,[5] adding a qualifying phrase that was necessary because it was possible for a Roman to be, like Ser. Sulpicius Rufus,[6] both a *nobilis* in the restricted sense as a descendant of consuls and legally an *eques*, since his branch of the family abstained from the *annua certamina venalis Campi*. Such prudent abstention from politics and corruption in the late Republic may have been less uncommon than we suppose, since in the nature of things we are unlikely to find it commemorated in our extant sources, and the example should suffice to remind us that, as I fear some prosopographers do not always keep steadily in mind, *nobilitas* in the restricted sense was, in Cicero's time, regarded as hereditary and inherent in the blood, like patrician status, and therefore not extinguished by abstention from senatorial careers through many generations.[7]

The possibility of ambiguity depends on the context, and Romans did not have the typographical devices that we use to distinguish between a nobleman and a noble man or between a republican government and a Republican administration. At the limit, therefore, the avoidance of ambiguity becomes a stylistic matter. Cicero, depreciating the achievements of Bibulus, says that he, in a mismanaged expedition, "cohortem primam totam perdidit centurionemque primi pili, nobilem sui generis, Asinium Dentonem," etc.[8] Here *nobilis* stands in the relationship that we describe in our normal grammatical terminology as that of a noun in apposition, so it could have been understood as *nobilis homo* in the restricted sense, and Cicero adds a qualifying phrase, probably indicating high distinction as the Roman equivalent of a non-commissioned officer,[9] which

---

[5] *Pro Sex. Roscio*, 6.17; *Pro Cluentio*, 39.109.

[6] *Pro Murena*, 7.16, a passage crucial for Republican standards.

[7] Not even by a lapse of approximately 320 years in the case of the younger Sulpicius, to whom Cicero specifically concedes *nobilitas*.

[8] *Ad Atticum*, V.20.4.

[9] This is the probable meaning. An ethnic application is most unlikely, since the cognomen is placed in the "sicher lateinische Gruppe" by Wilhelm Schulze, *Zur Geschichte*

he might have omitted, had he simply written *nobilemque centurionem, Asinium Dentonem,* making the adjectival force of the word and therefore its general sense more obvious. When Cicero draws a contrast between a furtive and nocturnal return to Rome and the pomp and brilliance of a *nobilis imperator*'s triumphal procession,[10] he is almost certainly using the adjective in its unrestricted sense and means "a distinguished general," although it so happens that the man in question was also the scion of a great consular family. Although I cannot point to a clear example, I think that Cicero would have seen nothing improper in describing a successful commander as a *nobilis imperator humili loco natus* or even as simply *nobilis imperator* if the immediately preceding context had precluded interpretation of the adjective as a reference to ancestry.

In short, as we should expect from what we know of linguistic development in other languages, the use of *nobilis* in a highly specialized sense with reference to a segment of Roman society never impaired or restricted use of the adjective with its normal meaning, and when we appeal to passages in which it is used with reference to Romans, we should first assure ourselves that the author—especially if he is a poet—is not indulging in a rhetorical amphibology, writing with unintended ambiguity, or simply making a statement that contemporaries would not have misunderstood, although it puzzles us.[11]

2. We are concerned only with the meaning of *nobilis* in the era of Roman history that runs from Augustus to Trajan, and particularly, of course, with the meaning in the histories of Tacitus. On purely *a priori* grounds we would think it likely that some change took place after the reign of Hadrian, which was, in so many aspects of Roman life, a great watershed in history; and since we know that the great families of the Republic became practically extinct in the second century, we could

---

lateinischer Eigennamen, Göttingen, 1904 (= Berlin, 1966), 315. The family cannot have been distinguished in any way. I note, by the way, that the *Oxford Latin Dictionary,* s.v. "nobilis," explicitly interprets Cicero's reference as to character ("one of nature's gentlemen"), with an assurance unseemly in lexicography.

10 *In Pisonem,* 22.53.

11 I therefore refuse to debate with Hill (*op. cit.,* 247) such questions as the ancestry of the Barea mentioned by Juvenal, 7.91. I think Syme is probably right in his identification and there is no way of *proving* that he is not, but granting Hill's claim that this man was a *novus homo,* how can we be certain that Juvenal did not intend a piquant contrast between the ancient nobility of the Camerini and men who had only recently attained great prominence, thus showing that neither class possessed the political influence of actors and dancers? And anyway, "faciunt imperite, qui . . . non ut a poëta sed ut a teste veritatem exigant."

predict with absolute certainty that in the society of the later Empire, *nobilis* either lost the specialized sense it had in earlier times and was used only with its primary and general meaning or that it acquired some new and different meaning when used of that society. Thus when Barnes thinks that he is producing a conclusive refutation by remarking that "the sociological implications of Gelzer's definition are also impossible; it becomes necessary to believe that by A.D. 200 there existed no senatorial nobility of any sort,"[12] he is merely calling attention to the obvious fact that when the hereditary *nobiles* died out, the adjective could be used without risk of ambiguity of distinguished contemporaries until it acquired a new specialized meaning in the later Empire, which, I am sure, Barnes has quite accurately defined, but which is of no interest to us in the present inquiry, to which it is entirely irrelevant.[13]

3. The *nobiles*, in the restricted sense of Gelzer's definition, must have formed a social class that was delimited by its own standards and by the recognition of those standards by a dominant part of the variegated group of wealthy and socially or politically prominent persons that we may call the upper class of the early Empire. The prestige of the *nobiles*, and hence such power as they had, undoubtedly depended in large part on their claim to be an aristocracy within the ever diminishing number of Romans in Rome,[14] and thus to have, so to speak, the rights of the founder and

---

[12] *Op. cit.*, 444.

[13] For all practical purposes, the great Roman families became extinct in the Second Century, and it would be a mere quibble to refer to Aelii who survived to the Fourth Century and may have owed their distinction to the ingenuity of genealogists. As is well known, the Romans of the Republic (even the late Republic) became practically extinct in the same period, and their Empire passed entirely into the hands of a conglomerate population of different ethnic and even racial origins and different mentality. But the odd notion that there was some kind of uniformity in the society of the Empire, from Augustus to Romulus Augustulus, still persists, partly as a latent premise in the thinking of writers who would not dare to affirm it explicitly.

[14] It is impossible to say precisely who were the Romans at the end of the Republic, when *Romani* obviously included not only descendants of the presumably more or less homogeneous population of ancient Latium, but also descendants of most, if not all, of the peoples of Italy south of the Po, who, despite great tribal and territorial animosities, were evidently of ethnic stocks that differed only slightly, if at all, from that found in Latium. I am extremely sceptical about the possibility of eliciting useful information about Roman times from the statistics of anthropometrical examination of the present populations of the various regions, as is attempted by Mario Cappieri, *Mankind Quarterly*, XV (1974–1975), 43–66, 100–116, 193–210. Even people less obtuse to ethnic differences than the Romans confuse anthropological fact with geographic, linguistic, and social accidentals, but it may be worth noting that in the time of Claudius the "conservatives" whose protests are

creator of an institution that is passing into the hands of outsiders. The *nobiles*, by virtue of their status as the heirs of the men who created the Roman Empire, claimed certain prescriptive rights to senatorial offices that were at times recognized by some principes and arrogantly flouted by others. We may be quite sure, from our knowledge of human societies, that the *nobiles'* claims to social precedence were resented by wealthy *parvenus* and other immigrants, whether or not they thought it expedient openly to behave with insolence or contempt, and they doubtless applauded Juvenal's "nobilitas sola est atque unica virtus," even though many or most of them would have fared worse by that new standard than by the old.

Since there was no legal definition of *nobilitas*, the social meaning of the word must have been determined by the *nobiles* themselves through some reasonable approximation to a consensus within their own ranks. It is more than likely that there was inconsistency in the application of their standards and dissent over many marginal cases, but for our purposes the *nobiles* must be those individuals whom the *nobiles* recognized as such, and we should not appeal from their verdict to either sociological theory[15] or historical truth. In particular, it does not matter to us whether a given individual, a Silius, for example, was a descendant of a Republican family; what matters is whether his contemporaries believed that he was or, at least, were willing to show him the courtesy that in recent times overlooked the prudent silences in the *Almanach de Gotha*.

---

recorded by Tacitus, *Ann.* XI.23.2, recognized most of the peoples of Italy (except the Veneti and the Insubres) as *consanguinei populi* who were in accord with, or even possessed, the *Romana indoles*, thus presumably including the Etruscans, whom the elder Tib. Sempronius Gracchus had denounced as aliens and *barbari* in 162 B.C., but excluding the Celtic Insubres and the "Illyrian" Veneti as well as the Celts of Gallia Comata. All these peoples were Aryans (including the Etruscans, to judge from their monuments rather than their language), and the ethnic differences are unlikely to have been greater than those that separate the Irish from the Anglo-Saxons; we are thus entitled to suspect that social manners and the recollection of wars in the recent past had much to do with deciding what populations were *consanguinei* at that time.

15 The statement, not infrequently found in British writers of the second half of the Nineteenth Century, that their countrymen are "mistaken" in identifying the nobility with the peerage, since the landed gentry "really belong" to the nobility, sprang from consideration of the social and economic position of leading families and their political influence, but was nonetheless absurd, since the landed gentry, though manifesting an aristocratic pride in lineage, did not think of themselves as noblemen and always recognized a generic difference of rank between themselves and the peers. I suspect that some reluctance to accept Gelzer's definition springs from a comparable tendency to impose on Roman society what it, in the writer's opinion, *ought* to have done.

4. We must frankly face and accept the fact, which has doubtless influenced the opinions of scholars who make no explicit use of it,[16] that at the end of the Republic the Roman attitude toward heredity became bivalent and even paradoxical. Whatever the origin of the patrician caste,[17] nothing is more certain than that in historical times a man could become a patrician only by being the son of a patrician father, yet, as we all know, Caesar by the Lex Cassia, Augustus by the Lex Saenia, and later Claudius by mere usurpation of a right that he pretended was censorial presumed to create patricians. We do not know what pretexts were officially used,[18] but whatever they were, and however acute may have been the need to provide for certain priesthoods and similar offices, the audacity of these measures is simply breath-taking and without modern analogy. The monarchs of Great Britain always had the power to convert the most scabrous scoundrel into a baron or a marquis or even a duke, but no monarch ever tried to bestow on a hero or favorite Norman ancestors—not, at least, by fiat. The Romans' genealogical miracle is made even more remarkable by the fact that the need for patricians was almost entirely religious, since the gods would not do business with *flamines*, *Salii*, and similar officers who were not of the divinely approved bloodline, and one would have supposed that superstitious persons would

[16] Gelzer, *Roman Nobility*, 153 f., frankly admits the paradox that while Domitian, for example, could convert Trajan's father into a Patrician, he could not make him a *nobilis*.

[17] Heaven forbid that we enter the interminable dispute, but I will confess that the balance of probability seems to me to incline sharply toward theories which regard the Patricians as a caste of conquerors (whether Sabine or other) roughly resembling the Normans in England, and explain the multiplicity of Plebeian families bearing Patrician *nomina* as the result of concubinage or marriage by a rite other than *confarreatio* between male Patricians and females of the indigenous population.

[18] It seems unlikely that even Caesar would have manufactured Patricians with the freedom with which British monarchs in recent decades have made the peerage ridiculous by adding to it beer barons, newspaper nabobs, and even less presentable individuals. So far as I know, the only specific grounds for a Caesarian creation are reported by Suetonius, *Aug.* 2.1, who says of the Octavii, "Ea gens a Tarquinio Prisco rege inter minores gentes adlecta in senatum, mox a Servio Tullio in patricias traducta, procedente tempore ad plebem se contulit." If all adlections into the Patriciate were given such fictitious justifications, the procedure becomes much less startling from the standpoint of a people eager to be credulous. The ancestry manufactured for Vitellius (Suet., *Vitel.* 1.2–3) suggests that Rome had expert genealogists, who, for a fee, could provide pedigrees with the assurance with which some Victorian practitioners were able to prove, step by step, the descent of Queen Victoria from a Jewish chieftain, from whom the noble line was easily traced back to the handiwork of Yahveh himself. It would be hazardous to infer from Tacitus, *Ann.* XI.25.2, anything concerning the provisions of the Leges Cassia and Saenia, but some concern for the real or supposed antiquity of a family is certainly implied.

have thought it dangerous to try to impose on the gods with spurious patricians, even though those divinities had been long accustomed not to notice or to overlook such minor frauds as a *bos cretatus*. Caesar may have acted with his wonted cynicism, but Augustus, who believed in the utility and perhaps the necessity of a national religion, must have had some assurance that the concept of hereditary differences had become so weakened that the pious would not be alarmed by possible consequences of the substitution.

If Iuppiter Optimus Maximus was not offended when he was saluted by a flamen who was a plebeian legally masquerading as a patrician, we must concede to Gelzer's opponents that it is intrinsically improbable that all the youths who participated in the ceremonial *ludus Troiae* had to produce pedigrees to prove their descent from Republican consuls.[19] And we must furthermore concede frankly that the prevalent *Weltanschauung* at Rome under the Principate was democratic in the sense that it rejected the concept of hereditary differences of quality between members of the same race.[20] A closed caste of *nobiles* under the Principate must have been an anomaly existing in opposition to the contemporary modes of thought and sentiment as well as to the actual organization of government, and it can be explained only on the supposition that there was some residual *pietas* toward the memory of the men who had created a Roman Empire

[19] Improbable, though not impossible; the few participants whose names we know were descendants of Republican consuls, and we may infer from Vergil, *Aen.* V.560 f., that only thirty-six young equestrians were needed for a *ludus* or twice that number, if we suppose a duplication to produce the two classes of *pueri minores* and *pueri maiores* implied . by Suetonius, *Tib.* 6.4. My point is that if the youths who exhibited their horsemanship were traditionally from consular families, the addition of other youths to the group by the time of Nero would not prevent a poet (Seneca, *Troades*, 779) from calling the grandson of the last King of Troy a *puer nobilis* and supposing that, had he lived, he would have been the leader in the performance of a *ludus Troiae*. In fact, even if we accept Hill's unwarranted assumption (*op. cit.*, 243 f.) that when the poet thinks of the *ludus* as a ceremony brought to Italy from Troy by Aeneas, he has in mind the performances of his own day rather than the one described by Vergil, all that Seneca says, strictly speaking, is that the youth who leads the companies (*agit turmas*) is *nobilis*, which, of course, is not a statement about the ranks of the other horsemen. Hill's other argument about the *ludus Troiae* (*op. cit.*, 231 f.), depends on the assumption that there can have been no "Republican" consuls after the assassination of Caesar.

[20] The causes, both biological and social, of the decadence of aristocracies, as of nations and races, are multiple, complex, and obscure, but among them must be numbered a loss of belief in their own superiority. An intensive study of the Roman conceptions of heredity, from families to races, is needed, if we are to understand the social (and perhaps the military) history of Rome, but it will have to be made at a time when objectivity in both research and publication has become possible.

that was recognized as a benefaction by the majority of its inhabitants, at least in the West.[21]

5. That there was such a closed caste is certain. Its members were the *posteri libertatis* of whom the younger Pliny spoke to Trajan,[22] and the *residui nobilium* mentioned by those who complained of Claudius's adlection of Gauls to the Senate,[23] since in this passage "what is left of the nobility" obviously presupposes a group to which there could be no further recruitment. What is legitimately in dispute is whether the words *nobiles* and *nobilitas*, when used of prominent Romans by Tacitus and presumably other writers of the early Principate, always refer to (a) that closed caste, excluding the descendants of persons who first attained senatorial (or consular) office after the end of the Republic, and (b) only descendants of Republican consuls, excluding the descendants of families whose members held lesser curule offices but never attained the consulship.

II

Gelzer's article, which may have been written in haste or affected by understandable perturbation after September, 1914, displays a really gross *bévue* on its very first page. He begins by quoting a passage from the younger Pliny with a widely accepted but implausible emendation, and then proceeds to twist that emendation—blandly and without argument— into a novel meaning which must have aroused misgivings in every reader who had a feeling for Latin style.

Since *Panegyricus*, 69.4–6, is not found in the exiguous fragments of the palimpsest, the text depends entirely on the lost Moguntinus, the source

[21] There is every indication, I believe, that the recognition of a caste of *nobiles* under the Principate was a part of Augustus's establishment of his own camouflaged monarchy. As Syme has concisely stated the situation (*The Roman Revolution*, Oxford, 1939 (= 1971), 510), "After a social revolution the primacy of the *nobiles* was a fraud as well as an anachronism—it rested upon support and subsidy by a military leader, the enemy of their class, acquired in return for the cession of their power and ambition. . . . Rome owed them a debt for their ancestors. It was paid by the Principate, under pretext of public service and distinction in oratory or law, but more and more for the sole reason of birth."

[22] In the passage quoted below.

[23] Tac., *Ann.*, XI.23.3–4. If I understand Hill correctly (*op. cit.*, 242 f.), he, in keeping with his Procrustean method of exegesis, would interpret the two words to mean "what would be left of the present-day Senate after it has been filled with Gauls." Cf. *Ann.*, XIII.18.2, where it is Agrippina's policy "nomina et virtutes nobilium, qui etiam tum supererant, in honore habere," where the reference must be to the *nobiles* who had survived to that time, but Hill (*loc. cit.*) thinks that it means "the senators whom Nero had not yet murdered." If that is what Tacitus meant, he is an author who should be classed with Symphosius.

of all extant copies, in which it appeared (except for orthographic minutiae, which I ignore) as follows:[24]

> An aliud a te quam senatus reverentia obtinuit ut iuvenibus clarissimae gentis debitum generi honorem, sed ante quam deberetur, offerres? Tandem ergo nobilitas non obscuratur sed illustratur a principe; tandem illos ingentium virorum nepotes, illos posteros libertatis, nec terret Caesar nec pavet: quin immo festinatis honoribus amplificat atque auget et maioribus suis reddit{us}. Si quid usquam stirpis antiquae, si quid residuae claritatis, hoc amplexatur ac refovet et in usum rei publicae promit. Sunt in honore hominum et in {hon}ore famae magna nomina ⟨excitata⟩ ex tenebris oblivionis indulgentia Caesaris, cuius haec intentio est, ut nobiles et conservet et †afficiat†.

In the last sentence there obviously were in the Moguntinus a dittography, an haplography, and a corruption at the end. The last word was emended, probably by Iohannes Aurispa,[25] to *efficiat*—and since he changed but one letter, the emendation should endear him to the hearts of the "conservative" critics of our time. The emendation was undoubtedly intended to mean that Trajan both preserved the existing *nobiles* and manufactured new ones, just as the monarchs of Western Europe were doing in the Fifteenth Century. The emendation was generally accepted, particularly since it was found in the text of the manuscripts generally consulted and was not recognized as an emendation, and it won the approbation of most or all of the early editors, including the most influential of all, Lipsius, who glossed it thus: "*efficiat*: iure annulorum dato, ingenuos facit; cumulatis honoribus, nobiles." This reading and interpretation appear to have been universally accepted until 1910.[26] What is even more astonishing, *efficiat*

[24] On the manuscript tradition see especially the younger Baehrens' dissertation, *Panegyricorum Latinorum editionis novae praefatio maior; accedit Plinii* Panegyricus, *exemplar editionis*, Groningae, *s.a.* [1910], and the prefaces by Schuster, Durry, and Mynors to their respective editions. I use the editions of Pliny's *Panegyricus* by Guilielmus Baehrens that I have cited and the one by Enrica Malcovati (1949); the editions of the *Panegyrici Latini* by the elder Baehrens (1874), his son (1911), and Mynors (1964); and the editions of Pliny by Müller (1903), Kukula (1908), Schuster (1933), Durry (1947), and Schuster (1952). There can be no doubt about the meaning of the passage I quote until we reach the word that I have obelized, and I have printed the emendations accepted by Mynors. For emendations that have been suggested as alternatives to *in {hon}ore famae* and *nomina ⟨excitata⟩*, but yield precisely the same meaning, see the editions I have listed above.

[25] It appears, so far as I can tell from the apparatus of the editions I have used, in all the manuscripts that are copied from his transcription of the Moguntinus. It is possible that Aurispa deleted the words *haec intentio*, which are missing in most or all of those copies, understanding *cuius est* to mean "it is the duty of a Caesar to preserve and create noblemen."

[26] Lipsius's gloss appears among the *notae variorum* of the Delphin edition by De la Baune, but no dissent or varying interpretation is recorded. As Lipsius's note shows, he thought of Trajan as forming *nobiles* from raw material, much as a sculptor might form a statue, or as training them by advancing them through the various steps of a senatorial career, but the metaphor is too much to load on a single verb in prose.

appears in the texts of Aemilius Baehrens, Müller, Kukula, Schuster (both editions), and Malcovati, all of whom were good Latinists.

Assuming that the meaning given by Lipsius is correct, viz. that Trajan's policy is to create new *nobiles*, the reading *efficiat* cannot stand. To convince yourself that Pliny would never have used the word in that sense, you have only to run your eyes over the columns in the new Oxford Dictionary in which the meanings of the word are nicely discriminated. Or, better yet, go to the Thesaurus, s.v. "efficio," 169.25, where the quotation from Pliny stands lonely in such embarrassing company as the Pseudo-Apuleian *Asclepius*, 22.2, which provides the closest parallel, "deus pater et dominus, cum post deos homines efficeret ex parte corruptiore mundi . . ." Pliny, who was a competent stylist, cannot have intended to say that Trajan constructed, completed, raised, or trained *nobiles*.

The younger Baehrens, I am sure, saw that something was stylistically wrong, although he speaks only of the requirements of a good *clausula*,[27] and emended the text to *faciat*. That does give the intended meaning, and the emendation was accepted by Durry and Mynors, who properly preferred it to Otto's *adiciat*. Their editions, however, raise a curious question of editorial procedure: is it proper to print and credit an emendation without informing the reader that its author later withdrew it? Baehrens revoked his *faciat* in 1918.[28]

Now, oddly enough, Gelzer quoted Pliny with the reading *efficiat*, which, in its accepted meaning, would negate the very thesis he is going to propound, and then glossed the passage as "Der Kaiser schafft keine neuen *nobiles*, dagegen erhält er ihren Bestand und läßt sie zur Geltung kommen."[29] He evidently understood Pliny to mean something like *ut eos non nomine tantum sed re vera nobiles efficiat qui summis in re publica honoribus perfungantur*. That, unfortunately, is not what the Latin says, and for the meaning that he reads into it Gelzer offers no support other than the observation that Pliny's style is pleonastic and that *et/ac* joins complementary verbs. That is quite true, but is inadequate in the absence of some instance of the use of the verb with the desired meaning. As Walter Otto promptly observed,[30] it will not do to impute to the verb a meaning unprecedented in Pliny and in good Latinity.

---

27 In his *praefatio maior*, p. 43.

28 *Berliner philologische Wochenschrift*, XXXVIII (1918), 502 f.

29 *Hermes*, 395 = *Kleine Schriften*, 136; Seager translates, "The emperor does not create new *nobiles*; he does on the other hand ensure their continued existence and secure them recognition."

30 *Hermes*, LI (1916), 77 ff.

Gelzer's remark about pleonasm is valid, however, and he could further have urged that throughout the passage, starting with *nobilitas* that was *obscurata* by earlier Principes (and therefore obviously was not the persons whom they raised to the consulship), and going down to *magna nomina excitata ex tenebris*, Pliny is talking about the *posteri libertatis*, whom Trajan is determined to honor and preserve. It would be an ineptitude inconceivable in Pliny to introduce an entirely different subject with his concluding verb. If, after praising Trajan for restoring the ancient nobility to prominence, Pliny had intended to praise him for founding a new nobility, that subject would have called for at least a paragraph of elaboration. Instead, as Gelzer did not fail to remark,[31] Pliny goes on to praise Trajan for encouraging the talents of men (such as himself, we understand) who deserve to be (but are not) *nobiles* and permitting them to attain in the state the same high offices that he bestows on the *nobiles*.[32]

It is really remarkable that the solution to the textual difficulty was not seen until Stein proposed a solution[33] which has oddly escaped modern editors: keep Pliny's habitual pleonasm, keep the manuscript reading *afficiat*, and assume a haplography similar to the one that obviously occurred in the earlier part of the same sentence: read *ut nobiles et conservet et ⟨honore⟩ afficiat*. Another supplement of the same basic meaning is, of course, possible,[34] but this treatment of the text is certainly superior, for both palaeographic probability and meaning, to Baehren's later emendation, *et conservet et stabiliat*.[35] Stein's solution has now been accepted by Gelzer.[36]

III

The gross defect of Gelzer's article and the one that has principally exercised his critics is his failure to define "Republican" as that concept was understood during the Principate. He nowhere states explicitly when

[31] *Nobility*, 141.

[32] 70.2: "Cur enim te principe, qui generis tui claritatem virtute superasti, deterior esset condicio eorum qui posteros habere nobiles mererentur, quam eorum qui parentes habuissent?"

[33] *Hermes*, LII (1917), 566, n. 1.

[34] I suppose that the logical ⟨*honoribus*⟩ *afficiat* is excluded by the clausula, and *afficiat* ⟨*honoribus*⟩, rhetorically weaker, is little better. One hesitates to suggest a lacuna of two words.

[35] See note 28 *supra*.

[36] According to Seager's note, *Nobility*, 142. One can only wonder why Gelzer did not find time, in more than fifty years, to revise a seriously defective article on a subject so important in all estimates of Roman society under the Principate.

the "Republic" was believed to have ended, although he does remark *ob iter* that "die *nobilitas* des Plancina, wohl zurückgehend auf den Vater oder Großvater L. Munatius Plancus, den Consul von 42 v. Chr., freilich schon 44 von Caesar bestimmt" justifies Tacitus's reference to her,[37] and that remark, taken in conjunction with his later statement that the consulship of Munatius Plancus "kann der Republik zugerechnet werden,"[38] certainly suggests that he not only thought that the Republic ended in 44 B.C., but also assumed that the *nobiles* of the Principate thought so, too. One is reluctant to attribute so thoughtless an opinion to a scholar of Gelzer's standing, but if he did not hold it, he at least laid himself open to the suspicion that he did.

The date, Idibus Martiis 710/-44, is a convenient terminal date for the inclusion of inscriptions in the first volume of the *Corpus inscriptionum Latinarum*, and doubtless serves as well as any other arbitrary date that might have been chosen, and when its editors speak of a *Libera Res Publica*, we understand what they mean. We all know, of course, that the assassination of Caesar marked, not the end of the Roman Republic, but the beginning of an attempt to restore it.

If we, looking back, try to decide when the Republic ended, we know that it was doomed when a Roman general invaded Roman territory with a Roman army, but we should have to conclude that the Republic was not destroyed until Pharsalus (706/-48) or even Munda (709/-45). Even then, however, as events proved, the Republic still had courageous and formidable advocates, so it would be best to lower the date to Philippi (712/-42). To speak of a republic as actually existing thereafter would be historically absurd, but, as Syme has demonstrated in *The Roman Revolution*, many men, who regretted the Republic and may have hoped for its eventual restoration, persisted in opposition to Octavian, embracing such courses of action as were feasible, and they were defeated only at Actium (723/-31). After the death of Antony, the world undoubtedly belonged to the cunning master of thirty legions, but his was a *de facto* and theoretically provisional rule until he regularized his position constitutionally in 27 B.C., so one could argue for that date as a theoretical terminus.

In the last age of what we call the Republic, Roman opinion naturally varied with men's conception of the unwritten and never systematically explained constitution of the state, and that, in turn, depended on their conception of historical events since the expulsion of the Kings and (since

---

[37] *Hermes*, 398 = *Kleine Schriften*, 139. Gelzer also suggests *nobilitas per matrem* for Plancina, noting the fact that her husband considered himself far superior to the sons of Tiberius.

[38] *Hermes*, 405 = *Kleine Schriften*, 145.

they were human) on what they wanted the state to become. The greatest Roman whose opinions on the subject we know assured his contemporaries in 703/–51 that the Republic no longer existed: "Nostris enim vitiis, non casu aliquo, rem publicam verbo retinemus, re ipsa vero iam pridem amisimus."[39] If we had the whole of his work, we might be able to say when, in his opinion, the Republic was finally lost; as it is, the dramatic date and the tenor of the extant dialogues permit us to say only that he probably placed in the time of Tib. Sempronius Gracchus, 621/–133, not the end, but the beginning of the end. This would agree roughly with the view of Sallust and many others, who saw in the final destruction of Carthage the beginning of the decay of Roman character and Roman institutions. It is likely that Cicero would have agreed in general with the brilliantly concise exposition of R. E. Smith in his *Failure of the Roman Republic*,[40] and have agreed in particular that the dissolution of the Republic was a gradual and protracted process that would make any specific date that might be fixed as its final end more or less arbitrary. But on any computation, Cicero was right in saying "iam pridem."

In the time of the Principate there was great and venerated authority for determining the end of the Republic, but it had to be disregarded for many reasons, one of which was the spiritual need to reckon Cicero, Cato, and even Pompey among the heroes of that Republic. As historians we may agree with Cicero and may even be able to prove conclusively that he was right, but Roman society in the First Century did not and, for obvious reasons, could not accept our criteria, and we are here interested only in what that society believed or was willing not to dispute.

A populace invariably accepts the most superficial indications of continuity in its government, especially the continued use of familiar words, however drastically their meaning may have changed. The original constitution of the United States, unlike the confused and often debatable traditions of Rome, can be precisely ascertained from written documents, although few take the trouble to do so. One has only to read the thirteen constitutions of the several states in 1789 and then read the treaty or covenant by which they formed a federation. It can be fairly argued that the constitution thus established lasted until 1861, when some of the states invaded, conquered, and subjugated the others and, as victors, imposed a

---

[39] *De rep.*, V.1.2. The text, to be sure, depends on Augustine, but there is no reason to suspect his quotation from a work that was evidently well known in his time, particularly since it is a long quotation and perfectly Ciceronian in diction throughout.

[40] Cambridge, 1955. He agrees with Cicero in identifying the beginning of the end, e.g., (165), "This was the final consequence of what the Gracchi did—the death of the Republic."

radically new conception of the constitution on the occupied states at gun-point and on themselves through their need to find a moral justification for their ruthless treatment of the vanquished. It is to the point, however, that it is now said and generally believed that the original constitution is still in force, even though several dates could be set for the end of the *second* republic that was established and enforced in 1865, and historians of the future may well decide that *that* republic did not last as long as the first, and came to an effective end in 1912 or 1918 or 1932. Indeed, according to one of the most prominent professors of what is called political science, Andrew Hacker, the question is no longer about the end of a republic, but about the end of a nation, and he is unwilling to date precisely the point at which a nation became a congeries of disparate and reciprocally antagonistic peoples inhabiting a geographical area to which they are confined by economic interests and the threat of force.[41] It is undeniable, however, that our population believes, with virtual unanimity, that the republic of 1789 still exists, and we may be certain that they will continue staunchly so to believe.

It is unlikely that the level of intelligence at Rome in 27 B.C. was very much higher than the level here, and while Octavian did not have modern technological equipment for herding the population, we must remember that when he pretended to have "restored the Republic," he made it very much to the interest of everyone, including the survivors of the great families of the past, to pretend to believe him. He certainly encouraged, for purposes of his own, continuation of the Republican concept of *nobilitas*, and we know that he tried to make the consulship appear to be an important, as well as a dignified, magistracy. We may assume that it was his intent that the attainment of that office in the "restored Republic" should confer *nobilitas* on the consul's posterity, as it had done in the past. And it would appear that he even permitted some semblance of the old elections, for men still canvassed for office and practiced bribery, evidently on the lavish scale that is normal in free elections, for when the Lex Iulia de ambitu proved no more effective than its many predecessors, Augustus, as late as 746/-8, had to impose new regulations and ignore the guilt of the consuls then in office to avoid marring the celebration of his return to Rome.[42] As Scullard observes, "men do not spend money when an issue is a foregone conclusion."[43] He could have added that men do not purchase offices that do not seem to them worth more, in graft, power, or prestige,

[41] Andrew Hacker, *The End of the American Era*, London, 1970. The author is Professor of Political Science in Cornell University.

[42] Cassius Dio, LV.5.2–3.

[43] H. H. Scullard, *From the Gracchi to Nero*, London, 1970, 233.

than the cost. Such competition for magistracies, in Augustus's time as in our own, encouraged the belief that the state was still a republic, since the people seemed to choose their own rulers in the usual way. It has often been observed that at least until 757/4, the majority of consuls came from the old Republican families, and even after that date those families seem to have enjoyed a large share of the eponymous consulships, while the suffect appointments went to men without ancestry to recommend them.[44] Augustus, who long observed the old formalities of candidacy when he chose to occupy a consulship himself, seems to have limited his covert and open control to making certain that only men acceptable to him became candidates for an office that was still theoretically one of political power, and to have encouraged strenuous competition between candidates, any one or two of whom would serve his purposes as well as any other. That policy, which not only masked quite effectively the reality of government but also provided the populace with the excitement and entertainment of hard-fought contests between Tweedledum and Tweedledee, was precisely what political sagacity, in which he was certainly not deficient, dictated in his situation. It was precisely what was needed to encourage among the masses and even among the less perspicacious candidates the illusion that the Republic had indeed been restored; and even the few who perceived what was hidden by the façade found it expedient to pretend that they did not. Even to the end of Augustus's disguised reign, perhaps, it is likely that in the *comitia*, as Tacitus says, "etsi potissima arbitrio principis, quaedam tamen studiis tribuum fiebant."[45] In other words, the popularity-contests that are the hallmark of popular government continued and must have been taken seriously by contemporaries.

[44] P. A. Brunt, *Journal of Roman Studies*, LI (1961), 71–83. What is not clear is whether the increase in the number of *novi homines* in the later years of Augustus's reign may not to some extent reflect a progressive disillusion on the part of the *nobiles* and hence a decrease in the number of men willing to deplete their fortunes by purchasing success in the *comitia*.

[45] *Ann.*, I.15.1. Tiberius must have had some good reason for abolishing the *annua certamina*, e.g., he may have felt that his adoptive father's acting in a solemn farce by pretending to solicit votes was personally degrading, or beyond his histrionic abilities. Or (more probably) he may have thought the late Augustan reforms inadequate to preclude a recurrence of the "crisis" at the end of 759/6, when, doubtless in the absence of Augustus, the political machinery slipped its cogs so badly that a potent clique (enemies of Tiberius, according to a plausible reconstruction by Barbara Levick, *Latomus*, XXXV [1976], 301–339) excited in some part of the populace political passions so strong that riots at the polls prevented the holding of elections. It is entirely possible, however, that there may have been a real lack of men of merit willing to spend lavishly for an increasingly unremunerative honor. When offices are elective, economic necessity normally obliges a successful candidate and his supporters not only to recover their investment but also to obtain a surplus at least sufficient to cover past and probable future losses.

To us, in our retrospective wisdom, it seems obvious that the rule of
Augustus was a camouflaged dictatorship (in the modern sense of that
word), and we may wonder that men strove for election to offices that, so
far as we know, offered little opportunity for extortion, peculation, and
the other perquisites of success at the polls, to say nothing of the kind of
power that might be desired for its own sake, but the evidence indicates
that they did. And so long as they did, superficial observers would believe
that they were living in a republic that had only been improved by a
minor amendment of the constitution.[46]

In other words, when we ask ourselves, not when the Roman Republic
ended in fact, but when contemporaries knew that it had, we must set a
date late in the reign of Augustus or, more probably, at the accession of
Tiberius.

On strictly historical grounds, therefore, we reach the conclusion that,
in the estimation of the survivors of the prepotent families of the Republic,
who necessarily regarded a consulship won by victory in a political contest
as a very high honor, and who may even have retained some belief in the
mystic efficacy of elections as expressions of the "will of the people," the
Republic ended in 767/14, when the *annua certamina* were abolished.[47] And,
as we all know, when we try to explain human behavior, men's illusions
and pretenses are far more important than the reality that they do not
perceive or choose to ignore.

We have answered the question that Gelzer should have propounded,
for he was led to it by the prosopographical evidence that he collected to
support his thesis, as Stein saw at once in an article in which he reaches
our answer by a different route.[48] To examine Gelzer's thesis fairly, we
must do so with Stein's modification of it, which is, of course, accepted by
Syme and others, but which is disregarded in the recent attacks on Gelzer
rather than the problem that Gelzer posed.[49]

---

[46] Which, as has often been observed, seemed to fill Cicero's prescription for a *rector*
who would restore the republic that "iam pridem amisimus," or at least arrest the
processes of corruption and dissolution.

[47] Possibly earlier, if the process of *destinatio* and the innovations implied in the Tabula
Hebana were thought of as destroying "free" elections, but Tacitus implies (*loc. cit.*) that
at the death of Augustus the people still had a *ius* they should have wanted to retain. The
official propaganda about a "restored republic" probably was accepted by the majority
of Romans during Augustus's lifetime. Intelligent men, of course, knew better, as did
Tacitus (*Ann.* I.3.7): "iuniores post Actiacam victoriam, etiam senes plerique inter bella
civium nati: quotus quisque reliquus qui rem publicam vidisset?"

[48] *Hermes*, LII (1917), 564–571.

[49] And, what is worse, Stein's amendment is rejected by Gelzer's translator, *Nobility*,
p. xiv, not necessarily with Gelzer's approval, which may not have extended to Seager's
preface. Cf. note 36 *supra*.

IV

Since we are dealing, not with a legally defined political status, but with an essentially social standard that must have been set in large measure by the *nobiles* themselves, we should not suppose that they lacked either the ability or the will to exercise some discrimination. Surely no one will believe that they regarded the descendants of C. Caninius Rebilus as ennobled by his few hours in the consulship and thus made the peers of the Cornelii Scipiones. If they had or professed a regard for electoral procedure, they can scarcely have been satisfied by the charismatic quality of consulships actually or virtually bestowed by appointment at the will of a *tyrannus*. And since they were human, we may be certain that they applied their criteria leniently when old Roman families of acceptable politics were concerned, and stringently against alien intruders, upstarts, and the lackeys of the *tyranni*.

Furthermore, they evidently made at some time an innovation in the reckoning of *nobilitas*, perhaps because so many male members of the consular aristocracy perished in the series of civil wars. The Etruscans, as their inscriptions show, considered maternal lineage as important as paternal, but while the Romans are unlikely to have regarded the mother as a mere incubator and genetically irrelevant, since females formed the bond of alliances between families, we hear nothing of claims to status based on maternal ancestry until late in the Republic.[50] Under the Principate, however, descent through women did bestow *nobilitas*.

Such acquisition of *nobilitas* is crucial to Gelzer's theory, and unfortunately for his opponents—perhaps I should say unfortunately for all of us who yearn for neat and precise solutions to such problems—denial of such acquisition is tantamount to a claim that Tacitus did not know what he was talking about.[51] When he says that a Calpurnius Piso was *nobilis utrimque*,[52] the only possible implication is that the man could have derived

[50] Antony boasted of his descent from the Iulii through his mother, which may not have been quite equivalent to claiming *nobilitas* through her, but Cicero's invective (*Phil.* III.6.17) shows that ancestry on the distaff side was already accepted as partly determining a man's claim to status.

[51] A possible argument, which I leave to those who may wish to exercise prosopographic ingenuity on it, would be a claim that *nobilitas materna* was transmitted only by an heiress who was the last of her family, so that she presumably transmitted its *sacra* to her husband or son, by a custom that may have been maintained in traditional families. This would take us to the question how it was *legally* possible for a M. Licinius Crassus to have a son named Cn. Pompeius Magnus—assuming that this was the legal *tria nomina* and not merely the most distinctive part of a name that anticipated the horrendous polyonymy of later times.

[52] *Hist.*, I.14.2; cf. 15.1.

that distinction from either his father's or his mother's ancestry as well as from both. If Rubellius Plautus had *nobilitas per matrem*,[53] he obviously acquired it from his mother. If another Calpurnius Piso is characterized as *multas insignesque familias paterna nobilitate complexus*,[54] the use of the adjective attests the existence of a *materna nobilitas* (whether or not this man had it), and furthermore, if the *multae familiae* contribute to the paternal nobility, the generally accepted reconstruction of his *stemma* shows that they did so through the maternal ancestry of some of his father's progenitors.[55]

The one great objection to *nobilitas materna* has been the ignobility that Tacitus ascribes to the infamous Sejanus, who, on the strength of a statement by Velleius Paterculus and an inscription that was connected with Sejanus by a conjectural restoration, was supposed to have had a mother who was *nobilis*, but that obstacle has been effectively removed by G. V. Sumner, who has provided, with as much certainty as can usually be attained in prosopography in the absence of documentary proof, a *stemma* that accounts for the man's origins.[56]

With this new fall of Sejanus, the case against *nobilitas materna* collapses. And we must frankly admit that we have thus opened another Pandora's box, to the endless woe of seekers for certainty. It will never be possible categorically to disprove Gelzer's thesis, and the corollary, of course, is that it cannot be proved either. After almost a century of diligent research, the *Prosopographia Imperii Romani* sets forth the ancestry of many prominent Romans in the male line with varying degrees of probability, the greatest single source of uncertainty being the possibility that there were brothers or sons of whom we have no record within the space of the few generations for which some evidence is available. But the maternal ancestry is seldom clear, wives are often unknown, and the possibility of daughters of whom no record has survived is almost always present. If X, a Roman without consular ancestors, marries Y, a woman descended from Republican

---

53 *Ann.*, XIV.22.1; cf. XIII.19.3. Gelzer's critics are, of course, right when they remark that a *nobilitas per matrem ex Iulia familia* does not prove the absence of a *nobilitas paterna*. Gelzer yielded more than once to the ever-present temptation to press evidence so far that it bends.

54 *Ann.*, XV.48.2.

55 See the family line set forth in the new edition of the *Prosopographia*, II, §C-284.

56 *Phoenix*, XIX (1965), 134–145. Now we shall have to ink out in all the reference books the elaborate conclusions that have been based on someone's guess about the identity of the *praefectus Aegypti* whose name was on the missing part of *C.I.L.*, XI.7283, and we shall have to cancel such remarks as Freeman Adams' conclusion (*American Journal of Philology*, LXXXVI (1955), 76 and n. 20) that "Tacitus' account of Sejanus' family . . . is deliberately misleading. He might have written, *cui nobilitas per matrem*." He might have, had he not known better!

consuls, their sons—and presumably their daughters also!—will be *nobiles*, and will transmit their now ichorous blood to their children, male and (presumably) female. To these genealogical ramifications there is no limit—except the practical one that the descendants must remain wealthy and able to assert a dignity that had otherwise best be forgotten. And if under the Republic the lapse of three centuries did not annul the nobility created when one man attained an office of consular dignity,[57] the dignity infused into the family by lady Y will presumably become extinct only with the death of the last of her descendants, male or female. One thinks of an analogy with the inheritance of titles in continental countries that have no rule of primogeniture, and one marvels that the *nobiles* of Republican consular descent could ever have become extinct. The answer, of course, must be, in addition to the practical consideration mentioned above and social refusal to recognize *mésalliances*, the limitation of offspring by numerous causes, ranging from parsimony and self-indulgence to lead poisoning[58] and biological exhaustion.

One need not extend the theory to its theoretical limit to see the consequences of the admission of *nobilitas materna*. Outside the Julio-Claudian line and a few generations of a few families of almost equal prominence, no genealogy is known with sufficient precision and detail to exclude the *possibility* of a female ancestor who brought nobility into a family that did not have it in the direct male line. That renders attempts conclusively to refute Gelzer simply hopeless.[59]

V

We need not rely on our inconclusive conclusion to deal with the references in Tacitus that have been used to impugn Gelzer's definition. Three of these can be disposed of quite summarily.

[57] Note 7 *supra*.

[58] S. C. Gilfillan, *Mankind Quarterly*, V (1965), 131–148; *Supplement to the Sociology of Invention*, San Francisco, [1971], 166 ff.; 217.

[59] And, of course, also prevents proof of the theory, since in a few cases it is necessary to assume a *nobilitas materna* for persons, such as Volusius Saturninus, whose *stemmata* are not sufficiently established to permit positive identification of the lady from whom the rank was derived. Since Republic consular ancestors cannot be certainly or probably identified for every *nobilis*, we cannot exclude, for example, the possibility that descent from certain ancient families that did not rise above a praetorship (especially, say, a praetor who triumphed) might have been accounted sources of *nobilitas*. For that matter, we cannot *prove* that in those cases Tacitus was not using the adjective in its general sense, committing a regrettable ambiguity, so that we should have to say of him, too, *quandoque dormitat*.

258 Illinois Classical Studies, III

Hist., I.78.2: Otho "creditus est etiam de celebranda Neronis memoria agitavisse spe volgum alliciendi: et fuere qui imagines Neronis proponerent; atque etiam Othoni quibusdam diebus populus et miles, tamquam nobilitatem ac decus adstruerent, Neroni Othoni adclamavit." Hill would have *adstruere* mean "to give more of the same thing,"[60] but what the words obviously mean is that the acclamations implied (as though it were a great honor!) that Nero had formally adopted Otho[61] and thus given him, as a member of the Julio-Claudian line, the ancestry that would entitle him to the Principate, an office which, thus far, had never been held by a man who was not *nobilis* in the restricted sense of that word.

Hist., II.48.2: Otho, discoursing shortly before his suicide, says, "satis sibi nominis, satis posteris suis nobilitatis quaesitum: post Iulios, Claudios, Servios, se primum in familiam novam imperium intulisse." This does not in the least suggest that "Tacitus thought it possible, in the year A.D. 69, for a family to be ennobled."[62] What it does show is that *Otho* believed that, as Pliny had suggested,[63] men of great achievement deserved to be the founders of a new nobility, and that *his* spectacular and memorable achievement as the first man who was not *nobilis* to attain the Principate and make himself the equal of the Julio-Claudians would bestow on *his* descendants a lustre fully as great as that enjoyed by descendants of Republican consuls.

Hist., II.76.3: Mucianus tells Vespasian, "confugiendum est ad imperium. An excidit trucidatus Corbulo? splendidior origine quam nos sumus, fateor, sed et Nero nobilitate natalium Vitellium anteibat ... et posse ab exercitu principem fieri sibi ipse Vitellius documento." Hill would take this to mean that Nero had more *nobilitas* than Vitellius, so that "Tacitus not only does not deny *nobilitas* to Vitellius, but implies that he

---

[60] Hill, *op. cit.*, 233 f., relying on Plin., *Paneg.*, 46.8, "omnibusque quos bonos facis hanc adstruis laudem ...," because, he says, there "is clearly no implication that the men concerned possessed no *laus* before." True, but what they did not possess was *hanc laudem*, the particular distinction which (according to Pliny) was conferred on them by Trajan, namely that their honesty was shown to be voluntary.—One could suppose that the *imagines Neronis* were to be added to Otho's *atrium*, but for the statement of Plutarch (*Otho*, 3.1) that these were statues set up in public.

[61] Plutarch, *Otho*, 3.2: Κλούβιος δὲ 'Ροῦφος εἰς 'Ιβηρίαν φησὶ κομισθῆναι διπλώματα, οἷς ἐκπέμπουσι τοὺς γραμματηφόρους, τὸ τοῦ Νέρωνος θετὸν ὄνομα προσγεγραμμένον ἔχοντα τῷ τοῦ "Οθωνος. Οὐ μὴν ἀλλὰ τοὺς πρώτους καὶ κρατίστους αἰσθόμενος ἐπὶ τούτῳ δυσχεραίνοντας, ἐπαύσατο. In the terminology of modern demagoguery, Otho, by instigating his claque to salute him as Nero, was sending up a trial balloon, and decided that a fake adoption was more than the upper classes would stomach.

[62] Hill, *op. cit.*, 234 f. The quotation from Eutropius is irrelevant; if that writer had used *nobilis* in the special sense that the word had in the early Principate, he would have had to explain it to his contemporaries.

[63] Note 32 *supra*.

possessed it."[64] If that were the meaning, what Tacitus would imply is that Mucianus was dithering and gabbling. He is encouraging Vespasian, who, as the son of a low-grade usurer, was *humili loco natus* (and some would have said *infimo*), to revolt and claim the Principate, and his argument is that (a) failure to revolt did not save another great general, Corbulo, from being murdered by Nero, and that was not because Corbulo had a more distinguished ancestry than you have, and (b) Vitellius, thanks to his army, attained the Principate, despite Nero's *nobilitas*. If, as Hill would have it, Vitellius was 50% as noble as Nero, his example proves that one has to have some *nobilitas* to claim the imperial office, and should therefore discourage Vespasian, whose nobility is 0 (if not −50%!).

The remaining instance, which has been offered to us as a "single passage" that alone "provides conclusive refutation" of Gelzer's thesis,[65] requires somewhat more extensive consideration.

Ann., XI.28.1: The *domus principis*, which means, for all practical purposes, the four powerful freedmen who manipulate Claudius, fear loss of their power, if Messalina's new husband, C. Silius, takes control: "nunc iuvenem nobilem dignitate forma[66] vi mentis ac propinquo consulatu maiorem ad spem accingi." Here there is an ambiguity, and we cannot be certain whether the four scoundrels are using the adjective in its specialized and quasi-technical sense (Silius is a *nobilis* whose ambitions are encouraged by his rank in Rome, his handsome bearing, his intellectual powers, and the fact that he will soon take office as consul) or in the common and general sense (Silius is a young man who, already eminent because of his rank, bearing, intellect, and coming consulship, is encouraged to cast his eyes much higher, now that he has married Claudius's wife).[67] If the latter is the meaning—and we must always remember that the word may always be used with its normal meaning by Tacitus or anyone else— then the passage is not relevant to our problem, although it may show that

[64] Hill, *op. cit.*, 235. We are also told (244) that Suetonius "supports the view" that Vitellius "did possess *nobilitas*." Suetonius says that some persons regarded Vitellius as *nobilis*, and he quotes a charming genealogy that traces the family to miscegenation between a goddess and a king, whose progeny were patricians in the Roman kingdom. I am prepared to believe that the offspring of goddesses were considered to be *nobiles*.

[65] T. D. Barnes, *Phoenix*, XXVIII (1974), 444 f.

[66] Lipsius's emendation, *forma⟨e⟩*, is generally accepted and may be right, but I retain the manuscript reading here because it favors the interpretation that I regard as the less probable.

[67] Since Silius was not an imbecile, we must assume that he had some hope that he, having become the stepfather of Claudius's son and heir, could supplant the old dolt (who is characterized in this passage as *hebes*), acting, perhaps, as protector of the boy during a regency, doubtless in conjunction with the mother. As the great-granddaughter of Mark Antony and Octavia, the sister of Augustus, she had certain hereditary claims to the Principate, and she was undoubtedly a very liberated woman.

Tacitus was guilty of a stylistic infelicity in failing to avoid a possible ambiguity.[68]

Was Silius a *nobilis* in the specialized sense? It is admitted that the ill-fated young man was the son of the P. Silius[69] who was consul in 766/13, and therefore the grandson of P. Silius Nerva, who was *ordinarius* in 734/-20 and the first of the Silii to hold the consulship. If, in the estimation of the Roman aristocracy of the First Century, the Republic ended in 767/14, Messalina's paramour was a *nobilis* by virtue of his father's office, and certainly *nobilis* by virtue of his grandfather's honor.[70]

Equally important for our purposes, perhaps, is the fact that the young man's mother was Sosia Gallia, and that she was probably[71] descended from the C. Sosius who triumphed *ex Iudaea* in 720/-34 and was, with Cn. Domitius Ahenobarbus, the legally elected consul in 722/-32, although he and his colleague, supporters of Antony, were driven from Rome by Octavian soon after they took office.[72] If *nobilitas* could be derived from an ancestor who held the consulship after Pharsalus, that social rank appertained to the posterity of C. Sosius, who had not only held the consulship but had attained the rarer and even more distinctively Republican honor of a triumph.[73] Thus we can say, with as much assurance as can commonly

---

[68] Strictly speaking, the word is used by the four freedmen, but we cannot suppose a blunder on their part. They owed their power to their adroitness in intrigue in the imperial court, and must certainly have been thoroughly acquainted with the social standards of their time.

[69] Who is commonly given the cognomina Caecina Largus as the result of an error in the chronological summary prefixed to Book LVI of Cassius Dio; the correction was made by Arthur E. and Joyce S. Gordon, *A.J.P.*, LXXIV (1953), 421 f., and has now reached *Der kleine Pauly* (s.v. "A. Caecina Largus"), whence, it is to be hoped, it will eventually pass to other reference works.

[70] These suffice; further claims to rank could be excogitated by a not unprecedented boldness in prosopographical speculation.

[71] Barnes (*loc. cit.*) concedes the probability, but errs in making Sosius a *suffectus*.

[72] He was legally elected, if anyone was during the Triumvirate. Naturally, Octavian, Antony, and Sex. Pompeius had agreed three years in advance that Sosius and his colleague would take office in 722/-32, as we know from Appian, *Bell. civ.*, V.73: Ἀπέφηναν δὲ τῆς ἐπιούσης ὑπάτους ἐς τετραετές, κ.τ.λ. Sosius and Ahenobarbus took office, and it is to the point that, according to Cassius Dio, L.2.2, when Sosius attacked Octavian in the senate, he commanded such support that he would have obtained a decree against Octavian, had not a tribune interceded, and that when Sosius and his colleague had to flee Octavian's armed retainers, a very large part of the senate accompanied or followed them. Sosius was therefore clearly on the "Republican" side.

[73] That descent from a daughter or granddaughter of Sosius was a great distinction, presumably conferring *nobilitas*, is obvious from *C.I.L.*, IX.4855: L·NONIVS· QVINTILIANVS·L·F·SEX·N·C·SOSI·COS·TRIVMPHAL·PRONEP. — Sex. Nonius Quintilianus was consul 761/8.

be attained in prosopography, that Claudius's rival was *nobilis utrimque*.[74]

It follows, therefore, that there is no evidence to show that Tacitus did not consistently use, when referring to prominent Romans of the Principate, the words *nobilis* and *nobilitas* in a highly specialized sense to indicate that they were members of a closed caste formed by the descendants of men who had held the consulship during the Republic, which was understood as meaning men who had been elected to that office by the people voting in ostensibly free elections. The available evidence very strongly suggests that he did, but it falls short of irrefragable proof because we do not possess complete genealogical records covering all the persons to whom he applies those words,[75] so that, as is so often our dolorous fate in scholarship, we must content ourselves with a fairly high degree of probability.

University of Illinois

[74] If we take literally Juvenal's statement (10.332) that C. Silius was "gentis patriciae," it would follow that either (a) a successfully forged genealogy, similar to one produced for Vitellius (note 64 *supra*), had been approved by Claudius when exercising his presumed censorial power, or that P. Silius Nerva, who was one of Augustus's boon companions (Augustus *ap.* Suet., *Aug.*, 71.2), was transformed into a Patrician under the provisions of the Lex Saenia of 724/–30. But Juvenal was a poet.

[75] Note 59 *supra*.

17

Three Textual Notes

CHAUNCEY E. FINCH

I. Citations from the *Topica* of Cicero in Codex Reg. Lat. 1048

Codex Vat. Reg. Lat. 1048 is an early Carolingian manuscript which contains in its first 20 folios Isidorus *Etymologiae* 5.1.1–5.27.38 and 9.4.1–9.6.22.[1] Most of the remainder of the manuscript is devoted to *Codex Theodosianus*. Folios 21ᵛ–35ᵛ are made up of lists of *capitula* of the various items which follow. Folios 36ʳ–124ʳ contain *Theodosiani Libri XVI* followed by (fols. 124ʳ–224ʳ) *Leges Novellae ad Theodosianum Pertinentes*. The concluding segment of the manuscript (fols. 224ᵛ–227ᵛ) is a trilingual glossary listing certain words in their Latin, Hebrew, and Greek forms. The entire document appears to have been written by a single hand, which is dated in the ninth or tenth century by Beeson in his catalogue of early Isidore manuscripts.[2] Codex Reg. Lat. 1048 has been discussed by Mommsen, who dates it in the tenth or eleventh century.[3] In his edition of *Leges Novellae ad Theodosianum Pertinentes* Paul M. Meyer described this manuscript in considerable detail, pointing out that it contains a marginal note which reads as follows: *Domino sanctissimo atque amantissimo Gualtrio episcoporum eximio humilis congregatio salutem in domino.*[4] Meyer thinks this note is by the original scribe and that the Gualtrius referred to is the Gualtrius (or Walterius) who was Bishop of Orléans 870–891. Hence he reaches the conclusion that the manuscript was copied in the late ninth century. This is a conclusion which is well supported by the palaeographical evidence.

---

1 The information about codex Vat. Reg. Lat. 1048 presented in this paper is based on a microfilm copy of the manuscript placed at my disposal by The Knights of Columbus Vatican Film Library at Saint Louis University.

2 Charles Henry Beeson, *Isidor-Studien* (Munich, 1913), 93.

3 Th. Mommsen, *Theodosiani Libri XVI Cum Constitutionibus Sirmondianis*, Pars Prior (Berlin, 1905), C.

4 Paulus M. Meyer, *Leges Novellae ad Theodosianum Pertinentes* (Berlin, 1905), xxxiv–xxxv. Meyer, probably by a typographical error, states that the entry is on fol. 205ʳ. Actually it is to be found on fol. 225ʳ.

Reg. Lat. 1048 contains a number of interlinear glosses and marginal scholia written in a Carolingian hand of the early tenth century under strong insular influence. Among indications of such insular influence are the frequent use of ÷ for *est*; exceedingly frequent use of angular *n*; the use of i-*longa* particularly in the preposition *in*; and confusion of *r* and *s*. The *ti* combination is quite similar to that used in pointed insular.

Two of these scholia are particularly interesting because they contain citations from the *Topica* of Cicero. The first is to be found on folio 78ʳ where it has been inserted in the lower margin to provide a commentary on *Theodosiani Libri* 4.8 (*De Liberali Causa*). The author of the scholion, in attempting to explain how, among the early Romans, persons could be restored from slavery to freedom, writes as follows:

> Priscis temporibus apud Romanos tribus modis dabatur libertas: censu, scilicet, vindicta et testamento. Censu, quoniam institutio fuerat Romanorum ut nullus ex servili genere infra VII miliaria in circuitu civitatis commaneret nisi servitutis vinculo solveretur. Et hoc erat censu fieri liberum, in coloniam transire Romanorum eos qui quondam censum solvebant ut dato censu civis diceretur Romanus. Est (et *in codice*) autem pars altera adipiscendae libertatis quae vindicta vocabatur. Vindicta erat quaedam virgula quam lector ei qui liberandus erat a servitio capiti inponens eundem servum in libertatem vocabat ac vindicabat dicens quaedam verba sollempnia et ideo illa vindicta vocabatur eo quod vindicabat in libertatem servum. Illa etiam pars faciendi liberi est, si quis suprema voluntate in testamenti serie servum suum liberum scripserit, quod et modo fieri solet. Unde Cicero in Topicis, volens monstrare eum quem servum esse constiterit non esse liberum factum, huius modi proponit syllogismum: Si neque censu neque vindicta neque testamento liber factus est, non est liber. Atqui nulla earum partium liber factus est. Non est igitur liber.

The citation from Cicero contained in this scholion corresponds to *Topica* 10.2–4, where the reading adopted by Bornecque in his critical edition is: Si neque censu nec vindicta nec testamento liber factus est, non est liber. Neque nulla est earum; non est igitur liber.[5]

The second scholion in Reg. Lat. 1048 containing a quotation from Cicero's *Topica* is to be found in the lower margin of folio 124ʳ. It takes the form of a commentary on the second section of *Liber Legum Novellarum Divi Theodosii A.*[6] The text of the scholion is as follows:

> Ius civile est quod quisque populus vel civitas sibi proprium in humanis divinisque rebus constituit. Cicero dicit in Topicis quod ius civile est aequitas constituta his qui eiusdem civitatis sunt ad res suas obtinendas. Eius autem aequitatis utilis cognitio est. Utilis est igitur iuris civilis scientia.

5 Henri Bornecque, *Cicéron: Divisions de l'Art Oratoire, Topiques* (Paris, 1925), 68.
6 Meyer (above, n. 4), 6.

The citation from Cicero here presented corresponds to *Topica* 9.3–6. The version of the passage found in Bornecque's critical edition reads: Ius civile est aequitas constituta eis qui eiusdem civitatis sunt, ad res suas obtinendas; eius autem aequitatis utilis est cognitio; utilis est ergo iuris civilis scientia.[7]

In both passages cited above it will be seen that the texts of portions of Cicero's *Topica* included in the scholia of Reg. Lat. 1048 agree very closely with the critical text of Bornecque. Those differences which do exist, however, assume very great importance for purposes of textual criticism by reason of the fact that these scholia are as early as the oldest extant manuscripts of the *Topica* and apparently stem from an insular version of the work. The question of whether this is an independent tradition becomes a significant one.

Editors of all recent critical editions of the *Topica* agree in dividing the manuscripts of this work into two families, fam. 1 and fam. 2. Fam. 1, according to these editors, is made up of two manuscripts: Vat. Ottob. Lat. 1406 (= O), dated in the critical editions as tenth-century, and Codex Vitebergensis (= f), *an*. 1432. Fam. 2, according to the same editors, is comprised of approximately ten manuscripts several of which are dated in the tenth century.[8] In an article published in *Classical Philology* in 1972,[9] I pointed out that O, which is a Beneventan manuscript, had been listed by E. A. Lowe in his *The Beneventan Script* as dating from the end of the eleventh century rather than from the tenth.[10] In the same article I also expanded the membership of fam. 1 by adding three new manuscripts to it: Vat. Lat. 1701, saec. xv (= h); Vat. Lat. 2110, saec. xv (= g); and Vat. Lat. 8591, saec. xi (= C) and provided a list of readings characteristic of the expanded fam. 1. (COghf) as opposed to fam. 2.[11]

A comparison of the texts of the two passages from Cicero's *Topica* quoted in the scholia of Reg. Lat. 1048 with the readings of representative manuscripts of fam. 1 and fam. 2 will show that the readings of the scholia (henceforth designated *schol.*) sometimes agree with fam. 1, sometimes with fam. 2, and sometimes with neither. In 10.2 the first *nec* of the Bornecque text follows fam. 2. This is matched in *schol.* by *necque* which is the reading of most of the fam. 1 manuscripts (Cgh). In the same line, the second *nec* is

---

[7] Bornecque (above, n. 5), 67–68.

[8] W. Friedrich, *M. Tullii Ciceronis Opera Rhetorica*, II (Leipzig, 1873), lxxvi; A. S. Wilkins, *M. Tullii Ciceronis Rhetorica*, II (Oxford, 1903), iii; Bornecque (above, n. 5), 61–62.

[9] Chauncey E. Finch, "Codices Vat. Lat. 1701, 2110, and 8591 as Sources for Cicero's *Topica*," *CP* LXVIII (1972), 112–117.

[10] E. A. Lowe, *The Beneventan Script* (Oxford, 1914), 366.

[11] Finch (above, n. 9), 113.

based on both fam. 1 and fam. 2 readings, but in *schol.* it is replaced by *neque*, which follows neither family. In 10.3 Bornecque has *neque nulla est earum*, which is the reading of fam. 2; the other editors follow the reading of fam. 1—*necque ulla est earum rerum*. *Schol.* has: *atqui nulla earum partium liber factus est*, which, though somewhat different from both fam. 1 and fam. 2, agrees more closely with the former. In this case it is rather difficult to determine whether the scholiast has rephrased the passage on his own initiative or has taken the text unchanged from an exemplar which perhaps belonged to a third family of manuscripts.

In the second citation from the *Topica* in Reg. Lat. 1048, the reading *his* appears in *schol.* for *eis* (9.4) in the Bornecque text. Here Bornecque is following fam. 2, whereas COg of fam. 1 have *his* in agreement with *schol.* In 9.6 Bornecque accepts the reading *est ergo* based on fam. 2. Other editors have *ergo est*, which is the reading of fam. 1. *Schol.* reads *est igitur* which follows the word-order of fam. 2 by placing *est* first, but disagrees with both families by substituting *igitur* for *ergo*, perhaps correctly. It is probably significant that according to the Index Verborum of Cicero's Rhetorical works by Abbott, Oldfather, and Canter, Cicero uses *ergo* only three times in the *Topica* while using *igitur* twenty-eight times.[12] In 9.5–6 the reading *cognitio est* of *schol.* is at variance with *est cognitio* found in both fam. 1 and fam. 2.

Since such a variety appears in the readings of *schol.*, with some agreeing with fam. 1, some with fam. 2, and some with neither, it seems certain that these citations have been taken from some manuscript which has been lost or, at least, is not among those previously utilized by editors of the *Topica*. Since the scholia themselves were written in the early part of the tenth century, the manuscript which was their source may very well have been earlier than any of those now extant and, in view of the insular influence present in the scholia, may have represented some thus far unknown insular tradition of the *Topica*. For these reasons the two citations, however brief, deserve the attention of future editors of the *Topica*.

II. Some New Manuscripts of *Anthologia Latina* (Riese) 392 and 798

Item 392 in *Anthologia Latina* (Riese) is a poem of eight verses, beginning with the line: *Ut belli sonuere tubae violenta peremit*. This was published without title by Riese in his 1894 edition on the basis of the following manuscripts: Vossianus q. 86, saec. ix (= V); Parisinus 8071, saec. ix–x (= B);

---

[12] Kenneth Morgan Abbott, William Abbott Oldfather, Howard Vernon Canter, *Index Verborum in Ciceronis Rhetorica* (Urbana, 1964), 427, 537.

Sangallensis 899, saec. ix (= G); Bruxellensis 10859, saec. ix (= D); Parisinus 8069, saec. x–xi (= C); Vossianus q. 33, saec. x (= L); Reg. Mus. Brit. 15 B 19, saec. ix–x (= R); Parisinus 13026, saec. x (= P); and numerous late documents.[13] The same poem had been published by Riese as item 392 in his earlier edition of *Anthologia Latina*[14] with the title, *Traiani Imperatoris: e bello Parthico versus decori*. In this earlier edition Riese had used codices VGDC from the group listed above and in addition had cited (with the designation *Maius*) readings from a copy of the poem published by Angelo Mai in his *Classici Auctores*[15] with no information about its source other than a statement that it had been found "in vetere admodum vaticano codice," from which he was also publishing in full a poem by Aldhelm entitled *De Basilica aedificata a Bugge* previously known from only fragmentary copies.[16] This Mai manuscript was disregarded by Riese in his later edition of item 392 presumably because, being unaware of its date and other identifying features, he assumed that it had been superseded by other early manuscripts which had come to light in the intervening period. Despite this fact, however, Mai's manuscript may be restored to its former position of prominence among the sources of this work since it can now definitely be identified as Vat. Reg. Lat. 251, fol. 11ʳ, saec. ix (henceforth designated M).[17] Aside from the fact that the text of M corresponds quite closely with the version of the poem printed by Mai, there are several other factors which confirm beyond a doubt the identification of this manuscript with Mai's unnamed source. Chief among these is the presence in Reg. Lat. 251, fols. 2ᵛ–4ᵛ, of the poem by Aldhelm referred to above as being included by Mai in the same volume of *Classici Auctores* (pp. 387–390). Furthermore, on folios 2ʳ and 4ᵛ of this codex notes appear in the margins in the writing of Angelo Mai with the signature *A. Maius*.

A description of codex Reg. Lat. 251 has been provided by Andreas Wilmart in the second volume of his catalogue of the first 500 Latin manuscripts of the Reginensis Collection.[18] In his description he indicates that M is a copy of *Anthologia Latina* 392, but does not identify it with Mai's text of the poem. He lists the title of M as *de tribus mulieribus victricibus atque*

[13] Alexander Riese, *Anthologia Latina*, Pars prior, Fasc. 1 (Leipzig, 1894), 306.

[14] Alexander Riese, *Anthologia Latina*, Pars prior, Fasc. 1 (Leipzig, 1869).

[15] Angelus Maius, *Classicorum Auctorum e Vaticanis Codicibus Editorum Tomus V* (Rome, 1833), 458.

[16] Maius (above, n. 15), 387.

[17] Information about this and other Vatican manuscripts discussed in this paper is based on microfilm copies of these documents placed at my disposal by The Knights of Columbus Vatican Film Library at Saint Louis University.

[18] Andreas Wilmart, *Codices Reginenses Latini*, Tomus II (Vatican City, 1945), 1–6.

ab eisdem de totidem viris interiectis. This is given by Mai as *de tribus mulieribus victricibus deque totidem viris interfectis ab eisdem.*[19] The wording actually found in M is *de tribus mulieribus victricibus atque ab eisdem de totidem viris interfectis.* In other words, the order as given by Wilmart agrees with the manuscript, but Mai was correct in reading *interfectis* in place of *interiectis.* Incidentally, the title given in M is almost identical with that found in D.

A comparison of M with the 1894 text of Riese shows the following variants: 2 *Hippolyte] ypolite Lyce] licae Alce] alcae*; 5 *Clonus] clonos* (corrected to *clonus* by a later hand); 7 *Iphicli] aepidi* or *aepicli Dorycli] doracli.* Mai has *Aepidii* as the first word of line 7; this does appear in the writing of M to be *aepidi,* but could just as easily be interpreted as *aepicli* in agreement with CD, since M frequently confuses *d* and *cl.* In line 3, for instance, the word which is clearly intended to be *Clonon* appears in M in a form which could easily be read as *donon.*

Another early copy of *Anthologia Latina* 392, apparently unknown to Riese, is to be found in codex Vat. Pal. Lat. 281, fol. 308ᵛ, saec. ix. The main body of this manuscript is made up of a copy of the *Etymologiae* of Isidore which was written in the ninth century, probably at Lorsch. It is described briefly by Henricus Stevenson Jr. in his catalogue of the first 921 of the Palatini Latini codices in the Vatican Library.[20] Stevenson refers briefly to the poem with the words: "Carmen paene deletum; inc. *Ut belli sonuere tubae,* f. 308ᵛ," but does not identify it as a poem in *Anthologia Latina.* Bernhard Bischoff discusses Pal. Lat. 281 in his recent monograph on the Lorsch manuscripts, pointing out that it resided in Lorsch in the ninth century and probably was corrected there.[21] He makes no references, however, to the copy of *Anthologia Latina* 392 contained in it. As indicated by Stevenson, the text of the poem has been almost completely obliterated. Apparently no title was ever included. Only the first few words of each line are legible, and for this reason any attempt to provide a systematic collation of the text is hopeless. Those words which can be read agree closely with the text of Riese. Perhaps the chief value of the manuscript for purposes of textual criticism lies in the fact that it provides evidence for the first two letters of *Hippolyte* in line 2. Manuscripts previously used have *yppolite* (with the symbol c over the *y* in G). M has *ypolite.* But Pal. Lat. 281 clearly reads *Hipolite* thus becoming the first document to provide manuscript evidence for the *Hi-* previously accepted into the text as an emendation. Enough of the original text of the poem as copied in Pal. Lat. 281 is

[19] Maius (above, n. 15), 458.

[20] Henricus Stevenson Iunior, *Codices Palatini Latini Bibliothecae Vaticanae,* Tomus I (Rome, 1886), 72.

[21] Bernhard Bischoff, *Lorsch im Spiegel seiner Handschriften* (Munich, 1974), 30, 110.

still visible to indicate that line 7 was completely omitted. This omission suggests a close affinity with codex B in which the same line is missing. This poses the interesting question: was B or any of its ancestors ever located in Lorsch? Certainly the presence of this poem in a Lorsch manuscript provides a small amount of additional proof of the richness and variety of the holdings of the Lorsch Library in the ninth century.

Item 798 of *Anthologia Latina* is a poem of twelve verses dealing with the seven planets and edited by Riese from a single manuscript of the thirteenth century—Parisinus 7461 (= P).[22] Two additional manuscripts of this poem have recently come to my attention: Vat. Pal. Lat. 1514, fol. 137^v, saec. xiii (= V) and Bodleian Canon. Misc. 517, fol. 52^r, saec. xv (= B).[23] Codex Pal. Lat. 1514 is a well-known manuscript of the *Tusculanae Disputationes* of Cicero and has been used in the preparation of numerous critical editions of this work. The first part, extending through *Non mihi videtur omni animi perturbatione posse sapiens vacare* (*Tusc.* 4.8.2–3), occupies the first 95 folios of the manuscript and was copied in a Carolingian hand usually dated at the end of the tenth century. The rest of the manuscript (fols. 96–137) contains the remaining portions of the *Tusculanae Disputationes* copied in two different thirteenth-century hands, with the first having written the first two folios of this segment and the second, the remainder of the codex. On fol. 137^v, immediately after the conclusion of the *Tusculanae Disputationes*, the second thirteenth-century hand added the text of *Anthologia Latina* 798. This is followed on the same folio without explanation, by a declension (with a few errors included) of the singular and plural, but not the dual, of the Greek definite article. In his Budé edition of *Tusculanae Disputationes*, Fohlen[24] has collated both the tenth-century portion of Pal. Lat. 1514 and the thirteenth-century portion, but neither he nor any other editor of Cicero calls attention to the copy of *Anth. Lat.* 798 at the end of the manuscript.

The Bodleian manuscript—B—is either a direct or an indirect copy of V, since it agrees with V in every detail with the exception that in line 8,

22 Alexander Riese, *Anthologia Latina*, Pars prior, Fasc. 2 (Leipzig, 1906), 274.

23 I wish to express my sincere gratitude to Dr. Ruth Joseph for securing a photograph of codex B for me from the Bodleian Library. I also wish to thank the Librarian of the Bodleian for permitting a photograph of the manuscript to be made for export. The first line of B, along with the title of the poem, is recorded by Lynn Thorndike and Pearl Kibre, *A Catalogue of Incipits of Mediaeval Scientific Writings in Latin* (Cambridge, Mass., 1963), 1503. Thorndike and Kibre do not, however, list any other manuscripts as containing the poem nor do they identify the poem with *Anthologia Latina* 798.

24 George Fohlen, *Cicéron Tusculanes*, Tome I (I–II); Tome II (III–V), with a French Translation by Jules Humbert (Paris, 1931).

where V has the correct *ast*, it has *astra*—apparently a scribal conjecture. All of the errors of V are to be found in B. Hence the two may be treated together in a discussion of their textual peculiarities. Both have the title, *De Septem (vii B) Planetis et Cursu eorum*, as opposed to P, which has no title. Both V and B omit line 7 in its entirety. In line 2, where Baehrens has conjectured that the reading should be *se sede*, V and B, like P, have *seseque*. In the same line, however, where P has *tenus*, both V and B have the correct *tenet*. V and B have *ciclus* in line 5 for *cursus*. As noted above, B has *astra* in line 8 where V and P have *ast*. In summary, then, the two new manuscripts have the effect of confirming Riese's conjecture that *tenet* is the correct reading for the *tenus* of P in line 2, and of establishing a title for the poem.

III. Two Unpublished Riddles in Codex Reg. Lat. 1260

The recto of the front flyleaf of codex Vat. Reg. Lat. 1260, which is parchment, contains two unpublished Latin riddles written near the top of the page in a twelfth-century Carolingian hand.[25] The text of the first is:

> Est domus in terris set vivit semper in undis.
> Si caput abstuleris, apparet fortis in armis.
> Si medium tollis, ictus mucrone patescit.
> Si finem abstuleris, volucer petit aethera pennis.

The four verses making up this riddle are encircled by a line to set them apart from the second riddle which follows immediately after the last line of the first, in the same hand, but in smaller writing. The text of the second is:

> Non sata conubio, nascor de virgine virgo.
> Nascor per coitum coitus et conscia non sum.

The remainder of the recto of the flyleaf is completely vacant except for the entry "1260 Reg." near the bottom in a much later hand. The verso of the same folio is completely blank.

The main body of codex Reg. Lat. 1260 is a Carolingian manuscript of the ninth century containing a variety of works dealing for the most part with astronomy and the arrangement of the calendar. The following is a list of the items to be found in this codex: (1) Beda, *De Natura Rerum* (fols. 1ʳ–7ᵛ); (2) Beda, *De Temporibus* (fols. 7ᵛ–10ʳ); (3) an anonymous tract on various ages of the world (fols. 10ʳ–12ʳ); (4) Beda, *Epistola ad Wicthedum*

---

[25] The information about codex Vat. Reg. Lat. 1260 provided in this paper is based on a microfilm copy of the manuscript placed at my disposal by The Knights of Columbus Vatican Film Library at Saint Louis University.

(fols. 12ʳ–14ᵛ); (5) paschal computations (fols. 14ᵛ–16ᵛ); (6) Isidorus, *De Natura Rerum* (fols. 17ʳ–44ʳ); (7) Hyginus, *De Astronomia* (fols. 44ᵛ–83ᵛ); (8) an anonymous work about the stars without title (fols. 84ʳ–86ʳ); (9) *Anthologia Latina* (Riese) 679, with musical notes, inserted in the eleventh century on a page previously left blank (fol. 86ᵛ); (10) an anonymous work entitled *Pauca de Ratione Conputandi secundum Solem et Lunam* accompanied by numerous paschal tables (fols. 87ʳ–124ᵛ); (11) Aethicus, *Cosmographia* (fols. 125ʳ–164ᵛ); (12) four glossaries of Greek and Latin medical terms (fols. 165ʳ–178ᵛ).

In the lower margin of fol. 1ʳ appears the entry "Petri Danielis Aurel." in Peter Daniel's own handwriting. This indicates that the manuscript is one of the famous collection which Peter Daniel owned at one time and that it, like many other manuscripts belonging to this collector, probably came from Fleury.

Codex Reg. Lat. 1260 was listed by Charles W. Jones in his edition of *Bedae Opera de Temporibus*[26] and by M. L. W. Laistner and H. H. King in their hand-list of Bede manuscripts.[27] It was described in greater detail by Charles Henry Beeson in his *Isidor-Studien*.[28] Both Laistner–King and Beeson assign the manuscript to Fleury, and Beeson calls attention to its having been owned at one time by Peter Daniel.

Whether the content of the main body of Reg. Lat. 1260 was in any way responsible for the insertion of two riddles on its flyleaf in the twelfth century is highly doubtful. In all probability this was a matter of accident. But it is just possible that there is some connection between the fact that the first part of the manuscript is made up of works of Bede and that five riddles of Symphosius[29] (in the order 1, 7, 77, 12, 10) and five of Aldhelm[30] (in the order 3, 90, 3, 4, 9) are to be found in the *Flores* of Pseudo-Bede.[31] If the twelfth-century scribe who copied the new riddles was by any chance familiar with the work of Pseudo-Bede, he may have been led by this to associate riddles with the name of Bede and thus may have considered a manuscript containing works by Bede a proper home for the riddles added on the flyleaf.

[26] Charles W. Jones, *Bedae Opera de Temporibus* (Cambridge, Mass., 1943), 167, 171.

[27] M. L. W. Laistner and H. H. King, *A Hand-List of Bede Manuscripts* (Ithaca, 1943), 121, 143, 147.

[28] Charles Henry Beeson, *Isidor-Studien* (Munich, 1913), 67.

[29] For the text of the riddles of Symphosius see Fr. Glorie, *Collectiones Aenigmatum Merovingicae Aetatis*, Corpus Christianorum, Series Latina CXXXIII A (Turnholt, 1968), 611–723. The Latin text in this edition is accompanied by the English translation originally published in Raymond Theodore Ohl, *The Enigmas of Symphosius* (Philadelphia, 1928).

[30] For the text of the riddles of Aldhelm see Glorie (above, n. 29), 359–540.

[31] Migne, *Patrologia Latina* 94, 543–548.

Be that as it may, there can be no doubt about the adherence of the new riddles to the Symphosius tradition. Symphosius is the name regularly assigned to a writer of the late fourth or early fifth century A.D. who produced a hundred riddles of three dactylic-hexameter lines each, dealing with a great variety of topics.[32] The riddles of Symphosius became quite popular in the middle ages, as is indicated by the large number of manuscripts of them which are now extant[33] and the presence of ten of them in *Historia Apollonii Regis Tyri*, which is thought to be a Latin adaptation of a lost Greek romance.[34]

One feature which very definitely connects the new riddles (written, incidentally, in dactylic-hexameter verses) with the Symphosius tradition is the identity of the first four words of the first riddle (*Est domus in terris*) with the first four words of Symphosius 12. The subject of Symphosius 12 is *Flumen et piscis* and its text is:

> Est domus in terris clara quae voce resultat.
> Ipsa domus resonat, tacitus sed non sonat hospes.
> Ambo tamen currunt, hospes simul et domus una.

Despite the similarity of the first new riddle in tone and meter to the riddles of Symphosius, the addition of a fourth line suggests some influence from Aldhelm, who was himself under the influence of Symphosius, as is indicated by his mention of Symphosius by name[35] in the prose prologue of his collection of 100 riddles produced in the late seventh century. The riddles of Aldhelm, which are also in dactylic hexameters, vary in length, but riddles 1–7, 9–17, 19, 51, 90 contain four lines each. Furthermore, the third line of riddle 16 (*Cum volucrum turma quoque scando per aethera pennis*) in its vocabulary resembles the fourth line of the first new riddle very closely, and almost certainly exercised considerable influence over the unknown composer of this riddle. The subject of Aldhelm 16 is Luligo, "Flying-fish."

The second new riddle, although made up of only two lines, is also distinctly reminiscent of the riddles of Symphosius. The fact that it is in the first person, as contrasted with the first, which is in the third person, is significant, since the vast majority of the 100 riddles of Symphosius are also in the first person with the only exceptions being 12, 24, 29, 30, 62, 72, 76, 79, 90, 95, and 96. The theme of "peculiar circumstances of

---

[32] For additional details see Chauncey E. Finch, "Codex Vat. Barb. Lat. 721 as a Source for the Riddles of Symphosius," *TAPA* 98 (1967), 173–179.

[33] Glorie (above, n. 29), 612–614. To the list of manuscripts provided by Glorie should be added Vat. Barb. Lat. 721. See Finch (above, n. 32).

[34] Alexander Riese, *Historia Apollonii Regis Tyri* (Leipzig, 1893).

[35] Glorie (above, n. 29), 371.1.

conception and birth" present in this new riddle is one which is popular with Symphosius, as can be seen in his riddles 14, 15, and 37.

I have no suggestion to offer with regard to the subjects of the new riddles. It should perhaps be noted that the two known riddles which have influenced the first of the new ones—Symphosius 12 and Aldhelm 16—both deal with fish. I find it hard to believe, however, that this is true of the first riddle in Reg. Lat. 1260.* Since in most manuscripts of riddles the subject of each is recorded as its title, it may be hoped that one or both of the new riddles will be found in other manuscripts where titles will be provided.

Saint Louis University

* [Vulturnus. *Editor.*]

Mark Naoumides (1931-1977):
List of Publications

MIROSLAV MARCOVICH

1. "*Εἰς τὸν ὅσιον καὶ δίκαιον Λάζαρον τὸν τετραήμερον Ὕμνος Βʹ,*" in *Ῥωμανοῦ τοῦ Μελωιδοῦ Ὕμνοι,* vol. 1 (Athens, Myrtides, 1952) 179–194.

2. *Τὰ Κοντακάρια τῆς Πάτμου. (Κώδικες 212 καὶ 213 ΙΑʹ αἰῶνος).* With P. G. Nikolopoulos. (= *Ῥωμανοῦ τοῦ Μελωιδοῦ Ὕμνοι,* vol. 2, part A), Athens, Myrtides, 1964, 393 pp.

3. "*Σωφρονίου Εὐστρατιάδου, Ῥωμανὸς ὁ Μελωιδὸς καὶ τὰ ποιητικὰ αὐτοῦ ἔργα,*" *Epeteris Hetaireias Byzantinon Spoudon* 25 (1955) 211–283.

4. "*Κοντάκιον τῶν τριῶν παίδων,*" in *Ῥωμανοῦ τοῦ Μελωιδοῦ Ὕμνοι,* vol. 3 (Athens, Myrtides, 1957) 207–285.

5. "The Papyrus of the Lexicon of Harpocration," *TAPA* 92 (1961) 384–388.

6. "Notes on Literary Papyri," *TAPA* 93 (1962) 240–252.

7. "*Βιβλιογραφικαὶ συμβολαὶ εἰς παπύρους καὶ ὄστρακα,*" *Athena* 66 (1962) 187–191.

8. "*Ὑμνογραφικὰ κείμενα εἰς παπύρους καὶ ὄστρακα,*" *Epet. Het. Byz. Sp.* 32 (1963) 60–93.

9. "*Ὁ P.Oxy. 1801 καὶ ὁ Θέων,*" in *Χάρις Κωνσταντίνωι Ἰ. Βουρβέρηι* (Athens, 1964) 327–335.

10. Review of A. Tovar, *Catalogus codicum Graecorum Universitatis Salamantinae,* I, in *Epet. Het. Byz. Sp.* 33 (1964) 315–320.

11. Review of R. A. Pack, *The Greek and Latin Literary Texts from Greco-Roman Egypt* (2nd ed.), in *AJP* 88 (1967) 352–355.

12. "New Fragments of Ancient Greek Poetry," *Greek, Roman and Byz. Studies* 9 (1968) 267–290.

13. "The Fragments of Greek Lexicography in the Papyri," in *Classical*

Studies presented to Ben Edwin Perry (Urbana, Illinois U.P., 1969) 181–202, 4 plates.

14. Review of K. Mitsakis, *Der byzantinische Alexanderroman nach dem Codex Vindob. Theol. gr.* 244, in *Comparative Literature Studies* 6 (1969) 334–337.

15. English version (with corrections and additions) of A. Komines, *Facsimiles of Dated Patmian Codices* (Athens, Myrtides, 1970), 129 pp., 176 plates.

16. Review of St. West, *The Ptolemaic Papyri of Homer*, in *AJP* 91 (1970) 375–378.

17. "Σύμμεικτα παλαιογραφικά," *Epet. Het. Byz. Sp.* 39–40 (1972–1973) 373–385 (= *Festschrift N. B. Tomadakis*).

18. "The Shorter Version of Pseudo-Zonaras, *Lexicon*," in *Serta Turyniana* (Urbana, Illinois U.P., 1974) 436–488.

19. "The Date, Scribe and Provenience of Cod. Holkham gr. 112 (*olim* 298)," *Scriptorium* 28 (1974) 65–68, 2 plates.

20. 'Ρητορικαὶ Λέξεις. *Editio princeps.* (*Athena*, Monogr. 20), Athens, 1975, 94 pp., 4 plates.

21. "Codex Athen. Mus. Byz. 186 and Photius," *Epet. Het. Byz. Sp.* 42 (1975–1976) 85–100.

22. Review of A. R. Littlewood, Ed., *The Progymnasmata of Joannes Geometres*, in *Phoenix* 30 (1976) 216–218.

23. Review of G. Berger, *Etymologicum Genuinum et Etymologicum Symeonis* (β), in *Amer. Class. Review* (in press).

24. "The v-Recension of St. Cyril's Lexicon," *Illinois Classical Studies* 4 (1979).